Taking SIDES

Clashing Views on Controversial Issues in Human Sexuality

Sixth Edition

Taking SIDES

Clashing Views on Controversial Issues in Human Sexuality

Sixth Edition

Edited, Selected, and with Introductions by

Robert T. Francoeur
Fairleigh Dickinson University
and
William J. Taverner

Dushkin/McGraw-Hill
A Division of The McGraw-Hill Companies

For my wife and daughters, Anna, Nicole, and Danielle, and other special friends who continually force me to ask new questions (R. T. F.)

For my wife, Denise Taverner, for her relentless support, encouragement, and insight (W. J. T.)

Photo Acknowledgments

Cover image: *Reddy #2* by Diana Ong/Super Stock

Cover Art Acknowledgment

Charles Vitelli

Library of Congress Cataloging-in-Publication Data

Main entry under title:
    Taking sides: clashing views on controversial issues in human sexuality/edited, selected, and with introductions by Robert T. Francoeur and William J. Taverner.—6th ed.
    Includes bibliographical references and index.
    1. Sex. 2. Sexual ethics. I. Francoeur, Robert T., *comp.* II. Taverner, William J., *comp.*

612.6

0-697-39145-0

Printed on Recycled Paper

PREFACE

In few areas of American society today are clashing views more evident than in the area of human sexual behavior. Almost daily, in the news media, in congressional hearings, and on the streets, we hear about Americans of all ages taking completely opposite positions on such issues as abortion, contraception, homosexuality, surrogate motherhood, teenage sexuality, and the like. Given the highly personal, emotional, and sensitive nature of these issues, sorting out the meaning of these controversies and fashioning a coherent position on them can be a difficult proposition. The purpose of this book, therefore, is to encourage meaningful critical thinking about current issues related to human sexuality, and the debates are designed to assist you in the task of clarifying your own personal values and identifying what society's are or should be in this area.

For this sixth edition of *Taking Sides: Clashing Views on Controversial Issues in Human Sexuality,* we have gathered 38 lively and thoughtful statements by articulate advocates on opposite sides of a variety of sexuality-related questions. For the questions debated in this volume, it is vital that you understand and appreciate the different positions other people take on these issues, as well as your own. You should respect other people's philosophical biases and religious beliefs and attempt to articulate your own. Democracies are strongest when they respect the rights and privileges of all citizens, be they conservative, liberal, or middle-of-the-road, religious or humanistic, of the majority or in the minority. Although you may disagree with one or even both of the arguments offered for each issue, it is important that you read each statement carefully and critically. Since this book is a tool to encourage critical thinking, you should not feel confined to the views expressed in the articles. You may see important points on both sides of an issue and may construct for yourself a new and creative approach, which may incorporate the best of both sides or provide an entirely new vantage point for understanding.

To assist you as you pursue the issues debated here, each issue has an issue *introduction*, which sets the stage for the debate, tells you something about each of the authors, and provides some historical background to the debate. Each issue concludes with a *postscript* that briefly ties the readings together and gives a detailed list of *suggested readings*, if you would like to further explore a topic.

Changes to this edition   This edition represents a considerable revision. There are 11 completely new issues: *Should We Accept Alternatives to Monogamy?* (Issue 1); *Is the Model of Normal and Vandalized Gendermaps/Lovemaps Biased?* (Issue 3); *Should Society Recognize Two Kinds of Marriage?* (Issue 4); *Are Men Really from Mars and Women from Venus?* (Issue 5); *Should Contractual Sex*

Be Legal? (Issue 8); *Should Late-Term Abortions Be Banned?* (Issue 9); *Should All Female Circumcision Be Banned?* (Issue 10); *Is Abstinence-Only Education Effective?* (Issue 11); *Is Chemical Castration an Acceptable Punishment for Male Sex Offenders?* (Issue 14); *Should Pornography Be Banned as a Threat to Women?* (Issue 15); and *Should Privacy Rights Yield to Public Health Concerns in Dealing With HIV Infection?* (Issue 18). In addition, for two of the issues retained from the previous edition—*Should Sex Be Banned on the Internet?* (Issue 12) and *Should Society Recognize Gay Marriages?* (Issue 13)—one or both of the selections have been replaced to provide a different perspective on the issue and to bring the issue up to date. In all, there are 25 new selections in this edition. We have also revised and updated the issue introductions and postscripts where necessary.

A word to the instructor   An *Instructor's Manual With Test Questions* (multiple-choice and essay) is available through the publisher for the instructor using *Taking Sides* in the classroom. A general guidebook, *Using Taking Sides in the Classroom*, which discusses methods and techniques for integrating the pro-con approach into any classroom setting, is also available. An online version of *Using Taking Sides in the Classroom* and a correspondence service for *Taking Sides* adopters can be found at www.cybsol.com/usingtakingsides/. For students, we offer a field guide to analyzing argumentative essays, *Analyzing Controversy: An Introductory Guide,* with exercises and techniques to help them to decipher genuine controversies.

   Taking Sides: Clashing Views on Issues in Human Sexuality is only one title in the Taking Sides series. If you are interested in seeing the table of contents for any of the other titles, please visit the Taking Sides Web site at http://www.dushkin.com/takingsides/.

Acknowledgments   The task of tracking down the best essays for inclusion in this collection is not easy, and we appreciate the useful suggestions from the many users of *Taking Sides* across the United States and Canada who communicated with the publisher. Special thanks go to those who responded with specific suggestions for the sixth edition:

Deborah Berke
Messiah College

David E. Corbin
University of
  Nebraska–Omaha

Corbin Fowler
Edinboro University of
  Pennsylvania

Donald W. Huffman
Cedar Crest College

Susan J. Massad
Springfield College

Jilline G. Seiver
Green River Community
  College

Colin J. Williams
Indiana University/Purdue
  University

Tina Winston
University of
  Wisconsin–Madison

We are also grateful to Herb Samuels for his insights on black sexuality, which were made use of in the Volume Introduction. We would also like to thank Terri Clark, for her assistance with the instructor's manual, and Joan Taverner, for her assistance with library research and the instructor's manual. Continue to write to us in care of Dushkin/McGraw-Hill with comments and suggestions for issues and readings.

Benjamin Franklin once remarked that democracies are built on compromises. But you cannot have healthy compromises unless people talk with each other and try to understand, appreciate, and respect their different ways of reasoning, their values, and their goals. Open and frank discussions of controversial issues is what this book is all about. Without healthy controversy and open exchange of different views, intolerance and bigotry could easily increase to the point where our democratic system could no longer function. Democracy thrives on controversy.

Robert T. Francoeur
Fairleigh Dickinson University

William J. Taverner

CONTENTS IN BRIEF

CONTENTS

Psychologist Deborah Anapol argues that our social environment has changed so much over the past century that monogamy can no longer function as the sole pattern for adult love and family. Anapol asserts that society would be much better off if we accepted a variety of marriage patterns, including exclusive monogamy, flexible, open forms of pair-bonding, and intimate networks. Therapist John Gray maintains that we should endorse and allow only strict monogamy because it is the one path to true love. He argues that we create distrust and destroy any chance of finding and keeping a soul mate when we allow our sexual energy to stray.

Simon LeVay and Dean H. Hamer, researchers in neuroanatomy and biochemistry, respectively, maintain that evidence of differences in the brain structures of gay and straight men indicate that genetic and/or hormonal factors play a role in the early development of sexual orientation. Neuroscientist William Byne argues that the origins of our sexual orientation lie "not within the biology of human brains but rather in the cultures those brains have created."

Pat Califia, a feminist and self-described sex radical, argues that John Money's concept of lovemaps reflects a high-handed, moralistic division of the world into "normal" and "abnormal" sexuality. She believes that many "differently-pleasured" persons, including homosexuals, are at risk because of the moralistic distinctions implicit in Money's model of lovemaps. John Money, an expert on gender development, argues that every society has taboos and establishes a sexual ethic and that the idea of a sexual democracy where people can love whomever they please in whatever fashion they please is unachievable because of those taboos.

Journalist James Carville applauds Louisiana's attempt to strengthen marriages and families by offering couples a choice between a traditional marriage with the possibility of no-fault divorce and a covenant marriage with much stricter limits on divorce. Clinical psychiatrist Peter D. Kramer maintains that creating two kinds of marriage invites couples to lash themselves to a morality of commitment that the broader culture does not support. He believes that the conventional form of modern marriage is much more in tune with the prevailing values of personal independence, autonomy, and fulfillment than is lifelong, exclusive monogamy.

Therapist John Gray argues that men and women can learn to communicate much better and have more loving relationships if they try to understand the consequences of their coming from two "different planets," meaning that they behave and react differently to the same situations and speak very different languages. Susan Hamson, a doctoral candidate at Temple University, rejects Gray's assertions of profound behavioral differences between men and women as being based solely on his intuitions and feedback from seminar audiences rather than on real research. She maintains that Gray's picture of male/female communications and his recommendations for better communication are loaded with patronizing sexist biases that degrade women.

The Center for Population Options, an organization that promotes healthy decision making about sexuality among youth, outlines what is known about the sexual behavior and the accompanying health risks of teens today, examines strategies for reducing these risks, and concludes that making condoms available to students through the schools with counseling and education is the best course of action. Professor of education Edwin J. Delattre identifies several flaws in the argument that we have a moral obligation to distribute condoms to save lives, and he discusses various moral issues involved in promoting casual sexual involvement, which he believes condom distribution does.

Martha Cornog, manager of Membership Services at the American College of Physicians in Philadelphia, Pennsylvania, maintains that public libraries that preserve and make available materials, including controversial sexuality materials, facilitate and promote debate, which is essential in the democratic process. James L. Sauer, a librarian at Eastern College in Phoenixville, Pennsylvania, claims that it is proper for libraries to use their censorship power to curb unfettered expression that violates or attacks the moral values of society.

Author James Bovard asserts that legalizing sex work would help stem the spread of AIDS and free up the police to focus on controlling violent crime. Anastasia Volkonsky, founding director of PROMISE, an organization dedicated to combating sexual exploitation, maintains that decriminalizing prostitution would only cause social harm, particularly to women.

Douglas Johnson, legislative director for the National Right to Life Committee, contends that President Clinton's insistence on including a clause allowing late-term abortion in the case of a serious threat to the mother's life or health will permit the thousands of partial-birth abortions being performed annually on healthy babies of healthy mothers to continue unabated. President William J. Clinton, in his notification to Congress, explains that although he abhors late-term abortions, he cannot sign a bill restricting this procedure unless it contains an exception in the case of a serious threat to the mother's life or health.

Loretta M. Kopelman, a professor of medical humanities, argues that certain moral absolutes apply to all cultures and that these, combined with the many serious health and cultural consequences of female circumcision, require that all forms of female genital mutilation be eliminated. P. Masila Mutisya, a professor of multicultural education, asserts that although most forms of female circumcision should be banned, the simplest form should be allowed as part of the rich heritage of rites of passage for newborn and pubertal girls in those cultures that have this tradition.

Thomas Lickona, a developmental psychologist and professor of education, argues that several studies show that teens who were given a value-free, nondirective, comprehensive sex education were significantly more likely to initiate sexual intercourse than teenagers whose sex education did not include discussion of contraceptives. Lickona concludes that only a program that stresses abstinence and does not discuss contraceptives will reduce premature sex, pregnancy, and sexual diseases among teenagers. Peggy Brick and Deborah M. Roffman, consultants and sexuality educator trainers, maintain that abstinence-only education "does not adequately address the developmental needs of children and adolescents, the reality of their lives, or the societal forces that condition their view of the world." They contend that only a comprehensive sex education that includes both abstinence education and contraceptive use can begin to meet the needs of young people.

Social commentator Simon Winchester argues that society must take measures to regulate and control the dissemination of sexual barbarism and criminal perversion on the over 5,000 online newsgroups and equally numerous chat groups on the Internet. Lisa Mason, a science fiction writer, concludes that Internet censorship will not work, based on the Internet's global nature, its complex and different functions, the limits we already have on free speech, the fact that free speech is not always pretty, and the Internet's ability to enhance the freedom of citizens in a democracy.

Philosophy professor Christine Pierce argues that lesbian and gay couples should not be denied the monetary and social benefits that married hetero-sexuals enjoy. She contends that allowing gay and lesbian couples to register as domestic partners but not to marry leaves homosexuals as second-class citizens with unequal rights. Robert H. Knight, director of cultural studies at the Family Research Council, argues that recognizing gay marriages would destroy society's traditional protection of marriage and family as the best environment for children, legitimize same-sex activity, allow homosexuals to adopt children, and undermine the crucial kinship structure that gives continuity, community, and stability to our society.

Douglas J. Besharov, a resident scholar at the American Enterprise Institute in Washington, D.C., argues that carefully conducted research in Europe and the United States shows that chemical castration is effective, more humane, and much less expensive than imprisonment for some convicted compulsive sex offenders. Andrew Vachhs, a juvenile justice advocate and novelist, asserts that chemical and surgical castration both fail to address aggression as an underlying motive for repeat sex offenders.

Feminist author Andrea Dworkin describes the numerous ways in which pornography is used by men in American culture to degrade women and to violate their civil rights. Professor of law Nadine Strossen argues that "po-litical correctness" movements on college campuses and misguided feminist assaults on pornography have resulted in the naive belief that pornography is a major weapon used by men to degrade and dominate women.

Eugene T. Gomulka, a commander in the U.S. Navy Chaplain Corps, argues that gays should be banned from the military because of the "behavioral problems" and tensions that come with housing gay and heterosexual personnel together in close quarters. Charles L. Davis, a political scientist, argues that any policy that does not grant full rights to gays to serve in the military fosters distrust and suspicion, which weakens the military and its effectiveness.

Professor of humanities Camille Paglia argues that feminists have grossly distorted the facts about date rape and that date rape propaganda actually puts women in greater danger of being raped. Robin Warshaw, a journalist who specializes in social issues, concludes that date rape is extremely pervasive but that relatively few victims are aware that they have been raped.

Tom A. Coburn, a Republican U.S. representative from Oklahoma, argues that we are not making as much progress as we should and could be making in controlling the spread of HIV, because we have given privacy rights priority over traditional, tried and proven tools of public health policy. Christopher DeMarco, an AIDS specialist, agrees that traditional public health measures will help reduce the spread of HIV infection. However, he maintains that some of these measures carry serious risks to the civil rights of infected individuals and that we must ensure equal access to medications and avoid reducing prevention education.

Catharine R. Stimpson, a former graduate dean of Rutgers University, claims that sexual harassment is epidemic in American society and will remain epidemic as long as males are in power and control. Gretchen Morgenson, senior editor of *Forbes* magazine, argues that statistics on the prevalence of sexual harassment are grossly exaggerated by "consultants" who make a good livelihood instituting corporate anti-harassment programs.

INTRODUCTION

Sexual Attitudes in Perspective

Robert T. Francoeur

How do we develop our attitudes, values, and stereotypes about what is proper and expected behavior for men and women? Where do we get our ideas and beliefs about the purposes of sexual intercourse, sexual behavior, the role and position of the child in the family, the role of the family in society, and countless other sexual issues?

In part, the newborn infant learns about gender roles and what is right or wrong in sexual relations through conditioning by his or her parents and by society. Sociologists call this conditioning process socialization, or social scripting. They study the processes whereby each newborn infant is introduced to the values and attitudes of his or her social group; sociologists start their examination with the family and branch out to include the broader community as well. Psychologists talk about the process of psychological conditioning and learned responses. Anthropologists speak of the process of enculturation and study how the infant becomes a person who can function within a particular culture, more or less adopting the values and attitudes characteristic of that culture. Educators talk about value-oriented education and values clarification. Religious leaders speak of divine revelations, commandments, and indoctrination with moral principles and values. Each of these perspectives gives us some clues as to how we develop as individuals with different sets of values and attitudes about sexuality and other aspects of human life.

Before we explore the contrasting views on specific controversial human sexuality issues contained in this volume, we should try to understand our own views, and those of others who take positions that are different from ours, by reviewing some key insights into our development as thinking persons. We can start with the insights of three developmental psychologists. Working from that base, we can move to a cultural perspective and consider some socioeconomic and ethnic factors that help to shape our attitudes about sex. To fill out our picture, we can briefly examine two religious perspectives that play a major role in the attitudes and values we adopt and come to defend with both tenacity and emotion.

THE INSIGHTS OF DEVELOPMENTAL PSYCHOLOGY

Jean Piaget
According to the theories of Jean Piaget (1896–1980), the famous Swiss developmental psychologist, we begin life as completely amoral, totally self-centered beings. For the first two years of life, we are only concerned with

our basic survival needs. The need for food, comfort, and security make us oblivious to the values of our parents. We do not understand nor do we care about what our families or culture have to say about our future roles as males or females and the kinds of relations and behaviors we might engage in. However, our parents are already conditioning and scripting us for our future roles. Parents and other adults generally treat boy and girl infants differently.

By age two, the child enters a stage of development Piaget calls the *egocentric stage*. For the next five years or so, the child has only a very general idea of what the rules are. As the child becomes aware of these rules, he or she tries to change them to accommodate personal needs and wants. A child's world is centered on itself. The child manipulates the world outside, then adjusts to the demands and expectations of parents and others.

By age seven, the child is ready to enter a new stage of development, which Piaget calls the *heteronomous stage*. In this stage, morality and what we see as right and wrong is based on outside authorities and a morality based on rules and laws. Guided by parents and other authority figures, the child begins to assert some degree of logical and moral control over his or her behavior. Between the ages of 7 and 12, the child begins to distinguish between valid and invalid ideas. Authority becomes a dominant concern, regardless of whether it is a parent, teacher, or older child who exerts it. The child often accepts an idea, attitude, or value without question, and issues tend to be seen in terms of black and white. There is little understanding of what is moral because of the total acceptance of the morality imposed by others.

As a young person enters the early teen years, he or she begins to comprehend values and apply them in original ways. This marks a transition, a turning point before one accepts full moral responsibility for one's life.

Finally, usually sometime after age 12, the young person starts moving into what Piaget calls an *autonomous stage*. At this level of moral development, we start thinking and acting as adults. We accept personal responsibility. We think in terms of cooperation rather than constraint. Peer interactions, discussions, criticisms, a sense of equality, and a respect for others help us to develop this sense of morality and values. We begin to see other perspectives on moral and ethical issues. We may question and struggle to verify rules and ideas. If we find a rule morally acceptable, we internalize it, making it an integral part of our values.

Lawrence Kohlberg

Lawrence Kohlberg, another influential developmental psychologist, built on Piaget's model of moral development and expanded it with further insights. Instead of Piaget's egocentric, heteronomous, and autonomous stages, Kohlberg speaks of preconventional, conventional, and postconventional stages. He then divides each of these stages into two substages.

On the level of *preconventional morality*, the child responds to cultural rules and the labels of good and bad. This level is divided into two stages: (1) punishment and obedience orientation and (2) instrumental relativist orientation.

At this level, the child expresses a total respect for the authority figure and has only a very primitive sense of morality. On the second level of preconventional morality, the child is concerned with satisfying its own needs rather than the needs of others or of society.

When we reach the level of *conventional morality*, our sense of values is characterized by conformity to and maintenance of the moral conventions that are expected by one's family, group, or nation (stage 3)—regardless of the consequences. When we first begin to think in terms of social conventions, we are labeled a good boy or nice girl if we conform our behavior to familial and societal norms. As we reach stage 4, our understanding of conventional morality matures, and we develop a sense of law and order, focusing on fixed rules and upholding the social order. On this level, moral behavior consists of respecting authority and maintaining the social order so that society can function smoothly.

Finally, Kohlberg describes a *postconventional morality*, which is very similar to Piaget's autonomous stage. At this stage, an individual tries to define his or her own morality apart from that of authoritative figures. Stage 5, the social contract stage, is reached when an individual puts an emphasis on what is legally binding but realizes that laws may change to meet social demands. The last stage of moral development is the level of universal ethical principle orientation. At this level, a person's conscience serves as the judge for moral dilemmas. Abstract qualities such as justice, human rights, respect for the dignity of human life, and equality become important in making decisions. For some people, adherence to an inner conscience may require them to break a law for a higher purpose.

While Kohlberg's theory is more detailed, it overlaps in many ways with Piaget's model. In a revision of his work, Kohlberg implies that a higher stage, such as stage 5 or 6, is not necessarily better than a lower stage, and that most people do not reach the sixth stage. In fact, Kohlberg's research suggests that most people seem to get "stuck" in stage 4, where law and order is the overriding orientation. What connections, if any, can you see between these two models of moral development and the value systems based on either a fixed or a process worldview?

Carol Gilligan

In 1982 Carol Gilligan, a Harvard psychologist, criticized Kohlberg's theory and its conclusions, and by implication the model suggested by Piaget. She suggests that these theories break down when applied to the ways in which women deal with moral issues. Studies have shown that when female solutions to hypothetical moral dilemmas are evaluated using Kohlberg's scheme, women appear to be "stuck" at the second level, that of conventional morality, where moral decisions are made in terms of pleasing and helping others. Gilligan rejects this conclusion. She contends that women are not deficient or immature in their moral development but that the standard against which they are measured is biased. Kohlberg's model was derived from a 20-year study of moral development in 84 boys and no girls, although the model has been generalized and applied to the moral sensitivity of both men and women.

As a result of some pilot studies of moral reasoning in women, Gilligan suggests that there is another, equally valid, moral perspective besides Kohlberg's "justice and rights" framework. She calls this second perspective the "care" perspective because it emphasizes relationships and connections between people rather than an abstract hierarchy of rules and rights. This framework stresses nurturance and responsibility to and for others. For Gilligan, the justice and the care perspectives of morality are different, but neither is superior to the other. Neither is more or less mature. Both are necessary for human survival.

Gilligan points out that the two moral frameworks are gender related, but not gender specific. For the most part, women seem to be more comfortable within the care perspective and men within the justice and rights perspective. However, in some instances, women reason from a justice/rights view and men from a care view.

SOCIAL AND ETHNIC FACTORS IN OUR VALUES

In our personal development, socioeconomic and ethnic factors play a major role in the sexual values and attitudes we incorporate into our lives.

The kinds of values and attitudes toward sex that we adopt in growing up are very much affected by our family's income level and general socioeconomic status. Studies have shown that, in general, there is more mutuality and sharing between men and women in the middle class than in the blue-collar working class. Working-class males are more reluctant to share in household duties and are more apt to segregate themselves from women at social functions. Working-class women tend toward passivity and nurturing and are more emotionally volatile than their middle-class counterparts. Studies have also indicated that one's occupation, educational level, and income are closely related to one's values, attitudes, role conceptions, child-rearing practices, and sexual identity.

Our values and attitudes about sex are also influenced by whether we are brought up in a rural, suburban, or large urban environment. Our ethnic background can be an important, if subtle, influence on our values and attitudes. In contrast to the vehement debates among white, middle-class Americans about pornography, for instance, Robert Staples, a professor of sociology at the University of California, San Francisco, says that among American blacks, pornography is a trivial issue. "Blacks," Staples explains, "have traditionally had a more naturalistic attitude toward human sexuality, seeing it as the normal expression of sexual attraction between men and women.... Rather than seeing the depiction of heterosexual intercourse or nudity as an inherent debasement of women, as a fringe group of [white] feminists claims, the black community would see women as having equal rights to the enjoyment of sexual stimuli.... Since the double [moral] standard has never attracted many American blacks, the claim that women are exploited by exhibiting their nude bodies or engaging in heterosexual intercourse lacks credibility" (quoted in Philip Nobile and Eric Nadler, *United States of America vs. Sex* [Minotaur Press, 1986]). While middle-class whites may be very concerned about pornography promoting sexual promiscuity, most black Americans are much more concerned about issues related to poverty and employment opportunities.

Similarly, attitudes toward homosexuality vary among white, black, and Latino cultures. In the macho tradition of Latin America, homosexual behavior is a sign that one cannot find a woman and have sexual relationships like a "real" man. In lower socioeconomic black cultures, this same judgment prevails in its own way. Understanding this ethnic value becomes very important in appreciating the ways in which blacks and Latinos respond to the crisis of AIDS and the presence of males with AIDS in their families. Often the family will deny that a son or husband has AIDS until the very end because others might interpret this admission as a confession that the man is homosexual.

Another example of differing ethnic values is the issue of single motherhood. In ethnic groups with a strong tradition of extended matrilineal families, the concept of an "illegitimate" or "illegal" child born "out-of-wedlock" may not even exist. Unmarried mothers in these cultures do not carry the same stigma often associated with single mothers in other, less-matrilineal cultures. When "outsiders" who do not share the particular ethnic values of a culture enter into such a subculture, they often cannot understand why birth control and family life educational programs do not produce any substantial change in attitudes. They overlook the basic social scripting that has already taken place.

Gender roles also vary from culture to culture. Muslim men and women who grow up in the Middle East and then emigrate to the United States have to adapt to the much greater freedom women have in the States. Similarly, American men and women who served in the armed forces in Saudi Arabia during the 1990 Persian Gulf War found they had to adapt to a very different Muslim culture, one that put many restrictions on the movement and dress of women, including Americans.

A boy who grows up among the East Bay Melanesians in the Southwestern Pacific is taught to avoid any social contact with girls from the age of three or four, even though he may run around naked and masturbate in public. Adolescent Melanesian boys and girls are not allowed to have sex with each other, but boys are expected to have sex both with an older male and with a boy of his own age. Their first heterosexual experiences come with marriage. In the Cook Islands, Mangaian boys are expected to have sex with many girls after an older woman teaches them about the art of sexual play. Mangaians also accept and expect both premarital and extramarital sex.

But one does not have to look to exotic anthropological studies to find evidence of the importance of ethnic values. Even within the United States, one can find subtle but important differences in sexual attitudes and values among people of French, German, Italian, Polish, Spanish, Portuguese, Dutch, Scandinavian, Irish, and English descent.

RELIGIOUS FACTORS IN OUR ATTITUDES TOWARD SEX

In the Middle Ages Christian theologians divided sexual behaviors into two categories: behaviors that were "natural" and those that were "unnatural." Since they believed that the natural function and goal of all sexual behavior and relations was reproduction, masturbation was unnatural because it frustrated the natural goal of conception and continuance of the species. Rape certainly was considered illicit because it was not within the marital bond, but since it was procreative, rape was considered a natural use of sex. The same system of distinction was applied to other sexual relations and behaviors. Premarital sex, adultery, and incest were natural uses of sexuality, while oral sex, anal sex, and contraception were unnatural. Homosexual relations, of course, were both illicit and unnatural. These religious values were based on the view that God created man and woman at the beginning of time and laid down certain rules and guidelines for sexual behavior and relations. This view is still very influential in our culture, even for those who are not active in any religious tradition.

In recent years several analysts have highlighted two philosophical or religious perspectives that appear throughout Judeo-Christian tradition and Western civilization.[1] Understanding these two perspectives is important in any attempt to debate controversial issues in human sexuality.

Let me introduce these two distinct worldviews by drawing on a non-Western example from history—the Islamic or Muslim world of the Middle East and the politics of Iran and Egypt. On one side of the spectrum are Muslims, who see the world as a process, an ever-changing scene in which they must struggle to reinterpret and apply the basic principles of the Koran (the sacred book of the teachings of Allah, or God) to new situations. On the opposing side of the spectrum are fundamentalist Muslims who, years ago, overthrew the shah of Iran and then tried to return Iran and the Muslim world to the authentic faith of Muhammed and the Koran. This meant purging Iran's Islamic society of all the Western and modern customs the shah had encouraged. Anwar Sadat, the late president of Egypt, was assassinated by Muslim fundamentalists who opposed his tolerance of Muslim women being employed outside the home and wearing Western dress instead of the traditional black, neck-to-ankle chador. These fundamentalists were also repulsed by the suggestion made by Sadat's wife that Muslim women should have the right to seek divorce and alimony. Nowadays Muslim women do have the right to divorce their husbands, but new issues that raise conflicts between the two worldviews continually arise in the Middle East, such as the 1993 election of Tansu Ciller as Turkey's first female prime minister.

These same two worldviews are equally obvious in the ongoing history of American culture. Religious fundamentalists, New Right politicians, and various members of the American Family Association, the Family Research Council of America, Focus on the Family, and the Eagle Forum believe that we need to return to traditional values. These distinct groups often share a conviction that the sexual revolution, changing attitudes toward masturbation and homosexuality, a tolerance of premarital and extramarital sex, sex education in the schools instead of in the homes, and the legality of abortion are contributing to a cultural decline and must be rejected.

At the same time, other Americans argue for legalized abortion, civil rights for homosexuals, decriminalization of prostitution, androgynous sex roles in child-rearing practices, and the abolition of all laws restricting the right to privacy for sexually active, consenting adults.

Recent efforts to analyze the dogma behind the fundamentalist and the "changing-world" value systems have revealed two distinct worldviews, or philosophies, tenuously coexisting for centuries within the Judaic, Christian, and Islamic traditions. When Ernst Mayr, a biologist at Harvard University, traced the history of biological theories, he concluded that no greater revolution has occurred in the history of human thought than the radical shift from a fixed worldview of cosmology rooted in unchanging archetypes to a dynamic, evolving cosmogenic worldview based on populations and individuals. While the process or evolutionary worldview may have gained dominance in Western cultures and religious traditions, the influences felt by such groups as the Moral Majority and religious New Right in the United States, the rise of Islamic fundamentalism in Iran and the Near East, and the growing vitality of orthodox Judaism provide ample evidence that the fixed worldview still has clear influence in moderating human behavior.

These two worldviews characteristically permeate and color the way we look at and see everything in our lives. One or the other view colors the way each of us approaches a particular political, economic, or moral issue, as well as the way we reach decisions about sexual issues and relationships. However, one must keep in mind that no one is ever fully and always on one or the other end of the spectrum. The spectrum of beliefs, attitudes, and values proposed here is an intellectual abstraction. Real life is not that simple. Still, it is a useful model that can help us to understand each other's positions on controversial issues provided we realize that the fixed and process worldviews are at the two ends of a continuum that includes a wide range of approaches to moral and sexual issues. While individuals often take a fixed position on one issue and a process position on a second issue, they generally tend to adopt one or the other approach and maintain a fairly consistent set of intertwined religious values and attitudes with respect to sexuality.

Either we view the world as a completely finished universe in which human nature was perfectly and completely created by some supreme being, unchanging in essence from the beginning, or we picture the world as continually changing with human nature constantly evolving as it struggles to reach its fuller potential, or what is called "to become by the deity." Either one believes that the first human beings were created by God as unchanging archetypes, thus determining standards of human behavior for all time, including our fixed roles as males and females, or one believes that human nature, behavior, and moral standards have been evolving since the beginning of the human race. In the former view, a supreme being created an unchanging human nature. In the latter view, the deity created human nature, then let it transform under human influences.

Coming out of these two views of the world and human nature, one finds two distinct views of the origins of evil and sexuality. If one believes that human nature and the nature of sexual relations were established in the beginning, then one also finds it congenial to believe that evil results from some original sin, a primeval fall of the first humans from a state of perfection and grace. If, on the other hand, one believes in an evolving human nature, then physical and moral evils are viewed as inevitable, natural growth pains that come as humans struggle toward the fullness of their creation.

The Work of James W. Prescott
One paradigm in particular is worth mentioning here to emphasize the importance of the two ways people view the world and their sexual attitudes, beliefs, and values. This model resulted from years of analyzing cross-cultural data, surveys of college students' attitudes, and voting patterns in state and federal governments. James W. Prescott, a noted neuropsychologist, began by examining the effects of the lack of nurturance and somatosensory stimulation on infant monkeys raised and studied by psychologists Harry and Margaret Harlow. In the Harlow studies, some monkeys were taken from their mothers immediately after birth and raised with only a wire mesh and a nursing bottle serving as a surrogate mother. Control infants remained with their natural mothers. Without the normal touching and cuddling of a parent, the test infants quickly became antisocial, withdrawn, and often autistic in their behavior. They were terrified at the approach of other monkeys and at the possibility of being touched. Infant monkeys nurtured and cuddled by a natural mother were peaceful and socially well adjusted when they grew up. Prescott then began to wonder whether or not these effects would be consistent with human child-rearing practices.[2]

From these varied biological, developmental, and cross-cultural studies, Prescott derived a behavioral/attitudinal pattern that links somatosensory affectional deprivation or positive nurturance in infancy and childhood with adult behaviors and attitudes. His statistical analysis reveals a causal connection between parental attitudes, child-rearing values, and the subsequent social adaptation, or lack of it, in the children when they grow up. In societies or families that encourage body pleasuring and somatosensory nurturance, parents commonly share a wide variety of nonviolent values, attitudes, and behavioral patterns for which their children are neurologically scripted by a high level of nurturing touch during infancy, childhood, and adolescence.

In subsequent statistical analyses using both contemporary American, Canadian, and European data, Prescott correlated the lack of childhood nurturance with negative attitudes toward gun control laws, nudity, sexual pleasure, masturbation, premarital and extramarital sex, breast-feeding, and women. Other values consistently associated with this perspective include a glorification of war and the frequent use of alcohol and drugs. Societal factors that were correlated with a high nurturance of infants include a lack of strong social stratification; prolonged breast-feeding; a strong sense of humor; an acceptance of abortion, premarital sex, and extramarital sex; low anxiety about sex; little sexual dysfunction; a negative view of war; and satisfying peer relationships between men and women.

Religious beliefs undoubtedly affect the child-rearing practices of our parents, which in turn color the way each of us views our sexuality and our attitudes toward different sexual behaviors and relationships. These same religious beliefs affect and color our social scripting and enculturation as we grow up and move through the stages of moral development outlined by Piaget, Kohlberg, and Gilligan. Along the way, we pick up values and attitudes that are peculiar to our ethnic and socioeconomic background.

APPROACHING THE ISSUES IN THIS VOLUME

As you consider the controversial issues in this volume of *Taking Sides*, think of how your parents, family, friends, and associates have helped to mold your opinions on specific issues. Try to be sensitive to how religious, racial, ethnic, and socioeconomic factors in your own background may affect the positions you take on different issues. At the same time, try to appreciate how these same factors may have influenced the people whose opinions clash with your own.

NOTES

1. Details of the perspectives offered in this introductory essay can be found in the author's chapter "Religious Reactions to Alternative Lifestyles," in E. D. Macklin and R. H. Rubin, eds., *Contemporary Families and Alternative Lifestyles: A Handbook on Research and Theory* (Sage Publications, 1983). In that chapter I summarize and give a complete comparison of seven models developed by researchers working independently in quite distinct disciplines. Included are a behavioral model based on a comparison of chimpanzee, baboon, and human social behavior by the British primatologist Michael Chance; a cultural/moral model based on an analysis of British and French arts, fashions, politics, lifestyles, and social structures proposed by British science writer and philosopher Gordon Rattray Taylor; a cross-cultural comparison based on child-rearing nurturance patterns and adult lifestyles by neuropsychologist James W. Prescott; a model relating lifestyles and values with technological and economic structures by economist/engineer Mario Kamenetzky; a model of open and closed marriages created by George and Nena O'Neill, authors of the 1972 best-seller *Open Marriage*; and my own model of "Hot and Cool Sexual Values," which I adapted from an insight by Marshall McLuhan and George B. Leonard.

2. J. W. Prescott, "Body Pleasure and the Origins of Violence," *The Futurist* (vol. 9, no. 2, 1975), pp. 64–74.

On the Internet . . .

Sacred Space Institute
The Sacred Space Institute is an organization that advocates "polyamourous" relationships, or what is commonly referred to as multiple-partner, or open, relationships. *http://www.lovewithoutlimits.com/*

Sex Information and Education Council of the United States
The Sex Information and Education Council of the United States (SIECUS) is a national, nonprofit organization that affirms that sexuality is a natural and healthy part of living. Incorporated in 1964, SIECUS develops, collects, and disseminates information, promotes comprehensive education about sexuality, and advocates the right of individuals to make responsible sexual choices. *http://www.siecus.org/*

The Gay and Lesbian Alliance Against Defamation (GLAAD) Web Site
GLAAD was formed in New York in 1985. Its mission is to improve the public's attitudes toward homosexuality and to put an end to violence and discrimination against lesbians and gay men. *http://www.glaad.org/glaad/*

The Intersex Society of North America
The Intersex Society of North America (ISNA) is a peer support, education, and advocacy group founded and operated by and for intersexuals, or individuals born with anatomy or physiology that differs from cultural ideals of male and female. *http://www.isna.org/*

Transgender Forum
This site offers information and links regarding transgender issues. *http://www.tgforum.com/*

PART 1

Biology, Behavior, and Human Sexuality

In Western civilization, a traditional belief has been that our ability to transcend emotion, think rationally, and experience love sets us apart from the world of brute animals, whose every behavior seems to be dictated by genes. Genes and hormones do play a role in human development, but are they relevant to how we experience gender, sexual orientation, sexual interactions, sexual drive, and pair-bonding? In this section we explore five aspects of the connection between nature—genes and hormones—and nurture, or our social conditioning and learning.

■ Should We Accept Alternatives to Monogamy?

■ Is Male Homosexuality Biologically Influenced?

■ Is the Model of Normal and Vandalized Gendermaps/ Lovemaps Biased?

■ Should Society Recognize Two Kinds of Marriage?

■ Are Men Really from Mars and Women from Venus?

ISSUE 1

Should We Accept Alternatives to Monogamy?

YES: Deborah Anapol, from "Monogamy: A Debate," *Free Spirit* (June/July 1995)

NO: John Gray, from "Monogamy: A Debate," *Free Spirit* (June/July 1995)

ISSUE SUMMARY

YES: Psychologist Deborah Anapol argues that our social environment has changed so much over the past century that monogamy can no longer function as the sole pattern for adult love and family. Anapol asserts that society would be much better off if we accepted a variety of marriage patterns, including exclusive monogamy, flexible, open forms of pair-bonding, and intimate networks.

NO: Therapist John Gray maintains that we should endorse and allow only strict monogamy because it is the one path to true love. He argues that we create distrust and destroy any chance of finding and keeping a soul mate when we allow our sexual energy to stray.

For many people, marriage means "forsaking all others... until death do us part." Single or married, young or old, religious or not, most Americans expect marriage to be a lifelong romance coupled with sexual and emotional exclusivity.

The reality of American marriages, however, seldom matches these expectations. Over half the marriages in the United States end in divorce. The average marriage lasts not a lifetime but seven years. Serial polygamy— divorce and remarriage, often repeated two, three, or more times—is more common than lifelong marriage to one spouse. The rate at which American couples of all ages live together without being married has tripled since 1960. And between one-quarter and one-half of all husbands and wives—perhaps more—stray into affairs. In reality, only 10–20 percent of Americans are truly monogamous.

Western religious leaders and politicians often claim that sexually exclusive monogamy is the highest level of social evolution, the hallmark of an advanced civilization, and the only acceptable form of marriage. But some of the most primitive cultures are much more strictly monogamous than some highly advanced cultures are. In addition, sociologists Clelland Ford and Frank Beech studied 185 contemporary cultures and found that only 29 cultures (less than 16 percent) restricted men and women to a single sexual partner for life. Equally important is the finding that less than one-third of the 29 monogamous cultures completely disapproved of both premarital and extramarital relations. And most of the monogamous cultures allowed men some freedom to engage in sex outside marriage.

History and anthropology indicate that each human society adapts the structure of marriage to meet its particular social environment, with its varied economic, political, and religious needs. And when this environment changes, whether rapidly or slowly, the structure of marriage also changes.

For centuries upper-class marriages were dynastic affairs, arranged by fathers whose sole motives were economics, social status, and extension of family alliances. Among the peasants, marriage was also a pragmatic arrangement. One thousand years ago, in southern France, the concept of courtly love —a passionate love for an unattainable woman, usually the wife of a nobleman—set the stage for two new patterns of marriage.

In Spain, Italy, and much of France, the traditional, family-arranged, economically based marriage was joined with the courtly love code. Since divorce was not possible in the dominant Catholic tradition, social customs evolved that protected marriage and the raising of children but accommodated the wanderlust of both husbands and wives in that extramarital affairs were allowed. The nobility of northern Europe and wealthy, upper-class Americans adopted this pattern.

In northern Europe the emerging middle class was uneasy with the Mediterranean acceptance of affairs. The solution was to shift a man's object of romance from the unattainable wife of another man to a single woman and then to his own wife. In this pattern, love and marriage were combined, and adultery was viewed as a lethal threat to marriage. However, divorce became acceptable as a remedy for infidelity. Middle-class Americans adopted this value system.

This history may seem irrelevant today, but the debate between Deborah Anapol and John Gray cannot be understood without it. Anapol asserts that recent changes in human life expectancy, people's sexual needs and expectations, women's liberation, contraceptive technologies, and mobility have so radically changed the social environment that individual men and women must be allowed to structure their intimate relationships and sexual lives however they can to best adapt to this complex and rapidly changing social system. Gray argues that one spouse for life and sexual fidelity before and during marriage are and will always be the only path to true love and the only acceptable pattern of marriage.

YES

Deborah Anapol

MONOGAMY: AN IDEA WHOSE TIME HAS PAST

Were human beings ever monogamous?

Not really. Monogamous marriage certainly has existed in the Western patriarchal culture but it existed with a behind-the-scenes recognition that men, particularly, were going to have other lovers and that this was okay.

Explain how our overemphasis on monogamy is the root of violence and marital discord.

Basically, the way I see it is this: Because we sanction only monogamy in this culture, those of us who want to be good, upstanding citizens and who believe the morality that we've been taught in our churches and schools are put in a position of denying our sexuality, which naturally wants to extend itself out beyond one partner. Particularly in a culture like the one we have now. You know, hundreds of years ago when most people only lived 30 or 40 years, they had to work very long hours under adverse conditions. And I think you didn't have the leisure time and the good health and the sexual and psychological sophistication and expectations that we have now. The average person back then was really involved in survival. The average person now is sexually frustrated largely because of our insistence on monogamy. Researchers such as James Prescott and Wilhelm Reich have made it very clear that violence and aggression are, in essence, frustrated sexual energy. It's redirected sexual energy. We have a choice really of directing our life force into love, pleasure and sexuality or directing it into violence, aggression and oppression or repression. So the fact is, very few people find one sexual partner to be totally satisfying for a lifetime or even for more than a few years. Some of the work that has come out recently looking at census data around the world shows a huge peak in the divorce rate after four years of marriage. The evidence that is being presented now says that brain chemistry actually changes after four years and that this seems to be tied to the length of time that a woman in a more natural society would conceive, give birth and wean a child. And they considered breast-feeding went on for two to four years, not six months or a year as we do it now.

If violence is caused by frustrated sexual energy mischanneled, what would need to be different for that scenario to change?

I think a whole shift from a sex-negative to a sex-positive ethic. A sex-positive point of view regards sexuality as something sacred, and holy. Beyond the '60s idea of if it feels good, do it, to a recognition that our sexual force is our life force. So we need to first educate our young people about how to have satisfying, fulfilling sexual encounters without transmitting diseases or having unplanned pregnancies. We need to provide and support opportunities for people of all ages to express themselves sexually.

How would that work?

Well, for example, in this culture, we attempt to prevent our young people from being sexually active by not allowing them the privacy in which to be sexual, by not providing them with condoms and other means of contraception and disease prevention. We don't initiate them, as has been done in some indigenous cultures, where not only are young people encouraged to become sexually active, they're actually instructed by those older and more experienced in how to do that. And then of course there is the whole social censure, particularly against adolescent girls, although it extends somewhat to boys, that basically says that nice girls don't.

Now, especially for older young adults, college students, people in their 20s, it's very acceptable for them to be sexually active, to live together without being married. That's changing quite a bit but I think most young people don't get that exposure and that experience until they've left home, till they've gone to college or moved out on their own. Very few parents are really willing to have their children's lovers come and spend the night.

Now let me switch to our overemphasis on monogamy causing marital discord. How does that work?

To put it very simply, infidelity is the leading cause of divorce and the next most common cause of divorce is domestic violence which frequently has to do with infidelity. There's an expectation that if you get married and if your partner really loves you, they're not attracted to anybody else. The reality is that even people who desire and choose to be monogamous are going to be attracted to others and many of them act on it, secretly, because they don't realize that perhaps they could have negotiated with their partner, that they could, with each other's consent, have other lovers. It doesn't even occur to them that it's a possibility to do it legitimately, and so they cheat. And the betrayal and the deception are very destructive to an intimate relationship. In many cases it does destroy it, as it should, I think. I wouldn't want to be in a marriage where my partner was lying and cheating, although I'd be happy to be in a relationship where my partner and I have agreed that it's okay to be sexual with others.

So you think the remedy is, rather than hopelessly trying to enforce monogamy, to throw it out? If people acknowledge that they're not going to be monogamous then they don't have a chance for betrayal?

Right. There are actually lots of alternatives. There are lots of ways to create a relationship that is loving, committed, responsible, honest, intimate, sexually satisfying; all of the things that people are looking for in monogamy but without the monogamy. And most people have no idea that these alternatives exist because we're not taught about them. And not only are we not taught about them, we're told that they're evil, that they're sinful, that they're unnatural, that they're not workable. I mean, every argument in the book has been used and is still being used to convince people to stick with monogamy. And yet if we were intended to be monogamous, we would be. There are a few animal species, not very many, that are monogamous. They don't cheat.

Are you saying that we're trying to do something that goes against our very nature? That we can't possibly succeed at? And the effort will cause us untold pain and problems, like violence and marital discord?

Exactly. It's the same thing as if we were insisting that everybody in the society be celibate, and we're sexual beings. And in fact I think that monogamy really evolved as a compromise position where the early Catholic church was holding up celibacy as an ideal. St. Augustine and others really wanted a celibate society but realized that most people couldn't do that. And besides, we needed to reproduce. So monogamy was sort of allowed. They couldn't get rid of sex altogether. They couldn't totally convince people to stop having sex, but at least it was kind of confined and restricted and a lot of the pleasure removed from it. And so today, a thousand or more years later, we are still living out a wrongheaded, antiwoman, and destructive philosophy that says that sexuality is something that

we want to have as little of as possible. We'll allow it basically with a license from the church with one person and nowhere else.

So give us an example, perhaps from your life, of how non-monogamy works.

I first married very young, especially for a baby-boomer. So by the time I was 30, I had been through two essentially monogamous marriages already, and many of my baby-boomer friends were still single and dating and having a great time. "Hey," I thought, "this monogamy stuff doesn't last long-term for me, anyway and I don't want to have 20 marriages by the time I'm 80." So I set out to see what else people were doing. And in fact, over the last 10 years I have talked with hundreds of people in group marriages, people who were in open marriages, couples who have outside relationships, and also intimate networks, which is really what I'm moving toward now myself. An intimate network being kind of a hybrid of all these other forms, I feel, is the best of all worlds.

Describe an intimate network. How does it work for a person?

Mine is made up of both single people and people who are in couples. Some of us live with each other, some of us live alone. And we're all close friends. But unlike an ordinary group of friends, some of us are sexual with each other. Most people in the network are sexual with several other people in the network, although just because you're in it doesn't mean that you have to be lovers with everybody who's in it. And there's a lot of freedom. There is also a lot of caring and commitment and the sense of an extended family. I mean in many ways it's like an extended family in the old days where people get together for birthdays, for holidays, they help each other out if they're having trouble, take care of each other's children. But there's none of the pressure and restrictions that existed in the old extended families. There's not as much emphasis on the group as there would be in a group marriage, where it's more like everybody does everything together and lives together under one roof. So it really allows a maximum of personal responsibility and independence as well as the support of the group.

Say you went to a birthday party and some or all of the members of the network were there, probably with a bunch of other people too. Would you suggest to somebody else in the network, a man who you wanted to hang out with for the whole evening and maybe spend the night with, "Let's go over to your house," or "Come to my house and maybe my husband will be going to someone else's house," or how would that work?

It does require a little bit of communication and planning, especially if people are sensitive about having privacy. I recently had a birthday party and four or five of my lovers were there as well as friends and other people and I didn't really have a plan about who I was going to sleep with that night. Other people might want to arrange it all beforehand with a specific person, that they're going to sleep with them in a specific place.

So does an evening like that almost always involve some angst for somebody who wanted but didn't get? I'd anticipate jealousy and competition and rivalry and ...

Right, it's the whole mentality of scarcity and ownership which is the conditioning that a lot of us have and which goes along with this concept. See, people think that they're going to get security out of monogamy 'cause that means that at least they know who they're with and that they're committed to each other and all of that. But really the way it works is that because people own each other and are exclusively committed to each other, it's easy to be left out. If you flip that mindset into one which is open and inclusive there is not just one person with whom you feel loving and intimate and who you permit yourself to be sexual with. If there are several such people, then if one of them is occupied, there's another one. And because you have several lovers in your life, if you happen to find yourself alone for an evening, it's like, oh, well great, I get some time for myself now. Instead of a sense of scarcity, there's a sense of abundance. There's a sense of many loving friends rather than only one who somebody else might take if I turn my back.

So, how did you make the decision that evening?

That evening it just sort of naturally evolved. One of the men whom I'm close to found himself exploring a new relationship with a woman friend of mine and so he went off with her. So I ended up with another man whom I love dearly and we had a wonderful time together.

Did he ask you or did it just happen?

Neither one, it just, there we were.

Some people think that it's their wiring that they are confronting. That more communication isn't going to change their feelings much. Because when the one they care the most about, or have had a child with, or depend on for income, is walking off with another woman, they're going to feel this thing in the middle of their gut that's always going to be there. That isn't the case?

I don't believe that this is hard-wired. I believe we're conditioned. If you look at our closest primate relative, what you see is a very fluid and open sexuality. The bonobo chimpanzees are bisexual. They pair, they mate with both males and females and they're very promiscuous. There is no evidence of jealousy or competition among them. Now I'm not saying that we're the same as chimpanzees but certainly if it were hard-wired, you'd expect to see it in our closest primate relatives, and you don't.

Maybe it is conditioned, but gosh, half the murders I've read about in the paper over the last year were ex-husbands or lovers killing their wife or their wife's new lovers, and often end [up] killing themselves.

Right. And this has been sanctioned. You're touching on the problem of domestic violence. That's where I started out. And that's what led me into exploring alternatives to monogamy and the nuclear family. I saw, through my doctoral research and years of working with victims of domestic violence, incest and child abuse, that it was the nuclear family system that was fostering that kind of extreme dependency. And that sexual repression does lead to violence.

If we could all be monogamous and be happy that way, that would be great. And we would have done it by now. Instead, we have been insisting on monogamy and what we're seeing is epidemic domestic violence and infidelity.

I realize if I start spinning out stories about my idyllic polyamorous life, most people will feel that's not something that they could turn right around and do.

But you have to realize that I've spent the last 15 years, and the people that I am relating with have spent the last five, 10, 15 years reconditioning ourselves. So we're able to be much freer than most people could immediately. But fortunately, it can be done in a step-like fashion. A couple can create an agreement which is what I did in my last marriage, which said that we each had veto power over any other person or occasion. So I wasn't totally giving up control. My husband wasn't totally giving up control. If he got jealous and he wanted me to not see somebody else, he could say so and that would prevail. And that happened very rarely actually. So there are ways for people to begin exploring this territory without putting themselves in an impossible situation.

Well, what would the instructions be in a starter kit for someone interested in testing this out?

I would say the first step is to have some very clear agreements and to have a total commitment to honesty with each other.

Does that mean telling your primary partner or all your partners who else you've been with?

Yes, unless they specifically say that they don't want to know. Some couples do make agreements that say, "You can do whatever you want as long as I don't know about it." That's not something that I would want to do myself but it works for some people. A good first step is an agreement to discuss and get permission before becoming sexual with another person. Some people want to meet that person first and be sure that the person really respects the marriage and is not thinking, "Oh well, she's letting her husband have a date with me, she must not really want to keep him around." And so a lot of people want to meet a new lover and make sure that that lover really understands and respects their relationship. They want a lot of communication so that if jealousy does come up, which it will for most people initially, they can get help with it. Because jealousy is just really like any other emotion: anger, fear, anxiety. We all have these emotions and we find ways to cope with them. Most parents get angry at their children at some time or another. It just kind of goes with the territory of being a parent. And a few people do decide not to have children because they're afraid they'll get so angry that they'll abuse them, especially if they were abused themselves. But most people go right ahead and have children knowing they're going to get angry at their children and knowing that they're going to handle it. Jealousy in an open marriage can be very much like that. You know it's going to come up and you're prepared to deal with it when it does.

Do you see any kind of a power in a relationship between two people? Could it be possible to sustain over many years a magnetic force or attraction and commitment between two people within this larger intimate network?

Yes. It's sort of hard to compare an intimate network with a one-on-one relationship. And part of my desire to let people know about alternatives to monogamy has to do with what I see as an evolutionary imperative to get beyond the couple. The isolated nuclear family is just not going to make it into the future and we're going [to] have no families at all, I feel, if we don't create room for more diverse forms of families and particularly,

multi-adult families. I just think that the two-adult family is doomed right now.

That extreme dependency... yes, there's a nice kind of romantic glow involved there, but there's also a very unhealthy dependency that I see leads directly to domestic violence. I mean that's when people really get threatened and really get violent when they have all their energy in this one other person. When they don't have a best friend. When they don't have colleagues, when they don't have other people who are very important in their inner life. But getting back to your question of in an intimate network, can this really survive over time? Yes. Very definitely. I think that this whole notion of focusing on one other person for a lifetime, I mean we're talking 60 or 80 years. That, I think, is something that we're just not equipped to do as human beings. We don't tend to have anything in our lives be consistent for that amount of time. As our lifespan increases and as our leisure time increases, few people want to do the same thing forever and ever and ever. I'm not against monogamy. If somebody wants to go off with their one partner and go deep for 60 years with that person, I think that's beautiful. I think it's very rare though. I think instead, most people go very deep for a couple of years, two, four, six, and then the whole thing falls apart. It's true of just about everybody I know. Most people find that the romantic glow just goes off the relationship after a few years. And those who I see who maintain it, frankly, are those who are non-monogamous.

So you've seen primary marriages keep that chemistry between the couple more when they're non-monogamous?

Yes. And that's certainly been true for me.

Are you in a primary relationship or a marriage now?

I am in the process of ending my third marriage. This one was an open marriage and it lasted twice as long as my monogamous marriages.

For families, raising kids, what model is practical?

What's practical for people raising children, I think, is, again, group marriages and intimate networks. I have two children myself and have been a parent essentially all of my adult life. And a good part of that time I was a single parent and I know that my life right now is a whole lot easier and my life in my open marriage was a whole lot easier than it ever was in my monogamous, nuclear family or as a single parent.

What most contributed to that greater ease?

The additional support on every level: Financial support, emotional support, somebody else for my child to spend the weekend with if I want to have some intimate time with a lover, my husband or somebody else. It also provides other children, because people are tending to have maybe one or two children, where they used to have three to five children, and so lots of children are growing up as only children. They could have brothers and sisters by combining with other families. That is not only a lot more fun for the children, it's a lot less stressful for the parents than trying to be both a parent and a playmate to your child all the time.

Aside from your unscientific survey of people you know, do you think this structure can be enduring?

By unscientific survey, I know of group marriages that have gone on for 25 years

and more. My impression is that once a group marriage really gets established, it's at least as stable, probably more stable, than a two-person marriage.

What about the idea that real monogamy, focusing your sexual energies, even your fantasies, on your partner, is a recipe to stay turned on by your partner for a long time? And when we're fantasizing and flirting with other women and possibly having affairs on the sly, then we're setting ourselves up? Because then we'll feel less attraction because of the coldness and distance our attitude creates in our partner?

It's a beautiful ideal but for me, while another person can be marvelous, mysterious, wondrous and magnificent, my ideal and what really excites me is that deep, deep kind of relationship with several people simultaneously who all love each other. I can't experience this energy of a group with one other person. And I can't experience a deep, loving relationship with both a man and a woman if I'm only with a man, and I can't experience the joy of seeing my two lovers really loving each other, sexually or not, if there's only one of them. And I can't experience the incredible power of the group mind and the group soul that's created when several people bond deeply and really open up to each.

But I don't want to tell anybody what the ideal form of a relationship is. I think one of the lessons that we've learned from the ecology movement is the lesson of diversity. A healthy ecosystem fosters a diversity of form. And I feel that we're lacking in diversity right now in the kinds of relationship forms and family forms that are imagined, let along legitimized, in our society. So I don't want to tell anybody that my way is the way.

To your knowledge, how widespread are intimate networks, polyamorous relationships, group marriages, those kinds of alternatives?

Well, it's awfully hard to come up with any hard numbers about that. Large surveys over the last few decades seem consistently to come up with about 10 percent of the adult population preferring a polyamorous type of relationship. Now that doesn't include all the people who say they prefer monogamy but who cheat. Those statistics are all over the map. You get anywhere from 30 on up to 80 percent of people who are cheating in monogamy. I feel that most of those people are polyamorous so that the monogamous population is probably around 30 percent or maybe 20 percent. I think that monogamy is actually a minority orientation. It's clear that with all the support that monogamy has received in our culture and all the indoctrination and all the legal advantages, the fact that so many people are non-monogamous demonstrates very clearly that that's not where most people are at.

John Gray has been an immensely successful author. His next book will be on monogamy. You don't think it will catch on? Do you think people are going to be quite frustrated when they attempt his kind of monogamy?

I think his book will be a bestseller. I think that he's speaking to the fantasy and the mythic image, the soulmate. Essentially all of us long for that. We've been raised with that. Our poplar songs reflect it. Our fairy tales, everything that we've known all our lives points us in the direction of that one other who's going to satisfy all of our needs and desires and be our soulmate for life. And I don't think it's realistic. So I think a lot of people are really being led astray. I think it's very sad

because of the pain and the frustration and the disillusionment that most people experience when they attempt to have that beautiful monogamous relationship and it just doesn't work out that way. Really just listening to our own bodies and our own hearts and our own souls is where I have found the possibility for a satisfying relationship.

When you look in that crystal ball, what do you see in 10, 15, 20 years? What will our society look like? Will it change in this direction do you think?

I definitely see it moving in this direction since I've been involved in this movement for 10 years. If I look ahead another 10 years I see more and more experimentation and diversity in the types of families and relationships that people are getting into. And I think as the baby-boomers get into retirement age and are less constrained by the geography that often keeps people tied to a particular location and a particular job, then we're going to see more and more group relationships, open relationships, intimate networks. We're going to see, instead of retirement homes where you get sent off by yourself, groups of seniors getting together and creating their own communal households where they can care for each other. People they've chosen to be with out of attraction and affinity rather than just being warehoused. I'm 43 and I have quite a few friends who are in their early 30s and then I see my daughter's generation in their early 20s. What I see is that many of those younger people have been raised by parents, such as myself, who are a little less rigid about sexual morality and who maybe encouraged them to be more sexually expressive at a younger age and who were experimenting with polyamorous relationships. And so we're starting to see a generation, actually a second generation, that does have different conditioning. They're much more able to negotiate these changes. And so I think that not only the senior citizens but the next generation growing up is a lot better equipped to pioneer these new forms of families. That's my rosy picture of the future.

My black picture of the future is that we're going to end up with no families at all. We're going to end up with test tube babies. We're going to end up with institutionalized child care from infancy, which is already the case actually, for far too many infants are being plunked into daycare at two, four, six months of age when they really need to be carried around on the body of their caretaker or they risk permanent neurological damage. I mean that's one of the scariest things to me about this emphasis on the nuclear family. Two incomes are really needed now for most people to support a family. And the family leave policies of our government are incredibly backward compared even to Europe and Japan and other industrialized societies. The black picture is that we're seeing infants who have not bonded with their parents because their parents are off working. Not only are they not going to bond with six people as in my ideal, or one person as in John Gray's ideal, they're not going to bond with anybody. We're going to have a nation of single people and we're going to become robotic and increasingly violent and ultimately do ourselves in. It's a choice point that we're at right now.

NO

John Gray

MONOGAMY IS ESSENTIAL TO KEEP LOVE'S SPARK ALIVE

What is your perspective on [monogamy]?

I think most men misunderstand or are not educated to the importance of monogamy for maintaining the passion in a marriage relationship. It is essential if you want to keep the marriage together and you want the passion and sex to stay alive. Why? Because for women to remain attractive to their partners, to put out that attractive energy, for a man to stay turned on to his partner, she needs to feel cherished and special. If she gets any messages that she's not the number one person in his life, then she will start to close up that part of her, and then after a while he'll stop being attracted to her, which reinforces his need to have affairs.

If he was to have an affair and not tell her, he assumes that as long as she doesn't find out, it's not going to affect the relationship. That's clearly not true in my perception. Intuitively she will feel the same feelings she would feel if she had known he was having an affair. She'll feel less special and close up.

The reason I know this to be true is that, as a counselor for 10 years, I would counsel women and I would know in some cases that the husband was having an affair. He would tell me, but not tell her. I would proceed to explore what was bothering her, and her feelings would be the same as a woman who knew her husband was having an affair. Feelings like, "I feel neglected," "I feel unimportant," "I don't feel special," "I don't feel loved."

And yet they can't really pin the reason for why they feel this way. They tend to displace these feelings on to other things and then overreact. For instance, let's say he's late for dinner. Instead of having a normal reaction to this, like "Why didn't you call?" the reaction will be stronger because it will be based on this deeper feeling of not being important or special, of being neglected. She'll say "his work is more important than me," but really she's reacting to his having sex with other women. Then he feels she's nuts because she's overreacting to things.

Couldn't that same statement from a woman, that "I'm not special enough to you," come from a lot of other things that go on in the relationship?

Sure, but when it is that intense it generally comes from an affair. If he's having affairs, something is missing inside the relationship. There's an actual attraction force, a magnetic force, and when you're feeling really attracted to your partner, she feels it. And when you're feeling attracted to other women, she doesn't feel that force anymore. She doesn't know what's going on, but just that something is missing. There is a connection there. I think the connection between parents and children is very instinctive, and I think it is also there between sexual partners.

I'd say men have it as well. It's just not as common for women to cheat on their men, although it does happen.

In our society the incidence of affairs is pretty high...

I'm not labelling any of this "sin." Men aren't educated into the understanding of sexual energy and how powerful it is to keep a relationship together. I advocate not only monogamy, but mental monogamy, which means that if you are thinking about another woman and you are turned on to her, then you go, "Great, my plumbing is working, I'm a guy, I'm attracted to other women. Now let me think about my wife." And you guide that energy back to your partner. If you are sitting there masturbating thinking about some other woman, then on an emotional level, your partner is going to start reacting to you as if you're having an affair. Maybe not as strongly, but in that direction. And repeatedly, that part of her closes off, and the cycle completes itself. Now you want to masturbate thinking of other women even more because you're not turned on to your partner. I'm not taking anything away from men, saying it's a sin or bad, I'm saying that if you are sending your sexual energy out to the left, it's not going to the right. But it is like a habit, a training, until after awhile you are always turned on to your wife. As your partner's body changes over the years, it remains the body that turns you on as opposed to the younger, firmer bodies, and you don't feel you are missing out on anything.

Is this a recipe for staying turned on to the woman you are with?

Exactly. What happens to a lot of couples is that he stops being turned on to her. It's a slow process. You get a healthy virile guy, and he thinks, "What's the harm in looking and enjoying?" There's no harm in looking and there's no harm in enjoying, as long as once you start getting aroused, or fantasizing sex with that woman, you catch yourself and say, "I'd rather do that with my wife," and bring it back to your wife. You bring the image of your wife's naked body into your mind and bring the energy back to her. I hardly have to do it anymore: I see a beautiful woman and I think about my wife. But it is not done by chastizing or judging the natural tendency of a man to be turned on visually by other women.

If this whole process is as potent as you are saying, it sounds like this is a central cause of all marital problems.

Yes, one of the major problems. There is another element which is equally important: a woman needs to feel special so that part of her that is attractive stays alive, the tender femininity, the vulnerability, that draws a man in and turns him on. The other element is communication. If a woman doesn't feel that she can communicate her innermost feelings with a man, she starts to close down as well. Those are the two arenas.

Given the youth-oriented, body-glorifying society we live in and the epidemic of extramarital affairs, can monogamy work?

It is very doable if you have good communication skills. Without them, the woman ends up feeling ignored and unheard, the man feels unappreciated and unacknowledged for what he does in the relationship, so neither partner feels loved. When you are not feeling loved, then you are not feeling turned on to your partner. If you are not feeling turned on to your partner and you are monogamous, it doesn't do anything. Monogamy comes into force as an extra power to supplement the power of your communication. Good communication creates arousal. Then, you control your arousal through monogamy.

You speak of men needing to move away at times and use the phrase, "I'll be back," which, as I interpret it, works if you are monogamous but is problematic if you are not.

Right, because when he pulls away, he could just go off and have an affair. And then he breaks the whole cycle.

So his phrase isn't believable if he isn't purely monogamous. Is that a really important thing, a vital part of sustaining a relationship, that men need to be able to say to their women, "I'll be back," and have it be believable?

Yes. Let's say I'm in a bad mood and I say, "I'm going for a drive. I'll be back." If she has the sense that I could get mad at her and go off and have an affair, we have a real problematic marriage. There is no way she can grow in love for me. She needs to feel that if I pull away and I do my business for me, which doesn't involve another woman, I will come back to her. Sexual monogamy is very important for that. When that happens it is important that he not panic and think "I'm not attracted to her, I'd better find somebody else." He should think, "I know the attraction will come back once the communication is working again."

What would you recommend to couples who are in a marriage and one partner has had an affair and they haven't told the other. But they like what you are saying and they want to change it. Should they tell each other about the affairs?

No. They need to change their actions and start practicing monogamy and things will get better. At some point when communication is really good, then tell your partner. I think honesty is always good, but if you don't have good communication, sometimes it will cause an unnecessary divorce because you don't know how to talk about the issue.

I suppose one's attraction to one's spouse takes time to rekindle.

Right, it does. You have to make the transition. If a man is not turned on to his wife, he may get turned on out in the world. Then he'll come home and not be turned on. He doesn't know how then to initiate sex without using fantasies. When he is out of the house and he finds himself getting turned on, he can take those feelings and write; "Dear Wife," and write out all his arousal feelings projected onto his wife in fantasy. Then you come home and say, "I was thinking about you today and these are some of my feelings. Would you read this letter?" She reads the letter out loud, and this has the very powerful effect of bringing the fantasy into reality. Suddenly now she is receiving all the energy that really wasn't fully directed towards her. He's just thrown the ball out there and she has caught it. When she catches that ball, part of her opens up and now his arousal will be towards her.

Another technique I use when the man is not turned on towards the woman is she says to him, "I understand you are real busy, working hard, you're not into sex right now, but I'm feeling really horny, so I'm just going to lie in bed tonight and fantasize making love to you and masturbate myself, and if any time you want to join in, you're welcome." As she gets closer to orgasm, he'll hear her breathing, and get turned on, and then he feels he's welcome to join in and does. And the connection is made again. It's a very powerful technique.

What about when the woman is not turned on?

If a man is not getting his sexual needs met, rather than masturbate alone, I suggest that he masturbate in his wife's presence or that she masturbate him. But the power is not as great on this side of it. If a woman is not into sex, it's for a different reason. It's because her communication need has to be satisfied. So the man needs to romance her. He needs to know how to listen to her, how to talk about her feelings without rejecting her feelings. That opens her up so she is more open to having sex with him. If he has different sexual frequencies than she, then the solution is not for him to go off alone and masturbate in the shower. Never masturbate when your wife is not around. Make sure that she is a part of that energy, because there is something very sacred when a man has his orgasm. He opens himself up, and when he is that open, it is very nurturing for the female to experience that part of him. It's central to my own success even.

How so?

Monogamy is a source of enormous power. Because monogamy creates trust, the woman will trust that you're there for her. She'll trust your love that says she's the most important person. When the woman who is closest to you trusts you, then the world trusts you. When the woman who is closest to you doesn't trust you, then as people get closer to you, they stop trusting you. That's why we say behind every great man is a very supportive woman. The reality is if my own wife can't trust me, why would anybody else trust me?

So from the male perspective, this can be the source of their success. And you're saying it's the source of yours?

Enormous source, I'd say it's the complete source of my success. My success only grows. Every year I put into this relationship, the love of my life grows stronger. My sexual energy stays controlled and directed towards my partner. I see that as a source of undying creativity.

You know, you see these people who start out very creative and then they lose their creativity after a certain point. I think it all has to do with how they're using their sexual energy. Because sexual energy is the creative force in the universe and this power, the power to create, is very important for men. If they're dissipating their sexual energy left and right, it weakens them. So I definitely see the link, and my marriage completely supports the success of my life. Love grows and builds over time. And the success of my life reflects that. And men don't realize it.

Why is communication so central to the sexual act?

If you look at the tantric teachings and all that stuff, they were supposed to be practiced with strangers. Meaning that you weren't supposed to know one woman at all. So what you were doing really was not having a personal relationship. You were communing with God, you were worshipping the Deva or the feminine presence of Mother Divine in the woman. And if you became personal, then it wouldn't work. I'm going at it from the other end. As you get your personal relationship over time through monogamy, you do find God in your partner, not in a stranger. So it's really a much more mature spiritual state than a lot of these mantra, taoist type things. They're all based on changing partners which is, to me, an immature spiritual space. But the real thing that people are looking for today is lasting relationship and then lasting passion and

great sex, and monogamy's the basis of it.

Why are these ideas so important now?

People are all wanting to come back to the home. There's been so much destruction and chaos based on divorce. People are saying, look, divorce is not an easy solution. Let's try to make it work. And my book offers fresh solutions for making it work.

What advice do you have for single people?

As far as being a single guy, I definitely believe in serial monogamy which means that when you're with a partner, make sure that it's just one partner. Because you're just fooling everybody if you're trying to have several partners at once. But to me it's always the search for the right person. Whenever you realize that this person is not a potential marriage partner, that's when I say stop having sex with them. Be monogamous with the person, with your soulmate. So if you're with somebody and you think this could be your soulmate, sex is great. But when you seriously realize this is not the person, then stop having sex with them. Save that energy for the right person. I think basically that there's a mate out there for almost every person. And part of our job here is to find that person. If someone seems to be that person, then sex is okay. But if I realize that the one I'm with is not that person, then I have no business having sex with them. So I'm holding my energy into always being focused, again even when I'm single, focusing that energy always toward that special person in my life.

And then you're saying you're more likely to find that person if that's what you're doing?

Right. You'll find the person sooner if that's what you're doing. Otherwise you're just wasting your energy and your time. And as far as what do you do if you're horny and you have sex, I mean I was celibate for nine years. I know it can be done. You take cold showers and if you masturbate, you don't shame yourself. But you know you might have put off finding the right person for a couple of days. So you want to keep that energy because the energy builds you up.

So you're suggesting even if you're single, as much as you possibly can, don't even masturbate.

Yes, if it's possible, don't masturbate or masturbate as little as possible. Because every time you masturbate, you're becoming your own soulmate. You're satisfying your need instead of finding that woman to satisfy that need. So I advocate celibacy until you find a woman who has the potential to be your soulmate.

POSTSCRIPT

Should We Accept Alternatives to Monogamy?

For 2,000 years moralists have cited ducks, swans, and other animals that mate for life and are sexually faithful as models of the true nature of marriage. Recently, however, biologists have used DNA fingerprinting to prove that most of the animal species that moralists assumed were monogamous and faithful do not live up to those expectations. When scientists checked the DNA fingerprints of the offspring of a variety of birds against the DNA of the mothers' mates, they found that about one-third of the offspring were fathered by birds other than the mates. Even mammals, who have never been a paragon of virtue, have proven to be only 2–4 percent sexually exclusive. It is now known that in most birds and mammals, both males and females commonly engage in sex with partners other than their mates.

Some scientists have suggested that sex outside the pair-bond promotes genetic diversity, increases the chances of the offspring's surviving, and brings significant advantages to the adventurous female. Whether or not this is the case with other animals, does it tell us anything about the prevalence of human polygamy? Considering all the species that engage in sex outside the pair-bond, can we ask whether the natural selection processes of evolution might have given humans a gene that makes us "mildly or ambiguously monogamous"?

As you weigh the arguments made by Anapol and Gray, ask yourself these questions: To what extent can and should we adapt our style or styles of marriage to radical changes in the social environment? Can we avoid becoming more flexible in our marriages? Regardless of how functional monogamous marriage was in the past, does it still work today?

SUGGESTED READINGS

D. M. Anapol, *Love Without Limits: Responsible Nonmonogamy and the Quest for Sustainable Intimate Relationships* (IntiNet Resource Center, 1992).

H. E. Fisher, *Anatomy of Love: The Natural History of Monogamy, Adultery, and Divorce* (W. W. Norton, 1992).

C. James, "Straying into Temptation in Prime Time," *The New York Times* (August 10, 1997), sec. 2, pp. 1, 32.

S. Johnson and H. Estroff Marano, "Love: The Immutable Longing for Contact," *Psychology Today* (March/April 1994).

G. K. Piorkowski, "Back Off!" *Psychology Today* (January/February 1994).

ISSUE 2

Is Male Homosexuality Biologically Influenced?

YES: Simon LeVay and Dean H. Hamer, from "Evidence for a Biological Influence in Male Homosexuality," *Scientific American* (May 1994)

NO: William Byne, from "The Biological Evidence Challenged," *Scientific American* (May 1994)

ISSUE SUMMARY

YES: Simon LeVay and Dean H. Hamer, researchers in neuroanatomy and biochemistry, respectively, maintain that evidence of differences in the brain structures of gay and straight men, along with differences in genetic markers and family pedigrees, is mounting. They conclude that some combination of genetic and/or hormonal factors plays a role in the early development of our sexual orientation.

NO: Neuroscientist William Byne argues that although all psychological phenomena, including sexual behavior and gender orientation, are ultimately based in our genes and hormones, biological theories of homosexuality hinge on assumptions of questionable validity. He believes that the most salient explanations about the origins of our sexual orientation lie "not within the biology of human brains but rather in the cultures those brains have created."

Twenty-five hundred years ago, in the first recorded symposium on sexuality, the Greek philosopher Plato reported that the human race originally had three sexes. Each sex consisted of a pair of humans; some pairs had two females, some two males, and others a male and a female. When the gods on Mount Olympus thought humans were becoming too powerful, Zeus decided to separate each pair to weaken them and teach them to fear the gods. This, Plato pointed out, explains why humans spend much of their time trying to find their lost perfect mate.

Today no one accepts Plato's explanation of why some people are homosexual, some heterosexual, and some bisexual. One accepted explanation is that the origin of our gender orientation is primarily biological and therefore beyond our control. Others are convinced that gender orientation is solely the product of our learning and social construction and therefore open to manipulation and control.

For centuries Western thinkers have approached questions about gender and personality in "either/or" terms. Either nature (genes, chromosomes, hormones, and neural encoding) is dominant in our development, or nurture (environmental factors such as learning, the influence of a domineering mother and an absent father, an early sexual trauma, or some combination of social environmental factors) is dominant.

Human development is more complex than the dichotomy of nature versus nurture. Our genetic constitution and hormones are modulated by the environmental factors we encounter and experience throughout our lives. It is this ongoing, lifelong interaction that shapes our characteristics and behavior.

The human brain is composed of three brains, one overlaying the other like three mushroom caps of increasing size and importance. The brain stem, or reptilian brain, is "hard-wired" for survival reflexes such as eating, fighting, fleeing, and mating. On top of the brain stem is the limbic system and hypothalamus. This limbic core expands the "hard-wired," reflexive drives and emotions of the primitive brain stem. Parts of the limbic brain are "soft-wired" and more open to modification than the brain stem. Finally, crowning the reptilian and limbic brains are the cerebral hemispheres that have infinitely flexible, "soft-wired," reprogrammable circuits that allow us to learn, think, and love.

The structure and circuits of the limbic brain, particularly the hypothalamus, are at the heart of the following selections on the origins of gender orientation. Simon LeVay and Dean H. Hamer support the position that structures in the brain determine whether a person will be homosexual or heterosexual. William Byne, in contrast, maintains that one's sexual orientation is determined mostly by environmental factors.

YES   Simon LeVay and Dean H. Hamer

EVIDENCE FOR A BIOLOGICAL INFLUENCE IN MALE HOMOSEXUALITY

Most men are sexually attracted to women, most women to men. To many people, this seems only the natural order of things—the appropriate manifestation of biological instinct, reinforced by education, religion and the law. Yet a significant minority of men and women—estimates range from 1 to 5 percent—are attracted exclusively to members of their own sex. Many others are drawn, in varying degrees, to both men and women.

How are we to understand such diversity in sexual orientation? Does it derive from variations in our genes or our physiology, from the intricacies of our personal history or from some confluence of these? Is it for that matter a choice rather than a compulsion?

Probably no one factor alone can elucidate so complex and variable a trait as sexual orientation. But recent laboratory studies, including our own, indicate that genes and brain development play a significant role. How, we do not yet know. It may be that genes influence the sexual differentiation of the brain and its interaction with the outside world, thus diversifying its already vast range of responses to sexual stimuli.

The search for biological roots of sexual orientation has run along two broad lines. The first draws on observations made in yet another hunt—that for physical differences between men's and women's brains. As we shall see, "gay" and "straight" brains may be differentiated in curiously analogous fashion. The second approach is to scout out genes by studying the patterns in which homosexuality occurs in families and by directly examining the hereditary material, DNA.

* * *

Researchers have long sought within the human brain some manifestation of the most obvious classes into which we are divided—male and female. Such sex differentiation of the brain's structure, called sexual dimorphism, proved hard to establish. On average, a man's brain has a slightly larger size that goes along with his larger body; other than that, casual inspection does not reveal any obvious dissimilarity between the sexes. Even under a microscope, the architecture of men's and women's brains is very similar. Nor surprisingly, the first significant observations of sexual dimorphism were made in laboratory animals.

Of particular importance is a study of rats conducted by Roger A. Gorski of the University of California at Los Angeles. In 1978 Gorski was inspecting the rat's hypothalamus, a region at the base of its brain that is involved in instinctive behaviors and the regulation of metabolism. He found that one group of cells near the front of the hypothalamus is several times larger in male than in female rats. Although this cell group is very small, less than a millimeter across even in males, the difference between the sexes is quite visible in appropriately stained slices of tissue, even without the aid of a microscope.

Gorski's finding was especially interesting because the general region of the hypothalamus in which this cell group occurs, known as the medial preoptic area, has been implicated in the generation of sexual behavior—in particular, behaviors typically displayed by males. For example, male monkeys with damaged medial preoptic areas are apparently indifferent to sex with female monkeys, and electrical stimulation of this region can make an inactive male monkey approach and mount a female. It should be said, however, that we have yet to find in monkeys a cell group analogous to the sexually dimorphic one occurring in rats.

Nor is the exact function of the rat's sexually dimorphic cell group known. What is known, from a study by Gorski and his co-workers, is that androgens —typical male hormones—play a key role in bringing about a dimorphism during development. Neurons within the cell group are rich in receptors for sex hormones, both for androgens—testosterone is the main representative —and for female hormones known as estrogens. Although male and female rats initially have about the same numbers of neurons in the medial preoptic area, a surge of testosterone secreted by the testes of male fetuses around the time of birth acts to stabilize their neuronal population. In females the lack of such a surge allows many neurons in this cell group to die, leading to the typically smaller structure. Interestingly, it is only for a few days before and after birth that the medial preoptic neurons are sensitive to androgen; removing androgens in an adult rat by castration does not cause the neurons to die.

Gorski and his colleagues at U.C.L.A., especially his student Laura S. Allen, have also found dimorphic structures in the human brain. A cell group named INAH3 (derived from "third interstitial nucleus of the anterior hypothalamus") in the medial preoptic region of the hypothalamus is about three times larger in men than in women. (Notably, however, size varies considerably even within one sex.)

In 1990 one of us (LeVay) decided to check whether INAH3 or some other cell group in the medial preoptic area varies in size with sexual orientation as well as with sex. This hypothesis was something of a long shot, given the prevailing notion that sexual orientation is a "high-level" aspect of personality molded by environment and culture. Information from such elevated sources is thought to be processed primarily by the cerebral cortex and not by "lower" centers such as the hypothalamus.

LeVay examined the hypothalamus in autopsy specimens from 19 homosexual men, all of whom had died of complications of AIDS, and 16 heterosexual men, six of whom had also died of AIDS. (The sexual orientation of those who had died of non-AIDS causes was not determined. But assuming a distribution similar to that of the general populace, no more than one or two of them were likely to have been gay.) LeVay also included specimens from six women whose sexual orientation was unknown.

After encoding the specimens to eliminate subjective bias, LeVay cut each hypothalamus into serial slices, stained these to mark the neuronal cell groups and measured their cross-sectional areas under a microscope. Armed with information about the areas, plus the thickness of the slices, he could readily calculate the volumes of each cell group. In addition to Allen and Gorski's sexually dimorphic nucleus INAH3, LeVay examined three other nearby groups—INAH1, INAH2 and INAH4.

Like Allen and Gorski, LeVay observed that INAH3 was more than twice as large in the men as in the women. But INHA3 was also between two and three times larger in the straight men than in the gay men. In some gay men, as in the example shown at the top of the opposite page, the cell group was altogether absent. Statistical analysis indicated that the probability of this result's being attributed to chance was about one in 1,000. In fact, there was no significant difference between volumes of INAH3 in the gay men and in the women. So the investigation suggested a dimorphism related to male sexual orientation about as great as that related to sex.

A primary concern in such a study is whether the observed structural differences are caused by some variable other than the one of interest. A major suspect here was AIDS. The AIDS virus itself, as well as other infectious agents that take advantage of a weakened immune system, can cause serious damage to brain cells. Was this the reason for the small size of INAH3 in the gay men, all of whom had died of AIDS?

Several lines of evidence indicate otherwise. First, the heterosexual men who died of AIDS had INAH3 volumes no different from those who died of other causes. Second, the AIDS victims with small INAH3s did not have case histories distinct from those with large INAH3s; for instance, they had not been ill longer before they died. Third, the other three cell groups in the medial preoptic area—INAH1, INAH2 and INAH4—turned out to be no smaller in the AIDS victims. If the disease were having a nonspecific destructive effect, one would have suspected otherwise. Finally, after completing the main study, LeVay obtained the hypothalamus of one gay man who had died of non-AIDS causes. This specimen, processed "blind" along with several specimens from heterosexual men of similar age, confirmed the main study: the volume of INAH3 in the gay man was less than half that of INAH3 in the heterosexual men.

One other feature in brains that is related to sexual orientation has been reported by Allen and Gorski. They found that the anterior commissure, a bundle of fibers running across the midline of the brain, is smallest in heterosexual men, larger in women and largest in gay men. After correcting for overall brain size, the anterior commissure in women and in gay men were comparable in size.

* * *

What might lie behind these apparent correlations between sexual orientation and brain structure? Logically, three possibilities exist. One is that the structural differences were present early in life—perhaps even before birth—and helped to establish the men's sexual orientation. The second is that the differences arose in adult life as a result of the men's sexual feelings or behavior. The third possibility is that there is no causal connection, but both sexual orientation and the brain structures in question are linked to some third variable, such as a developmental event during uterine or early postnatal life.

We cannot decide among these possibilities with any certainty. On the basis of animal research, however, we find the second scenario, that the structural differences came about in adulthood, unlikely. In rats, for example, the sexually dimorphic cell group in the medial preoptic area appears plastic in its response to androgens during early brain development but later is largely resistant to change. We favor the first possibility, that the structural differences arose during the period of brain development and consequently contributed to sexual behavior. Because the medial preoptic region of the hypothalamus is implicated in sexual behavior in monkeys, the size of INAH3 in men may indeed influence sexual orientation. But such a causal connection is speculative at this point.

Assuming that some of the structural differences related to sexual orientation were present at birth in certain individuals, how did they arise? One candidate is the interaction between gonadal steroids and the developing brain; this interaction is responsible for differences in the structure of male and female brains. A number of scientists have speculated that atypical levels of circulating androgens in some fetuses cause them to grow into homosexual adults. Specifically, they suggest that androgen levels are unusually low in male fetuses that become gay and unusually high in female fetuses that become lesbian.

A more likely possibility is that there are intrinsic differences in the way individual brains respond to androgens during development, even when the hormone levels are themselves no different. This response requires a complex molecular machinery, starting with the androgens receptors but presumably including a variety of proteins and genes whose identity and roles are still unknown.

At first glance, the very notion of gay genes might seem absurd. How could genes that draw men or women to members of the same sex survive the Darwinian screening for reproductive fitness? Surely the parents of most gay men and lesbians are heterosexual? In view of such apparent incongruities, research focuses on genes that sway rather than determine sexual orientation. The two main approaches to seeking such genes are twin and family studies and DNA linkage analysis.

* * *

Twin and family tree studies are based on the principle that genetically influenced traits run in families. The first modern study on the patterns of homosexuality within families was published in 1985 by Richard C. Pillard and James D. Weinrich of Boston University. Since then, five other systematic studies on the twins and siblings of gay men and lesbians have been reported.

The pooled data for men show that about 57 percent of identical twins, 24 percent of fraternal twins and 13 percent of brothers of gay men are also gay. For women, approximately 50 percent of identical twins, 16 percent of fraternal twins and 13 percent of sisters of lesbians are also lesbian. When these data are compared with baseline rates of homosexuality, a good amount of family clustering of sexual orientation becomes evident for both sexes. In fact, J. Michael Bailey of Northwestern University and his co-workers estimate that the overall heritability of sexual orientation—that proportion of the variance in a trait that comes from genes—is about 53 percent for men and 52 percent for women. (The family clustering is most obvious for relatives of the same sex, less so for male-female pairs.)

To evaluate the genetic component of sexual orientation and to clarify its mode of inheritance, we need a systematic survey of the extended families of gay men and lesbians. One of us (Hamer), Stella Hu, Victoria L. Magnuson, Nan Hu and Angela M. L. Pattatucci of the National Institutes of Health [NIH] have initiated such a study. It is part of a larger one by the National Cancer Institute to investigate risk factors for certain cancers that are more frequent in some segments of the gay population.

Hamer and his colleagues' initial survey of males confirmed the sibling results of Pillard and Weinrich. A brother of a gay man had a 14 percent likelihood of being gay as compared with 2 percent for the men without gay brothers. (The study used an unusually stringent definition of homosexuality, leading to the low average rate.) Among more distant relatives, an unexpected pattern showed up: maternal uncles had a 7 percent chance of being gay, whereas sons of maternal aunts had an 8 percent chance. Fathers, paternal uncles and the three other types of cousins showed no correlation at all.

Although this study pointed to a genetic component, homosexuality occurred much less frequently than a single gene inherited in simple Mendelian fashion would suggest. One interpretation, that genes are more important in some families than in others, is borne out by looking at families having two gay brothers. Compared with randomly chosen families, rates of homosexuality in maternal uncles increased from 7 to 10 percent and in maternal cousins from 8 to 13 percent. This familial clustering, even in relatives outside the nuclear family, presents an additional argument for a genetic root to sexual orientation.

* * *

Why are most gay male relatives of gay men on the mother's side of the family? One possibility—that the subjects somehow knew more about their maternal relatives—seems unlikely because opposite-sex gay relatives of gay males and lesbians were equally distributed between both sides of the family. Another explanation is that homosexuality, while being transmitted by both parents, is expressed only in one sex—in this case, males. When expressed, the trait reduces the reproductive rate and must therefore be disproportionately passed on by the mother. Such an effect may partially account for the concentration of gay men's gay relatives on the maternal side of the family. But proof of this hypothesis will require finding an appropriate gene on an autosomal chromosome, which is inherited from either parent.

A third possibility is X chromosome linkage. A man has two sex chromosomes: a Y, inherited from his father, and an X, cut and pasted from the two X chromosomes carried by his mother. Therefore, any trait that is influenced by a gene on the X chromosome will tend to be inherited through the mother's side and will be preferentially observed in brothers, maternal uncles and maternal cousins, which is exactly the observed pattern.

To test this hypothesis, Hamer and his colleagues embarked on a linkage study of the X chromosome in gay men. Linkage analysis is based on two principles of genetics. If a trait is genetically influenced, then relatives who share the trait will share the gene more often than is expected by chance—this is true even if the gene plays only a small part. Also, genes that are close together on a chromosome are almost always inherited together. Therefore, if there is a gene that influences sexual orientation, it should be "linked" to a nearby DNA marker that tends to travel along with it in families. For traits affected by only one gene, linkage can precisely locate the gene on a chromosome. But for complex traits such as sexual orientation, linkage also helps to determine whether a genetic component really exists.

To initiate a linkage analysis of male sexual orientation, the first requirement was to find informative markers, segments of DNA that flag locations on a chromosome. Fortunately, the Human Genome Project has already generated a large catalogue of markers spanning all of the X chromosomes. The most useful ones are short, repeated DNA sequences that have slightly different lengths in different persons. To detect the markers, the researchers used the polymerase chain reaction to make several billion copies of specific regions of the chromosome and then separated the different fragments by the method of gel electrophoresis.

The second step in the linkage analysis was to locate suitable families. When scientists study simple traits such as color blindness or sickle cell anemia—which involve a single gene—they tend to analyze large, multigenerational families in which each member clearly either has or does not have the trait. Such an approach was unsuited for studying sexual orientation. First, identifying someone as not homosexual is tricky; the person may be concealing his or her true orientation or may not be aware of it. Because homosexuality was even more stigmatized in the past, multigenerational families are especially problematic in this regard. Moreover, genetic modeling shows that for traits that involve several different genes expressed at varying levels, studying large families can actually decrease the chances of finding a linked gene: too many exceptions are included.

For these reasons, Hamer and his coworkers decided to focus on nuclear families with two gay sons. One advantage of this approach is that individuals who say they are homosexual are unlikely to be mistaken. Furthermore, the approach can detect a single linked gene even if other genes or noninherited factors are required for its expression. For instance, suppose that being gay requires an X chromosome gene together with another gene on an autosome, plus some set of environmental circumstances. Studying gay brothers would give a clear-cut result because both would have the X chromosome gene. In contrast, heterosexual brothers of gay men would sometimes share the X chromosome gene and sometimes not, leading to confusing results.

Genetic analysts now believe that studying siblings is the key to traits that are affected by many elements. Because Hamer and his colleagues were most interested in finding a gene that expresses itself only in men but is transmitted through women, they restricted their search to families with gay men but no gay father–gay son pairs.

Forty such families were recruited. DNA samples were prepared from the gay brothers and, where possible, from their mother or sisters. The samples were typed for 22 markers that span the X chromosome from the tip of the short arm to the end of the long arm. At each marker, a pair of gay brothers was scored as concordant if they inherited identical markers from their mothers or as discordant if they inherited different ones. Fifty percent of the markers were expected to be identical by chance. Corrections were also made for the possibility of the mother's having two copies of the same marker.

The results of this study were striking. Over most of the X chromosome the markers were randomly distributed between the gay brothers. But at the tip of the long arm of the X chromosome, in a region known as Xq28, there was a considerable excess of concordant brothers: 33 pairs shared the same marker, whereas only 7 pairs did not. Although the same size was not large, the result was statistically significant: the probability of such a skewed ratio occurring by chance alone is less than one in 200. In a control group of 314 randomly selected pairs of brothers, most of whom can be presumed to be heterosexual, Xq28 markers were randomly distributed.

The most straightforward interpretation of the finding is that chomosomal region Xq28 contains a gene that influences male sexual orientation. The study provides the strongest evidence to date that human sexuality is influenced by heredity because it directly examines the genetic information, the DNA. But as with all initial studies, there are some caveats.

First, the result needs to be replicated: several other claims of finding genes related to personality traits have proved controversial. Second, the gene itself has not yet been isolated. The study locates it within a region of the X chromosome that is about four million base pairs in length. This region represents less than 0.2 percent of the total human genome, but it is still large enough to contain several hundred genes. Finding the needle in this haystack will require either large numbers of families or more complete information about the DNA sequence to identify all possible coding regions. As it happens, Xq28 is extraordinarily rich in genetic loci and will probably be one of the first regions of the human genome to be sequenced in its entirety.

A third caveat is that researchers do not know quantitatively how important a role Xq28 plays in male sexual orientation. Within the population of gay brothers studied, seven of 40 brothers did not share markers. Assuming that 20 siblings should inherit identical markers by chance alone, 36 percent of gay brothers show no link between homosexuality and Xq28. Perhaps these men inherited different genes or were influenced by nongenetic physiological factors or by the environment. Among all gay men—most of whom do not have gay brothers—the influence of Xq28 is even less clear. Also unknown is the role of Xq28, and other genetic loci, in female sexual orientation.

How might a genetic locus at Xq28 affect sexuality? One idea is that the hypothetical gene affects hormone synthesis or metabolism. A candidate for such a gene was the androgen receptor locus, which encodes a protein essential for masculinization of the human brain and is, moreover, located on the X chromosome. To test this idea, Jeremy Nathans, Jennifer P. Macke, Van L. King and Terry R. Brown of John Hopkins University teamed up with Bailey of Northwestern and Hamer, Hu and Hu of the NIH. They compared the molecular structure of the androgen receptor gene in 197 homosexual men and 213 predominantly heterosexual men. But no significant variations in the protein coding sequences were found. Also, linkage studies showed no correlation between homosexuality in brothers and inheritance of the androgen receptor locus. Most significant of all, the locus turned out to be at Xq11, far from the Xq28 region. This study excludes the androgen receptor from playing a significant role in male sexual orientation.

A second idea is that the hypothetical gene acts indirectly, through personality or temperament, rather than directly on sexual-object choice. For example, people who are genetically self-reliant might be more likely to acknowledge and act on same-sex feelings than are people who are dependent on the approval of others.

Finally, the intriguing possibility arises that the Xq28 gene product bears directly on the development of sexually dimorphic brain regions such as INAH3. At the simplest level, such an agent could act autonomously, perhaps in the womb, by stimulating the survival of specific neurons in preheterosexual males or by promoting their death in females and prehomosexual men. In a more complex model, the gene product could change the sensitivity of a neuronal circuit in the hypothalamus to stimulation by environmental cues—perhaps in the first few years of life. Here the genes serve to predispose rather than to predetermine. Whether this fanciful notion contains a grain of truth remains to be seen. It is in fact experimentally testable, using current tools of molecular genetics and neurobiology.

* * *

Our research has attracted an extraordinary degree of public attention, not so much because of any conceptual breakthrough—the idea that genes and the brain are involved in human behavior is hardly new—but because it touches on a deep conflict in contemporary American society. We believe scientific research can help dispel some of the myths about homosexuality that in the past have clouded the image of lesbians and gay men. We also recognize, however, that increasing knowledge of biology may eventually bring with it the power to infringe on the natural rights of individuals and to impoverish the world of its human diversity. It is important that our society expand discussions of how new scientific information should be used to benefit the human race in its entirety.

NO
William Byne

THE BIOLOGICAL EVIDENCE CHALLENGED

Human-rights activists, religious organizations and all three branches of the U.S. government are debating whether sexual orientation is biological. The discussion has grabbed headlines, but behavioral scientists find it passé. The salient question about biology and sexual orientation is not whether biology is involved but how it is involved. All psychological phenomena are ultimately biological.

Even if the public debate were more precisely framed, it would still be misguided. Most of the links in the chain of reasoning from biology to sexual orientation and social policy do not hold up under scrutiny. At the political level, a requirement that an unconventional trait be inborn or immutable is an inhumane criterion for a society to use in deciding which of its nonconformists it will grant tolerance. Even if homosexuality were entirely a matter of choice, attempts to extirpate it by social and criminal sanctions devalue basic human freedoms and diversity.

Furthermore, the notion that homosexuality must be either inborn and immutable or freely chosen is in turn misinformed. Consider the white-crowned sparrow, a bird that learns its native song during a limited period of development. Most sparrows exposed to a variety of songs, including that of their own species, will learn their species's song, but some do not. After a bird has learned a song, it can neither unlearn that song nor acquire a new one. Although sexual orientation is not a matter of mimicry, it is clear that learned behavior can nonetheless be immutable.

Finally, what evidence exists thus far of innate biological traits underlying homosexuality is flawed. Genetic studies suffer from the inevitable confounding of nature and nurture that plagues attempts to study heritability of psychological traits. Investigations of the brain rely on doubtful hypotheses about differences between the brains of men and women. Biological mechanisms that have been proposed to explain the existence of gay men often cannot be generalized to explain the existence of lesbians (whom studies have largely neglected). And the continuously graded nature of most biological variables is at odds with the paucity of adult bisexuals suggested by most surveys.

* * *

To understand how biological factors influence sexual orientation, one must first define orientation. Many researchers, most conspicuously Simon LeVay, treat it as a sexually dimorphic trait: men are generally "programmed" for attraction to women, and women are generally programmed for attraction to men. Male homosexuals, according to this framework, have female programming. Some researchers suggest that this programming is accomplished by biological agents, perhaps even before birth; others believe it occurs after birth in response to social factors and subjective experiences. As a function of the brain is undoubtedly linked to its structure and physiology, it follows that homosexuals' brains might exhibit some features typical of the opposite sex.

The validity of this "intersex" expectation is questionable. For one, sexual orientation is not dimorphic; it has many forms. The conscious and unconscious motivations associated with sexual attraction are diverse even among people of the same sex and orientation. Myriad experiences (and subjective interpretations of those experiences) could interact to lead different people to the same relative degree of sexual attraction to men or to women. Different people could be sexually attracted to men for different reasons; for example, there is no a priori reason that everyone attracted to men should share some particular brain structure.

Indeed, the notion that gay men are feminized and lesbians masculinized may tell us more about our culture than about the biology or erotic responsiveness. Some Greek myths held that heterosexual rather than homosexual desire had intersex origins: those with predominately same-sex desires were considered the most manly of men and womanly of women. In contrast, those who desired the opposite sex supposedly mixed masculine and feminine in their being. Classical culture celebrated the homosexual exploits of archetypally masculine heroes such as Zeus, Hercules and Julius Caesar. Until a decade ago (when missionaries repudiated the practice), boys among the Sambia of New Guinea would form attachments to men and fellate them; no one considered that behavior a female trait. Indeed, the Sambia believed ingesting semen to be necessary for attaining strength and virility.

But there is a more tangible problem for this intersex assumption; the traits of which homosexuals ostensibly have opposite-sex versions have not been conclusively shown to differ between men and women. Of the many supposed sex differences in the human brain reported over the past century, only one has proved consistently replicable: brain size varies with body size. Thus, men tend to have slightly larger brains than women. This situation contrasts sharply with that for other animals, where many researchers have consistently demonstrated a variety of sex differences.

If brains are indeed wired or otherwise programmed for sexual orientation, what forces are responsible? Three possibilities come into play: The direct model of biological causation asserts that genes, hormones or other factors act directly on the developing brain, probably before birth, to wire it for sexual orientation. Alternatively, the social learning model suggests that biology provides a blank slate of neural circuitry on which experience inscribes orientation. In the indirect model, biological factors do not wire the brain for orientation; instead they predispose individuals toward certain personality traits that influence the relationships and experiences that ultimately shape sexuality.

During past decades, much of the speculation about biology and orientation focused on the role of hormones. Workers once thought an adult's androgen and estrogen levels determined orientation, but this hypothesis withered for lack of support. Researchers have since pursued the notion that hormones wire the brain for sexual orientation during the prenatal period.

According to this hypothesis, high prenatal androgen levels during the appropriate critical period cause heterosexuality in men and homosexuality in women. Conversely, low fetal androgen levels lead to homosexuality in men and heterosexuality in women. This hypothesis rests largely on the observation that in rodents early exposure to hormones determines the balance between male and female patterns of mating behaviors displayed by adults. Female rodents that were exposed to androgens early in development show more male-typical mounting behavior than do normal adult females. Males deprived of androgens by castration during the same critical period display a female mating posture called lordosis (bending of the back) when they are mounted.

Many researchers consider the castrated male rat that shows lordosis when mounted by another male to be a homosexual (as is the female rat that mounts others). Lordosis, however, is little more than a reflex: the male will take the same posture when a handler strokes its back. Furthermore, the male that mounts another male is considered to be heterosexual, as is the female that displays lordosis when mounted by another female. Applying such logic to humans would imply that of two people of the same sex engaged in intercourse only one is homosexual—and which member of the couple it is depends on the positions they assume.

In addition to determining rodent mating patterns, early hormonal exposure determines whether an animal's brain can regulate normal ovarian function. A male rat's brain cannot respond to estrogen by triggering a chain of events, called positive feedback, that culminates in the abrupt increase of luteinizing hormone in the bloodstream, which in turn triggers ovulation. Some researchers reasoned from this fact to the idea that homosexual men (whose brains they allege to be insufficiently masculinized) might have a stronger positive-feedback reaction that do heterosexual men.

Two laboratories reported that this was the case, but carefully designed and executed studies, most notably those of Luis J. G. Gooren of the Free University in Amsterdam, disproved those findings. Furthermore, the feedback mechanism turns out to be irrelevant to human sexual orientation: workers have since found that the positive-feedback mechanism is not sexually dimorphic in primates, including humans. If this mechanism is indistinguishable in men and women, it is illogical to suggest that it should be "feminized" in gay men.

Moreover, a corollary of the expectation that luteinizing hormone responses should be feminized in homosexual men is that they should be "masculinized" in lesbians. If that were true, homosexual women would neither menstruate nor bear children. The overwhelming proportion of lesbians with normal menstrual cycles and the growing number of openly lesbian mothers attest to the fallacy of that idea.

* * *

If the prenatal hormonal hypothesis were correct, one might expect that a large proportion of men with medical conditions known to involve prenatal androgen deficiency would be homosexual, as would be women exposed prenatally to excess androgens. That is not the case.

Because androgens are necessary for development of normal external genitals in males, the sex of affected individuals may not be apparent at birth. Males may be born with female-appearing genitals, and females with male-appearing ones. These individuals often require plastic surgery to construct normal-appearing genitals, and the decision to raise them as boys or as girls is sometimes based not on genetic sex but on the possibilities for genital reconstruction.

Research into the sexual orientation of such individuals tends to support the social learning model. Regardless of their genetic sex or the nature of their prenatal hormonal exposure, they usually become heterosexual with respect to the sex their parents raise them as, provided the sex assignment is made unambiguously before the age of three.

Nevertheless, some studies report an increase in homosexual fantasies or behavior among women who were exposed to androgens as fetuses. In accordance with the notion of direct biological effects, these studies are often interpreted as evidence that prenatal androgen exposure wires the brain for sexual attraction to women. The neurobiologist and feminist scholar Ruth H. Bleier has offered an alternative interpretation. Rather than reflecting an effect of masculinizing hormones on the sexual differentiation of the brain, the adaptations of prenatally masculinized women may reflect the impact of having been born with masculinized genitalia or the knowledge that they had been exposed to aberrant levels of sex hormones during development. "Gender must seem a fragile and arbitrary construct," Bleier concluded, "if it depends upon plastic surgery."

* * *

Stephen Jay Gould of Harvard University has written of the way that the search for brain differences related to sex and other social categories was for the most part discredited during the past century by anatomists who deluded themselves into believing that their brain measurements justified the social prejudices of their day. The search for sex differences in the human brain was revitalized in the late 1970s, when Roger A. Gorski's team at the University of California at Los Angeles discovered a group of cells in the preoptic part of the rat hypothalamus that was much larger in males than in females. The researchers designated this cell group the sexually dimorphic nucleus of the preoptic area (SDN-POA). The preoptic area has long been implicated in the regulation of sexual behavior.

Like the sex differences in mating behaviors and luteinizing hormone regulatory mechanisms, the difference in the size of the SDN-POA was found to result from differences in early exposure to androgens. Shortly thereafter, Bleier and I, working at the University of Wisconsin at Madison, examined the hypothalamus of several rodent species and found that the SDN-POA is only one part of a sexual dimorphism involving several additional hypothalamic nuclei.

Three laboratories have recently sought sexually dimorphic nuclei in the human hypothalamus. Laura S. Allen, working in Gorski's lab, identified four possible candidates as potential homologues of the rat's SDN-POA and designated them as the interstitial nuclei of the anterior hypothalamus (INAH1-INAH4). Different laboratories that have measured these nuclei, however, have produced conflicting results: Dick F. Swaab's group at the Netherlands Institute for Brain Research in Amsterdam, for example, found INAH1 to be larger in men that in women, whereas Allen found no difference in that nucleus but reported that INAH2 and INAH3 were larger in men. Most recently, LeVay found no sex difference in either INAH1 or INAH2 but corroborated Allen's finding of a larger INAH3 in men. LeVay also reported that INAH3 in homosexual men tends to be small, like that of women. (Neurologist Clifford Saper of Harvard and I are in the process of measuring the interstitial nuclei; at present, we have no definitive results.)

LeVay's study has been widely interpreted as strong evidence that biological factors directly wire the brain for sexual orientation. Several considerations militate against that conclusion. First, his work has not been replicated, and human neuroanatomical studies of this kind have a very poor track record for reproducibility. Indeed, procedures similar to those LeVay used to identify the nuclei have previously led researchers astray.

Manfred Gahr, now at the Max Planck Institute for Animal Physiology in Seewiesen, Germany, used a cell-staining technique similar to LeVay's to observe what appeared to be seasonal variations in the size of a nucleus involved in singing in canaries. Two more specific staining methods, however, revealed that the size of the nucleus did not change. Gahr suggested that the less specific method might have been influenced by seasonal hormonal variations that altered the properties of the cells in the nucleus.

Furthermore, in LeVay's published study, all the brains of gay men came from AIDS patients. His inclusion of a few brains from heterosexual men with AIDS did not adequately address the fact that at the time of death virtually all men with AIDS have decreased testosterone levels as the result of the disease itself or the side effects of particular treatments. To date, LeVay has examined the brain of only one gay man who did not die of AIDS. Thus, it is possible that the effects on the size of INAH3 that he attributed to sexual orientation were actually caused by the hormonal abnormalities associated with AIDS. Work by Deborah Commins and Pauline I. Yahr of the University of California at Irvine supports precisely this hypothesis. The two found that the size of a structure in mongolian gerbils apparently comparable to the SDN-POA varies with the amount of testosterone in the bloodstream.

A final problem with the popular interpretation of LeVay's study is that it is founded on an imprecise analysis of the relevant animal research. LeVay has suggested that INAH3, like the rat's SDN-POA, is situated in a region of the hypothalamus known to participate in the generation of male sexual behavior. Yet studies in a variety of species have consistently shown that the precise hypothalamic region involved in male sexual behavior is not the one occupied by these nuclei. Indeed, Gorski and Gary W. Arendash, now at the University of South Florida, found that destroying the

SDN-POA on both sides of a male rat's brain did not impair sexual behavior.

Jefferson C. Slimp performed experiments in Robert W. Goy's laboratory at the Wisconsin Regional Primate Research Center (shortly before I joined that group) that suggested that the precise region involved in sexual behavior in male rhesus monkeys is located about the area comparable to that occupied by INAH3 in humans. Males with lesions in that region mounted females less frequently than they did before being operated on, but their frequency of masturbation did not change. Although some have taken these observations to mean that the lesions selectively decreased heterosexual drive, their conclusion is unwarranted; male monkeys pressed a lever for access to females more often after their operations than before. Unfortunately, these males had no opportunity to interact with other males, and so the study tells us nothing about effects on homosexual as opposed to heterosexual motivation or behavior.

Interstitial hypothalamic nuclei are not the only parts of the brain to have come under scrutiny for links to sexual orientation. Neuroanatomists have also reported potentially interesting differences in regions not directly involved in sexual behaviors. Swaab and his co-worker Michel A. Hofman found that another hypothalamic nucleus, the suprachiasmatic nucleus, is larger in homosexual than in heterosexual men. The size of this structure, however, does not vary with sex, and so even if this finding can be replicated it would not support the assumption that homosexuals have intersexed brains.

Allen of U.C.L.A., meanwhile, has reported that the anterior commissure, a structure that participates in relaying information from one side of the brain to the other, is larger in women than in men. More recently, she concluded that the anterior commissure of gay men is feminized—that is, larger than in heterosexual men. Steven Demeter, Robert W. Doty and James L. Ringo of the University of Rochester, however, found just the opposite: anterior commissures larger in men than in women. Furthermore, even if Allen's findings are correct, the size of the anterior commissure alone would say nothing about an individual's sexual orientation. Although she found a statistically significant difference in the average size of the commissures of gay men and heterosexual men, 27 of the 30 homosexual men in her study had anterior commissures within the same size range as the 30 heterosexual men with whom she compared them.

* * *

Some researchers have turned to genetics instead of brain structure in the search for a biological link to sexual orientation. Several recent studies suggest that the brothers of homosexual men are more likely to be homosexual than are men without gay brothers. Of these, only the study by J. Michael Bailey of Northwestern University and Richard C. Pillard of Boston University included both nontwin biological brothers and adopted (unrelated) brothers in addition to identical and fraternal twins.

Their investigation yielded paradoxical results: some statistics support a genetic hypothesis, and others refute it. Identical twins were most likely to both be gay; 52 percent were concordant for homosexuality, as compared with 22 percent of fraternal twins. This result would support a genetic interpretation because identical twins share all of their genes, whereas fraternal twins share only half of theirs. Nontwin brothers of homosexuals, however, share the same proportion of genes as fraternal twins; however, only 9 percent of them were concordant for homosexuality. The genetic hypothesis predicts that their rates should be equal.

Moreover, Bailey and Pillard found that the incidence of homosexuality in the adopted brothers of homosexuals (11 percent) was much higher than recent estimates for the rate of homosexuality in the population (1 to 5 percent). In fact, it was equal to the rate for nontwin biological brothers. This study clearly challenges a simple genetic hypothesis and strongly suggests that environment contributes significantly to sexual orientation.

Two of three other recent studies also detected an increased rate of homosexuality among the identical as opposed to fraternal twins of homosexuals. In every case, however, the twins were reared together. Without knowing what developmental experiences contribute to sexual orientation—and whether those experiences are more similar between identical twins that between fraternal twins—the effects of common genes and common environments are difficult to disentangle. Resolving this issue requires studies of twins raised apart.

Indeed, perhaps the major finding of these heritability studies is that despite having all of their genes in common and having prenatal and postnatal environments as close to identical as possible, approximately half of the identical twins were nonetheless discordant for orientation. This finding underscores just how little is known about the origins of sexual orientation.

Dean H. Hamer's team at the National Institutes of Health has found the most direct evidence that sexual orientation may be influenced by specific genes.

The team focused on a small part of the X chromosome known as the Xq28 region, which contains hundreds of genes. Women have two X chromosomes and so two Xq28 regions, but they pass a copy of only one to a son (who has a single X chromosome). The theoretical probability of two sons receiving a copy of the same Xq28 from their mother is thus 50 percent. Hamer found that of his 40 pairs of gay siblings, 33 instead of the expected 20 had received the same Xq28 region from their mother.

Hamer's finding is often misinterpreted as showing that all 66 men from these 33 pairs shared the same Xq28 sequence. That is quite different from what the study showed: Each member of the 33 concordant pairs shared his Xq28 region only with his brother—not with any of the other 32 pairs. No single, specific Xq28 sequence (a putative "gay gene") was identified in all 66 men.

Unfortunately, Hamer's team did not examine the Xq28 region of its gay subjects' heterosexual brothers to see how many shared the same sequence. Hamer suggests that inclusion of heterosexual siblings would have confounded his analysis because the gene associated with homosexuality might be "incompletely penetrant"—that is to say, heterosexual men could carry the gene without expressing it. In other words, inclusion of heterosexual brothers might have revealed that something other than genes is responsible for sexual orientation.

Finally, Neil J. Risch of Yale University, one of the developers of the statistical techniques that Hamer used, has questioned whether Hamer's results are statistically significant. Risch has argued that until we have more details about the familial clustering of homosexuality, the implications of studies such as Hamer's will remain unclear.

* * *

Studies that mark homosexuality as a heritable trait (assuming that they can be replicated) do not say anything about how that heritability might operate. Genes in themselves specify proteins, not behavior or psychological phenomena. Although we know virtually nothing about how complex psychological phenomena are embodied in the brain, it is conceivable that particular DNA sequences might somehow cause the brain to be wired specifically for homosexual orientation. Significantly, however, heritability requires no such mechanism.

Instead particular genes might influence personality traits that could in turn influence the relationships and subjective experiences that contribute to the social learning of sexual orientation. One can imagine many ways in which a temperamental difference could give rise to different orientations in different environments.

The *Achillea* plant serves as a useful metaphor: genetic variations yield disparate phenotypes depending on elevation. The altitude at which a cutting of *Achillea* grows does not have a linear effect on the plant's growth, however, nor is the impact limited to a single attribute. Height, number of leaves and stems, and branching pattern are all affected. If a plant can display such a complex response to its environment, then what of a far more complex organism that can modify its surroundings at will?

The possible interaction between genes and environment in the development of sexual orientation can be sketched here only in the most oversimplified of ways. For example, many researchers believe aversion to rough-and-tumble play in boys is moderately predictive of homosexual development. (Direct-model theorists argue this aversion is merely the childhood expression of a brain that has been wired for homosexuality.) Meanwhile psychoanalysts have noted that of those gay men who seek therapy, many report having had poor rapport with their fathers. They thus suggest that an impaired father-son relationship leads to homosexuality.

One could combine these observations to speculate that a genetically based aversion to rough-and-tumble play in boys could impair rapport with fathers who demand that they adhere to rigid sex-role stereotypes. Fathers who make no much demands would maintain a rapport with their sons. As a result, the hypothetical gene in question could affect sexual orientation in some cases but not in others. Even such a reductionist example (based on traits that reflect cultural stereotypes rather than biology) shows how neither temperament nor family environment might be decisive. Studies focusing on either one or the other would yield inconclusive results.

* * *

These speculations reemphasize how far researchers must go before they understand the factors—both biological and experiential—that contribute to sexual orientation. Even if the size of certain brain structures does turn out to be correlated with sexual orientation, current understanding of the brain is inadequate to explain how such quantitative differences could generate qualitative differences in a psychological phenomenon as complex as sexual orientation. Similarly, confirmation of genetic research purporting to show that homosexuality is heritable makes clear neither what is inherited nor how it influences sexual orientation. For the foreseeable future, then, interpretation of these results will continue to hinge on assumptions of questionable validity.

While attempts to replicate these preliminary findings continue, researchers and the public must resist the temptation to consider them in any but the most tentative fashion. Perhaps more important, we should also be asking ourselves why we as a society are so emotionally invested in this research. Will it—or should it—make any difference in the way we perceive ourselves and others or how we live our lives and allow others to live theirs? Perhaps the answers to the most salient questions in this debate lie not within the biology of human brains but rather in the cultures those brains have created.

POSTSCRIPT

Is Male Homosexuality Biologically Influenced?

One answer to the question of where sexual orientation originates is offered by Alan Bell, Martin Weinberg, and Sue Hammersmith in their 1981 study *Sexual Preference: Its Development in Men and Women*. After examining a variety of environmental and learning factors, these sexologists found that there is no evidence that homosexuality is caused by unresolved Oedipal feelings, lack of sufficient heterosexual opportunities, rape (for lesbianism), seductive opposite-sex parents, seduction by older same-sex persons, a domineering mother or a weak father, or labeling by others. They concluded that "if a biological basis exists—and this study points in that direction—it is probably stronger for exclusive homosexuals than for bisexuals."

Everything we know about the development of biological organisms is that nature and nurture constantly interact to channel the individual at critical periods in his or her development. Elsewhere, William Byne has written, "Genetic factors can be conceptualized as indirectly influencing the development of sexual orientation without supposing that they either directly influence or determine sexual orientation per se. Similarly, one could imagine that prenatal hormones influence particular personality dimensions or temperamental traits which, in turn, influence the emergence of sexual orientation."

As the debate continues over possible biological influences on sexual orientation, it is important to remember that biological explanations of homosexuality and heterosexuality carry with them hidden implications for our religious institutions, moral judgments, legal structures, and social policies.

SUGGESTED READINGS

P. Bereano, "The Mystique of the Phantom 'Gay Gene,' " *Gay Community News* (Spring 1997).

C. Burr, "Homosexuality and Biology," *The Atlantic Monthly* (March 1993).

D. Hammer and P. Copeland, *The Science of Desire: The Search for the Gay Gene and the Biology of Behavior* (Simon & Schuster, 1994).

S. LeVay, *Queer Science: The Use and Abuse of Research into Homosexuality* (MIT Press, 1996).

J. Paulk, "Overcoming the 'Biological Imperative,' " *The Wall Street Journal* (February 4, 1997), p. A19.

R. Pool, *Eve's Rib: Searching for the Biological Roots of Sex Differences* (Crown Publishers, 1994).

ISSUE 3

Is the Model of Normal and Vandalized Gendermaps/Lovemaps Biased?

YES: Pat Califia, from *Sex Changes: The Politics of Transgenderism* (Cleis Press, 1997)

NO: John Money, from "An Interview With John Money," *Omni* (April 1996)

ISSUE SUMMARY

YES: Pat Califia, a feminist and self-described sex radical, argues that John Money's concept of lovemaps reflects a high-handed, moralistic division of the world into "normal" and "abnormal" sexuality. She believes that many "differently-pleasured" persons, including homosexuals, are at risk because of the moralistic distinctions implicit in Money's model of lovemaps.

NO: John Money, an expert on gender development, argues that every society has taboos and establishes a sexual ethic and that the idea of a sexual democracy where people can love whomever they please in whatever fashion they please is unachievable because of those taboos.

The cover story of the March/April 1993 issue of *The Sciences* was "The Five Sexes: Why Male and Female Are Not Enough." The author of the article, medical biologist Anne Fausto-Sterling, argued that "biologically speaking, there are many gradations running from female to male; along that spectrum lie at least five sexes—perhaps even more." Along with males and females, Fausto-Sterling counted the 4 percent of babies who are born hermaphrodites (herms), female pseudo-hermaphrodites (ferms), or male pseudo-hermaphrodites (merms).

If a person's gender identity is relevant to the question "How many sexes are there?" then we can add to Fausto-Sterling's list of sexes people who describe themselves as transgendered—transvestites (or cross-dressers) and transsexuals, or people whose psyche (gender identity) conflicts with their sexual bodies. If one's "gender orientation" is part of one's "sex," then we may need to consider people who are sexually attracted to people of their own sex or gender, those who fall in love with people of the opposite sex, people who are sexually attracted to both sexes, and asexual people, who have no interest in sexual intimacy at all. And then we have to figure out where people who enjoy fetishes and unconventional sexual outlets fit into our schema.

"How many sexes are there?" is not a simple question, because it cannot have a simple answer. It is now known that a person's sexual nature is not a simple given, male or female, set at conception, birth, or any other point in time. Most experts believe that a person's sex is the result of both nature (genes, hormones, and anatomy) and nurture (learning) interacting from conception to death.

Few scientists have contributed more to the understanding of human sexual development than John Money. For 50 years Money has studied "nature's experiments," the not-so-rare children with anomalies of sex organs and hormone systems. Money views the complex path that people follow as they develop their gender identity, gender role, and gender orientation as a "gendermap." Part of this gendermap is a "lovemap."

As described in the introduction to the *Omni* interview with Money that is reprinted in the second selection of this issue, the concept of a lovemap represents the personal template, or imprint, of all the neural pathways that develop in the brain. Its development is influenced by hormones, genes, and learning. Its contours affect who we are sexually attracted to, who we fall in love with, and what kind of sex we like, including when, how often, and under what circumstances. In adulthood individuals seek to match their lovemaps with someone else's to form pair-bonding relationships.

When a child is subjected to traumatic experiences, his or her lovemap may be vandalized, or distorted. Thwarted childhood sex play can also vandalize a lovemap. If this happens adult functioning of the sex organs in lovemaking may be impaired; there may be no sex at all. Or, conversely, the lovemap owner may use the sex organs with compulsive frequency. Another possibility is the development of a paraphilia. In paraphilia, both love and lust are compromised. The genitals will work but only in the presence of some special substitute imagery, object, or ritual. This is because in the lovemap of the paraphiliac, where love and lust cannot be reconciled, the solution is to find a way to reconcile them temporarily. The means can be as benign as a shoe fetish, as complex as cross-dressing, or as deadly as autoerotic asphyxiation (purposely cutting off one's air supply while masturbating).

This brings us to the issue raised by Pat Califia, who argues in the following selection that Money's concept of lovemaps discriminates against people whose lovemap does not fit the conventional expectations of society. Califia suggests that terms like *vandalized, abnormal, deviant,* and *distorted* are cultural constructs that unnecessarily stigmatize some individuals. Money counters that every society has its taboos, so these terms are unavoidable, even though we must constantly reevaluate and challenge them in the light of new knowledge.

YES

Pat Califia

SEX CHANGES: THE POLITICS OF TRANSGENDERISM

[John] Money (with his collaborators) is the author of hundreds of scientific papers and more than two dozen books in the field of sexology and psychoendocrinology. He is an enormously influential intellectual and researcher who clearly sees himself as a humanitarian who advocates better treatment for those he views as being less sexually fortunate than normal people. But he does not seem to understand how precarious the scientific basis is for his high-handed division of the world into "normal sexuality" and "paraphilias." Money is essentially a moralist masquerading as a scientist, and he gets away with it because of his medical credentials and his prolific output of technical-sounding publications about sexuality. In fact, it is the sort of attitudes toward sex, gender, and pleasure that he promotes which are the underpinnings of such things as sodomy laws and psychiatric incarceration of "differently-pleasured" people.

Nowhere is this moralism made more clear than in Money and Margaret Lamacz's 1989 *Vandalized Lovemaps: Paraphilic Outcome of Seven Cases in Pediatric Sexology. . . .* Money and Lamacz advocate intervention in the lives of sexually different children without conclusive proof that such interventions have any impact on adult sexual orientation, gender identity, or pleasure-seeking behavior. In fact, the dedication of this book is to "Those whose lovemaps will be paraphilia-free in the twenty-first century if this book promotes the founding of pediatric sexology clinics and research centers, worldwide, as we hope." The prospect makes me shudder.

Money says:

The lovemap is the personal imprint or template of whatever turns a person on. The beginning topography of the lovemap evolves in the womb, where the developing brain is open to the influence of the sex hormones. Spontaneous erections begin in the womb. And throughout childhood erotic play for most youngsters seldom voluntarily stops. The main contours of the lovemap are etched during this childhood sex-rehearsal play; when the lovemap is allowed to grow naturally, the child at puberty matures into a healthy lover. In adulthood an individual seeks to match lovemaps with someone else in a pair-bonding relationship.

This explanation of the genesis of the lovemap has as much to do with objective reality as the fad that swept the country a few years ago for female ejaculation, which supposedly took place because of the G-spot, a mythical organ that no anatomist could even find in the female body. All Money is really doing is recycling a bunch of very questionable assumptions about the genesis of pleasure-seeking behavior in adults. He moves readily from the "circulating fetal hormones" explanation of the structure of the lovemap to a "traumatic childhood event" explanation, without managing to document that either one is true. This is his "theory" about the etiology of sadomasochism: "The classic example is the kid who gets a hard-on while in a state of abject terror because he's been called down to the principal's office for punishment.... Suddenly you've got the connection between an erection, sexual feeling, and getting beaten up. So you've got a sadomasochist in the making."

Money, of course, is not troubled by the fact that there are plenty of sadomasochists who had little or no childhood experience with corporal punishment. Nor does it occur to him to ask why the kid who is about to be punished has a hard-on in the first place. Perhaps a predisposition to enjoy exposure, verbal rebukes, and a blow upon the buttocks existed before this make-believe teenager was chastised—or perhaps the potential to respond with arousal to this set of circumstances exists in all of us. The right

question to ask may not be, "Why do some people grow up to be perverts?" but "Why doesn't everybody grow up with more sexual diversity and the ability to enjoy polymorphous pleasure?"

Though sexually conservative, Money does not consciously refer to the Bible or English common law to justify his fairly traditional views about what constitutes appropriate sexual conduct. Instead, he makes reference to the secular religion of the West, romantic love. It is the inability to enjoy romantic fulfillment that makes Money's paraphile a sad figure. The paraphiliac, according to Money, has accomplished a triumph in spite of the tragedy of having her or (more often) his lovemap defaced. The paraphiliac rescues lust from total wreckage and obliteration and constructs a new map that gives the erotic side of relationships a new chance. But there is a terrible price to be paid. In Money's world view, paraphiliacs cannot have both love and lust; they sacrifice committed, intimate, romantic partnerships in order to have their strange pleasures.

Having known many people Money would call "paraphiliacs" who do indeed enjoy romance and committed relationships, this generalization seems dubious to me. But Money has a double-bind to cover any exceptions to his rule. He simply pathologizes any relationships that sexually-different people might construct. In an interview, he typified such relationships as "spooky" and added, "I have never really gotten to the bottom of this strange collusional business between a paraphile and the partner. Do they smell each other out at the time of courtship? Does one grow into the paraphilia of the other—or a bit of both? Well, I have to call it a spooky collusional relationship. They know what they're doing. They're not ignorant, but both are powerless to not do it."

As powerless, perhaps, as two heterosexual vanilla people who are deeply in love? When he enters the shadow side of human sexuality, Money leaves Occam's Razor at home.

In case being threatened with the loss of love doesn't convince us that the intense pleasures of the paraphilias are to be shunned, he makes ominous references to epilepsy among paraphiliacs and warns us that it is "terribly dangerous" to have "people who've got too much power" (i.e., politicians) with hidden paraphilias. In an interview, he equated the use of atomic weapons with fetishism and masochism. This, and his attempt to make paraphiliac sex sound radically different from vanilla heterosexual lovemaking, fall rather flat. He says there "must be neurochemical changes" when paraphiliacs "go into a trance-like state and carry out their rituals. . . . They have no self-governance over their behavior" —as if neurochemical changes do not take place during all sexual activity! Money has absolutely no evidence that a fetishist, sadomasochist, or transsexual is in any more of a "trance," engaging in a "ritual," or lacking self-control than a teenage boy who's getting some at a drive-in movie or a couple of newlyweds during their first night in the honeymoon hotel.

By the way, according to the 1996 edition of *Who's Who*, Money never married and has no children. It seems that what's sauce for the goose is not sauce for the sexologist. I guess it would verge on ad hominem to speculate about what might have happened to *his* lovemap.

Money has gotten big street cred in academia for boldly and calmly confronting dreadful things. He says he made a decision to allow the first sex-change surgery in the United States to take place in February of 1965 at Johns Hopkins because he was interested in the welfare of transsexuals and wanted to change the medical profession's attitude toward people with sexual problems. This kind of talk has made some people see Money as an advocate for positive social change. But the fact is, he wants to get rid of all the weird, scary people who made him so esteemed and famous. When asked by an interviewer if transsexuals would still seek sex reassignment in a "sexual democracy," Money replied, "I have a very strong suspicion that if we had a genuine sexual democracy, we would not create all of these problems in our children." Conformity, not increased tolerance, is Money's recipe for the Sexually Great Society.

Money believes that societies such as an aboriginal community in north central Australia, have no "paraphilias or even bisexual or homosexual stuff either. They had no sexual taboo; the kids were allowed to play sex-rehearsal games without being punished." He continues:

We need a better ethnographic survey of peoples who don't have sexual taboos to find out to what extent we're actually creating these paraphilias by so zealously trying to beat out sex from the development of young children. Perfectly reasonable, nice mothers and fathers go berserk when they encounter the first appearance of normal sexual rehearsal play in their children. If we were truly committed to having our children grow up to be plain, ordinary heterosexuals, we'd treat them exactly as if we wanted them to be athletes—get them practicing and reward them every time we saw them doing it.

It never seems to have occurred to him that small, isolated groups of people are able to do a much better job of controlling and repressing unacceptable sexual conduct than a handful of vice cops and fundamentalist preachers in a big, modern city. Nor has he considered the possibility that the respondents may have lied to whoever was studying them, or not understood the sexual categories used by Westerners. While I can certainly support Money's goal to get parents to stop punishing their children for age-appropriate sex play, it seems intellectually dishonest for him to simply overlook the large amount of such childish "sexual rehearsal" that is unconventional, to say the least. Piaget may not have noticed that, but Freud certainly did. I can't say I relish the prospect of "normal" sex-play being imposed on homosexual or transsexual children as a form of behavioral therapy. Money doesn't prescribe this specifically, but it seems consistent with his philosophy.

... The overwhelming sense that I get from this examination of the history of transsexuality and sex reassignment is that "help" from doctors is truly a double-edged sword for sexual minorities.

Transsexuals became the abused darlings of sexologists and medical doctors because they could be "cured" by using hormones and surgery. Those who see themselves as gender scientists are invested in trying to discover a physiological explanation for human sexual variation. Instead of simply accepting this variation as a normal part of the spectrum of human experience, and seeing its intrinsic worth, these people inappropriately apply a medical model of health versus disease to gender identity and pleasure-seeking behavior.

Once sex hormones were discovered, doctors tried to use them to treat every sex disorder from impotence to homosexuality; in no case were they successful enough to set up a treatment industry. Transsexuality is an exception. By creating a "treatment" process that is intended to churn out feminine heterosexual women and masculine heterosexual men, the gender scientists have turned their backs on the most liberating and revolutionary implications of what they call "gender dysphoria"—the possibility that the categories of "male" and "female" are unrealistic and smothering us all.

It doesn't matter whether sex deviation is caused by social learning or biology; or at least it doesn't matter to the "deviate." If it weren't for loneliness, discrimination, and stigma, most sexual-minority members would never consider giving up or altering their fantasies and pleasures. But it does matter to the doctors and scientists and researchers because these issues give them government grants, publishing contracts, and tenure at universities. We need to question the so-called experts who are too quick to pathologize behavior or self-concepts that are not inherently self-destructive and that don't necessarily interfere with people's ability to love or pleasure one another. We can only do that if we jettison our own guilt and apply the same intellectual standards to sex research that we would apply to a piece of research in the field of astronomy or physics.

Queer activists who believe it would be politically advantageous for us to be able to prove that homosexuality has a genetic basis should consider transsexuals' experience with the father figures of gender science. Doctors have believed that transsexuality is a medical problem with a biological cause for nearly two decades, and the position of transgendered people in society has barely advanced a notch or two. Transsexuals are still perceived as the tragic victims of a delusion that may or may not have a chromosomal or hormonal origin. Not a single recognized authority on this issue has said that transgendered people have intrinsic value and worth, or something important to contribute to the rest of us and our understanding of what it means to be human. Money [and his colleagues] would have absolutely no ethical problem with genetically engineering transsexuals out of existence. It would be interesting to see what their recommendations might be if amniocentesis could detect the potential for transgenderism in a fetus.

Gay men, lesbians, and bisexuals would be foolish and deluded if we imagined the gender scientists have a more positive picture of us than they do of transsexuals. To them, we are all manifestations of the same disease, gender identity disorder. As long as we are operating in a social context where sexual or gender difference is seen as a bad thing, the medical model will further stigmatize homosexuals as sick or developmentally flawed people in need of a cure—not equal civil rights. It is very possible that homosexuality does have a biological basis. But the belief that our difference springs from our genes, hormones, or brain chemistry is no guarantee that social policy toward us will be liberalized.

Finally, how very sad it is that even the people who viewed themselves as transsexuals' allies and advocates at the same time saw them as sick, delusional, and inferior people.... And how frustrating it is that... lengthy technical texts were constructed to explain gender dysphoria and justify sex reassignment, when the thing that really needs to be explained is our insistence on gender dimorphism, despite all the hard medical evidence that this is not uniformly natural to our species. It is our fear and hatred of people who are differently-gendered that need to be cured, not their synthesis of the qualities we think of as maleness and femaleness, masculinity and femininity.

NO

John Money

AN INTERVIEW WITH JOHN MONEY

OMNI: Why have the sexual passions so long been considered anarchistic, dangerous, something to suppress?

MONEY: At the recent Seventh World Congress of Sexology, in India, quite a clear contrast emerged for me between the sexual philosophy of the Kama Sutra and that of Ayurvedic medicine. This traditional Indian herbal medicine, totally in contrast with the celebration of joy and sex in the Kama Sutra, espouses the conservation of "vital fluids," that is, semen. This is a teaching of extreme antiquity and is widespread in Asia and Africa, probably antedating the discovery of writing. While we'll never know when taboos originated, I associate their invention with this concept of seminal retention. In my imagination I place taboo as a means of controlling human behavior in the hands of some priestly rulers in the Magdalenian Age, when the drawings were done in the caves of Lascaux and Altamira.

It's a pretty simple piece of psychology that if you terrorize small children, making them afraid of doing something the human organism normally does in healthy development, then you've put in place a lever of guilt and shame. All you need to do after that is pull the lever and they jump to attention and do whatever you tell them. So taboos are extremely widespread, the most common by far being the taboo against sex. While some tribes in New Guinea, Melanesia, or Amazonia still may exist without a taboo, the Polynesians, covering a large part of the earth's surface, are the prime example of a people who've managed not to have a sexual taboo. They raise teenagers with a totally different morality for sex. But they have a fearful taboo about the desecration of the bodies, spirits, and burial places of the dead.

OMNI: Is there evidence that taboos enable societies to function in orderly ways?

MONEY: It would be challenging to find out, with comparative ethnographic studies, why humans invented the concept of taboo, used it to raise their children, and adhered to it so wonderfully all these millennia. Still, we can say that every society establishes a sexual ethic, regardless of the conditions and constraints. This century reevaluated the sexual ethic in the presence of contraception. The contraception revolution that got going around 1870 simply *dictated* this change to us. It's not the whimsy of a bunch of pointy-eared Easterners, as some Bible Belt people would have it. The so-called sexual revolution was necessitated by the universalization of birth control, which culminated in the discovery of the pill. Although the diaphragm had been in existence for ages, the pill's incredible value was that you put it in your mouth, not your vagina. So it wasn't sex. It was so completely de-eroticized, it was acceptable.

OMNI: Do you think there's a struggle going on now over sexual morality?

MONEY: The rules of social behavior tend to be self-perpetuating except when something new—a cultural artifact either invented or borrowed—comes in to upset the balance. The American automobile changed the landscape, really everything. And there's almost a complete chronological overlap with the invention of the automobile and of birth control. The pivotal factor of the universalization of birth control was the vending machine. It was very important that young people could drive up to a gas station, slip in a quarter, and get a condom; and avoid a red-faced confrontation at a counter, especially with a female clerk. Even today some people will risk pregnancy rather than the humiliation of asking for birth control in public.

OMNI: Are there new strategies for love as a result of this historical imperative?

MONEY: Historically, there are different traditions of pair-bonding in establishing marriages, breeding relationships. The familiar European one, endorsed by the Church, came through Imperial Rome, by way of the Middle East. This system of the arranged marriage, the virgin bride, and the double standard was also adapted by the Moslems. In contrast was the pre-Roman, pre-Christian European one

that I call the betrothal system. It's still intact in Iceland and parts of the Arctic north in Scandinavia. In the betrothal system lasting relationships were based on a ritualistic sequence of the love affair, falling in love.

The breeding customs of any society are almost in the Marxist sense intimately related to the method of production and distribution of wealth. The betrothal system was a natural for a society of small farmers, fishermen, and woodspeople, where the family was the production unit. In the Middle East the system evolved with the growth of cities. Very rich and powerful people would commandeer the girls for their harems, leaving the public harem—the whorehouse—to take care of all the unattached men.

Today's college students, without necessarily any blueprint for it, have resumed the pattern of the betrothal by living together before getting married. Birth control, of course, has made the system viable again. You don't live together to try for a pregnancy but to see how well you make it as a sexual couple in advance of the contractual obligations of marriage. Many young people are vaguely aware that they grew up in erotically rather joyless families, and they are searching for a better way. Many people, being so obsessed with sex and conformity to the old mores, forget that people fall in love, and the romantic affair is as important a part of the equation as the sex-organ relationship. Young people are very much involved in romantic love attraction to one another.

OMNI: Can a sexual democracy—where people can love whomever they please, in whatever fashion they please—exist?

MONEY: Yes, but it would cause a kaleidoscopic reshuffling, because everything within a society is integrated with everything else. All the institutions have their feelers out interdigitating with one another. Some of the Moral Majority expect young people to have no sex, not even to masturbate, until they're old enough to marry at twenty-eight. But a true sexual democracy doesn't dictate to children. With adequate economic support, there's a perfectly good argument for young parenthood.

OMNI: Will AIDS have an effect on this historical progression?

MONEY: Yes, AIDS has already made a big, big change in sexual-life patterns. But not big enough to stop the spread of AIDS; it never will. Nothing ever stopped people from spreading syphilis and gonorrhea. In the eighteenth century [Swiss physician Simon André] Tissot was obsessed with the terrifying effects of the social vice. Syphilis and gonorrhea were considered one disease. His book on the terrible dangers of onanism said it's not only losing your vital seminal fluids (women were problematic vis-à-vis vital fluids), but it's also yielding to your concupiscent thoughts and letting your passions go wild that gets you out on the streets with the whores and catching the disease. Tissot was really tangling with issues of sexual behavior and morality as related to disease. The great appeal of his teaching, summed up as degeneracy theory, was that it gave doctors an explanation for disease. You degenerated yourself, and then you were vulnerable to everything. After the previous theory—the demon possession theory, which faded when the Inquisition burned itself out—the medical profession had no theory of health or disease until Tissot formulated this wonderful degeneracy theory.

His book was profoundly influential, in America particularly through Sylvester Graham, who had many followers in the 1830's. By 1870 Kellogg made his mark with degeneracy theory. Kellogg is important historically because he sat on the fence between degeneracy theory and germ theory. He couldn't make change and absorb germ theory, so he became a sort of mastodon of medical theory embalmed in ice. Yet his antisexual teachings are still explicitly used by the Seventh Day Adventists and Jehovah's Witnesses in their books on sex education. Neither differ much from the Mormons.

OMNI: In a sexual democracy, will transsexuals and others with complex gender identity/roles still try to make sex changes?

MONEY: At the New Delhi Congress, Margaret Lamacz and I ran a symposium on gender transposition. Gender transposition means that as compared with the standard stereotypes, which may or may not be biologically, historically, or culturally based, some people are transposed away from what you'd expect if you looked only at their sex organs. Instead of being male, they're committed to a whole lot that's female, and vice versa. Since there was a terminological problem, I suggested we use the concept of miming, so you get men who are gynemimetic, impersonating women; and women who are andromimetic, impersonating men.

In India you find the hijra, whose history is lost in the mists of time, but essentially these people replenish their ranks with teenagers who run away from home because they are disgracing their families by being too effeminate. They like to have sex with men and want to be women—they're obsessed with it, the same as our patients here are. The ultimate stage of the hijra is to get up the courage to go through with amputation of penis and testicles. They had no anesthetic. No hormone treatment. So in their ancient ways, they looked like men impersonating women. Now some of them are beginning to take hormones.

I have a large group of gynemimetic patients—so does anybody who deals with gender problems—who do *not* want their penises removed, do *not* want a vagina constructed, and the corresponding is true for the women-to-men. They simply want to take hormones and live their lives as members of the opposite sex. Now if we had a sexual democracy, we'd have a place for both kinds of people. A book called *The Transsexual Empire* argues that it's only these cruel, vicious, and heartless members of the medical profession who are forcing these poor darlings to go and get themselves cut up and mutilated, whereas we should leave them alone. Well, I have news for whoever wrote that book: You'd have lots of patients willing to get a gun and blow off their own genitals if you don't do it. I've had several who got knives and cut themselves trying to get rid of their sex organs. That's their obsession!

Then there are the transvestophiles, who dress up occasionally, often doing incredibly good impressions of the other sex. It's almost always men who cross-dress, and it gives them a real thrill, but that's not why they do it. The major reason is that it's the only way they can get an erection and reach orgasm. Ideally, one finds a partner who's as turned on by your dressing up as you are. It's incredibly hard to find. I've never met a woman partner who was really turned on by having her man with his legs and body shaved, wearing perfumes and ladies' clothing. It just makes her go

sexually, erotically dead. Numb. I've met those who go along with it, but basically it's a nasty taste in their mouths. That's transvestophilia.

Now with a partial degree of transposition you have people whom you'd never recognize as being gender transposed. Everything, except their choice of sex partner, conforms to the stereotypes of masculinity or femininity. Many a person is surprised to discover the boyfriend, husband, brother, or guy at work is gay. They don't look or act gay in social situations. The only way you know they are—like the big football player who comes out and announces himself on TV—is that he's said he likes to have a boyfriend he sucks penis with. In terms of total life pattern, that is a minor degree of transposition because it only applies to the sexual activity and not to the other trimmings and trappings of acting masculine or not. Then you have bisexual people.... Now all I've dealt with is gender transposition, and I haven't even gone through the whole list of them. So in a sexual democracy, you'd find a place for all of those people. But I have a very strong suspicion that if we had a genuine sexual democracy, we would not create all of these problems in our children.

OMNI: Your critics note that you talk about these people as if their behavior is natural, and yet you say they've got problems. Do they have problems?

MONEY: Why don't you just define problem! Whose criterion? Many people with varying degrees of gender transportation do experience it in some contexts of their lives as a problem. I've seen many a youngish person in a panic about whether he or she's gay. For some, the biggest help is for someone to tell them, yes, you can find a niche for yourself in life as a gay person. Others will blow up, practically pull a gun if you tell them it's okay to be gay. Because their attitude is: Nobody's going to tell me that, damn it; you've got to change me! A big part of this business is whether people define themselves as having a problem or not.

OMNI: Why the variety of lovemaps, gender identifications, and paraphilias?

MONEY: I've never found an explanation for why the human race has so many languages. When the brain became a language brain, it obviously needed to develop an intense degree of plasticity. Such plasticity allows languages to be logical, coherent systems and yet be extremely variable. The same brain that thinks in words and symbols is also a brain that has to be freed up with regard to sexual turn-on and partnering. God knows why sex attitudes have been subject to the corresponding degrees of modification and variety as language. I suspect there's a close parallel between the two.

The brain doesn't seem incredibly efficient with regard to sex. I can't find a rational or sensible explanation for why a man needs his partner to dress him in diapers, feed him a baby bottle, let him pee in his diapers, smack his bottom, and tell him what a naughty boy he is—so that then and only then he can get a hard-on and come. I have patients like that, and I can go through my list of forty-odd paraphilias and say, Okay, why should I inveigh against people who have to wear diapers to copulate, or any of the others? But I really can't recommend that person to a partner because I haven't yet met any woman who really gets turned on by diapering her husband.

It's all right if you've a perfect match. And those who do sometimes match are the paraphiliacs of amputation, who get turned on by the stumps. That is, if they don't feel too guilty once they actually admit their paraphilia to an amputee! Perhaps all they can do is establish a friendship; many can't allow it to become erotic, but a few make it wonderfully by marrying an amputee.

OMNI: Would there be any paraphilias in a sexual democracy?

MONEY: I made a study of an aboriginal community way up in north central Australia. I could not find any paraphilias or even bisexual or homosexual stuff either. They had no sexual taboo; the kids were allowed to play sexual-rehearsal games without being punished. My big surprise was that this play was inconspicuous, socially unobtrusive. Their taboo was about with whom you were allowed to use your vocal chords, not your sex organs. And if you weren't allowed to talk to them, you weren't allowed to have sex with them. In some relationships, usually an uncle/nephew relationship, the child could talk to him only if he used a joking relationship, and all the jokes were sexual.

We need a better ethnographic survey of peoples who don't have sexual taboos to find out to what extent we're actually creating these paraphilias by so zealously trying to beat out sex from the development of young children. Perfectly reasonable, nice mothers and fathers go berserk when they encounter the first appearance of normal sexual rehearsal play in their children. If we were truly committed to having our children grow up to be plain, ordinary heterosexuals, we'd treat them exactly as if we wanted them to be athletes—get them practicing and reward them every time we saw them doing it.

But you can't say things like that in this society without convincing people you're an idiot! Yet there's not a single university hospital in the Western world with a department of adult or pediatric sexual health. Children in trouble with their healthy sexual development have no experts and no clinic to go to. Piaget never dealt with sexual, erotic, or genital concepts. He never wrote about boys and girls, really. And he certainly never got down between their legs and looked at their concepts of themselves that way. It's quite an accomplishment, to live to Piaget's age and wear horse blinders about sexual concepts in the development of childhood.

OMNI: The fertilized egg is basically hermaphroditic, undifferentiated, but by the eighth week, depending on chromosomal sex, one set of sexual apparatus grows and the other atrophies. Why does nature have a dual pattern like that?

MONEY: I don't know, but I use that question as a challenge to think about which pattern is used in the development of the sexual part of the brain. The best evidence now says that within the brain, the biochemical—mainly hormonal—process of differentiation occurs so that both masculinizing and feminizing are able to take place together. It has now been established that masculinizing and feminizing and demasculinizing and defeminizing are four processes. The fool who jumps in where angels fear to tread would say that the opposite of masculine is feminine, but it's not; it's demasculine. And that's probably crucial for understanding bisexual feelings and dispositions in love affairs—that people can have either or both. I don't think we can escape the evidence that there's a sexual disposition shaped by hormones influencing the brain.

OMNI: What do you think of East German endocrinologist Gunter Dörner's attempt to prove that homosexuality is caused by hormonal differences? In 1980

he tried to show that gay males have a bigger response to estrogen injections than do straight males.

MONEY: Dörner reported that the effect of estrogen shots on LH [luteinizing hormones, a pituitary regulator that triggers the gonads to secrete sex steroids] in homosexuals resembled that of heterosexual women and differed from that of heterosexual and bisexual men. In 1984 Brian Gladue of Stony Brook obtained similar findings. But this year L. Gooren in Amsterdam not only failed to replicate these findings but showed that the difference in receptivity was due to a previously neglected variable. He showed that abnormal response to the estrogen might result from poor functioning of the hormone-producing cells in the testicles [Leydig cells]. This phenomenon appeared in both hetero- and homosexual men.

Gooren went one step further. He had an additional test group: male-to-female transsexual applicants who were not yet on hormonal therapy. They did not show the higher sensitivity to the estrogen injections, nor the weak Leydig cell function. Since then, he told me, he's been able to repeat this same test on transsexuals before they had their testicles removed and after. When they had their testicles, they didn't show the higher sensitivity. And after, when, of course, they'd lost their Leydig cells along with their testicles, their response was up to females' levels. So Gooren has gone further and pinned it down to the Leydig cells instead of something in the brain. He found it didn't make any difference if they were gay or straight.

It's hard to know if, in your group of homosexuals, you're going to pick up some who may have damaged Leydig cells. Dörner wasn't too fussy about reviewing his patients for unexpected contamination from, for instance, regular drug use. The question is: Is there a greater proportion of gays to straights with Leydig cell impairment? And how will you test for it?

OMNI: Isn't science a bit deterministic in insisting on a purely physiological cause?

MONEY: Yes, and I don't know why. But I get attacked from both sides of the fence. Some homosexuals want to make it all a matter of moral choice, and I tell them they're crazy. They couldn't fall in love with a woman if they got a million dollars. They might be able to fuck her, but falling in love is *the* key. You can't force yourself if you don't have your heart and soul in it.

The problem reduces itself to a simple scientific issue: How do you get your gender status, a lovemap that makes you fall in love with your own sex? When, and through what channel, does it get into the body? Through your genes, your prenatal hormones, the kind of food your mother ate when she was pregnant, the food you ate in your first years, pollutants in the air? Or does it get in through your eyes, ears, and skin senses? And it doesn't really matter, does it? What matters is that science has been totally defeated in being able to change straight people into gays, and vice versa.

OMNI: Could we create new human genders from the procreation of groups with the same sexual anomalies?

MONEY: Such as girls with precocious onsets of puberty? Would we create a class of three-year-old whores? Why not capitalize on what could be a new development in the human species and put all the early-developing children together to breed so that you have a new subspecies? Why not make it into a total irony by having a kennel-club show every year and see who gets the prize in each category of human subspecies? It's provocative to suggest that instead of viewing these conditions as pathological diseases to be attacked, you could twist it around and say maybe this is a new design in nature that we should help her with, exploit. And then, it's fascinating to pursue all the implications of abolishing childhood.

OMNI: Do paraphiles have more intense erotic or love experiences?

MONEY: Something I find scientifically provoking beyond my capability to deal with since I haven't big money for PET [positron emission tomography] scanning and such, is what happens to so many of these paraphiles when they go into a trancelike state and carry out their rituals. There must be neurochemical changes. But it's not terribly different from how far out we go when we're in a hopeless love affair. And we can get pretty carried away with a really good sexual experience. So paraphiles probably are not terribly different from ordinary people. They have no self-governance over their behavior once it takes over because it's the only intensity they know.

OMNI: Why do suppressed paraphilias sometimes explode during a midlife crisis?

MONEY: Usually they haven't been suppressed in mental imagery, fantasy, or erotic dreams. Most paraphilias appear to be developmentally induced, except where tumors screw up the sexual pathways in the brain. Paraphilias are induced mostly by biochemical malfunctions, not by three-dimensional lesions in the brain. The paraphilia is somehow a response to stress at a critical period of childhood when sexual-rehearsal play was handicapped, or even induced prematurely under wrong conditions. Years later, when there's gigantic stress in a person's life, this accommodation to the earlier stress reaffirms itself as an answer to the present stress.

Many years ago, I saw a sixty-something-year-old transsexual-candidate applicant. He had spent years of his adult life married to a woman physician, and they had raised two children to college age. He had invested very successfully on the stock market, so he could stay at home on a small farm that he ran, as well as invest. He established that life because he dressed as a lady every day, just about.

In his early sixties he developed abdominal cancer, had surgery, and was apparently okay for several years —no recurrence or metastases. But his response to the life-threatening tragedy of cancer was a complete blowup of his cross-dressing into an obsession with becoming a transsexual. Always able to keep that at bay by dressing up as a lady, he now had to go all the way to surgery. The first clinic turned him down, saying it was merely a depressive reaction to his close brush with death. And like all good transsexuals, he got his dander up and told them he was going to teach them a lesson or two.

He finally got through the barricades down here. I told him, "If you think this is going to be the salvation of your life, then you've got to get your affairs in order for a major change. You can't go into this lightly; you've got to pass the two-year real-life test [the act of living and passing in the role of the opposite sex]. You've got to get your wife in here to talk to me."
OMNI: Was she against it?
MONEY: Not exactly. Not for it, either. It was spooky. I have never really gotten to the bottom of this strange collusional business between a paraphile and the partner. Do they smell each other out at the time of courtship? Does one grow into the paraphilia of the other—or a bit of both? Well, I have to call it a spooky collusional relationship. They know what they're doing. They're not ignorant, but both are powerless to not do it.

Anyway, considering the pragmatics of marriage, it worked out marvelously for this physician to have someone doing the housekeeping, bookwork, and accounting. And I admire him for the deftness of his shenanigans: He finally got the evaluations he needed and managed to get the surgery done on Canadian national insurance. That's just one of many stories illustrating the point that he would've spent his whole life as just a cross-dresser, except for the stress of cancer that precipitated the complete transsexualism. I could see it as plain as day: He wasn't changing into a sixty-five-year-old lady; he changed to be a little girl. Talk about Alice in Wonderland or Scarlett O'Hara! This was the formula for rescue....

OMNI: Maybe future societies will allow love and lovesickness as an excuse for missing an exam or not coming to work for a week.

MONEY: It's an important speculation because the amount of time spent at work is obviously going to be diminished as everything becomes microchips. What else is there left in life, really, when you get down to absolute fundamentals, except food, shelter, clothing, and love and lust?

POSTSCRIPT

Is the Model of Normal and Vandalized Gendermaps/Lovemaps Biased?

What criteria should psychologists and society use in deciding how to treat people who are described as having "transposed" or "cross-coded" gender identities (transsexuals) or cross-coded gender roles (transvestites). How should people who engage in sadomasochistic sexual behavior or some other paraphilic behavior that injures no one and the partners enjoy (whom Money would label as having a "vandelized lovemap") be treated?

Money and most other gender specialists talk about some people having a gendermap or lovemap with a gender identity, gender role, or gender orientation that somewhere in the developmental process became "cross-coded" or "transposed" from the male path to the female path (or vice versa), or from a heterosexual to a homosexual or bisexual orientation, or from "normophilic" to "paraphilic." Califia objects to Money's terminology as judgmental, discriminatory, biased, unjustified, and moralistic. She asks us to consider "the possibility that the categories of 'male' and 'female' are unrealistic and smothering us all." She feels that "differently-pleasured" people are just as normal and functional as "conventionally pleasured" people.

In a similar vein, members of the Intersex Society of North America recently began describing themselves as "gender fluid." In their newsletter *Hermaphrodites With Attitude*, they argue that infants born with ambiguous genitals or an intersex condition should not be forced by doctors or their parents into undergoing sex-change surgery or other forms of treatment. Instead, society should accept their conditions and allow them to make their own decisions about possible treatment when they are adults.

SUGGESTED READINGS

A. Fausto-Sterling, "The Five Sexes: Why Male and Female Are Not Enough," *The Sciences* (March/April 1993).

A. Fausto-Sterling, "How Many Sexes Are There?" *The New York Times* (March 12, 1993), p. A29.

R. T. Francoeur, *Becoming a Sexual Person*, 2d ed. (Macmillan, 1991), chapter 4.

J. Money, *Gendermaps: Social Constructionism, Feminism, and Sexosophical History* (Continuum, 1995).

J. Money, *Reinterpreting the Unspeakable: Human Sexuality 2000* (Continuum, 1994).

ISSUE 4

Should Society Recognize Two Kinds of Marriage?

YES: James Carville, from "It'll Make You Think Twice: Louisiana's Conservative New 'Covenant Marriage' Law Ain't More Than Half Bad," *Salon Magazine* (June 30, 1997)

NO: Peter D. Kramer, from "Divorce and Our National Values," *The New York Times* (August 29, 1997)

ISSUE SUMMARY

YES: Journalist James Carville applauds Louisiana's attempt to strengthen marriages and families by offering couples a choice between a traditional marriage with the possibility of no-fault divorce and a covenant marriage with much stricter limits on divorce.

NO: Clinical psychiatrist Peter D. Kramer maintains that creating two kinds of marriage invites couples to lash themselves to a morality of commitment that the broader culture does not support. He believes that the conventional form of modern marriage is much more in tune with the prevailing values of personal independence, autonomy, and fulfillment than is lifelong, exclusive monogamy.

The problem faced by married couples in the United States today is serious: between 1970 and 1990 the divorce rate jumped 34 percent. In those two decades, practically every state adopted a no-fault divorce policy. With half of all marriages now ending in divorce, compared with about one-third in 1970, about 1.2 million American couples get divorced each year. Despite the popular inclination to blame no-fault divorce laws for this increase in divorce, experts are not sure how much of the increase is due to the ease with which divorces can be obtained. Other factors may have equal or perhaps greater impact on the divorce rate. In past centuries, for example, a couple's personal expectations of married bliss were much more limited than they are for Americans today. In earlier times, women could expect to spend most of their adult lives rearing children and providing domestic support for their husbands, who worked from sunup to sundown six or seven days a week. It wasn't until 1945 that 50 percent of the American workforce began to enjoy a 40-hour, five-day workweek. Also, with an average life expectancy somewhere between 35 and 47 years, and with one in five mothers dying during childbirth, years ago death often brought a marriage to an early end. With the current average life expectancy pushing 80, divorce now ends marriages more often than death does.

The current issue focuses on a law enacted by the state of Louisiana in the summer of 1997. Following the failed attempts by several states to revoke no-fault divorce legislation, Louisiana lawmakers adopted a new tactic in an attempt "to slow down the hemorrhaging of the American family through the no-fault divorce system." The new law recognizes two kinds of marriage and requires couples to choose between a traditional marriage that can be dissolved by a no-fault divorce and a new kind of marriage, called a "covenant marriage," with stricter limits on both separation and divorce.

Before entering a covenant marriage, a couple must get premarital counseling and discuss the requirements of a covenant marriage with a member of the clergy or other counselor. If a covenant marriage goes sour, the couple can be granted a separation only if there is proof that one spouse committed adultery, has abandoned the matrimonial home for at least a year, has been sentenced to prison or death for a felony, or has physically or sexually abused the spouse or a child. A separation can also be granted if there is proof of "cruel treatment" or "habitual intemperance" by one spouse. A divorce can only be granted if the couple have been legally separated for at least one year —18 months if the couple have a minor child—or if they have lived apart for two years. The grounds for a divorce in a covenant marriage are limited to proven adultery, imprisonment, abandonment for a year, or physical or sexual abuse.

A Louisiana couple who choose a traditional marriage, on the other hand, can be granted a no-fault divorce either after they have lived apart for six months or immediately if one spouse is guilty of adultery or has been sentenced to prison or death for a felony.

Tony Perkins, a Republican state representative, sponsored the bill, hoping that it will force couples to consider their compatibility before getting married and starting a family.

In the first of the following essays, James Carville supports the Louisiana legislation and looks forward to other states enacting similar legislation. Such legislation, he argues, is more likely to be passed in the South, where conservative Christians and profamily activists have long fought without success to revoke the no-fault divorce laws. On the other side, Peter D. Kramer opposes the idea of a covenant marriage because it is unrealistic and completely out of touch with the most important and basic values of American culture. Kramer contends that lifelong marriage is not supported by America's long history of celebrating and promoting self-expression, self-fulfillment, and self-reliance.

YES   James Carville

IT'LL MAKE YOU THINK TWICE

Get this: Lazy ol' Louisiana, my home state, has raced to the forefront of a new social movement. It's not exactly the most progressive of social movements, mind you—the Christian Coalition's misguided masses are behind this thing all the way. But there's something to be said for Louisiana being out front in something other than humidity and corruption. It also happens to be that Louisiana's movement makes some sense.

The movement I refer to is an attempt to strengthen the ties of matrimony. [Recently], the Louisiana House and Senate voted overwhelmingly—there was only one opponent in the two houses—to create a new form of marriage that will be much harder to wriggle out of than the standard no-fault marriage available throughout the rest of the nation. The new bond is called a "covenant marriage," and its name has religious overtones for a reason: the grounds for divorce look much more biblical than they used to.

To get a divorce today in Louisiana, all you need to show is that you and your spouse have lived apart for six months. Under the new law, a couple could get a divorce only if one partner commits adultery, abandons the family for a year, physically or sexually abuses the other spouse or a child, gets sent to prison for a felony, or if the couple has been informally separated for two years or legally separated for a year (18 months if they have a kid). The goal, of course, is to make people think twice or three times before they tie the knot.

When the bill goes into effect, on Aug. 15, [1997], covenant marriages will not be mandatory. Couples will have a choice between a covenant marriage and a no-fault marriage. At least in theory. Mary and I got hitched in Louisiana. I can just imagine what would have happened if, after my year of stalling, I finally asked Mary to be my wife but then told her I wanted to go with Marriage Option B—the quickie kind. Or worse yet: What if I asked Mary to be my wife and *she* only wanted Option B?! You see what I mean? I suspect that legions of young Louisiana lovers will avoid the so-called choice altogether by hopping in the Chevy and heading for Las Vegas.

That being said, I think the Louisiana Legislature has got it partially right. Bringing attention to the issue of divorce is an admirable idea. More than half of all marriages end in divorce, and that's just way too high for any society to bear. I doubt that no-fault marriages are the cause of the divorce epidemic, but they sure haven't done much to help, either. Louisiana is right to try a new approach.

But here's where they went wrong: they made almost no distinction between marriages with children and without. The way I look at it, unless we're talking about a case of abuse, the state's got very little business meddling in a marriage that hasn't produced any kids. But when there are kids, especially young ones, that's a whole different story. Far too many kids are growing up in single-parent families. Far too many of those single-parent kids are growing up with lasting scars.

It used to be possible—hell, it was downright fashionable—to say that kids could do just fine with one parent. Not anymore. The weight of evidence —from scholars associated with both the left and the right—is overwhelming: there ain't no substitute for a stable, two-parent family. I suppose we could choose to ignore this consensus and pretend that family break-up has no social consequences, but at this point in the debate, we might as well claim that smoking doesn't cause cancer. Sure, plenty of kids from single-parent families turn out just fine. And some smokers run marathons and live to be 90 years old. But does that mean that growing up without a daddy or smoking a pack a day isn't harmful to most people? Of course not. The cause-and-effect relationships here are simply beyond dispute. Even the live-and-let-live liberals have gotten that message loud and clear.

If I were writing Louisiana's covenant marriage bill, I would have done it very differently. In fact, some might say my version would be even more dramatic than theirs. I say, forget this voluntary crap. I think every marriage ought to become a covenant marriage... the moment the couple has any kids. That's the point when the state begins to have a compelling interest in making it difficult for a couple to simply call it quits. That's when a stricter definition of marriage is justifiable. That's when a state could make a real social difference.

This issue ain't going away any time soon. I suspect that we'll see several other states—most of them Southern— adopt versions of the Louisiana law over the course of the next year. I'd like to think Democrats will get actively involved in shaping these efforts. As for me, any honest bill that makes couples with children think longer and harder about getting divorced will have my eager support.

NO

Peter D. Kramer

DIVORCE AND OUR NATIONAL VALUES

How shall we resolve a marital crisis? Consider an example from the advice column of Ann Landers. An "Iowa Wife" wrote to ask what she should do about her husband's habit, after 30 years of marriage, of reading magazines at table when the couple dined out. Ann Landers advised the wife to engage her husband by studying subjects of interest to him.

Readers from around the country protested. A "14-Year-Old Girl in Pennsylvania" crystallized the objections: "You told the wife to read up on sports or business, whatever he was interested in, even though it might be boring to her. Doesn't that defeat the basic idea of being your own self?" Chastened, Ann Landers changed course, updated her stance: Reading at table is a hostile act, perhaps even grounds for divorce.

When it comes to marriage, Ann Landers seems a reasonable barometer of our values. In practical terms, reading the sports pages might work for some Iowa wife—but we do not believe that is how spouses ought to behave. Only the second response, consider divorce, expresses our overriding respect for autonomy, for the unique and separate self.

Look south now from Iowa and Pennsylvania to Louisiana, where a new law allows couples to opt for a "covenant marriage"—terminable only after a lengthy separation or because of adultery, abandonment, abuse or imprisonment. The law has been praised by many as an expedient against the epidemic of divorce and an incarnation of our "traditional values."

Whether the law will lower the divorce rate is an empirical question to be decided in the future, but it is not too soon to ask: Does covenant marriage express the values we live by?

History seems to say no. American literature's one great self-help book is "Walden," a paean to self-reliance and an homage to Henry David Thoreau's favorite preacher, Ralph Waldo Emerson, who declaimed: "Say to them, O father, O mother, O wife, O brother, O friend, I have lived with you after appearances hitherto. Henceforward, I am the truth's.... I must be myself. I cannot break my self any longer for you, or you."

The economic philosophy we proudly export, fundamentalist capitalism, says that society functions best when members act in a self-interested manner. The nation's founding document is a bill of divorcement. Autonomy is the characteristic American virtue.

As a psychiatrist, I see this value embedded in our psychotherapy, the craft that both shapes and expresses the prevailing common sense. In the early 1970's, Carl Rogers, known as the "Psychologist of America," encapsulated the post–World War II version of our ideals: A successful marriage is one that increases the "self-actualization" of each member. Of a failed union, he wrote: "If Jennifer had from the first insisted on being her true self, the marriage would have had much more strife and much more hope."

Rogers was expressing the predominant viewpoint; for most of the past 50 years, enhanced autonomy has been a goal of pyschotherapy. Erik Erikson began the trend by boldly proclaiming that the search for identity had become as important in his time as the study of sexuality was in Freud's. Later, Murray Bowen, a founder of family therapy, invoked a scale of maturity whose measure is a person's ability to maintain his or her beliefs in the face of family pressures. The useful response to crises within couples, Bowen suggested, is to hold fast to your values and challenge your partner to rise to meet your level of maturity.

But autonomy was a value for men only, and largely it was pseudo-autonomy, the successful man propped up by the indentured wife and overburdened mother. (No doubt Thoreau sent his clothes home for laundering.)

The self-help movement, beginning in the 1970's, extended this American ideal to women. Once both partners are allowed to be autonomous, the continuation of marriage becomes more truly voluntary. In this sense, an increase in divorce signals social progress.

It signals social progress, except that divorce is itself destructive. So it seems to me the question is whether any other compelling value counterbalances the siren song of self-improvement.

Turning again to psychotherapy, we do hear arguments for a different type of American value. Answering Erickson's call for individual identity, Helen Merrell Lynd, a sociologist at Sarah Lawrence College, wrote, "Nor must complete finding of oneself... precede finding oneself in and through other persons."

Her belief entered psychiatry through the writings of her pupil, Jean Baker Miller. A professor of psychiatry at Boston University, Dr. Miller faults most psychotherapy for elevating autonomy at the expense of qualities important to women, such as mutuality. To feel connected (when there is genuine give-and-take) is to feel worth. Miller wants a transformed culture in which mutuality "is valued as highly as, or more highly than, self-enhancement."

Mutuality is an ideal the culture believes it should honor but does not quite. Ours is a society that does a half-hearted job of inculcating compromise, which is to say that we still teach these skills mainly to women. Much of psychotherapy addressed the troubles of those who make great efforts at compromise only to be taken advantage of by selfish partners.

Often the more vulnerable spouse requires rescue through the sort of move Ann Landers recommends, vigorous self-assertion, and even divorce.

Mutuality is a worthy ideal, one that might serve as a fit complement and counterbalance to our celebration of the self. But if we do not reward it elsewhere—if in the school and office and marketplace, we celebrate self-assertion—it seems worrisome to ask the institution of marriage to play by different rules.

What is insidious about Louisiana's covenant marriage is that, contrary to claims on its behalf, it is out of touch with our traditional values: self-expression, self-fulfillment, self-reliance.

* * *

The Louisiana law invites couples to lash themselves to a morality the broader culture does not support, an arrangement that creates a potential for terrible tensions.

Though we profess abhorrence of divorce, I suspect that the divorce rate reflects our national values with great exactness, and that conventional modern marriage—an eternal commitment with loopholes galore—expresses precisely the degree of loss of autonomy that we are able to tolerate.

POSTSCRIPT

Should Society Recognize Two Kinds of Marriage?

Originally, the church and the state became involved in regulating marriage in the interest of providing security for the children on whom the future stability of society would depend and to clarify inheritance. Nowadays the interests of children in the permanence of marriage seems to have taken second place to the desire of the divorcing parents for self-expression, self-fulfillment, and self-reliance. In recent decades the divorce rate for couples with children has gone up much faster than the divorce rate for childless couples. Today most divorces involve children, and every year more than 1 million youngsters are involved in divorce.

Debates rage about the short- and long-term effects of parental divorce on children. Most studies focus on the negative impact of divorce on many areas of children's lives as they struggle to cope with the breakup. Other studies have found that some children who have had to deal with parental divorce have shown enhanced maturity, self-esteem, and empathy, as well as less rigid gender roles.

Similar debates rage over the alleged disadvantages experienced by children in single-parent families. Psychologist June Stephenson, for instance, has reported on her research indicating that the case for two-parent families being "the best" is grossly overstated. Her studies show that a variety of family forms, including single-parent families, can produce children who are as well-adjusted as or better adjusted than those reared in two-parent families.

SUGGESTED READINGS

R. T. Francoeur, "Covenants, Intimacy, and Marital Diversity," *Humanistic Judaism* (Winter 1994).

D. Gately and A. I. Schwebel, "Favorable Outcomes in Children After Parental Divorce," *Journal of Divorce and Remarriage* (vol .18, no. 3, 1992).

J. Stephenson, *The Two-Parent Family Is Not the Best* (Diemer, Smith, 1991).

B. D. Whitehead, "Dan Quayle Was Right," *The Atlantic Monthly* (April 1993).

K. Zinsmeister, "Divorce's Toll on Children," *The American Enterprise* (May/June 1996).

ISSUE 5

Are Men Really from Mars and Women from Venus?

YES: John Gray, from *Men Are from Mars, Women Are from Venus* (Harper-Collins, 1992)

NO: Susan Hamson, from "The Rebuttal from Uranus: Enough Already! Men and Women Are from Earth!" An Original Essay Written for This Volume (November 1997)

ISSUE SUMMARY

YES: Therapist John Gray argues that men and women can learn to communicate much better and have more loving relationships if they try to understand the consequences of their coming from two "different planets," meaning that they behave and react differently to the same situations and speak very different languages.

NO: Susan Hamson, a doctoral candidate at Temple University, rejects Gray's assertions of profound behavioral differences between men and women as being based solely on his intuitions and feedback from seminar audiences rather than on real research. She maintains that Gray's picture of male/female communications and his recommendations for better communication are loaded with patronizing sexist biases that degrade women.

For 3,000 years Western thinkers have viewed human development as the result of two separate, parallel, noninteracting influences. Nature—genes, hormones, and anatomy—was believed to be the dominant influence before birth and irrelevant after birth. And it was assumed that nurture—learning and social influences—had hardly any effect during pregnancy but guided development completely between birth and death.

This splitting of nature and nurture grew out of the philosophical and religious split between body and soul popularized by the French philosopher René Descartes. Historically, this split has been used to support a variety of personal, political, and religious purposes based on "this is better than that." On one side of the split is spirit and spiritual rewards, the rational intellect and analytical thought, and independent action—traits that are traditionally considered characteristic of males. On the other side is the body, which, with its sensual and erotic pleasures, is emotional, intuitive, and given to responses that depend on others and a nurturing passivity. These traits have traditionally been assigned to females.

In the twentieth century adherents of communism decided that nature was irrelevant and that any differences that were seen between the sexes and the way they are treated were created by capitalism, which is based on male dominance. The German philosopher Karl Marx believed that the solution to this gender divide was to create a sexless, genderless, socialist system (i.e., communism) in which all distinctions—whether sexual, gender-oriented, economic, or social—are rooted out and eliminated. Soviet science adopted the theory that traits acquired during one's life could be passed on to one's offspring, a theory proposed 200 years ago by the French biologist Jean-Baptiste Lamarck. The dangers of this one-sided approach, however, have been well demonstrated by the bankruptcy of Marxist economics, agriculture, and social policy, and by the fact that in many ways women were still subordinate to men in the communist reality.

In recent years the traditional dichotomy of nature-versus-nurture has been gradually supplanted by the theory that there is a lifelong developmental interaction of genes, hormones, and anatomy with the environment of our developing bodies, experiences, and learning.

In the following selections, John Gray tells an allegorical tale about Martians (men) and Venusians (women) getting together on Earth and selectively forgetting that because they come from two different planets, men and women speak different languages. Susan Hamson charges that Gray's view of male-female communications is not based on scientific research but on his patronizing view of women as intuitive, emotional, nurturing people who seek validation of their views from men and passively respond to others, rather than taking the initiative as self-sufficient, independent people.

YES   John Gray

MEN ARE FROM MARS, WOMEN ARE FROM VENUS

MEN ARE FROM MARS WOMEN ARE FROM VENUS

Imagine that men are from Mars and women are from Venus. One day long ago the Martians, looking through their telescopes, discovered the Venusians. Just glimpsing the Venusians awakened feelings they had never known. They fell in love and quickly invented space travel and flew to Venus.

The Venusians welcomed the Martians with open arms. They had intuitively known that this day would come. Their hearts opened wide to a love they had never felt before.

The love between the Venusians and Martians was magical. They delighted in being together, doing things together, and sharing together. Though from different worlds, they reveled in their differences. They spent months learning about each other, exploring and appreciating their different needs, preferences, and behavior patterns. For years they lived together in love and harmony.

Then they decided to fly to Earth. In the beginning everything was wonderful and beautiful. But the effects of Earth's atmosphere took hold, and one morning everyone woke up with a peculiar kind of amnesia-*selective amnesia!*

Both the Martians and Venusians forgot that they were from different planets and were supposed to be different. In one morning everything they had learned about their differences was erased from their memory. And since that day men and women have been in conflict.

Remembering Our Differences

Without the awareness that we are supposed to be different, men and women are at odds with each other. We usually become angry or frustrated with the opposite sex because we have forgotten this important truth. We expect the opposite sex to be more like ourselves. We desire them to "want what we want" and "feel the way we feel."

We mistakenly assume that if our partners love us they will react and behave in certain ways—the ways we react and behave when we love someone.

This attitude sets us up to be disappointed again and again and prevents us from taking the necessary time to communicate lovingly about our differences.

Men mistakenly expect women to think, communicate and react the way men do; women mistakenly expect men to feel, communicate, and respond the way women do. We have forgotten that men and women are supposed to be different. As a result our relationships are filled with unnecessary friction and conflict.

Clearly recognizing and respecting these differences dramatically reduce confusion when dealing with the opposite sex. When you remember that men are from Mars and women are from Venus, everything can be explained....

Good Intentions Are Not Enough

Falling in love is always magical. It feel eternal, as if love will last forever. We naïvely believe that somehow we are exempt from the problems our parents had, free from the odds that love will die, assured that it is meant to be and that we are destined to live happily ever after.

But as the magic recedes and daily life takes over, it emerges that men continue to expect women to think and react like men, and women expect men to feel and behave like women. Without a clear awareness of our differences, we do not take the time to understand and respect each other. We become demanding, resentful, judgmental, and intolerant.

With the best and most loving intentions love continues to die. Somehow the problems creep in. The resentments build. Communication breaks down. Mistrust increases. Rejection and repression result. The magic of love is lost.

We ask ourselves:
How does it happen?
Why does it happen?
Why does it happen to us?

To answer these questions our greatest minds have developed brilliant and complex philosophical and psychological models. Yet still the old patterns return. Love dies. It happens to almost everyone.

Each day millions of individuals are searching for a partner to experience that special loving feeling. Each year, millions of couples join together in love and then painfully separate because they have lost that loving feeling. From those who are able to sustain love long enough to get married, only 50 percent stay married. Out of those who stay together, possibly another 50 percent are not fulfilled. They stay together out of loyalty and obligation or from the fear of starting over.

Very few people, indeed, are able to grow in love. Yet, it does happen. When men and women are able to respect and accept their differences then love has a chance to blossom.

Through understanding the hidden differences of the opposite sex we can more successfully give and receive the love that is in our hearts. By validating and accepting our differences, creative solutions can be discovered whereby we can succeed in getting what we want. And, more important, we can learn how to best love and support the people we care about.

Love is magical, and it can last, if we remember our differences....

MEN GO TO THEIR CAVES AND WOMEN TALK

One of the biggest differences between men and women is how they cope with stress. Men become increasingly focused and withdrawn while women become increasingly overwhelmed and emotionally involved. At these times, a man's needs for feeling good are different from a woman's. He feels better by solving problems while she feels better by talking about problems. Not understanding and accepting these differences creates unnecessary friction in our relationships. Let's look at a common example.

When Tom comes home, he want to relax and unwind by quietly reading the news. He is stressed by the unsolved problems of his day and finds relief through forgetting them.

His wife, Mary, also wants to relax from her stressful day. She, however, want to find relief by talking about the problems of her day. The tension slowly building between them gradually becomes resentment.

Tom secretly thinks Mary talks too much, while Mary feels ignored. Without understanding their differences they will grow further apart.

You probably can recognize this situation because it is just one of many examples where men and women are at odds. This problem is not just Tom and Mary's but is present in almost every relationship.

Solving this problem for Tom and Mary depends not on how much they loved each other but on how much they understood the opposite sex.

Without knowing that women really do need to talk about problems to feel better, Tom would continue to think Mary talked too much and resist listening to her. Without knowing that Tom was reading the news to feel better, Mary would feel ignored and neglected. She would persist in trying to get him to talk when he didn't want to.

These two differences can be resolved by first understanding in greater detail how men and women cope with stress. Let's again observe life on Mars and Venus and glean some insights about men and women.

Coping With Stress on Mars and Venus
When a Martian gets upset he never talks about what is bothering him. He would never burden another Martian with his problem unless his friend's assistance was necessary to solve the problem. Instead he becomes very quiet and goes to his private cave to think about his problem, mulling it over to find a solution. When he has found a solution, he feels much better and comes out of his cave.

If he can't find a solution then he does something to forget his problems, like reading the news or playing a game. By disengaging his mind from the problems of his day, gradually he can relax. If his stress is really great it takes getting involved with something even more challenging, like racing his car, competing in a contest, or climbing a mountain.

When a Venusian becomes upset or is stressed by her day, to find relief, she seeks out someone she trusts and then talks in great detail about the problems of her day. When Venusians share feelings of being overwhelmed, they suddenly feel better. This is the Venusian way.

On Venus sharing your problems with another actually is considered a sign of love and trust and not a burden. Venusians are not ashamed of having problems. Their egos are dependent not on looking "competent" but rather on being in loving relationships. They openly share feelings of being overwhelmed, confused, hopeless, and exhausted.

A Venusian feels good about herself when she has loving friends with whom to share her feelings and problems. A Martian feels good when he can solve his problems on his own in his cave. These secrets of feeling good are still applicable today.

Finding Relief in the Cave

When a man is stressed he will withdraw into the cave of his mind and focus on solving a problem. He generally picks the most urgent problem or the most difficult. He becomes so focused on solving this one problem that he temporarily loses awareness of everything else. Other problems and responsibilities fade into the background.

At such times, he becomes increasingly distant, forgetful, unresponsive, and preoccupied in his relationships. For example, when having a conversation with him at home, it seems as if only 5 percent of his mind is available for the relationship while the other 95 percent is still at work.

His full awareness is not present because he is mulling over his problem, hoping to find a solution. The more stressed he is the more gripped by the problem he will be. At such times he is incapable of giving a woman the attention and feeling that she normally receives and certainly deserves. His mind is preoccupied, and he is powerless to release it. If, however, he can find a solution, instantly he will feel much better and come out of his cave; suddenly he is available for being in a relationship again.

However, if he cannot find a solution to his problem, then he remains stuck in the cave. To get unstuck he is drawn to solving little problems, like reading the news, watching TV, driving his car, doing physical exercise, watching a football game, playing basketball, and so forth. Any challenging activity that initially requires only 5 percent of his mind can assist him in forgetting his problems and becoming unstuck. Then the next day he can redirect his focus to his problem with greater success.

Let's explore in greater detail a few examples. Jim commonly uses reading the newspaper to forget his problems. When he reads the paper he is no longer being confronted with the problems of his day. With the 5 percent of his mind that is not focused on his work problems, he begins forming opinions and finding solutions for the world's problems. Gradually his mind becomes increasingly involved with the problems in the news and he forgets his own. In this way he makes the transition from being focused on his problems at work to focusing on the many problems of the world (for which he is not directly responsible). This process releases his mind from the gripping problems of work so he can focus on his wife and family again.

Tom watches a football game to release his stress and unwind. He releases his mind from trying to solve his own problems by solving the problems of his favorite team. Through watching sports he can vicariously feel he has solved a problem with each play. When his team scores points or wins, he enjoys the feeling of success. If his team loses, he suffers their loss as his own. In either case, however, his mind is released from the grip of his real problems.

For Tom and many men the inevitable release of tension that occurs at the completion of any sporting event, news event, or movie provides a release from the tension he feels in his life.

How Women React to the Cave
When a man is stuck in his cave, he is powerless to give his partner the quality attention she deserves. It is hard for her to be accepting of him at these times because she doesn't know how stressed he is. If he were to come home and talk about all his problems, then she could be more compassionate. Instead he doesn't talk about his problems, and she feels he is ignoring her. She can tell he is upset but mistakenly assumes he doesn't care about her because he isn't talking to her.

Women generally do not understand how Martians cope with stress. They expect men to open up and talk about all their problems the way Venusians do. When a man is stuck in his cave, a woman resents his not being more open. She feels hurt when he turns on the news or goes outside to play some basketball and ignores her.

To expect a man who is in his cave instantly to become open, responsive, and loving is as unrealistic as expecting a woman who is upset immediately to calm down and make complete sense. It is a mistake to expect a man to always be in touch with his loving feelings just as it is a mistake to expect a woman's feelings to always be rational and logical.

When Martians go to their caves they tend to forget that their friends may be having problems too. An instinct takes over that says before you can take care of anybody else, you must first take care of yourself. When a woman sees a man react in his way, she generally resists it and resents the man.

She may ask for his support in a demanding tone, as if she has to fight for her rights with this uncaring man.

By remembering that men and from Mars, a woman can correctly interpret his reaction to stress as his coping mechanism rather than as an expression of how her feels about her. She can begin to cooperate with him to get what she needs instead of resisting him.

On the other side, men generally have little awareness of how distant they become when they are in the cave. As a man recognizes how withdrawing into his cave may affect women, he can be compassionate when she feels neglected and unimportant. Remembering that women are from Venus helps him to be more understanding and respectful of her reactions and feelings. Without understanding the validity of her reactions, a man commonly defends himself, and they argue. These are five common misunderstandings:

1. When she says "You don't listen," he says "What do you mean I don't listen. I can tell you everything you said."

   When a man is in the cave he can record what she is saying with the 5 percent of mind that is listening. A man reasons that if he is listening with 5 percent, then he is listening. However, what she is asking for is his full undivided attention.

2. When she says "I feel like you are not even here," he says "What do you mean I'm not here? Of course I am here. Don't you see my body?"

   He reasons that if his body is present then she shouldn't say he is not there. However, though his body is present, she doesn't feel his full presence, and that is what she means.

3. When she says "You don't care about me," he says "Of course I care about you. Why do you think I am trying to solve this problem?"

He reasons that because he is preoccupied with solving a problem that will in some way benefit her, she should know he cares for her. However, she needs to feel his direct attention and caring, and that is what she is really asking for.

4. When she says "I feel like I am not important to you," he says "That's ridiculous. Of course you are important."

He reasons that her feelings are invalid because he is solving problems to benefit her. He doesn't realize that when he focuses on one problem and ignores the problems she is bothered by that almost any woman would have the same reaction and take it personally and feel unimportant.

5. When she says "You have no feelings. You are in your head," he says "What's wrong with that? How else do you expect me to solve this problem?"

He reasons that she is being too critical and demanding because he is doing something that is essential for him to solve problems. He feels unappreciated. In addition he doesn't recognize the validity of her feelings. Men generally don't realize how extremely and quickly they may shift from being warm and feeling to being unresponsive and distant. In his cave a man is preoccupied with solving his problem and is unaware of how his indifferent attitude might feel to others.

To increase cooperation both men and women need to understand each other better. When a man begins to ignore his wife, she often takes it personally. Knowing that he is coping with stress in his own way is extremely helpful but does not always help her alleviate the pain.

At such times she may feel the need to talk about these feelings. This is when it is important for the man to validate her feelings. He needs to understand that she has a right to talk about her feelings of being ignored and unsupported just as he has a right to withdraw into his cave and not talk. If she does not feel understood then it is difficult for her to release her hurt.

Finding Relief Through Talking

When a woman is stressed she instinctively feels a need to talk about her feelings and all the possible problems that are associated with her feelings. When she begins talking she does not prioritize the significance of any problem. If she is upset, then she is upset about it all, big and small. She is not immediately concerned with finding solutions to her problems but rather seeks relief by expressing herself and being understood. By randomly talking about her problems, she becomes less upset.

As a man under stress tends to focus on one problem and forget others, a woman under stress tends to expand and become overwhelmed by all problems. By talking about all possible problems without focusing on problem solving she feels better. Through exploring her feelings in this process she gains a greater awareness of what is really bothering her, and then suddenly she is no longer so overwhelmed.

To feel better, women talk about past problems, future problems, potential problems, even problems that have no solutions. The more talk and exploration, the better they feel. This is the way women operate. To expect otherwise is to deny a woman her sense of self.

When a woman is overwhelmed she finds relief through talking in great detail about her various problems. Gradually, if she feels she is being heard, her stress disappears. After talking about one topic she will pause and then move on to the next. In this way she continues to expand talking about problems, worries, disappointments, and frustrations. These topics need not be in any order and tend to be logically unrelated. If she feels she is not being understood, her awareness may expand even further, and she may become upset about more problems.

Just as a man who is stuck in the cave needs little problems to distract him, a woman who doesn't feel heard will need to talk about other problems that are less immediate to feel relief. To forget her own painful feelings she may become emotionally involved in the problems of others. In addition she may find relief through discussing the problems of her friends, relatives, and associates. Whether she is talking about her problems or others' problems, talking is a natural and healthy Venusian reaction to stress.

How Men React When Women Need to Talk
When women talk about problems, men usually resist. A man assumes she is talking with him about her problems because she is holding him responsible. The more problems, the more he feels blamed. He does not realize that she is talking to feel better. A man doesn't know that she will appreciate it if he just listens.

Martians talk about problems for only two reasons: they are blaming someone or they are seeking advice. If a woman is really upset a man assumes she is blaming him. If she seems less upset, then he assumes she is asking for advice.

If he assumes she is asking for advice, then he puts on his Mr. Fix-It hat to solve her problems. If he assumes she is blaming him, then he draws his sword to protect himself from attack. In both cases, he soon finds it difficult to listen.

If he offers solutions to her problems, she just continues talking about more problems. After offering two or three solutions, he expects her to feel better. This is because Martians themselves feel better with solutions, as long as they have asked for a solution to be offered. When she doesn't feel better, he feels his solutions have been rejected, and he feels unappreciated.

On the other hand, if he feels attacked, then he begins to defend himself. He thinks if he explains himself that she will stop blaming him. The more he defends himself, however, the more upset she becomes. He doesn't realize that explanations are not what she needs. She needs him to understand her feelings and let her move on to talk about more problems. If he is wise and just listens, then a few moments after she is complaining about him, she will change the subject and talk about other problems as well.

Men also become particularly frustrated when a woman talks about problems that he can do nothing about. For example, when a woman is stressed she could complain:

- "I'm not getting paid enough at work."
- "My Aunt Louise is getting sicker and sicker, each year she gets sicker."
- "Our house just isn't big enough."
- "This is such a dry season. When is it going to rain?"
- "We are almost overdrawn in our bank account."

A woman might make any of the above comments as a way of expressing her worries, disappointments, and frustrations. She may know that nothing more can be done to solve these problems, but to find relief she still needs to talk about them. She feels supported if the listener relates to her frustration and disappointment. She may, however, frustrate her male partner-unless he understands that she just needs to talk about it and then she will feel better.

Men also become impatient when women talk about problems in great detail. A man mistakenly assumes that when a woman talks in great detail that all the details are necessary for him to find a solution to her problem. He struggles to find their relevance and becomes impatient. Again he doesn't realize that she is looking not for a solution from him but for his caring and understanding.

In addition, listening is difficult for a man because he mistakenly assumes there is a logical order when she randomly changes from one problem to another. After she has shared three or four problems he becomes extremely frustrated and confused trying logically to relate these problems.

Another reason a man may resist listening is that he is looking for the bottom line. He cannot begin formulating his solution until he knows the outcome. The more details she gives the more he is frustrated while listening. His frustration is lessened if he can remember that she is greatly benefiting by talking about the details. If he can remember that talking in detail is helping her to feel good, then he can relax. Just as a man is fulfilled through working out the intricate details of solving a problem, a woman is fulfilled through talking about the details of her problems.

Something a woman can do to make it a little easier for a man is to let him know in advance the outcome of the story and then go back and give the details. Avoid keeping him in suspense. Women commonly enjoy letting the suspense build because it brings more feeling into the story. Another woman appreciates this buildup, but a man can be easily frustrated.

The degree to which a man does not understand a woman is the degree to which he will resist her when she is talking about problems. As a man learns more how to fulfill a woman and provide her emotional support he discovers that listening is not so difficult. More important, if a woman can remind a man that she just wants to talk about her problems and that he doesn't have to solve any of them, it can help him to relax and listen.

How the Martians and Venusians Found Peace

The Martians and Venusians lived together in peace because they were able to respect their differences. The Martians learned to respect that Venusians needed to talk to feel better. Even if he didn't have much to say, he learned that by listening he could be very supportive. The Venusians learned to respect that Martians needed to withdraw to cope with stress. The cave was no longer a great mystery or cause for alarm.

What the Martians Learned

The Martians realized that even when they felt they were being attacked, blamed, or criticized by the Venusians it was only temporary; soon the Venusians would suddenly feel better and be very appreciative and accepting. By learning to listen, the Martians discovered how much the Venusians really thrived on talking about problems.

Each Martian found peace of mind when he finally understood that a Venusian's need to talk about her problems was not because he was failing her in some way. In addition he learned that once a Venusian feels heard she stops dwelling on her problems and becomes very positive. With this awareness, a Martian was able to listen without feeling responsible for solving all her problems.

Many men and even women are very judgmental of the need to talk about problems because they have never experienced how healing it can be. They have not seen how a woman who feels heard suddenly can change, feel better, and sustain a positive attitude. Generally they have seen how a woman (probably their mother) who did not feel heard continued to dwell on her problems. This happens to women when they do not feel loved or heard over an extended period of time. The real problem, however, is that she feels unloved, not that she is talking about problems.

After the Martians learned how to listen they made a most amazing discovery. They began to realize that listening to a Venusian talk about problems could actually help them come out of their caves in the same way as watching the news on TV or reading a newspaper.

Similarly, as men learn to listen without feeling blamed or responsible, listening becomes much easier. As a man gets good at listening, he realizes that listening can be an excellent way to forget the problems of his day as well as bring a lot of fulfillment to his partner. But on days when he is really stressed he may need to be in his cave and slowly come out by some other distraction, like the news or a competitive sport.

What the Venusians Learned

The Venusians also found peace of mind when they finally understood that a Martian going into his cave was not a sign that he didn't love her as much. They learned to be more accepting of him at these times because he was experiencing a lot of stress.

The Venusians were not offended when Martians were easily distracted. When a Venusian talked and a Martian became distracted, she would very politely stop talking, stand there, and wait for him to notice. Then she would begin talking again. She understood that sometimes it was hard for him to give his full attention. The Venusians discovered that by asking for the Martians' attention in a relaxed and accepting manner the Martians were happy to redirect their attention.

When the Martians were completely preoccupied and in their caves, the Venusians also did not take it personally. They learned that this was not the time to have intimate conversations but a time to talk about problems with their friends or have fun and go shopping. When the Martians thereby felt loved and accepted, the Venusians discovered that the Martians would more quickly come out of their caves.

NO

Susan Hamson

THE REBUTTAL FROM URANUS: ENOUGH ALREADY! MEN AND WOMEN ARE FROM EARTH!

WHY JOHN GRAY?

I am aware that there are virtually thousands of self-help books on the market written by psychologists, psychiatrists, and psychotherapists that profess to help individuals find some peace with, or gain control over, some aspect of their lives. Judging by the space devoted to the genre, there is no doubt a substantial demand for such reading material, thus my concerns lie not with the need to occasionally seek the opinions of others, but the degree to which individuals question the material they are reading.

Men Are from Mars, Women Are from Venus: A Practical Guide for Improving Communication and Getting What You Want in Your Relationships (New York: HarperCollins, 1992) came to my attention through a friend of mine who had been experiencing a very draining and depressing marriage. On the precipice of divorce, her husband arrived home one evening with John Gray's book. He had underlined a number of passages and suggested she read the book in an effort to improve their communication (the source, he believed, of their marital discord). Always open-minded, she thought it was at least worth the old college try. She proceeded to read the introduction and the first two chapters—at which point she closed the book, walked into another room and laughed out loud. Her impression? "It's ridiculous," she said to me. "It's sexist and demeaning. You have *got* to read this."

Within a few months another friend called me. She told me that a co-worker had received the book from her sister as a "gag gift" and brought it into work. It quickly became the focus of laughter and, later, real concern. The consensus among this group of women held that *Men Are from Mars, Women Are from Venus* was, at best, demeaning and sexist. At worst, it dangerously bordered on the misogynist. Misogyny? It was time to read the book.

As of this writing, I have read the book. Over eight times. The first time I was, to say the least, amused. It was rich fodder for laughs, but as I thought

Copyright © 1998 by Susan Hamson.

75

about it, I realized how destructive the information really was. It was certainly a book that professed to improve communication—but at what cost? The underlying message was not one of mutual respect, but an obvious endorsement of passivity on the part of women. Women needed to settle for less, shut up, and pull back when men needed time to themselves. Lists abound for the improvement of women, but what of those for men? Was this really an improvement? Beyond the clever, but quickly overused, Martian-Venusian metaphor was the theme of female subordination. This book, clearly aimed at a female audience, was patronizing and downright insulting. How had this book become so popular?

As a woman, I had serious questions about its proposed methods for better communication. I spoke with colleagues as well as other friends and acquaintances—male *and* female—and found an overwhelming dislike for the book. They dismissed it as harmless pop-psychology. What I found so unnerving in this general dismissal of the material was a belief that most people were intelligent enough to reject it and move on. While I agree that this is certainly the case with some individuals, those who are hurting may not always see through clever presentations that comouflage ugly realities. I began to feel that this book—with its erroneous assumptions, patriarchial basis, and lack of scholarly documentation—was well posed to take advantage of such individuals.

Without having read every self-help book on the market, it is probably safe to say that John Gray is not the only author with whom I might have cause to disagree, but he is one of a few that I have read. And, judging by his apparent fondness for self-promotion, I think that it is important to have another voice rise to seriously question his ideas. True enlightenment, regardless of the subject matter, comes when an individual has had the opportunity to look at two sides of an issue and reach some sort of synthesis. Should you find this critique unwarranted, I respect your right to disagree, but only if you have at least read the concerns presented on this page before making your decision.

INTRODUCTION/CHAPTER ONE: MEN ARE FROM MARS, WOMEN ARE FROM VENUS

It is best to begin a critical analysis of this celestial travesty by combining its introduction and first chapter. While questionable editing has separated into two chapters what should have been a comprehensive introduction, it is here that John Gray lays down the foundation on which he constructs the remainder of his sexist and demeaning observations regarding the relationships between men and women.

He begins by establishing for himself a position of authority in which he claims to have conducted "seven years of research" leading to the concepts explored in *Men Are from Mars, Women Are from Venus*. What is missing, unfortunately, are any references to work that Gray may have published for the scholarly community. This would be tremendously helpful in both assessing his claims and possibly his standing within the profession as a whole (sans infomercial endorsements). What *is* provided, however, are numerous references to his seminars. These self-serving advertisements raise more questions than they answer, specifically in regard to the "more than 25,000" attendees who were questioned at these various seminars.

I ask you, have these surveys been published anywhere or scholarly and critically analyzed? In what form was this survey (if any) distributed (formal or informal)? What questions were asked? Was it distributed before or after the seminar? Does it take into account class, ethnic, religious, or regional/national differences? Was age taken into account? Are answers separated on the basis of gender, marital status, or length of relationship? Exactly how many individuals were questioned? And, equally important, was there any long term follow-up among any, or all, of the participants? This is crucial information. Certainly Gray should have provided more than his claim of thousands of seminar participants or success stories in order to buttress the broad, and often insulting, generalizations made in this book.

Also established in the book's introduction is the inference that women must have outside validation in order to feel somewhat content within their relationships. Gray claims that after reading this book men are relieved to find that nothing is wrong with them, while women are relieved that someone is validating them. This is the beginning of what I refer to as the "Active-Passive" control mechanism that Gray will consistently use throughout this book. It first becomes obvious in Chapter One where Gray's Mars/Venus metaphor instantaneously disintegrates from a hardly humorous comparison that highlights the author's weak ideas regarding the nature of gender to a miserable, and unfortunate, reinforcement of destructive gender stereotypes.

According to Gray's Metaphor, "Martians (i.e., men) *discovered* the Venusians (i.e., women)" and, after falling in love,

"quickly *invented*" space travel (enhancements mine). Women (excuse me, Venusians), on the other hand, happily *received* the arrival of the Martians for "they had intuitively known that this day would come." The basis of this shallow metaphor is the belief that men are actively pursuing what they want by controlling their environments and relationships, while women sit passively waiting to be rescued by the proverbial knight in shining armor who, because of his intelligence and wisdom, will make their lives content, worry-free and, I suppose, validate them.

Here lies Gray's central thesis: Men fulfill active roles and are seen as ambitious and powerful. Women, however, satisfy passive roles and, although the author may grudgingly admit that women are cognizant human beings, they must necessarily take a back seat to the dominant male in their lives in order to routinely accommodate his wants and desires. I ask you, is this the study of situation comedies or serious scholarship (in itself a questionable claim) regarding the relationships among rational beings?

CHAPTER THREE: MEN GO TO THEIR CAVES AND WOMEN TALK

Having already established in previous chapters what he believes are the inherent behaviors of men and women, John Gray confidently attempts in this third nebulous chapter to enlighten the reader on how men and women manage stress. By further elaborating on the active/passive control mechanism that is the foundation of his book, Gray tells us that stress makes "men... increasingly focused and withdrawn while women become increasingly overwhelmed and emotionally involved." Notice that by *fo-

cusing on his problems, a man takes a pro-active stance. Women adopt a passive response by becoming *overwhelmed*. The implication here, of course, is that men can deal with problems and women cannot.

Tom and Mary, two Stepford hopefuls, make their appearance as exemplars of a typical evening encounter after a hard day's work. But who is working? We are told that when Tom arrives home, "he wants to relax and unwind by quietly reading the news. He is stressed by the unsolved problems of his day and finds relief through forgetting them." Stop and think about this for one moment: Tom *comes home,* which implies that he has been working outside the home. But where has Mary been all day? It seems that she also has some problems, but she has not come from any particular place; she must have been home all day waiting for Tom to arrive from his job. Naturally, Gray's sexist proclivities would not have allowed for Mary to have *come home* from a stressful day's work outside of the home.

In an attempt to deal with their problems, Gray tells us that "Tom *thinks* Mary talks too much [and] Mary *feels* ignored." Again, who is being proactive here? Tom is, of course. Tom is the initiator of his own thoughts and opinions. Mary is the passive recipient of her perceived reality.

Once again, we are propelled into this overused metaphor of "going back" to our so-called "home planets" in order to find out how our ancestors developed this gender-specific behavior. (What is frightening for me is that I almost feel as if some people actually believe it at this point.) Gray tells us that a man faced with a perplexing dilemma "becomes very quiet and goes to his private cave

to think about his problem, mulling it over to find a solution." When a solution has been found, "he feels much better and comes out of his cave." Indeed, a man "feels good when he can solve his problems on his own in his cave." Following Gray's established gender-specific behavior patterns, a man actually *enters* his cave. He is independent. Self-reliant. Self-motivated. He possesses all the answers. However, when he is aware that he needs help, Gray states that he will seek out the advice of his friends. (Hmm, but not his spouse. Interesting.)

But the ways of the woman are not so bold, I am afraid. Why? Well, according to Gray, a woman's ego is "dependent not on looking 'competent,' but rather on being in loving relationships." To that end, a woman will look to "someone she trusts and [then talk] in great detail about the problems of her day." Indeed, women "openly share feelings of being overwhelmed, confused, hopeless, and exhausted".

What I like best about this particular author is that there is much more communicated in what he does *not* say than what he actually *does* say. For example, Gray has devoted a good deal of space to the discussion of a man's problems, but women are just "overwhelmed, confused, hopeless, and exhausted." So, are men not also vulnerable to feeling "overwhelmed, confused, hopeless, and exhausted?" I suppose if they were, *then* such feelings would be problems. Of course, these words also convey a sense of powerlessness as well. Having long established that it is women who are passive, Gray could not assign such an image to men. Or could he?

When men are in their caves, Gray argues that they are "incapable of giving a woman the attention and feeling that she normally receives and deserves. [Their minds] are preoccupied and [they] are powerless to release it." This is clearly an example of powerlessness, but not because they are "overwhelmed, confused, hopeless, and exhausted," but because they have *declared* that they are powerless. But a man's powerlessness at such times fits perfectly into Gray's gender paradigm because this is an active response to a problem, and thus the proper response for a man.

That all individuals need time to themselves in which to sort out problems or just reflect on things is a given as far as this writer is concerned. Whether you want to call it a "cave" or just "private time," all couples need to recognize that their partners may need time alone to sort out life's ever-present complexities. The problem, then, is not that a man or woman might (forgive me) "cave," it is Gray's erroneous assessment of gender-based behavior which is so problematic.

"To expect a man who is in his cave to instantly become open, responsive and loving," asserts Gray, "is as unrealistic as expecting a woman who is upset to immediately calm down and make complete sense." Now I would *like* to think that I did not see this, but it *is* written down in black and white. Wait! Perhaps he phrased it in a better way! "It is a mistake to expect a man to always be in touch with his loving feelings as it is a mistake to expect a woman's feelings to always be rational and logical." So what is Gray telling us? Again, when the man is silent he speaks volumes! It is the *man* who is always rational and logical. Men always make complete sense. They may not be loving at all times, but they always make sense. And women? Well, these two sentences infer that women

are hysterical, rambling, illogical half-wits who can *sometimes* be rational and logical. Now are women supposed to be loving and responsible while being irrational and not making sense? Does a certain someone feel a little put out when a woman is not devoting all her time to his happiness? In other words, Gray infers that the only things a woman should be thinking about are the needs of her partner. If she has something else on her mind, her partner feels cheated because it isn't him and thus becomes resentful.

Since Gray seems bent on nurturing the male stereotype of the uncommunicative Neanderthal, should we be surprised that women are portrayed as talkative, nonsensical, illogical beings? Mr. Spock would have more compassion for the female sex than this author seems to possess. Gray tells us that "when [a woman] begins talking she does not prioritize the significance of any problem.... She is not immediately concerned with finding solutions to her problems... by randomly talking about her problems, she becomes less upset." Well, why should we be surprised that big, strong, testosterone-laden men experiencing stress tend to "focus on one problem and forget others," yet women "become overwhelmed by all problems." This is Gray's primary thesis rearing its ugly head again, ladies and gentlemen. Men are pro-active; they determine the course of their lives, their relationships, and their reactions to stress. Women, however, are the passive victims. Powerless, they are easily overwhelmed by past, present, and future problems. Overwhelmed to the point that they can't even decide which of their problems is more or less important than the other.

Gray draws on his gender paradigm time and time again in this chapter. "Martians talk about problems for only two reasons," we are told, "they are blaming someone or they are seeking advice." Again, men are being pro-active. They are determining why they are talking: blame (an active response) or seeking advice (an active response). "Just as a man is fulfilled through working out [active!] the intricate details of solving a problem," writes Gray, "a woman is fulfilled through talking about [passive!] the details of her problems." There is that active/passive control mechanism again! A man actively works out his problems, a woman just passively talks about them.

Now, I should not shortchange the author completely. I mean, women are not completely passive, they can help their man by reminding him that he does not have to solve any of her problems. Gray argues that this "can help him to relax and listen." This is important, for "a woman who feels heard suddenly can change, feel better, and sustain a positive attitude." I see, women do not want any of their problems solved. Indeed, Gray takes us deep into the minds of men and tells us that they have usually seen "how a woman (probably their mother) who did not feel heard continued to dwell on her problems.... The real problem, however, is that she feels unloved, not that she is talking about problems." How could we be so blind? Women do not want any of their problems solved because they do not have any problems to begin with! This revelation could change the way we operate in the world! Think about it! Do you need a raise? No! All your boss has to do is love you a little more and your "problem" will have resolved itself instantly! Unable to come up with the rent? Do not take it

personally, your landlord wants to kick you out because he/she is just not capable of loving you more! It's not really a problem! Problems? What, me worry? No! Me's just not loved enough, so I'll just chatter on about it while I live in my car!

Ultimately the lesson the author would like us to take away from Chapter Three is that when men have retreated to their caves, women should not take it so personally. "They [women] learned that this was not the time to have intimate conversations but a time to talk about problems with their friends or go shopping." Yes, shopping. Another gender-specific behavior. However, there are two lingering questions that I would like to consider.

First, Gray says nothing about the length of time or frequency that a man might remain in his cave. This is an important consideration. The importance that Gray assigns to the cave left me with the impression that this was a place where a man would occasionally retreat for a lengthy period of time to mull over some really heavy problems. However, if reading a newspaper is but one manifestation of a man caving, then it seems as if the cave has the potential for being a convenient excuse to avoid communicating. In this vein it behooves the cave aficionado to be aware that if he stays in his cave long enough, he might emerge to find that his partner has gone. Of course, given Gray's sexist bias, he would probably not have considered that a woman would actually take such a pro-active stance regarding the course of her life and relationships. Did the author ever consider that maybe the solution is not to convince women to *live with* his cave concept, but to get men to be more open with their problem solving?

Second, you think the good "doctor" would have at least provided his readers with some sort of warning regarding clinical depression or other disorders. Individuals who are hurting read a book like this and think that following its suggestions will help them along the road to a healthy relationship. However, if the partner with whom you are dealing suffers from clinical depression or manic-depressive disorder, you are left thinking that this man is mulling over problems when he could be suffering from a very serious medical condition. This is irresponsible to be sure, but as we have already seen (and will continue to see) this is only par for the course as far as John Gray is concerned.

"Silver bullet" solutions to complex problems make self-help books and videos bestsellers. The problem is that simplistic solutions to complex questions can easily mislead and are often danger-ous. John Gray's simplistic analysis of hu-man communication may contain a few cells of common sense observation with which men and women can identify, but his solutions are as insidious as a can-cer. *Men Are from Mars, Women Are from Venus* is not do-it-yourself therapy, but a prescriptive manual utilizing the notion of "differences" to perpetuate essentialist notions of gender. By the end of his third chapter, Gray has defined what *he believes* are the roles that men and women satisfy in society. The language he has chosen to use clearly establishes that men are active doers and women passive receivers. Why is the use of a simple verb or adjective so significant? Because words are very pow-erful. In Gray's case they unquestionably betray the unethical, indeed, patriarchal, view that in heterosexual relationships the man should be the boss.

In the end, however, *Mars and Venus* is not about "differences." That men and women manifest variations in communi-cation is hardly surprising given that we are socialized differently, but perpetuat-ing stereotypical archetypes of what is thought to be inherently masculine and feminine is hardly a positive step for-ward. This book, then, is completely use-less as a "fix," but its popularity is invalu-able for what it tells us about ourselves as a society. Given the amount of press that this book has received, ask yourself: How far have we come in recognizing that men and women are equally feel-ing, equally rational and equally deserv-ing human beings? As I see it, not terribly far. As a contributor to this Rebuttal once observed, "The Dr.'s' sexism... is hardly incidental to the book: it's the very reason he's raking in millions."

POSTSCRIPT

Are Men Really from Mars and Women from Venus?

In 1983 Alice Rossi, the incoming president of the American Sociological Association, warned that attempts to explain human behavior and to create therapies that seek to change problem behavior "carry a high risk of eventual irrelevance" if they "neglect the fundamental biological and neural differences between the sexes" and "the mounting evidence of sexual dimorphism from the biological and neural sciences."

Gray finds so many differences in the ways in which men and women communicate that he is willing to picture them as coming from two distinct planets, each speaking a language that the other sex just does not understand. He does not, however, offer any explanation for how these differences arise. Are they due to inescapable genetic and hormonal differences in the development of male and female brains during pregnancy? If so, will Gray's suggestion for better understanding really work? Or are the differences due to the ways in which boys and girls are reared? If this is the case, should the way in which boys and girls are socialized be changed? If "diversity is a biological fact," as Rossi warns, then gender equality "is a political, ethical, and social precept." The diversity that Gray seems to accept goes much deeper than just a man and a woman trying to communicate better. He seems to accept and even celebrate fundamental differences between men and women that, however subtly, consistently put women at a disadvantage and lower on the social status scale than men.

Hamson focuses her essay on what she sees as Gray's implicitly derogatory and patently sexist interpretation of women's communication style. What do you think about her critique? How accurate is her interpretation of Gray's analysis? Where do you agree or disagree with her critique?

As the biological and neuropsychological evidence supporting the existence of significant differences between the genders continues to grow, we need to be especially careful in how we interpret the meaning and significance of these differences. How do we avoid implying that some of these differences fit conveniently with our inclination to view this as better than that, or this as good and that as not so good? People tend to view racial, religious, ethnic, and gender differences not as part of human diversity but in superior-inferior or good-bad terms. Human diversity does not deny or obstruct human equality, because human equality is a political, moral, and social concern. However we decide this issue and whatever gender differences we are willing to recognize, can we accept the equality of the genders, or do we use the emerging evidence of gender diversity to maintain traditional patriarchal prerogatives?

SUGGESTED READINGS

N. Angier, "How Biology Affects Behavior and Vice Versa," *The New York Times* (May 30, 1995), pp. C1, C5.

N. Angier, "Man's World, Woman's World? Brain Studies Point to Differences," *The New York Times* (February 28, 1995), pp. C1, C7.

D. Blum, *Sex on the Brain: The Biological Differences Between Men and Women* (Viking, 1997).

A. Fausto-Sterling, *Myths of Gender: Biological Theories About Women and Men*, 2d ed. (Basic Books, 1992).

C. Gorman, "Sizing Up the Sexes," *Time* (January 20, 1992), pp. 42–51.

J. Gray and H. Estroff Marano, "When Planets Collide," *Psychology Today* (May/June 1997).

D. Kimura, "Sex Differences in the Brain," *Scientific American* (September 1992).

R. Pool, *Eve's Rib: Searching for the Biological Roots of Sex Differences* (Crown Publishers, 1994).

D. Tannen, *You Just Don't Understand: Women and Men in Conversation* (William Morrow, 1990).

C. Tavris, *The Mismeasure of Woman* (Simon & Schuster, 1992).

On the Internet ...

http://www.dushkin.com

A Forum for Women's Health
This Internet resource hosts a collection of information, advice, and suggestions for helping women to deal with their health concerns. This helpful site covers birth control and pregnancy issues, as well as many others.
http://www.womenshealth.org/

ACT UP/New York Chapter
The AIDS Coalition to Unleash Power (ACT UP) is a diverse, nonpartisan group of individuals united in anger and committed to direct action to end the AIDS crisis.
http://www.actupny.org/

Men's Health
This site links to information on issues concerning men's health and sexual concerns, including circumcision, contraception, infertility, hair loss, male sexuality, and prostate conditions.
http://www.health-library.com/men/index.html

NARAL Online
This is the home page of the National Abortion and Reproductive Rights Action League (NARAL), an organization that works to promote reproductive freedom and dignity for women and their families.
http://www.naral.org/

The Femal Genital Mutilation Research Home Page
This site is dedicated to research pertaining to female genital mutilation.
http://www.hollyfeld.org/fgm/

The Ultimate Pro-Life Resource List
The Ultimate Pro-Life Resource List is the most comprehensive listing of right-to-life resources on the Internet.
http://www.prolife.org/ultimate/

PART 2

Issues in Reproduction and Health

Modern medical technology allows us to engage in sexual intercourse without the risk of pregnancy, to terminate an unwanted pregnancy when one occurs, and to reduce the risk of and control sexually transmitted diseases. This technology raises many moral and social issues, such as, What are the privacy and education rights of sexually mature teenagers? Who is responsible for the sexuality education of our youth? How do we balance the rights of the fetus developing in the womb and the rights of the pregnant woman? And should prostitutes be allowed to practice their trade? This section also explores the sensitive cross-cultural issue of female circumcision, a centuries-old tradition that many immigrants bring to the West from their homelands in Africa and the Middle East.

■ Should Schools Distribute Condoms?

■ Should Public Libraries Provide Sexuality Materials?

■ Should Contractual Sex Be Legal?

■ Should Late-Term Abortions Be Banned?

■ Should All Female Circumcision Be Banned?

■ Is Abstinence-Only Education Effective?

ISSUE 6

Should Schools Distribute Condoms?

YES: Center for Population Options, from *Condom Availability in Schools: A Guide for Programs* (Center for Population Options, 1993)

NO: Edwin J. Delattre, from "Condoms and Coercion: The Maturity of Self Determination," *Vital Speeches of the Day* (April 15, 1992)

ISSUE SUMMARY

YES: The Center for Population Options, an organization that promotes healthy decision making about sexuality among youth, outlines what is known about the sexual behavior and the accompanying health risks of teens today and then examines strategies for reducing these risks—specifically, encouraging abstinence and condom use. Considering all the options and all the risks, the center concludes that making condoms available to students through the schools with counseling and education is the best course of action.

NO: Professor of education Edwin J. Delattre, in opposing condom distribution in schools, identifies several flaws in the argument that we have a moral obligation to distribute condoms to save lives. He dismisses the claim that this is purely a health issue, and he discusses various moral issues involved in promoting casual sexual involvement, which he believes condom distribution does.

Seventy-two percent of American high school seniors have engaged in sexual intercourse. This percentage is likely higher in large cities and their suburbs.

With the highest rate of teenage pregnancy and abortion in North America and Europe, and with young people rapidly becoming the highest risk group for HIV (human immunodeficiency virus) infection, American parents, educators, and health care professionals have to decide how to deal with these problems. Some advocate teaching abstinence and saying nothing about contraceptives and other ways of reducing the risk of contracting sexually transmitted diseases (STDs) and HIV infections. Others advocate educating and counseling: "You don't have to be sexually active, but if you are, this is what you can do to protect yourself." But in some schools, the problem is so serious, some advocate offering students free condoms. School boards in New York, Baltimore, Chicago, Los Angeles, San Francisco, Philadelphia, Miami, and other cities have opted to allow school nurses and school-based health clinics to distribute free condoms to students, usually without requiring parental notification or permission.

Dr. Alma Rose George, president of the National Medical Association, opposes schools giving condoms to teens without their parents knowing about it: "When you give condoms out to teens, you are promoting sexual activity. It's saying that it's all right. We shouldn't make it so easy for them." Faye Wattleton, former president of the Planned Parenthood Federation of America, approves of schools distributing condoms and maintains that "mandatory parental consent would be counterproductive and meaningless."

Some detect overtones of racism in condom distribution programs. "When most of the decisions are made, it's by a White majority for schools predominantly Black," says Dolores Grier, noted black historian and vice chancellor of community relations for the Catholic Archdiocese of New York. "They introduce a lot of Black and Hispanic children to this like they're animals. I consider it racist to give condoms to children." Elijah Mohammed, founder of the Black Nation of Islam, has condemned condom distribution as racist genocide.

This debate requires the consideration of several distinct issues, as the two selections here clearly reveal. We have to take a position on the morality, implied endorsement, and encouragement of premarital sex. We have to decide on the roles of the school and those of the parents in dealing with the evident and growing risks of STDs and HIV infection. We have to consider the psychological, emotional, and social issue of "how early is too early" for initiating sexually intimate relationships. And we need to reach a general agreement on the timing, content, philosophy, and objectives of sex education in the schools. That is no easy task, but the issue—debated in the following selections by the Center for Population Options and Edwin J. Delattre—and our answers will affect the lives of millions of young people.

YES

Center for Population Options

MAKING THE CASE

I. YOUTH AT RISK

Confronted with rising levels of adolescent pregnancy and the growing incidence among adolescents of sexually transmitted diseases (STDs), including the HIV virus that cause AIDS, most adults agree these threats to young people's health have reached crisis proportions. Strong interventions are needed to protect adolescents.

For many teens, schools are the primary source of accurate information about STDs: almost all states encourage or require HIV/AIDS prevention education in their schools. Comprehensive health and sexuality programs can also help teens delay initiation of sexual intercourse. But while education is critical for changing attitudes, it does not, alone, change the behaviors that put sexually active teens at risk of infection and unintended pregnancy. Teens also need to be provided the means to protect themselves and to be taught effective ways of discussing protection with their partners.

Many school personnel, public health officials and policymakers are suggesting that high schools make latex condoms available to sexually active students. They reason that schools are uniquely positioned to provide two-part health and sexuality programs that include education and access to barrier methods that protect against disease and unintended pregnancy.

Through these programs, those charged with educating adolescents hope to empower them to change their risk-taking, and sometimes life-threatening, sexual behavior.

A. Behaviors and Risks of Sexually Active Adolescents
Adolescents have a sense of omnipotence and invulnerability as they move toward independence. Their fearlessness can lead to dangerous behaviors, such as using drugs (including alcohol and tobacco) and having sex without contraception and/or protection....

Large Numbers of Adolescents Engage in Sexual Activity. Surveys of adolescent sexual behavior indicate that young people are engaging in sexual intercourse at early ages. Seventy-seven percent of females and 86 percent of males are sexually active by age 20.

Sexually Active Adolescents Are at Risk for Unintended Pregnancy.   Over one million teenage girls—one in 10—become pregnant every year. Four out of 10 teenagers will become pregnant before turning 20. At least 82 percent of teen pregnancies are unintended. One out of four adolescents does not use an effective means of contraception.

Adolescents Are at Risk for STDs.   For reasons related to their physiological development, adolescent women are more vulnerable to infection when exposed to STDs than are adult women. Rates of chlamydia, gonorrhea and syphilis for adolescent women are higher than for adult women. Over three million sexually active adolescents are infected with an STD annually, representing one-fifth of all STD cases in the nation. The American Medical Association estimates that one out of four teens will have an STD before high school graduation. The estimate is even higher for youth who are not in school.[1] Left untreated, STDs can cause pelvic inflammatory disease, which is a cause of infertility and increases vulnerability to HIV.

Adolescents Are Also at Risk of Contracting HIV.   Adolescents are just as vulnerable to contracting HIV as adults, and perhaps more so. Individuals already infected with an STD may have breakdowns of skin and mucosal barriers and thus are more vulnerable to HIV infection. Currently, almost 20 percent of people diagnosed with AIDS in the United States are in their 20s. Because the latency period between HIV infection and onset of symptoms is about 10 years, many were probably exposed to HIV as adolescents. From 1990 to 1992, the number of youth ages 13 to 24 who were diagnosed with AIDS increased by 77 percent.[2] ...

II. STRATEGIES FOR REDUCING THE RISK

A. Encouraging Abstinence

Only complete abstinence from risky sexual behaviors and judgement-impairing substances—such as alcohol and drugs —entirely eliminates the risk of pregnancy and STD infection. Comprehensive health education or HIV/AIDS prevention programs encourage young people to abstain from or delay sexual intercourse, and suggest substituting other forms of non-risky sexual activity.

Research has shown that some programs are effective in helping teens postpone intercourse. The "Postponing Sexual Involvement" (PSI) program developed at Grady Memorial Hospital in Atlanta, has been shown to increase the percentage of students who had not yet initiated intercourse by the end of the ninth grade from 61 percent (in the control group) to 76 percent (among program participants). By the end of eighth grade, students who did not participate in the program were as much as five times more likely to have initiated sexual intercourse than were PSI participants.[3] In contrast, the program demonstrated little, if any, impact on the behavior of teens who were already sexually active.

The Grady program uses the "social inoculation" model of outreach. This model assumes that young people engage in negative behaviors partly because of social influences and pressures, arising both generally and from their peers. Such programs use activities that help participants identify the origin of these pressures and develop skills to respond to them positively and effectively. Such programs also rely on peers—slightly older teens—to present information, lead group activities and discuss issues and problems.

Another program using social inoculation is "Reducing the Risk" (RTR), implemented and evaluated at 13 California high schools. RTR stresses that students should avoid unprotected intercourse—either through abstinence or contraception. RTR also encourages parent-child communication on subjects such as birth control and abstinence. The program significantly increased participants' knowledge of abstinence and contraception, and their communication about these topics with their parents. Participants who had not yet initiated intercourse indicated a significantly-reduced likelihood that they would have had intercourse 18 months later. Further, a survey of parents found broad support for RTR, as well as a belief that the program had had positive effects.[4]

Some adults believe teens should not be taught or shown methods of contraception and protection, and that sexuality education should focus exclusively on abstinence for unmarried adolescents. Numerous "abstinence-only" curricula are being promoted for use in schools that present opinion as fact, convey insufficient, inaccurate or biased information, rely on scare tactics, reinforce gender stereotypes and are insensitive to cultural and economic differences. These programs have not been adequately evaluated and should not be confused with the curricula mentioned here that have demonstrated a measure of success. . . .

There is little evidence that programs which promote abstinence alone are ef-

fective with adolescents who have already initiated sexual intercourse. Evaluations of even the most promising abstinence-based curricula reveal that substantial proportions of participants continue to engage in intercourse. These adolescents are at risk of pregnancy and STDs, including HIV.

Even the more successful abstinence-based curricula promote the delay of sexual activity but seldom prevent sexual intercourse until marriage. Most adolescents will eventually become sexually active. Therefore, all students must be taught the information and skills necessary to make healthy decisions and to accept personal responsibility.

B. Encouraging Condom Use

A majority of teens are sexually active. According to the CDC's 1990 Youth Risk Behavior Survey, 39.6 percent of ninth graders, 47.6 percent of tenth graders, 57.3 percent of eleventh graders and 71.9 percent of twelfth graders report they have had intercourse. Programs must help sexually active teens reduce the potential for negative consequences associated with unprotected intercourse.

Next to abstinence, latex condoms are the most effective method for reducing STDs and the sexual transmission of HIV infection. When properly used, latex condoms are also effective at reducing the risk of pregnancy. Promoting correct and consistent condom use by sexually active teens is an important strategy in curbing the national epidemics of HIV, other STDs and too-early childbearing.

The National Research Council, in its landmark 1987 report, *Risking the Future: Adolescent Sexuality, Pregnancy and Childbearing*, recommended "the development, implementation and evaluation of condom distribution programs."

An important U.S. National Health Promotion and Disease Prevention Objective is to increase the use of condoms at last intercourse by sexually active females aged 15–19 from 25 percent in 1988 to 60 percent by the year 2000. For sexually active males ages 15–19, the year 2000 target is 75 percent.[5]

III. BARRIERS TO CONDOM ACCESS AND USE

Adolescents have a legal right to purchase condoms. Ensuring a minor's right to contraception does not, however, translate into easy access. Condoms may appear to be widely available, but a number of factors inhibit young people's ability to acquire and effectively use them.

Surveys have found that lack of availability is one of the most frequently cited reasons sexually active adolescents fail to use condoms. Furthermore, adolescents' desire for confidentiality often overshadows their concerns for health. While fear that others will learn they are sexually active does not keep teens from having intercourse, it does apparently inhibit them from purchasing condoms. Other factors, many of which are associated with low self-esteem, that teens perceive as barriers to regular condom use include:

- peer or partner pressure
- fear of loss of relationship
- fear of decreased sexual pleasure
- cultural expectations for gender-related behavior and roles
- denial of sexual activity
- alcohol and drugs which impair judgement, often contribute to risky behavior and failure to use condoms properly or at all

- anxiety about being seen by parents, friends or neighbors when purchasing condoms
- cost

A 1988 survey by members of the Center for Population Options (CPO) Teen Council examined the accessibility of contraception in drugstores and convenience stores in Washington, D.C. and found that:

- One-third of the stores kept condoms behind the counter, forcing teens to ask for them.
- Only 13 percent of the stores had signs that clearly marked where contraceptives were shelved.
- Adolescent girls asking for assistance encountered resistance or condemnation from store clerks 40 percent of the time.

For adolescents, these obstacles are significant barriers to contraceptive access. Evidence from other parts of the country suggests that D.C. is not unique.

Even in areas where health departments or family planning clinics provide condoms free of charge and without appointments, school or work obligations may combine with clinic schedules to make it difficult or impossible for adolescents to take advantage of these services. Rural youth, in particular, have concerns about transportation and privacy—being seen at the drug store or clinic by someone they or their parents know is more likely in a small town or rural community.

IV. FACTORS THAT INCREASE LATEX CONDOM USE

Logistical barriers to condom use can be addressed by making condoms widely and freely available; however, successful strategies to help teens use latex condoms properly and consistently must address *both* physical and psychological access. Psychological and emotional barriers to condom use are embedded in the culture and are harder to address. Access is enhanced with increased knowledge, social and physical skills, perception of personal risk and perceived peer and societal norms.

Among the factors specifically cited by teens that would tend to increase condom use are condoms' acceptability among peers and a perception that they are easy to use and permit spontaneity. Teens who believe condoms help prevent HIV transmission are also more likely to report consistent use.[6] Another survey of teenagers found that providing condoms free of cost and making them easy to obtain are crucial elements in increasing adolescent use.

V. A PREVENTION STRATEGY THAT MAKES SENSE

Condoms are currently available to teens from a variety of sources: drugstores, family planning clinics, health clinics, supermarkets, convenience stores and vending machines. Making condoms available within schools does not introduce an otherwise unobtainable commodity to students. Rather, it expands the range of sources and facilitates teens' access to an important health aid. Adults understand that social endorsement by adults and society is a critical factor in normalizing condom use, and large majorities support giving teens access to condoms in school.

By making condoms available to students who choose to engage in sexual activity, schools let students know the community cares about their health and well-being. School programs reinforce that there are adults who will address adolescent sexual behavior, rather than deny it is a reality. While adults may prefer that young people refrain from sexual intercourse, it is important to help those teens who do not to avoid the negative consequences of HIV and other STDs, as well as unplanned pregnancy.

Condom availability programs eliminate some of the most significant barriers to condom use, including lack of access. By making condoms available in schools, caring adults can reach at-risk adolescents in a familiar and comfortable setting. Furthermore, programs can be designed specifically to reduce other barriers to condom use.

Several studies have shown that sexually active teens are more likely to use condoms if they believe their peers are using them. Condom availability in schools promotes positive and open attitudes toward condoms, increasing the likelihood that teens not only will acquire the condoms they need to protect themselves, but will also use them.

Schools are in a unique position to help teens address issues that are clearly associated with inappropriate risk-taking behaviors. Schools can provide opportunities for students to increase self-esteem and to practice decision-making, negotiation and conflict-resolution skills. Thus, school condom availability programs supported by comprehensive life skills training are uniquely able to help students gain and practice the skills necessary for successful condom use.

Despite fears to the contrary, research clearly demonstrates that students in schools which make condoms and other contraceptives available through school-based health centers are no more likely to be sexually experienced than students in

> According to a 1988 Harris poll, 73 percent of adults favor making contraceptives available in schools. A 1991 Roper poll found that 64 percent of adults say condoms should be available in high schools. According to a Gallup poll released in August, 1992, adult support for condom availability has grown to 68 percent.[7] In April, 1992, a National Scholastic Survey also found that 81 percent of high school seniors felt condoms should be available; 78 percent felt condom availability programs do not encourage sexual activity.

schools without these services available. In fact, at some schools with centers making contraception available, teens' mean age at first intercourse was older —and already sexually active teens' frequency of intercourse was lower— than at schools without contraception availability.[8]

VI. CONDOM AVAILABILITY AS PART OF A COMPREHENSIVE PROGRAM

It is important to remember that condom availability can be most effective only if it is part of a comprehensive health, sexuality education, HIV/AIDS and pregnancy prevention program. To affect adolescent behavior it is necessary to address teens' attitudes and knowledge of reproductive health issues, as well as their ability to access and use condoms and contraceptives effectively. Strategies must also seek to improve teens' capacity to abstain from or delay sexual intercourse. Outreach to at-risk teens, education, counseling and follow-up are all necessary components of a program.

As a result, school condom availability programs typically involve collaborative efforts among schools, health agencies, youth-serving organizations and community members.

A surprising but important benefit of the debate over condom availability is the way the issue has engaged entire communities and increased public awareness. Schools are conducting surveys of teenagers to determine their level of risk-taking behavior. Students themselves are speaking out on the issue, sometimes being heard for the first time. Parents and community members are becoming more involved in the early stages of the debate and are helping to design these programs. Schools and communities are also taking the opportunity to evaluate whether the health education programs that already exist are comprehensive and teach decision-making skills as well as impart information.

The complex strands of cultural influence, socio-economic status, environment and individual personality that determine why people do the things they do are not easily disentangled. No single approach—sexuality education, condom availability or abstinence programs —can alone eliminate STDs and too-early childbearing among adolescents. These components combined can help teens to develop attitudes, skills and behavior patterns that will protect them from unnecessary risks throughout their lives.

NOTES

1. Janet Gans, Ph.D. et al. *America's Adolescents: How Healthy Are They?* (Chicago, IL: The American Medical Association, 1990).

2. U.S. House of Representatives, Select Committee on Children, Youth and Families, *A Decade of Denial: Teens and AIDS in America* (Washington, DC: U.S. Government Printing Office, April 12, 1992).

3. Marion Howard and Judith Blamey McCabe, "Helping Teenagers Postpone Sexual Involvement," *Family Planning Perspectives* 22:1 (January/February 1990).

4. Douglas Kirby et al., "Reducing the Risk: Impact of a New Curriculum on Sexual Risk-Taking," *Family Planning Perspectives,* 23:6 (November/December 1991).

5. U.S. Department of Health and Human Services, Public Health Service. *Healthy People 2000* (Washington, DC: U.S. Government Printing Office, 1990) p. 503.

6. Ralph DiClemente et al., "Determinants of Condom Use Among Junior High School Students in a Minority, Inner-City School District," *Pediatrics* 89:2 (February 1992).

7. Stanley E. Ealm, Lowell C. Rose and Alex M. Gallup, "24th Annual Gallup Poll/Phi Delta Kappa Poll of the Public's Attitudes Towards the Public Schools" (September 1992).

8. Doug Kirby, Cindy Waszak and J. Ziegler, *An Assessment of Six School-Based Clinics: Services, Impact and Potential* (Washington, DC: The Center for Population Options, 1989). See also: L. S. Zabin et al., "Evaluation of a Pregnancy Prevention Program for Urban Teenagers," *Family Planning Perspectives* 18:3 (May/June, 1986).

NO

Edwin J. Delattre

CONDOMS AND COERCION: THE MATURITY OF SELF DETERMINATION

We [are] told . . . by condom distribution advocates that school distribution of condoms is not a moral issue but rather an issue of life and death. We [are] told, by the same people, that we have a moral obligation to do everything in our power, at all times, to save lives. The incoherence—indeed, contradiction—between these claims reflects the failure of condom distribution advocates to perceive the fact that *all* life-and-death issues are morally consequential; that questions of what schools have the right and the duty to do in the interest of their students are irreducibly moral questions; and that *how* schools should endorse and sustain the honorable conduct of personal life is a moral issue of the most basic and profound sort.

The plain fact is that if our only moral duty were to save lives—at whatever cost to other ideals of life—on statistical grounds, we would have to raise the legal age for acquiring a driver's license to at least twenty-five; we would have to reduce interstate highway speed limits to 35 mph or less; we would have to force everyone in America to undergo an annual physical examination; we would have to outlaw foods that contribute to bad health; we would have to prohibit the use of tobacco and advertisements for it, and spend huge resources to enforce those laws; we would have to eliminate rights of privacy in the home in order to minimize the possibility of domestic violence; we would have to establish laws to determine who can safely bear children, and therefore who is allowed to become pregnant; we would have to make AIDS and drug testing mandatory for all citizens at regular intervals; we would have to do away with the rights of suspects to due process in order to eliminate open-air drug marketplaces in our cities; we would have to incarcerate, on a permanent basis, all prostitutes who test HIV positive; we would have to announce publicly the name of every person who tests HIV positive in order to safeguard others from possible exposure through sexual activity. And so on.

Saving lives is not the only moral concern of human beings. The prevention of needless suffering among adults, youths, children, infants and unborn babies; the avoidance of self-inflicted heartache; and the creation of

From Edwin J. Delattre, "Condoms and Coercion: The Maturity of Self Determination," *Vital Speeches of the Day*, vol. 58, no. 13 (April 15, 1992). Copyright © 1992 by Edwin J. Delattre. Reprinted by permission.

opportunities for fulfilling work and for happiness in an environment of safety and justice all merit moral attention as well. And even if saving lives were our only moral concern, there is no reason to believe that distributing condoms in schools is the best way to save lives. Certainly, the distribution of condoms is an unreliable substitute for the creation of a school environment that conveys the unequivocal message that abstinence has greater life-saving power than any piece of latex can have.

Furthermore, even if condoms were the best means of saving lives, there would be no compelling reason for schools rather than parents to distribute condoms; no reason for schools to be implicated in the distribution of condoms when others are willing and eager to do so; no reason for schools to assent to the highly questionable claim that *if* they distribute condoms, they will, in fact, save lives.

We have a duty to make clear to our students... the implications of sexual involvement with other people who are ignorant of the dangers of sexual transmission of diseases or uncaring about any threat they may pose to the safety of the innocent. Our students need to grasp that if any one of us becomes sexually involved with someone and truly needs a condom or a dental dam because neither we nor the other person knows how much danger of exposure to AIDS that person may be subjecting us to, then we are sleeping with a person who is either staggeringly ignorant of the dangers involved or else is, in principle, willing to kill us. Such a person has not even the decency to wait long enough for informative medical tests to be conducted that would have a chance of disclosing an HIV positive condition; not even the decency to place

saving our lives, or anyone else's, above personal gratification. Obviously, if we behave in this way, we, too, are guilty of profound wrongdoing.

This is so inescapably a moral issue— about saving lives—that its omission by condom distribution advocates astounds the imagination. They have said nothing about the kinds of people who are unworthy of romantic love and personal trust, who conceal or ignore the danger they may pose to another's life, even with a condom. These considerations prove yet another fundamental fact of human life: the only things casual about casual sex are its casual indifference to the seriousness of sexual life, its casual dismissal of the need for warranted trust between one individual and another, and its casual disregard and contempt for our personal duty to protect others from harm or death.

We have a duty to explain to students that there is no mystery about discovering and saying what is morally wrong. It is morally wrong to cause needless suffering, and it is morally wrong to be indifferent to the suffering we may cause by our actions. On both counts, sexual promiscuity is conspicuously wrong.

Sexual promiscuity, casual sexual involvement, whether in youth or adulthood, is an affront to all moral seriousness about one's own life and the lives of others. Exposing oneself and others to possible affliction with sexually transmitted diseases is itself morally indefensible, but even where this danger is not present, sexual promiscuity reveals a grave failure of personal character.

A person who is sexually promiscuous inevitably treats other people as mere objects to be *used* for personal gratification, and routinely ignores the possibility of pregnancies that may result in unwanted children whose lot in life will be unfair from the beginning. This is morally wrong; it is an affront to the dignity of human beings, an affront to their right to be treated with concern for their feelings, hopes, and happiness, as well as their safety.

Where promiscuity is shrewdly calculated, it is crudely exploitative and selfish; where promiscuity is impulsive, it is immature and marks a failure of self-control. In either case, promiscuity is incompatible with moral seriousness, because wherever there is promiscuity, there is necessarily an absence of the emotional and spiritual intimacy that anchor genuine love among human beings, love that is healthfully expressed among morally mature people in nonpromiscuous sexual intimacy.

Those who are sexually promiscuous —or want to become promiscuous by successfully persuading others to gratify their desires—routinely seek to exert peer pressure in favor of sexual indulgence, as surely as drug users seek to impose peer pressure in favor of drug and alcohol consumption. Anyone who believes that such persons will not try to overcome resistance to sexual involvement by insisting that the school distributes condoms; that the Health Center says condoms increase your safety, or at least make sex "less dangerous"; that sexual activity is *only* a health issue and not a moral issue, and that condoms eliminate the health problem—anyone so naive ignores entirely, or does not know, the practices of seduction, the manipulativeness among people who treat others as objects to be used for their own pleasure, or the coercive power of adverse peer pressure.

We also have a duty to describe to our students the very real dangers of promiscuity even with condoms. According to

research conducted by Planned Parenthood, condoms have a vastly greater rate of failure in preventing pregnancy when used by young unmarried women—36.3 percent—than has been reported by condom distribution advocates. The Family Research Council stresses that this figure is probably low where condom failure may involve possible exposure to AIDS, since the HIV virus is $1/450$ the size of a sperm and is less than $1/10$ the size of open channels that routinely pass entirely through latex products such as gloves.

The behavior of health professionals with respect to "less dangerous" sex ought to be described to students as well. As reported in the Richmond, Virginia, *Times-Dispatch* ten days ago:

"Dr. Theresa Crenshaw, a member of the national AIDS Commission and past president of the American Association of Sex Education, Counselors, and Therapists, told a Washington conference of having addressed an international meeting of 800 sexologists: 'Most of them,' she said, 'recommended condoms to their clients and students. I asked them if they had available the partner of their dreams, and knew that person carried the virus, would they have sex, depending on a condom for protection? No one raised their hand. After a long delay, one timid hand surfaced from the back of the room. I told them that it was irresponsible to give advice to others that they would not follow themselves. The point is, putting a mere balloon between a healthy body and a deadly disease is not safe.' " [January 4, 1992, p. A-10]

These reasons of principle and of fact ought to be sufficient to show the hazards.... But there is more to the moral dimension of school distribution of condoms, and those who have claimed otherwise deserve a further account with respect to sexual life itself.

In being forced to distribute condoms... to children and adolescents whose emotional and intellectual maturity remain, for the most part, in the balance—we are made to convey to the young the false message that we do not know these things about basic decency, about safety, about the high price of putting everything at risk for instant pleasure. And we are also giving youths whose judgment is still being formed the impression that we do not particularly care about the moral dimensions of sexual life, and that there is no particular reason for them to do so either.

Remember: we have been told... by adults and youths alike that there *is* no moral issue at stake. The acquiescence of the School... in condom distribution tacitly affirms that pronouncement. Their message betrays fidelity to high standards of ethics in education and sensitivity to more comprehensive dimensions of respect for justice, self-control, courage, and regard for persons in the articulation of institutional policy and the conduct of personal life.

Those who have told us that we are not faced with a moral issue transparently lack understanding of the fundamentals of moral maturity and character excellence. Their judgement, shallow as it is, betrays the young to a supposed, but implausible, expediency.

We will be told that all this will be covered by conscientious counseling of youths who request condoms. But, despite the best efforts of our well-intentioned health care professionals, it will not be adequately covered—and it will certainly not be covered for the students, and their former classmates who have dropped out of school, who are subject to peer pressure but never seek condoms themselves.

Condom distribution in the schools, even under the most carefully considered conditions, lends itself to the theme we have heard here: that profound dimensions of moral life, including decent treatment of others, have nothing to do with morality. It is not simply that this position is morally incompetent; it is also cruel in its licensing of peer pressure to become sexually active, peer pressure that can be, and often is, selfish, intolerant, even downright vicious.

The School... has sanctioned such peer pressure and has thereby given approval to forms of behavior and manipulation that cause, among the young, enormous suffering. Condom distribution advocates behave as though they know nothing of human nature and nothing of the unfair pressures to which the young are routinely subjected. The School['s] decision has now implicated us in teaching the young that we, too, are ignorant of these facts of life as they apply in youth.

The reply of condom distribution advocates to my reasoning is predictable. Sexual activity among the young is inevitable, they will say, even natural, and for reasons of birth control, avoidance of unwanted teenage pregnancies and protection from sexually transmitted diseases, including AIDS, it is better that students should use condoms than not. They will insist that the availability of condoms does not increase the likelihood of sexual activity and that, in any case, many students who use the condoms will be selectively active rather than promiscuous.

The counterarguments are equally straightforward. If we teach the young that sexual activity is what we expect of them, at least some of them will come to expect it of themselves. We have no right to exhibit, or to have, such low expectations—especially toward those whose decisions about whether to become sexually active remain in the balance or who hope to live in an environment where restraint is not only respected but genuinely admired.

And for those who *are* sexually promiscuous—for whatever motives—whether they act in this way to aggrandize themselves; or to exert power over others; or to gain prestige, or physical pleasure, or peer approval; whether they are sexually active because of a desperate and doomed hope of securing affection and attention; or from failure to grasp alternatives; or from ignorance of consequences of promiscuity; or from a mistaken belief that intercourse and intimacy are the same—for all of them, if it is better that they should use condoms than not, how does it follow that *we* should give them the condoms *in* the High School?

In logic—and in fact—it does *not* follow. Even if it is true that promiscuity with condoms and dental dams is physically less dangerous than promiscuity without them, this ostensible fact in no way suggests or implies that *we* should be in the business of distributing condoms—as surely as the fact that filtered cigarettes are less harmful than unfiltered ones does not imply that we should be distributing free filtered cigarettes in the . . . Public Schools. We should instead be standing on the side of peer pressure against casual sex, and we should be providing resolute support for such peer pressure because it is morally right and because it has a distinctive and irreplaceable power to save lives.

Some condom distribution advocates insist that because we now have a health clinic in the High School, we are obliged to defer to the judgment of experts in health care on this subject. They claim that these experts do not try to tell us what we should do as educators, and we should not tell them what to do in matters of health and health-related services.

This artificial and illusory bifurcation of education and health is based on the false premise that what health officials do in the High School contains no educational lessons and teaches nothing about institutional policy or the decent conduct of personal life.

In this particular matter, health experts have clearly attempted to teach the public—including students—that the High School is an appropriate condom distribution site, while dismissing as irrelevant questions of educational mission and duty; and social service agency leaders have advocated that policy by pandering to and proselytizing for the view naively expressed by the students that there are no moral issues implicit in the policy. They have exceeded their competence in questions of morals.

Furthermore, it is well understood by all of us that condoms are fallible. We have not adequately addressed problems of potential legal liability for . . . the City . . . , the . . . Public Schools, and the School Committee. Yet both health professionals and social service personnel have . . . explicitly dismissed as trivial the prospect of legal liability for our institutions, as though they were qualified not only in matters of ethics but also in matters of law. In both respects, they have acted as educators—miseducators.

In doing so, they have potentially undermined the achievement of healthy levels of self-assertion by students, putting that achievement at risk from dangerous peer pressure. They have likewise jeopardized the achievement of self-respect among students by teaching them that even a questionable expediency is more important than mature judgment, personal restraint, and respect for the well-being of other people.

These are the facts of our present situation. We have been brought to a moment with we are no longer able to do what we ought to do in the High School, but are forced to do what is educationally wrong. We have been driven to this condition by a collection of flawed arguments about educational policy, about ethical life, and about law.

POSTSCRIPT

Should Schools Distribute Condoms?

The debate over whether or not public schools should distribute condoms to students clearly reflects the opposing philosophical and moral positions of fixed versus process value systems. The fixed world view places a top priority on opposing all sexual activity outside marriage. A process world view maintains that we can and should encourage sexual abstinence for teens but that we must also provide them with the knowledge and ways of reducing health risks when they do decide to engage in sex.

Obviously, contraception is a sensitive issue where young people are concerned. In Saint Clair Shores, Michigan, five students were suspended from school for wearing buttons promoting condom use. In Seattle, Washington, activists handing out condoms and risk-reduction pamphlets at local high schools have been threatened with arrest for public obscenity.

In addition, sex-related health problems among adolescents continue to grow. One quarter of all Americans who currently have AIDS (acquired immunodeficiency syndrome) were infected during their teen years. In some areas, the rate of HIV infection among teens is doubling every 16 to 18 months. In some schools, the rate of STD infection is over 20 percent. And pregnancies in the fifth grade are not unheard of.

By mid-1993 the debate over distributing condoms in the schools as a way of reducing teenage pregnancy, STDs, and HIV infections was further complicated by debates in a dozen states about schools providing students with the five-year contraceptive implant, Norplant. Seen by some as a panacea for the problem of teenage pregnancy, school distribution of Norplant is feared by others because it may reduce the effectiveness of condom programs aimed at reducing the risk of STDs and HIV infection.

SUGGESTED READINGS

S. Guttmaher et al., "Condom Availability in New York City Public High Schools: Relationships to Condom Use and Sexual Behavior," *American Journal of Public Health* (September 1997).

"None—Not Safer—Is the Real Answer," *Insight on the News* (May 9, 1994).

L. Richardson, "When Sex Is Just a Matter of Fact: To High School Students, Free Condoms Seem Normal, Not Debatable," *The New York Times* (October 16, 1997), pp. B1, B6.

J. Seligmann, "Condoms in the Classroom," *Newsweek* (December 9, 1991).

B. Wright and K. Cranston, "Condom Availability in a Small Town: Lessons from Falmouth, Massachusetts," *SIECUS Report* (October/November 1992).

ISSUE 7

Should Public Libraries Provide Sexuality Materials?

YES: Martha Cornog, from "Is Sex Safe in Your Library? How to Fight Censorship," *Library Journal* (August 1993)

NO: James L. Sauer, from "In Defense of Censorship," *The Christian Librarian* (February 1993)

ISSUE SUMMARY

YES: Martha Cornog, manager of Membership Services at the American College of Physicians in Philadelphia, Pennsylvania, maintains that public libraries have a responsibility to preserve all literature that is part of our cultural heritage for patrons and future generations. Public libraries that preserve and make available materials, including controversial sexuality materials, facilitate and promote debate, which is essential in the democratic process.

NO: James L. Sauer, a librarian at Eastern College in Phoenixville, Pennsylvania, claims that free speech is not unlimited—it is governed by and must serve the moral order. Thus, it is proper for libraries to use their censorship power to curb unfettered expression that violates or attacks the moral values of society.

Gershon Legman, writing in "The Lure of the Forbidden," in Martha Cornog, ed., *Libraries, Erotica, and Pornography* (Oryx Press, 1991), makes this statement:

> The libraries' censorship, except at the provincial lending level... has paradoxically had the opposite effect: that of preserving, in many cases, the very books that would otherwise have been destroyed.... For essentially, the libraries' effort is to protect the books for and sometimes against the readers, and not to protect the readers from the books.

The role of the library in deciding what materials should and should not be made available to the public—or even if libraries have the right to refrain from providing certain material—is the focus of this issue. Censorship in any form has always raised controversy in countries in which freedom of speech is a valued right. The issue becomes even more complicated when the speech in question is sexual in nature, as the following examples illustrate.

In 1985 Congressman Chalmers P. Wylie (R-Ohio) added an amendment to the Library of Congress appropriations bill that would have reduced the library's budget by the exact amount it would cost to have *Playboy* magazine put into Braille and made available through the National Library Service for the Blind and Physically Handicapped. After the Librarian of Congress withdrew *Playboy* from the list of magazines to be put into Braille, Playboy Enterprises, several blind individuals and advocacy organizations, and the American Library Association sued successfully for full funding.

In 1993 libraries across the nation had to decide whether or not to purchase pop singer Madonna's sexually explicit picture book *Sex*. Some libraries faced massive demonstrations, letter and phone campaigns, and interventions by civic leaders. Nearly all retained the book despite the protests. The anti-*Sex* contingent cited as reasons for not carrying the book its lack of enduring value, poor binding, high price, and self-promotional ballyhoo. The pro-*Sex* contingent denounced censorship and cited as reasons for carrying the book its ranking as a best-seller, public interest, the author's popularity, and a desire to spare patrons the cost of satisfying their curiosity.

Since 1992 the Fairfax County, Virginia, Public Library Board of Trustees has been locked in a disagreement with the Fairfax County Board of Supervisors. At issue is the policy of having free copies of the *Washington Blade,* a gay newspaper, available along with other free information in library lobbies. Responding to complaints from patrons and conservative Christian activists, county supervisors have pressured the library to remove the *Blade* or to restrict access to it. The library board twice voted to retain the newspaper, which, in the interim, moved its sexually explicit personal ads to a separate section not included with library copies. County supervisors threatened to abolish the library board but lacked the authority to do so. More recently, one supervisor proposed prohibiting county employees from participating in any activity that might encourage violation of the state's rarely enforced antisodomy law, which would make those who put the *Blade* in the lobbies subject to being fired. Other efforts focused on encouraging the selection of antigay board members.

Meanwhile, the Fairfax library system purchased 11 titles suggested by Christian activists to balance the over 100 gay books in its collection. These titles offer the conservative Christian perspective that homosexuality can be "cured" or "reformed" through counseling and changes in lifestyle. The Fairfax Lesbian and Gay Citizens Association responded by donating 78 titles to counter the antigay books.

The tensions public libraries face in these and similar debates over the censorship of sexuality materials are likely to increase as the gap grows between religious conservatives who favor censorship to preserve moral values and liberals who favor free speech and open debate.

In the following selections, Martha Cornog criticizes the censors and argues that public libraries have a responsibility to make available informative, if controversial, sexuality materials. James L. Sauer defends censorship as a valuable process through which the morals of society may be preserved.

YES
Martha Cornog

IS SEX SAFE IN YOUR LIBRARY?
HOW TO FIGHT CENSORSHIP

When most of us think of free libraries, we think of free books, even books that have been described as *improper, questionable, controversial, objectionable,* or as exotic, erotic literature—all euphemisms for books about sex. Of the three historical arenas for censorship—sex, religion, and politics—only sex has maintained enough widespread power to evoke the censor as we enter the 21st century. We have laws against sexual expression but not against religious or political expression. Thus, librarians cannot avoid censorship battles about sex, especially at a time when sexual issues saturate the media and sexual problems beset patrons who desperately need information about sexual harassment, AIDS, sex education, abortion, or homosexuality.

Yet library censorship, especially of sexuality materials, has proliferated in the last 25 years. Where is censorship headed? What does it mean for libraries?

Censorship of sexuality and other controversial materials has increased partly because there is so much more to censor. The most visible tension currently centers on gay and lesbian materials. One freedom to read expert who requested anonymity suggested, "homosexuality has replaced communism as the scapegoat for the right of center." Conservative groups are working to pass laws against governmental "promoting" of homosexuality, and librarians in both Colorado and Oregon have reported increased challenges to gay materials even though Colorado's Amendment 2 did pass and Oregon's Measure 9 did not.

However, sharp rises in the incidence of homosexuality-based censorship are not endemic to Colorado and Oregon. Gay books now make up as much as one-third of sex-related library challenges nationwide.

The percentage of libraries reporting challenges on *all* material has more than doubled since 1980—when library surveys indicated 20 percent of those surveyed reporting challenges—to between 40 and 50 percent reporting challenges today. Still, the American Library Association's Office for Intellectual Freedom estimates only *15 percent* of censorship attempts ever reach tabulation.

Access by children and young adults represents a large percentage of the challenges to sexuality materials. This author's analysis of such challenges in both school and public libraries from 1991 to 1993 shows that 70–90 percent of sex-related challenges involved access by younger people. Censorship attempts relating to sex and to "objectionable language" appear to differ in one important way from other attempts: they are more likely to result in removal of books, whether in school or public libraries.

GETTING WORSE BEFORE IT GETS BETTER

Controversy over sex books will get worse before it gets better. "If you can't deal with the fact that these groups are here, then you're in the wrong job," said Dennis Day, director of the Salt Lake City Public Library. To make matters more complex, groups that traditionally support censorship are at odds. At a recent conference of the Association of Christian Librarians, Craighton Hippenhammer reported results of an intellectual freedom survey of Christian college and Bible college librarians. There was, he said, a divergence of opinion, with some supporting censorship and others dead set against it. Though feminists are against sexism, they do not agree on whether censorship is an acceptable means to that end. Two feminist groups, Feminists for Free Expression and Women Against Pornography, oppose each other over censorship of sexuality materials. With many censors, each opposing one another, no consensus emerges, resulting in a lot of confusion and little clear dialog.

For some librarians, censorship cases are, at best, irritants, distractions—annoyances best ignored, pacified, and dealt with quickly and quietly, even in advance with self-imposed censorship—to make way for the "real business" of librarianship. "[Censorship] is not as important as the meat and potatoes of our profession, which is getting people to read," and James Casey, director of the Oak Lawn Public Library, IL. But censors intrinsically oppose the major goal of librarianship by impeding reading and therefore must be taken very seriously. No longer sedate, passive temples, libraries can be vital and exciting places to learn about all sides of controversial issues. Librarians can capitalize on censorship attempts by transforming their libraries into major players in the community, a place of importance in the public mind, a resource for democracy.

POTENT PR

Moreover, controversy can be potent public relations. When the right to read is threatened, supporters come out of the woodwork. Patrons, too. Officials at the Fort Vancouver Public Library, WA, reported that after they added Madonna's Sex in reference, more than 900 people came to see the controversial book for themselves. Many expressed appreciation at being able to see what young people are exposed to.

Most censorship incidents, however, do not elicit the spectacular and daunting tactics used recently by groups to attack Sex and Daddy's Roommate and the libraries that carry them: massive telephone campaigns, bomb threats, and media blitzes. Many complaints can be settled with active listening and civil discussion. Yet the range of tactics and scenarios for which librarians must be prepared has certainly expanded:

- The Downers Grove Public Library, IL, and the Austin Public Library, TX, received notice from their respective state attorney's offices that Madonna's *Sex* might violate laws prohibiting distribution of pornography to minors, and the Casa Grande PL, AZ, received a similar notice from the police about *Truly Tasteless Jokes*. All three libraries immediately restricted the books to those age 18 and over.
- A lobbyist-attorney, retained by the Arizona State Library Association to assist in passing a library exemption to state anti-obscenity laws, faced daily harassment from a local minister who set up a stand outside state buildings and loudly trumpeted the names of all who were expected to vote for the exemption. The exemption bill did not pass.
- In three California high school libraries, vice principals removed *Annie on My Mind* and *All American Boys*, donated by a gay group, and did not return them to the shelves despite repeated requests from librarians.
- In Florida, members of the American Family Association mobilized an extensive campaign against a gay and lesbian film festival held by the Leon County PL, with appeals to the library board, radio exhortations, threatening and obscene telephone calls, and disruptive protesters. The festival had been approved by three separate library board votes.

AIN'T SEEN NOTHIN' YET

Still, in the estimation of one anonymous censorship veteran, librarians haven't seen anything yet. "I believe we'll see in the next few years the same type of tactics used against libraries that were used against abortion clinics." But statistics show that the extremists may be beating their heads against the wall. This author's analysis of 222 sexual censorship cases from 1991 to 1993 in school and public libraries suggests that more extreme tactics do not necessarily result in the removal of books.

While libraries use a variety of formal and informal reconsideration procedures, what *is* associated with removal of books is avoidance of established process—decisions made unilaterally by a library director or administrator. Conversely, retention of sexuality materials seems to be associated with use of a formal process, particularly a "two-tiered" system: review by a reconsideration committee of some type, followed by final decision by an administrator or board.

By smartening up and becoming wiser to the ways of their opponents as well as more media-savvy, libraries across the country are confronting the controversy surrounding censorship issues head on—and winning:

- Downers Grove PL, which had restricted Madonna's *Sex* after notice from the State Attorney's office, later requested a written opinion from that office as to whether or not giving the book to minors violated the state's Harmful Material Act. When the library found out it was within the law, it made *Sex* available to all patrons but added an option to its circulation policy allowing parents to restrict their own children's borrowing privileges.
- In Oak Law, another public library successfully fought two censorship attempts in two years to keep Gershon

Legman's bawdy classic *The Limerick* off its shelves—the first attempt from a school principal, the second from a Catholic organization. The library jump-started its public relations program, hiring a full-time staff member who edited a semimonthly newsletter, wrote columns and press releases for local newspapers, and planned numerous adult and youth programs. Since the newsletter began, library circulation and program participation has risen dramatically.

- The Fort Vancouver PL responded proactively to the Madonna book with an open letter to patrons, explaining reasons for purchase and the freedom to read. Similarly, Carolyn Anthony, director of the Skokie PL, IL, sent a memo to staff providing background information on the book, why it was ordered, and how to defend it against complaints. Both libraries have retained the title....

CONTROVERSY A HEALTHY SIGN

Librarians must be willing to see controversy about sexuality materials as part of the democratic process and as an opportunity to enlarge the library's role in that process. Rather than looking at censorship as confusion among noisy and conflicting demands, the best course may be to view the controversy as a healthy sign of debate and involvement in which the library can provide materials on all sides of the issue. Controversy can be used to facilitate the mission of the library.

So when the library announces loudly that, yes, we have *Sex*, and *Daddy's Roommate*, and dictionaries with dirty words, and *Playboy*, and *Changing Bodies, Changing Lives*—and books about sex from religious, feminist, and minority viewpoints as well—then patrons and readers can only increase, because people need to become informed about sexuality to make their own decisions about sexual issues. Libraries can use censorship to encourage people to read, and they must take the risks that come with the controversy. If they do not, the library dwindles in books and in influence, to a small, sanitized, and quite trivial retreat from reality.

NO

James L. Sauer

IN DEFENSE OF CENSORSHIP

The "great debate" of civil life is really about control of various "pulpits."
Parenthood is a pulpit, as is a Newspaper. Schools are pulpits. The church
is an obvious pulpit. A public library is a pulpit. Television is an ubiquitous
pulpit. And the Presidency is a bully pulpit.

The current conflict is really about who shall control these "pulpits." It is a
battle of power and control over the soul of society. The issue has two facets.
First, who shall be included on a given pulpit—who shall have the right to
rule in the family; to pontificate in the schools; to choose books in the public
library. It is the power of the pulpit committee; it is the function of selection.
And second, who shall be excluded from speaking. This power deals with the
limitation of debate. It exercises suppressive powers, and is best known by
the label of censorship. The selective and censorial functions in our society are
under the power of the knowledge professions: teachers, librarians, media
powers, psychologists, and talk show hosts. Ideas and actions are advocated;
other world views are denigrated. It is a commonplace notion of modern life
that censorship is an evil. As Joel Belz has pointed out, "Our society fervently
rejects censorship as a bad thing. No one doing a word search of the last 1,000
uses of 'censorship' in the major media is likely to find a single case where
reference is positive. We just tend to assume that censorship is wrong."

I do not make that assumption. Censorship is a natural part of the communication process by which we include and exclude information from life's
great debate. To act is to select; to choose is to censor. Only certain modes of
censorship are inherently wrong; those modes which attempt to control the
pulpits of others by deceit and force—which cross governmental lines and
abrogate the order of God's creation for family, society, and state. Selection
has its proper role, censorship its rightful limit.

As the devouring statism of our century grows in power and control, we
seem to be losing any sense of when selection and censorship are just or
unjust. Censorship is attacked in order to advance vice; and selection rights
are asserted in order to repress virtue. We have lost Edmund Burke's notion
of a "liberty connected with order: that not only exists along with order and
virtue, but which cannot exist at all without them."

From James L. Sauer, "In Defense of Censorship," *The Christian Librarian* (February 1993).
Copyright © 1993 by James L. Sauer. Reprinted by permission.

It may startle practitioners of professional information services to know that librarians, editors, publishers, news men, and teachers, are the chief censors of our society. They select ideas—they funnel and shape the terms of contemporary life. Not only do they select what shall be discussed and censor what shall not be seen, but they do so, usually, without the consent of the communities they serve. The citizen's group which boycotts a movie theatre showing the Last Temptation of Christ is far less of a censor than the librarian who excludes popular religious titles from the public library collection. The citizen's group is expressing a consumer's choice; the librarian is ignoring a community's values.

DEFINING THE C WORD

Perhaps the first thing we must do is to eliminate the largely negative view we hold of the word "censorship." We approach this label in a biased manner. Censorship has had a number of emotionally neutral meanings throughout history which we might well remember.

In Roman society, the censor was one who acted as an inspector of public morals. The censor was a protector of civil, social, and religious order. The censors were also census takers and property assessors. They also had the power to tax, which as we know in our day, is the power to destroy.

In modern life, a censor is any official who examines publications for objectionable material. For example, an editor or library book reviewer is such a figure; as is a policeman on the vice squad. It is a secondary question as to what they are finding objectionable.

A censor also monitors forbidden communication. Such censorship was a common task during the last two world wars when the correspondence of soldiers was monitored to preserve security. Such censorship is practiced in totalitarian lands during times of peace.

Finally, self censorship is a psychological mechanism that represses unacceptable notions before they reach fruition. Before we dismiss this psychological notion, it is wise to realize that such censorship is practiced by every human mind. It is an absolute necessity. We cannot survive psychologically without repressing anti-social thoughts and acts. And by analogy, if we must suppress violence and a wanton libido in our own minds and actions, does it not give some credence to the notion of suppressing such evils in the body politic.

WHERE DO OUR RIGHTS COME FROM?

It is a common presupposition of the information masters that we have an absolute right to full self-expression and unfettered freedom of speech and press, and that no one has the right to restrict this. Though professing relativistic ignorance of all other moral values, the modernist is absolutely sure of one thing: censorship is wrong.

But where does this absolute right of expression come from? There are in fact only three possible sources: God, nature, or society.

First, if God is the author of our rights, and specifically, our right to self-expression then it should be revealed in Scripture and Christian tradition. But in fact it is not so revealed. Instead, we find two opposite principles: the suppression of evil and the encouragement of virtue. Suppression of evil ideas, words, and actions is a central focus of Scripture.

From the Ten Commandments to the holy prophets, to Christ's extension of morality to our thought life, you have in the Biblical worldview full liberty to do good, but you do not have a concomitant right to sin.

Second, it is futile to look to nature as the source of rights. Nature can be viewed in two ways: as an expression of a divine will (Providence) or as a unwilled expression of chance relationships (evolution). If we look to providential nature (the nature's God of our founding fathers), we are turned back to the Judeo-Christian tradition. Natural law and reason are seen in service to a revealed order; a gentlemen's religion, a kind of moralistic deism. If we look to evolutionary nature we wind up with rights in process, not fixed rights at all. Instead, we find notions of efficiency, power, and biological fitness. One does not have rights in nature, one merely survives.

Third, if society grants us our rights by the social contract, then those rights exist in two patterns. First, we find legal rights in a static pattern as expressed, for instance, in our Constitution. This pattern involves relatively fixed, nonarbitrary law structures, and can only be altered by changing the law. Without a moral order behind these constitutional rights, we find that such rights have no absolute nature. Amendments can be made to add to or take away from our rights. This makes such rights in actuality privileges. When we speak of rights, we mean provisional rights; when we speak of unalienable rights, we mean God-given rights.

The second pattern is through evolutionary, sociological law. This pattern suggests that our rights evolve, that science, public opinion, and changing mores alter the meaning of law. Hence, the so called "right of privacy" discovered by our Supreme Court in 1973. Rights can appear and disappear almost overnight using "sociological law." The notion of an evolving synthetic law system is present in the Marxist worldview. A right defined in such a society changes colors with the seasons.

A right to free speech, therefore, in so far as it exists, must have its foundation in the Judeo-Christian tradition. It cannot be separated from that tradition's view of moral order. Separate from that tradition, it is but an idea which evolves with nature and society.

CENSORSHIP IN SOCIETY

If we do not have a right to full self-expression—since such a right can only spring absolutely from God—then by what criteria can self-expression and freedom of speech be reasonably curtailed? Up until the last century in the West, the following restrictions on the right of free speech were considered natural and self-evident.

1. The Suppression of Evil, especially pornography. Every good society will desire to repress anti-social acts which demean life and human sexuality. The censorship of pornography is necessary not because we are repelled by it, but because we are overwhelmingly attracted to it. Pornography is anti-woman and anti-child. Destructive to familial happiness, it feeds a fantasy world of mechanical sex and abusive domination. No one who truly understands masculine psychology or who has read the terrible acts described in a book like *Pornography's Victims* can believe that pornography is harmless.

2. Suppression of Slander and Libel. No just society willingly condones lies, especially harmful lies told about its citizens.

3. Suppression of Acts of Symbolic Desecration. No one should have a right to paint swastikas on synagogues, to defecate on the Bible, or to burn a flag.

4. Suppression of Anti-Social Acts. It is a general truism accepted by most human beings that your neighbor does not have the right to shout at the top of his lungs into your ear. It is a cliche of law that no one has the right to scream fire in a crowded theatre. Flashers do not have the right to "express" themselves in public.

5. Suppression of National Secrets. Certainly, this last area is liable to abuse. We can all imagine a Pentagon official classifying laundry lists as top secret; or a politician hiding his crimes behind national security. Nevertheless, any society which wishes to preserve itself from its enemies must censor information needed for its existence.

WHO SHOULD CENSOR?

All the spheres of life are governed. Without these governments civil life could not function. Proper censorship involves the suppressive function at its appropriate level. Where then does censorship begin and who should act as censor?

1. Censorship begins with the individual. Self censorship is the psychological repression of interior evil and the resisting of exterior temptation. Turning off the television, for instance, is an act of self censorship. Some older people have the habit of turning down their hearing aids—one of the benefits of old age.

2. Family censorship involves repressing evils in this fundamental institution. For example, you might not merely turn the TV off, you might actually throw the one-eyed god out. Familial censorship is also illustrated in parental control of children's reading. One of the contributing factors in the dissolution of the modern family has been our inability to control the invasion of destructive values into our homes.

3. Specific communities also exercise censorship in their own narrow areas of control. For instance, we have churches defining the doctrinal material found in their church libraries. Organizations, businesses, and civic groups set guidelines for the values expressed in their publications. The local peace group logically offers only pacifist materials from its book table. Academic libraries define for themselves what is and what is not scholarly material.

4. Censorship takes place in the general community. Public libraries develop their own ordering and discarding policies. Such policies may be set by local governments, library boards, librarians, or citizens. What librarians often deplore as censorship is when someone besides the "professionals" want to have a say in establishing selection policies. It is a battle for control of the "pulpit committee."

5. State officials sometimes censor by setting guidelines and restrictions on the use of tax money. As a purchaser and provider of services, shouldn't the elected officials of a state have a say in how the tax dollars are to be used? If they say that "x" dollars

can be used for purchasing a certain type of material, and "y" dollars cannot be used to further a particular partisan worldview, is this not a just use of state money, which is to say, taxpayer's money?

6. The federal government's situation is exactly like that of the state's. It is perfectly proper for the federal government to use its censorship power by determining the nature of the art it is going to purchase. Most citizens do not believe that a crucifix submerged in urine is creativity worthy of civic support. Mr. Maplethorpe, and other so called artists, can take any number of pictures of men with objects thrust into their anal cavities but that is no reason why the people should be forced to pay for these unique acts of "self expression." Censorship and selection, like the freedom of speech itself, have their natural limits. The citizen properly uses his suppressive powers through his exercise of speech, freedom of press, letter writing, and voting. He acts in community through petitions, pickets, and boycotts. And he acts collectively in the state through the ultimate sanctions of fines, the seizing of materials, and arrests. All is done according to the moral framework of Western society and by the rule of law.

JUST CENSORSHIP

When the *Information Class Tribune* of the ACLU hysterically tells us that "If we let them ban *Teen Slut* today, they'll be burning the Mona Lisa tomorrow," we can be assured that we are not dealing with reason but with an absolutist ideology. Our society banned pornography until the last 40 years; and the people produced in those earlier decades were more virtuous, more chaste, more honest, more cultured, and more literate than the current masses. It was a Catholic culture that produced the Mona Lisa. It was a Reformed Protestant culture that produced the Miltonic defense of free speech found in the Areopagitica. Only a society which censors *Teen Slut* will preserve a world in which the Mona Lisa is valued; only a nation which suppresses evil will conserve a world in which the Miltonic freedom of thought can have any meaning. In a sense, the censorship issue bears a close resemblance to the just war theory debate. Just as militarists believe that war is always good and pacifists believe that war is always bad, so we find similar extremes in the censorship controversy. The totalitarian believes that everything should come under the scrutiny of the new order; the anti-censorship activist believes that nothing—no matter how vile, destructive or crude—should be suppressed. And just as the just war theory seeks to develop some rational and accepted moral framework to limit the evils of war, so a just censorship view attempts to curb the evils of unfettered expression and totalitarian thought control by defining the limits of liberty. The object sought is the golden mean. The aim is freedom in a civil, social, and humane society. As the writer of Ecclesiastes says, "There is a time to be silent, and a time to speak." Proper selection allows each of us to speak in his sphere. Proper censorship defines when it is time to be silent.

POSTSCRIPT

Should Public Libraries Provide Sexuality Materials?

The role of the library as a repository for sexuality materials dates back to the early 1880s and the "Enfer" or "Hell" collection of the National Library in Paris. This library was unique in listing its erotic holdings in its printed catalog. Among English-speaking countries, the earliest erotic collection is the "Private Case" in the British Museum Library. The catalog of books in this collection was tightly guarded. Censorship, restricted circulation, and book burning served the Victorian notion that silence was the best way to deal with sexuality. American public libraries commonly took their role as guardians of social morals quite seriously, refusing to put certain books on their shelves.

In 1910 a growing concern in the United States about good health prompted the American Medical Association and the Society of Sanitary and Moral Prophylaxis to support libraries' circulating a few approved books on sexual education and health. While most libraries did buy books of "physiological information," they usually restricted the books' circulation.

When sexologist Alfred Kinsey and his colleagues published *Sexual Behavior in the Human Male* in 1948 and *Sexual Behavior in the Human Female* in 1953, many libraries restricted their circulation to physicians and psychologists.

From the birth of public libraries to the present, sexuality materials have posed a problem. In the past, the emphasis on censorship favored the library's role as guardian of society's morality. More recently this has shifted to favoring the individual's right to read whatever he or she chooses, as expressed in the American Library Association's *Intellectual Freedom Manual*.

SUGGESTED READINGS

American Library Association, *Intellectual Freedom Manual*, 4th ed. (American Library Association, 1992).

S. C. Brubaker, "In Praise of Censorship," *The Public Interest* (Winter 1994).

M. Cornog, ed., *Libraries, Erotica, and Pornography* (Oryx Press, 1991).

M. Cornog and T. Perper, *For Sex Education, See Librarian: A Guide to Issues and Resources* (Greenwood Press, 1996).

D. F. Ring, "Defending the Intended Mission," *Public Libraries* (July–August 1994).

M. Stover, "Libraries, Censorship, and Social Protest," *American Libraries* (November 1994).

ISSUE 8

Should Contractual Sex Be Legal?

YES: James Bovard, from "Safeguard Public Health: Legalize Contractual Sex," *Insight on the News* (February 27, 1995)

NO: Anastasia Volkonsky, from "Legalizing the 'Profession' Would Sanction the Abuse," *Insight on the News* (February 27, 1995)

ISSUE SUMMARY

YES: Author James Bovard asserts that legalizing sex work would help stem the spread of AIDS and free up the police to focus on controlling violent crime.

NO: Anastasia Volkonsky, founding director of PROMISE, an organization dedicated to combating sexual exploitation, maintains that decriminalizing prostitution would only cause social harm, particularly to women.

In maintaining prostitution's criminal status, the United States has ignored two alternatives adopted by many other countries: legalization and decriminalization.

Prior to the Civil War, prostitution was tolerated in America to a limited extent, even though it was socially frowned upon. Few states had specific laws making prostitution a crime. After the Civil War, however, some states passed laws to segregate and license prostitutes operating in "red light districts." In 1910 Congress tried to eliminate the importation of young women from Asia and South America for purposes of prostitution by passing the Mann Act, which prohibited any male from accompanying a female across a state border for the purpose of prostitution, debauchery, or any other immoral purpose. During World War I concern for the morals and health of U.S. soldiers led the U.S. surgeon general to close down all houses of prostitution near military training camps, especially the famous whorehouses of the French Quarter and Storyville, New Orleans. By 1925 every state had enacted an antiprostitution law.

The effectiveness and the social and economic costs of criminalizing prostitution have been continually questioned. The sexual revolution and the women's movement have added new controversies to the debate. Some advocates of women's rights and equality condemn prostitution as male exploitation of women and their bodies. Others champion the rights of women to control their own bodies, including the right to exchange sexual favors for money. This new attitude is reflected in the term *sex worker*, which has recently begun to replace *prostitute*. New social problems confuse the issue further: the growing concern over drug abuse, the risk of human immunodeficiency virus (HIV) infection among street prostitutes, and the exploitation of teenage girls and boys.

European countries have taken different approaches to prostitution. In Germany, where prostitution is legal and regulated, there are efficient and convenient drive-in motels—often owned and run by women—where customers can arrange a pleasant, safe encounter with a sex worker. Italy and France, longtime bastions of regulated prostitution, have abandoned this approach because of organized efforts of women to abolish it and evidence that other approaches to prostitution could reduce the spread of venereal disease more effectively than legalization and regulation. Since 1959 solicitation on the streets of Great Britain has been a crime, but prostitution per se is no longer against the law. The British authorities have concluded that prostitution cannot be controlled simply by making it a crime. However, they do have laws prohibiting sex workers from advertising their services by posting their business cards in public phone booths. After the collapse of the Soviet Union, sex work in Russia and abroad became an acceptable career choice for many young women.

There are a number of ways in which lawmakers could deal with the "world's oldest profession":

- Outlaw prostitution and throw valuable resources into a legal campaign to eliminate it entirely.
- Outlaw some behavior associated with prostitution, such as street solicitation or loitering, but this can raise difficult distinctions. When, for instance, does casual flirtation and overt come-ons to a stranger become illegal solicitation?
- Legalize sex work and control it by licensing "body work therapists," requiring regular medical checkups, and setting aside specific areas where sex workers can ply their trade.
- Decriminalize all sexual activities between consenting adults, whether or not money changes hands. Advertising and solicitation could be limited by social propriety, and minors could be protected against recruitment and exploitation by the laws regulating age of consent and child abuse that are already in effect.

In the following selections, James Bovard advocates legalizing sex work to help stem the spread of AIDS and to allow police to focus their time and energy on violent crimes. Anastasia Volkonsky argues that decriminalizing sex work would hurt society in general and allow males to continue exploiting women, particularly those who are poor and vulnerable.

YES

James Bovard

SAFEGUARD PUBLIC HEALTH: LEGALIZE CONTRACTUAL SEX

The call to legalize prostitution once again is becoming a hot issue. Columnists have been complaining about the conviction of Heidi Fleiss, the "Hollywood madam," saying it is unfair that the law punishes her but not her clients. San Francisco has appointed a task force to analyze the issue of legalizing prostitution. (A similar task force in Atlanta recommended legalization in 1986, but the city has not changed its policies.)

As more people fear the spread of AIDS, the legalization of prostitution offers one of the easiest means of limiting the spread of the disease and of improving the quality of law enforcement in this country.

Prostitution long has been illegal in all but one state. Unfortunately, laws against it often bring out the worse among the nation's law-enforcement agencies. Since neither prostitutes nor their customers routinely run to the police to complain about the other's conduct, police rely on trickery and deceit to arrest people.

In 1983, for example, police in Albuquerque, N.M., placed a classified advertisement in a local paper for men to work as paid escorts—and then arrested 50 men who responded for violating laws against prostitution. In 1985, Honolulu police paid private citizens to pick up prostitutes in their cars, have sex with them and then drive them to nearby police cars for arrest. (One convicted prostitute's lawyer complained: "You can now serve your community by fornicating. Once the word gets out there will be no shortage of volunteers.") In San Francisco, the police have wired rooms in the city's leading hotels to make videotapes of prostitutes servicing their customers. But given the minimal control over the videotaping operation, there was little to stop local police from watching and videotaping other hotel guests in bed.

Many prostitution-related entrapment operations make doubtful contributions to preserving public safety. In 1985, eight Fairfax County, Va., police officers rented two $88-a-night Holiday Inn rooms, purchased an ample supply of liquor and then phoned across the Potomac River to Washington to hire a professional stripper for a bachelor party. The stripper came, stripped and was busted for indecent exposure. She faced fines of up to $1,000 and 12 months in jail. Fairfax County police justified the sting operation by claiming it was necessary to fight prostitution. But the department had made only 11 arrests on prostitution charges in the previous year—all with similar sting operations.

In 1992, police in Des Moines, Wash., hired a convicted rapist to have sex with masseuses. The local police explained that they hired the felon after plainclothes police officers could not persuade women at the local Body Care Center to have intercourse. Martin Pratt, police chief in the Seattle suburb, claimed that the ex-rapist was uniquely qualified for the job and, when asked why the police instructed the felon to consummate the acts with the alleged prostitutes, Pratt explained that stopping short "wouldn't have been appropriate."

A New York sting operation [in 1994] indirectly could have helped out the New York Mets: Two San Diego Padres baseball players were arrested after speaking to a female undercover officer. A Seattle journalist who also was busted described the police procedure to *Newsday*: "He said that he was stuck in traffic when he discovered that a miniskirted woman in a low-cut blouse was causing the jam, approaching the cars that were stopped. 'She came up to the windows, kind of swaggering,' he said. He said that she offered him sex, he made a suggestive reply, and the next thing he knew he was surrounded by police officers who dragged him out of his car and arrested him."

Many police appear to prefer chasing naked women than pursuing dangerous felons. As Lt. Bill Young of the Las Vegas Metro Police told Canada's *Vancouver Sun*, "You get up in a penthouse at Caesar's Palace with six naked women frolicking in the room and then say: 'Hey,

baby, you're busted!' That's fun." (Las Vegas arrests between 300 to 400 prostitutes a month.) In August 1993, Charles County, Md., police were embarrassed by reports that an undercover officer visiting a strip joint had had intercourse while receiving a "personal lap dance."

In some cities, laws against prostitution are transforming local police officers into de facto car thieves. Female officers masquerade as prostitutes; when a customer stops to negotiate, other police rush out and confiscate the person's car under local asset-forfeiture laws. Such programs are operating in Detroit, Washington, New York and Portland, Ore. The female officers who masquerade as prostitutes are, in some ways, worse than the prostitutes—since, at least, the hookers will exchange services for payment, while the police simply intend to shake down would-be customers.

Shortly after the Washington police began their car-grabbing program in 1992, one driver sped off after a plainclothes officer tried to force his way into the car after the driver spoke to an undercover female officer. One officer's foot was slightly injured, and police fired six shots into the rear of the car. The police volley could have killed two or three people—but apparently the Washington police consider the possibility of killing citizens a small price to pay for slightly and temporarily decreasing the rate of prostitution in one selected neighborhood.

The same tired, failed antiprostitution tactics tend to be repeated ad nauseam around the country. Aurora, Colo., recently announced plans to buy newspaper ads showing pictures of accused johns. The plan hit a rough spot when the *Denver Post* refused to publish the ads, choosing not to be an arm of the criminal-justice system. One Aurora councilman told local radio host Mike Rosen that the city wanted to publish the pictures of the accused (and not wait until after convictions) because some of them might be found not guilty "because of some legal technicality."

In recent years, the Washington police force has tried one trick after another to suppress prostitution—including passing out tens of thousands of tickets to drivers for making right turns onto selected streets known to be venues of solicitation. (Didn't they see the tiny print on the street sign saying that right turns are illegal between 5 p.m. and 2 a.m.?) Yet, at the same time, the murder rate in Washington has skyrocketed and the city's arrest and conviction rates for murders have fallen by more than 50 percent.

The futile fight against prostitution is a major drain on local law-enforcement resources. A study published in the *Hastings Law Journal* in 1987 is perhaps the most reliable estimate of the cost to major cities. Author Julie Pearl observed: "This study focuses on sixteen of the nation's largest cities, in which only 28 percent of reported violent crimes result in arrest. On average, police in these cities made as many arrests for prostitution as for all violent offenses.

Last year, police in Boston, Cleveland, and Houston arrested twice as many people for prostitution as they did for all homicides, rapes, robberies, and assaults combined, while perpetrators evaded arrest for 90 percent of these violent crimes. Cleveland officers spent eighteen hours —the equivalent of two workdays—on prostitution duty for every violent offense failing to yield an arrest." The average cost per bust was almost $2,000 and "the average big-city police department spent 213 man-hours a day enforcing prostitution laws." Pearl estimated that 16 large American cities spent more than $120 million to suppress prostitution in 1985. In 1993, one Los Angeles official estimated that prostitution enforcement was costing the city more than $100 million a year.

Locking up prostitutes and their customers is especially irrational at a time when more than 35 states are under court orders to reduce prison overcrowding. Gerald Arenberg, executive director of the National Association of the Chiefs of Police, has come out in favor of legalizing prostitution. Dennis Martin, president of the same association, declared that prostitution law enforcement is "much too time-consuming, and police forces are short-staffed." Maryland Judge Darryl Russell observed: "We have to explore other alternatives to solving this problem because this eats up a lot of manpower of the police. We're just putting out brush fires while the forest is blazing." National surveys have shown that 94 percent of citizens believe that police do not respond quickly enough to calls for help, and the endless pursuit of prostitution is one factor that slows down many police departments from responding to other crimes.

Another good reason for reforming prostitution laws is to safeguard public health: Regulated prostitutes tend to be cleaner prostitutes. HIV-infection rates tend to be stratospheric among the nation's streetwalkers. In Newark, 57 percent of prostitutes were found to be HIV positive, according to a *Congressional Quarterly* report. In New York City, 35 percent of prostitutes were HIV-positive; in Washington, almost half.

In contrast, brothels, which are legal in 12 rural Nevada counties, tend to be comparative paragons of public safety. The University of California at Berkeley School of Public Health studied the health of legal Nevada brothel workers compared with that of jailed Nevada streetwalkers. None of the brothel workers had AIDS, while 6 percent of the unregulated streetwalkers did. Brothel owners had a strong incentive to police the health of their employees, since they could face liability if an infection were passed to a customer.

Prostitution is legal in several countries in Western Europe. In Hamburg, Germany, which some believe has a model program of legalized prostitution, streetwalkers are sanctioned in certain well-defined areas and prostitutes must undergo frequent health checks. Women with contagious diseases are strictly prohibited from plying their trade. (While some consider Amsterdam a model for legalization, the system there actually has serious problems. A spokesman for the association of Dutch brothels recently told the Associated Press: "The prostitutes these days are not so professional any more. In the past, prostitutes had more skills and they offered better services. Most of them now work only one or two evenings per week, and that's not enough time for them to become good.")

Bans on prostitution actually generate public disorder—streetwalkers, police chases, pervasive disrespect for the law and condoms littering lawns. As long as people have both money and sexual frustration, some will continue paying others to gratify their desires. The issue is not whether prostitution is immoral, but whether police suppression of prostitution will make society a safer place. The ultimate question to ask about a crackdown on prostitution is: How many murders are occurring while police are chasing after people who only want to spend a few bucks for pleasure?

In 1858, San Francisco Police Chief Martin Burke complained: "It is impossible to suppress prostitution altogether, yet it can, and ought to be regulated so as to limit the injury done to society, as much as possible." Vices are not crimes. Despite centuries of attempts to suppress prostitution, the profession continues to flourish. Simply because prostitution may be immoral is no reason for police to waste their time in a futile effort to suppress the oldest profession.

NO
Anastasia Volkonsky

LEGALIZING THE 'PROFESSION' WOULD SANCTION THE ABUSE

Prostitution commonly is referred to as "the world's oldest profession." It's an emblematic statement about the status of women, for whom being sexually available and submissive to men is the oldest form of survival.

As the "world's oldest," prostitution is presented as an accepted fact of history, something that will always be with us that we cannot eradicate. As a "profession," selling access to one's body is being promoted as a viable choice for women. In an era in which the human-rights movement is taking on some of history's most deeply rooted oppressions and an era in which women have made unprecedented strides in politics and the professions, this soft-selling of prostitution is especially intolerable.

Calls for legalization and decriminalization of prostitution put forth by civil libertarians are not forward-thinking reforms. They represent acceptance and normalization of the traffic in human beings. Moreover, the civil-libertarian portrayal of the prostitute as a sexually free, consenting adult hides the vast network of traffickers, organized-crime syndicates, pimps, procurers and brothel keepers, as well as the customer demand that ultimately controls the trade.

In studies replicated in major cities throughout the United States, the conditions of this "profession" are revealed to be extreme sexual, physical and psychological abuse. Approximately 70 percent of prostitutes are raped repeatedly by their customers—an average of 31 times per year, according to a study in a 1993 issue of the *Cardozo Women's Law Journal*. In addition, 65 percent are physically assaulted repeatedly by customers and more by pimps. A majority (65 percent and higher) are drug addicts. Increasingly, prostituted women are HIV positive. Survivors testify to severe violence, torture and attempted murders. The mortality rate for prostitutes, according to Justice Department statistics from 1982, is 40 times the national average.

What can be said of a "profession" with such a job description? How can it be said that women freely choose sexual assault, harassment, abuse and the risk of death as a profession? Such a term might be appealing for women who are trapped in the life, as a last-ditch effort to regain some self-respect and identify with the promises of excitement and glamor that may have lured them into prostitution in the first place. A substantial portion of street-walkers are homeless or living below the poverty line. Even most women who work in outcall or escort services have no control over their income because they are at the mercy of a pimp or pusher. Most will leave prostitution without savings.

Prostitution is not a profession selected from among other options by today's career women. It comes as no surprise that the ranks of prostitutes both in the United States and globally are filled with society's most vulnerable members, those least able to resist recruitment. They are those most displaced and disadvantaged in the job market: women, especially the poor; the working class; racial and ethnic minorities; mothers with young children to support; battered women fleeing abuse; refugees; and illegal immigrants. Women are brought to the United States from Asia and Eastern Europe for prostitution. In a foreign country, with no contacts or language skills and fearing arrest or deportation, they are at the mercy of pimps and crime syndicates.

Most tellingly, the largest group of recruits to prostitution are children. The average age of entry into prostitution in the United States is approximately 14, sociologists Mimi Silbert and Ayala Pines found in a study performed for the Delancey Foundation in San Francisco. More than 65 percent of these child prostitutes are runaways. Most have experienced a major trauma: incest, domestic violence, rape or parental abandonment. At an age widely considered too young to handle activities such as voting, drinking alcohol, driving or holding down a job, these children survive by selling their bodies to strangers. These formative years will leave them with deep scars—should they survive to adulthood.

* * *

Sensing this contradiction between the reality of prostitution and the rhetoric of sexual freedom and consensual crime, some proposals to decriminalize prostitution attempt to draw a distinction between "forced" prostitution and "free" prostitution. A June 1993 *Time* article about the international sex industry notes that "faced with the difficulty of sorting out which women are prostitutes by choice and which are coerced, many officials shrug off the problem," implying that when one enters prostitution, it is a free choice. The distinction between force and freedom ends in assigning blame to an already victimized woman for "choosing" to accept prostitution in her circumstances.

"People take acceptance of the money as her consent to be violated," says Susan Hunter, executive director of the Council for Prostitution Alternatives, a Portland, Ore.-based social-service agency that has helped hundreds of women from around the country recover from the effects of prostitution. She likens prostituted women to battered women. When battered women live with their batterer or repeatedly go back to the batterer, we do not take this as a legal consent to battering. A woman's acceptance of money in prostitution should not be taken as her agreement to prostitution. She may take the money because she must survive, because it is the only recompense she will get for the harm that has been done to her and because she has been socialized to believe that this is her role in life. Just as battered women's actions now are understood in light of the effects of trauma and battered woman syndrome, prostituted women suffer psychologically in the aftermath of repeated physical and sexual assaults.

To make an informed choice about prostitution, says Hunter, women need to recover their safety, sobriety and self-esteem and learn about their options. The women in her program leave prostitution, she asserts, "not because we offer them high salaries, but because we offer them hope.... Woman are not voluntarily returning to prostitution."

Proponents of a "consensual crime" approach hold that the dangers associated with prostitution are a result of its illegality. Legal prostitution will be safe, clean and professional, they argue; the related crimes will disappear.

Yet wherever there is regulated prostitution, it is matched by a flourishing black market. Despite the fact that prostitution is legal in 12 Nevada counties, prostitutes continue to work illegally in casinos to avoid the isolation and control of the legal brothels. Even the legal brothels maintain a business link with the illegal pimping circuit by paying a finder's fee to pimps for bringing in new women.

Ironically, legalization, which frequently is touted as an alternative to spending money on police vice squads, creates its own set of regulations to be monitored. To get prostitutes and pimps to comply with licensing rules, the penalties must be heightened and policing increased—adding to law-enforcement costs.

Behind the facade of a regulated industry, brothel prostitutes in Nevada are captive in conditions analogous to slavery. Women often are procured for the brothels from other areas by pimps who dump them at the house in order to collect the referral fee. Women report working in shifts commonly as long as 12 hours, even when ill, menstruating or pregnant, with no right to refuse a customer who has requested them or to refuse the sexual act for which he has paid. The dozen or so prostitutes I interviewed said they are expected to pay the brothel room and board and a percentage of their earnings —sometimes up to 50 percent. They also must pay for mandatory extras such as medical exams, assigned clothing and fines incurred for breaking house rules. And, contrary to the common claim that the brothel will protect women from the dangerous, crazy clients on the streets, rapes and assaults by customers are covered up by the management.

Local ordinances of questionable constitutionality restrict the women's activities even outside the brothel. They may be confined to certain sections of town and permitted out only on certain days, according to Barbara Hobson, author of *Uneasy Virtue*. Ordinances require that brothels must be located in uninhabited areas at least five miles from any city, town, mobile-home park or residential area. Physically isolated in remote areas, their behavior monitored by brothel managers, without ties to the community and with little money or resources of their own, the Nevada prostitutes often are virtual prisoners. Local legal codes describe the woman as "inmates."

Merely decriminalizing prostitution would not remove its stigma and liberate women in the trade. Rather, the fiction that prostitution is freely chosen would become encoded into the law's approach to prostitution. Decriminalization would render prostitution an invisible crime without a name. "The exchange of money [in prostitution] somehow makes the crime of rape invisible" to society, says Hunter.

Amy Fries, director of the National Organization For Women's International Women's Rights Task Force, speaks from experience in studying and combating the sex trade both internationally and in the Washington area. Decriminalization, she says, does not address the market forces at work in prostitution: "[Prostitution] is based on supply and demand. As the demand goes way up, [the pimps] have to meet it with a supply by bringing in more girls."

Ultimately, changing the laws will benefit the customer, not the prostitute. Legalization advocates identify the arrest as the most obvious example of the abuse of prostitutes. But, surprisingly, former prostitutes and prostitutes' advocates say the threat of jail is not a top concern. Considering the absence of any other refuge or shelter, jail provides a temporary safe haven, at the very least providing a bunk, a square meal and a brief respite from johns, pimps and drugs. This is not to make light of abuses of state and police power or the seriousness of jail—the fact that for many women jail is an improvement speaks volumes about their lives on the streets.

It is the customers who have the most to lose from arrest, who fear jail, the stigma of the arrest record and the loss of their anonymity. The argument that prostitution laws invade the privacy of consenting adults is geared toward protecting customers. Prostitutes, working on the streets or in brothels controlled by pimps, have little to no privacy. Furthermore, decriminalization of prostitution is a gateway to decriminalizing pandering, pimping and patronizing—together, decriminalizing many forms of sexual and economic exploitation of women. A 1986 proposal advocated by the New York Bar Association included repeal of such associated laws and the lowering of the age of consent for "voluntary" prostitution. Despite the assertion that prostitutes actively support decriminalization, many women who have escaped prostitution testify that their pimps coerced them into signing such petitions.

Of the many interests contributing to the power of the sex industry—the pimps, the panderers and the patrons— the acts of individual prostitutes are the least influential. Yet, unfortunately, there are incentives for law enforcement to target prostitutes for arrest, rather than aggressively enforcing laws against pimps, johns and traffickers. It is quicker and less costly to round up the women than to pursue pimps and traffickers in elaborate sting operations. The prostitutes are relatively powerless to fight arrest; it is the pimps and johns who can afford private attorneys. And, sadly, it is easier to get a public outcry and convictions against prostitutes, who are marginalized women, than against the wealthier males who are the majority of pimps and johns.

Prostitution is big business. Right now, economics provide an incentive for procuring and pimping women. In all the debates about prostitution, the factor most ignored is the demand. But it is the customers—who have jobs, money, status in the community, clean arrest records and anonymity—who have the most to lose. New legal reforms are beginning to recognize that. An increasing number of communities across the country, from Portland to Baltimore, are adopting car-seizure laws, which allow police to impound the automobiles of those who drive around soliciting prostitutes. This approach recognizes that johns degrade not only women who are prostitutes, but also others by assuming that any females in a given area are for sale. Other towns have instituted, legally or as community efforts, measures designed to publicize and shame would-be johns by publishing their names or pictures and stepping up arrests.

Globally, a pending U.N. Convention Against All Forms of Sexual Exploitation would address the modern forms of prostitution with mechanisms that target pimps and johns and that hold governments accountable for their policies.

Hunter supports the use of civil as well as criminal sanctions against johns, modeled after sexual harassment lawsuits. "People will change their behavior because of economics," she points out, using recent changes in governmental and corporate policy toward sexual harassment as an example of how the fear of lawsuits and financial loss can create social change.

At the heart of the matter, prostitution is buying the right to use a woman's body. The "profession" of prostitution means bearing the infliction of repeated, unwanted sexual acts in order to keep one's "job." It is forced sex as a condition of employment, the very definition of rape and sexual harassment. Cecilie Hoigard and Liv Finstad, who authored the 1992 book *Backstreets*, chronicling 15 years of research on prostitution survivors, stress that it is not any individual act, but the buildup of sexual and emotional violation as a daily occurrence, that determines the trauma of prostitution.

Cleaning up the surrounding conditions won't mask the ugliness of a trade in human beings.

POSTSCRIPT

Should Contractual Sex Be Legal?

Some years ago, a United Nations study team came up with a sophisticated list of arguments for and against the treatment of prostitution as a crime. Among the reasons the team listed for continuing to treat prostitution as a criminal offense punishable by fines and imprisonment were (1) It is the responsibility of the government to regulate public morals in the interest of the public good and, therefore, to declare prostitution a punishable offense; (2) If prostitution per se is not made a punishable offense, the abolition of the regulation of prostitution will merely replace controlled prostitution with clandestine prostitution; (3) It will be difficult to enforce strictly legal provisions proscribing the exploitation of the prostitution of others when prostitution itself is not considered a punishable offense; and (4) Many women and girls on the borderline may be encouraged to take up prostitution if the law does not proscribe such a calling.

Among the study team's arguments in favor of decriminalizing contractual sex between consenting adults were (1) To make prostitution a crime requires defining this activity; (2) Laws against prostitution, even when written to include both parties, in practice penalize only one party: the woman; (3) There is only a difference of degree between prostitution and other sexual relations outside wedlock, and it is unjust to limit the penalty only to persons who meet the arbitrary criteria set forth in the legal definition of prostitution; and (4) Criminalization of prostitution does not reduce or eliminate it. Instead it promotes a ruthless underworld organization that increases exploitation and crime.

What is your opinion on this issue now? Which of the arguments sketched out by the United Nations study team add any light to the debate between Bovard and Volkonsky?

SUGGESTED READINGS

S. Bell, *Reading, Writing, and Rewriting the Prostitute Body* (Indiana University Press, 1994).

H. Moody and A. Carmen, *Working Women: The Subterranean World of Street Prostitution* (Little, Brown, 1995).

L. Shrage, *Moral Dilemmas of Feminism: Prostitution, Adultery, and Abortion* (Routledge, 1994).

L. Shrage, "Prostitution and the Case for Decriminalization," *Dissent* (Spring 1996).

ISSUE 9

Should Late-Term Abortions Be Banned?

YES: Douglas Johnson, from "President Clinton's Deception on Partial-Birth Abortion 'Ban' Continues," A National Right to Life Press Release (February 28, 1997)

NO: William J. Clinton, from "To the House of Representatives," White House Press Release (April 10, 1996)

ISSUE SUMMARY

YES: Douglas Johnson, legislative director for the National Right to Life Committee, contends that President Clinton's insistence on including a clause allowing late-term abortion in the case of a serious threat to the mother's life or health will permit the thousands of partial-birth abortions being performed annually on healthy babies of healthy mothers to continue unabated.

NO: President William J. Clinton, in his notification to Congress, explains that although he abhors late-term abortions, he cannot sign a bill restricting this procedure unless it contains an exception in the case of a serious threat to the mother's life or health.

From 1995 to June 1997 Congress fought over two bills to ban late-term, or partial-birth, abortions. During the debate this procedure, known medically as D&X (intact dilation and extraction), was given two new names—"partial-birth abortion," which was used by pro-life advocates, and "late-term abortion," which was used by pro-choice advocates.

The ongoing debate has been bitter, emotional, and burdened with partial truths. In the March 24, 1997, edition of *Time* magazine, Margaret Carlson characterized the debate bluntly: "He lied, she lied, they lied, we all lie, to ourselves and one another, in hearings and in print, at dinner and on *Nightline*, lest we give one inch in a war over abortion that rages on.... The truth eludes not just those on the extremes but also those in the middle." Still, after two years and presidential vetos of abortion bills in 1995 and 1997, some basic facts have surfaced.

About 1.8 million abortions, over 90 percent of all abortions, are performed in the first two months of pregnancy. About 9 percent (180,000) second-trimester abortions are performed each year, usually because of a serious genetic defect in the fetus. Medical intervention to terminate the life of a healthy, viable fetus in the last three months of pregnancy is rare and usually illegal after 21 weeks unless required to save the life of the mother or to avoid serious health consequences.

In a D&X the woman's cervix is dilated and the fetus is partially removed from the womb, feet first. The surgeon punctures the back of the fetus's head and inserts a tube through which the brains are extracted. When the head contracts, the fetus can be more easily removed from the womb. The best estimate puts the number of D&X abortions at 3,000–4,000 annually, or about 10 per day.

D&X is not performed in the first trimester. In the fifth and sixth months of pregnancy, D&X may be performed before the fetus is viable outside the womb, usually for maternal health reasons (including mental health) or because the fetus is badly malformed or genetically defective. Physicians use D&X in the third trimester to save the life of or to avoid serious damage to the mother. The only alternative in this situation is hysterotomy, which is similar to but more serious than a Cesarean section. But hysterotomy requires a competent physician with state-of-the-art skill in managing high-risk pregnancies. Since many, if not most, physicians lack this level of skill, they resort to D&X.

These facts may help you to weigh the arguments raised by Douglas Johnson and William J. Clinton in the selections that follow.

YES

Douglas Johnson

PRESIDENT CLINTON'S DECEPTION ON PARTIAL-BIRTH ABORTION "BAN" CONTINUES

Even in light of this week's startling developments in the partial-birth abortion debate, President Clinton and his agents are maintaining a deceptive public posture that relies heavily on verbal diversionary tactics. So far, they've gotten away with it.

On April 10, 1996, President Clinton vetoed the Partial-Birth Abortion Ban Act, which would have banned partial-birth abortions except to save the life of the mother. The bill defined partial-birth abortion as "an abortion in which the person performing the abortion partially vaginally delivers a living fetus before killing the fetus and completing the delivery." The vetoed bill contained no reference to the developmental age of the baby, but from the time the bill was introduced in June, 1995, both bill author Rep. Charles Canady (R-FL.) and NRLC (National Right to Life Committee) consistently emphasized that most partial-birth abortions are performed in the fifth and sixth months of pregnancy, *not* during the third trimester. [Documentation will be provided on request, or please view the revealing report titled "Partial Truth" in the January edition of *Media Matters*, a Corporation for Public Broadcasting–funded mediacriticism TV documentary program.]

At his December 13 news conference and on other occasions, President Clinton said that he *would have signed* the Partial-Birth Abortion Ban Act if Congress had only bowed to his demand to expand the life-of-mother exception in order to allow the procedure to be used for certain "health" considerations, variously described. (The medical implausibilities of Mr. Clinton's "health"-based arguments are not addressed in this memo, but are thoroughly critiqued in other materials available from NRLC and from the Physicians' Ad Hoc Coalition for Truth.) In mid-October the Clinton campaign ran ads on about 100 Christian radio stations that stated, "President Clinton wants a complete ban on late-term abortions except when the mother's life is in danger or faces severe health risks, such as the inability to have another child."

From Douglas Johnson, "President Clinton's Deception on Partial-Birth Abortion 'Ban' Continues," A National Right to Life Press Release [electronic document] (1997). Copyright © 1997 by National Right to Life. Reprinted by permission. This document can be found at http://www.nrlc.org/.

In all of these public statements by Mr. Clinton and his agents that he would have signed "the bill" with a health exception, the President is being gravely deceptive, and here is why: the legislative language on which Mr. Clinton quietly insists contains an additional, radical difference from the vetoed bill: *the President's bill would apply only in the seventh month of pregnancy and later.*

This is no nuance. It means that the vast majority of partial-birth abortions would continue without any limitation, because they occur *before* the third trimester. (The remainder, those performed in the seventh month and later, would be allowed by the elasticity of Mr. Clinton's "health" exception; a point discussed in other NRLC materials but not here.)

So far, the President and his agents have been largely successful in diverting the news media's attention away from the "timeline" gutting revision but when *NBC News* Bureau Chief Tim Russert directly pressed White House Chief of Staff Leon Panetta on the December 15 edition of *Meet the Press*, Panetta admitted that the Clinton proposal would *not* apply to second trimester partial-birth abortions. A proposal advocated by Senator Tom Daschle (D-SD) has the same key characteristics.

In much publicized interviews earlier this week, Ron Fitzsimmons, executive director of the National Coalition of Abortion Providers (NCAP), admitted that he and leaders of other proabortion groups knew all along that partial-birth abortions are performed routinely during the fifth and sixth months, and that few involve any medical problem of the mother or the baby. "What abortion rights supporters failed to acknowledge," Fitzsimmons said, "is that the vast majority of these abortions are performed in the 20-plus-week range on healthy fetuses and healthy mothers." ("Abortion Rights Leader Urges End to 'Half Truths'," by Diane Gianelli, *American Medical News*, March 3, 1997, page 54.)

Yet, at the White House, the deception continues. *Even over the past two days* President Clinton's spokespersons have reiterated commitments to sign the "ban" if Mr. Clinton is accommodated on the "health" issue.

On Wednesday, February 26, White House spokeswoman Mary Ellen Glynn said, "If this procedure is being used on an elective basis, where there's another procedure available, *the president would be happy to sign legislation that would ban it.*" [emphasis added] On Thursday, February 27, White House Press Secretary Mike McCurry said, "[President Clinton] indicated at the time he corresponded last with Congress that *he would sign legislation banning that procedure if it had that [health] exception. That continues to be his position...*" [emphasis added]

How long can this deception be sustained? It is simply false for President Clinton or his agents to say that he will "sign legislation banning that procedure," or will sign "that legislation" or "the ban," when he is really insisting on a radically different and entirely hollow bill. Under the Clinton-Daschle bill, the thousands of partial-birth abortions being performed annually on healthy babies of healthy mothers would continue without restriction.

NO

William J. Clinton

TO THE HOUSE OF REPRESENTATIVES

I am returning herewith without my approval H.R. 1833, which would prohibit doctors from performing a certain kind of abortion. I do so because the bill does not allow women to protect themselves from serious threats to their health. By refusing to permit women, in reliance on their doctors' best medical judgment, to use this procedure when their lives are threatened or when their health is put in serious jeopardy, the Congress has fashioned a bill that is consistent neither with the Constitution nor with sound public policy.

I have always believed that the decision to have an abortion generally should be between a woman, her doctor, her conscience, and her God. I support the decision to Roe v. Wade protecting a woman's right to choose, and I believe that the abortions protected by that decision should be safe and rare. Consistent with that decision, I have long opposed late-term abortions except where necessary to protect the life or health of the mother. In fact, as Governor of Arkansas, I signed into law a bill that barred third trimester abortions, with an appropriate exception for life or health.

The procedure described in H.R. 1833 has troubled me deeply, as it has many people. I cannot support use of that procedure on an elective basis, where the abortion is being performed for non-health related reasons and there are equally safe medical procedures available.

There are, however, rare and tragic situations that can occur in a woman's pregnancy in which, in a doctor's medical judgment, the use of this procedure may be necessary to save a woman's life or to protect her against serious injury to her health. In these situations, in which a woman and her family must make an awful choice, the Constitution requires, as it should, that the ability to choose this procedure be protected.

In the past several months, I have heard from women who desperately wanted to have their babies, who were devastated to learn that their babies had fatal conditions and would not live, who wanted anything other than an abortion, but who were advised by their doctors that this procedure was their best chance to avert the risk of death or grave harm which, in some cases, would have included an inability to ever bear children again. For these women, this was not about choice—not about deciding against having a child.

From William J. Clinton, "To the House of Representatives," Office of the Press Secretary, The White House (April 10, 1996).

These babies were certain to perish before, during or shortly after birth, and the only question was how much grave damage was going to be done to the woman.

I cannot sign H.R. 1833, as passed, because it fails to protect women in such dire circumstances—because by treating doctors who perform the procedure in these tragic cases as criminals, the bill poses a danger of serious harm to women. This bill, in curtailing the ability of women and their doctors to choose the procedure for sound medical reasons, violates the constitutional command that any law regulating abortion protect both the life and the health of the woman. The bill's overbroad criminal prohibition risks that women will suffer serious injury.

That is why I implored Congress to add an exemption for the small number of compelling cases where selection of the procedure, in the medical judgment of the attending physician, was necessary to preserve the life of the woman or avert serious adverse consequences to her health. The life exception in the current bill only covers cases where the doctor believes that the woman will die. It fails to cover cases where, absent the procedure, serious physical harm, often including losing the ability to have more children, is very likely to occur. I told Congress that I would sign H.R. 1833 if it were amended to add an exception for serious health consequences. A bill amended in this way would strike a proper balance, remedying the constitutional and human defect of H.R. 1833. If such a bill were presented to me, I would sign it now.

I understand the desire to eliminate the use of a procedure that appears inhumane. But to eliminate it without taking into consideration the rare and tragic circumstances in which its use may be necessary would be even more inhumane.

The Congress chose not to adopt the sensible and constitutionally appropriate proposal I made, instead leaving women unprotected against serious health risks. As a result of this Congressional indifference to women's health, I cannot, in good conscience and consistent with my responsibility to uphold the law, sign this legislation.

POSTSCRIPT

Should Late-Term Abortions Be Banned?

In one of his "Focus on the Family" radio broadcasts, James Dobson referred to D&X as "Nazi era experimentation" in which doctors "suck the brain matter out of a living, viable baby for use in medical experiments." The impression was that researchers eager to study brain structure were asking doctors to select about-to-be-born fetuses at random and kill them to obtain more research material. This misrepresentation of the actual situation was never corrected, but it did unleash a flood of calls to the White House and Congress. Ron Fitzsimmons, a national pro-choice spokesperson, originally told Congress that only about 450 D&Xs were performed annually. He later admitted being carried away by the rhetoric on both sides and said that the figure was more like 3,000–4,000.

Some testimony in Congress revealed that state laws concerning third-trimester abortions and/or state medical society regulations have been violated by physicians and that partial-birth abortions had been conducted for elective reasons, for example, because the woman was suicidally depressed. Others testified that D&Xs were only done when the fetus was dead or hopelessly malformed, or when the woman's life or her long-term health were at risk. Some testified that fetuses are anesthetized during a D&X and cannot feel pain. Others said the opposite: that the anesthetic cannot pass the placental barrier and affect the fetus. Some authorities testified that fetuses cannot feel pain under any conditions; others said that fetuses can feel pain early in pregnancy. Obviously, it is not easy to break through the curtain of intentional or unintentional misinformation and detect reality.

Still, congressional debate revealed some areas of agreement. For instance, most in Congress would allow D&X when it is necessary to save the woman's life or if the fetus is dead. The consensus is that D&X should not be allowed for ordinary health reasons, in cases of rape or incest, or in cases where the fetus is very severely malformed and will die within hours or days of birth. Major differences of opinion exist where the woman's life is not in jeopardy but where she would be disabled or suffer some very serious long-term health problems.

SUGGESTED READINGS

S. C. Busey, "Contra Crushing Fetal Skulls," *Human Life Review* (vol. 22, no. 3, 1996), pp. 93–107.

M. Carlson, "Partial-Truth Abortion," *Time* (March 24, 1997), p. 40.

R. F. Drinan, "Late-Term Abortion Veto Merits Analysis," *National Catholic Reporter* (May 31, 1996), p. 16.

D. Johnson, Testimony before the National Right to Life Committee on the Partial-Birth Abortion Ban Act (H.R. 929, S. 6) at a Joint Hearing before the U.S. Senate Judiciary Committee and the Constitution Subcommittee of the U.S. House Judiciary Committee (March 11, 1997).

R. Kerrison, "Bill's Abortion Stand Is Heartless," *Human Life Review* (Winter 1996).

"Veto the Abortion Ban," *The New York Times* (May 21, 1997), p. 22.

ISSUE 10

Should All Female Circumcision Be Banned?

YES: Loretta M. Kopelman, from "Female Circumcision/Genital Mutilation and Ethical Relativism," *Second Opinion* (October 1994)

NO: P. Masila Mutisya, from "A Symbolic Form of Female Circumcision Should Be Allowed for Those Who Want It," An Original Essay Written for This Volume (November 1997)

ISSUE SUMMARY

YES: Loretta M. Kopelman, a professor of medical humanities, argues that certain moral absolutes apply to all cultures and that these, combined with the many serious health and cultural consequences of female circumcision, require that all forms of female genital mutilation be eliminated.

NO: P. Masila Mutisya, a professor of multicultural education, asserts that although most forms of female circumcision should be banned, the simplest form should be allowed as part of the rich heritage of rites of passage for newborn and pubertal girls in those cultures that have this tradition.

Each year in central and northern Africa and southern Arabia, 4–5 million girls have parts of their external genitals surgically removed in ceremonies intended to honor and welcome the girls into their communities or into womanhood. About 80 million living women have had this surgery performed sometime between infancy and puberty in ancient rituals said to promote chastity, religion, group identity, cleanliness, health, family values, and marriage goals. Female circumcision (FC) is deeply embedded in the cultures of many countries, including Ethiopia, Sudan, Somalia, Sierra Leone, Kenya, Tanzania, Chad, Gambia, Liberia, Mali, Senegal, Eritrea, Ivory Coast, Upper Volta, Mauritania, Nigeria, and Egypt.

Opponents of FC call it female genital mutilation (FGM) because the usual ways of performing FC frequently cause serious health problems, such as hemorrhaging, urinary and pelvic infection, painful intercourse (for both partners), infertility, complications giving birth, and even death. Besides denying women orgasm, the health consequences of FC also strain the overburdened, limited health care systems in the developing nations in which it is practiced.

In Type 1 FC, the simplest form, the clitoral hood is pricked or removed. Type 1 FC should not preclude orgasms in later life, but it can when performed on the tiny genitals of infants with the pins, scissors, and knives that traditional practitioners commonly use. In Type 2 (intermediate) FC, the clitoris and most or all of the minor labia are removed. In Type 3 FC, known as pharonic circumcision, or infibulation, the clitoris, minor labia, and parts of the major labia are removed. The vulval wound is stitched closed, leaving only a small opening for passage of urine and menstrual flow. Traditional practitioners often use sharpened or hot stones or unsterilized razors or knives, frequently without anesthesia or antibiotics. Thorns are sometimes used to stitch up the wound, and a twig is often inserted to keep the passage open. Healing can take a month or more. In southern Arabia, Sudan, Somalia, Ethiopia, and other African nations, more than three-quarters of the girls undergo Type 2 or 3 FC.

Impassioned cultural clashes erupt when families migrate from countries where FC is customary to North America and Europe. In their new homes immigrant parents use traditional practitioners or ask local health professionals to perform FC. Some doctors and nurses perform FC for large fees; others do it because they are concerned about the unhygienic techniques of traditional practitioners. In the United Kingdom about 2,000 girls undergo FC each year, even though it is legally considered child abuse. Many international agencies, such as UNICEF, the International Federation of Gynecology and Obstetrics, and the World Health Organization (WHO), openly condemn and try to stop FC. France, Canada, and the United Kingdom have banned FC; the American Medical Association has denounced it; and the U.S. Congress has made all FC illegal.

The question discussed here is whether or not the traditional pluralism and openness of American culture can make some accommodation that would allow thousands of immigrants to maintain the essence of their ancient, traditional rites of passage for young girls in some symbolic way. Some commentators argue that we should prohibit Types 2 and 3 circumcision for health reasons but allow some symbolic ritual nicking of the clitoral hood as a major element in the extensive ceremonies and educational rites of passage that surround a girl's birth into her family and community or her passage to womanhood in these African and Arabic cultures. In the following selections, Loretta M. Kopelman advocates a ban on all female circumcision. P. Masila Mutisya advocates allowing a symbolic female circumcision, similar to the removal of the male foreskin (prepuce), with modern medical safeguards.

YES

Loretta M. Kopelman

FEMALE CIRCUMCISION/GENITAL MUTILATION AND ETHICAL RELATIVISM

REASONS GIVEN FOR FEMALE CIRCUMCISION/GENITAL MUTILATION

According to four independent series of studies conducted by investigators from countries where female circumcision is widely practiced (El Dareer 1982; Ntiri 1993; Koso-Thomas 1987; Abdalla 1982), the primary reason given for performing this ritual surgery are that it (1) meets a religious requirement, (2) preserves group identity, (3) helps to maintain cleanliness and health, (4) preserves virginity and family honor and prevents immorality, and (5) furthers marriage goals including greater sexual pleasure for men.

El Dareer conducted her studies in the Sudan, Dr. Olayinka Koso-Thomas in and around Sierra Leone, and Raquiya Haji Dualeh Abdalla and Daphne Williams Ntiri in Somalia. They argue that the reasons for continuing this practice in their respective countries float on a sea of false beliefs, beliefs that thrive because of a lack of education and open discussion about reproduction and sexuality. Insofar as intercultural methods for evaluating factual and logical statements exist, people from other cultures should at least be able to understand these inconsistencies or mistaken factual beliefs and use them as basis for making some judgments having intercultural *moral* authority.

First, according to these studies the main reason given for performing female circumcision/genital mutilation is that it is regarded as a religious requirement. Most of the people practicing this ritual are Muslims, but it is not a practice required by the Koran (El Dareer 1982; Ntiri 1993). El Dareer writes: "Circumcision of women is not explicitly enjoined in the Koran, but there are two implicit sayings of the Prophet Mohammed: 'Circumcision is an ordinance in men and an embellishment in women' and, reportedly Mohammed said to Om Attiya, a woman who circumcised girls in El Medina, 'Do not go deep. It is more illuminating to the face and more enjoyable to the husband.' Another version says, 'Reduce but do not destroy. This is enjoyable to the woman and preferable to the man.' But there is nothing in the Koran to suggest that the Prophet commanded that women be circumcised. He advised that it was important to both sexes that very little should be taken" (1992:72). Female circumcision/genital mutilation, moreover, is not practiced in the spiritual center of Islam, Saudi Arabia (Calder et al. 1993). Another reason for questioning this as a Muslim practice is that clitoridectomy and infibulation predate Islam, going back to the time of the pharaohs (Abdalla 1982; El Dareer 1992).

Second, many argue that the practice helps to preserve group identity. When Christian colonialists in Kenya introduced laws opposing the practice of female circumcision in the 1930s, African leader Kenyatta expressed a view still popular today: "This operation is still regarded as the very essence of an institution which has enormous educational, social, moral and religious implications, quite apart from the operation itself. For the present, it is impossible for a member of the [Kikuyu] tribe to imagine an initiation without clitoridectomy ... the abolition of IRUA [the ritual operation] will destroy the tribal symbol which identifies the age group and prevent the Kikuyu from perpetuating that spirit of collectivism and national solidarity which they have been able to maintain from time immemorial" (Scheper-Hughes 1991:27). In addition, the practice is of social and economic importance to older women who are paid for performing the rituals (El Dareer 1982; Koso-Thomas 1987; Abdalla 1982; Ginsberg 1991).

Drs. Koso-Thomas, El Dareer, and Abdalla agree that people in these countries support female circumcision as a good practice, but only because they do not understand that it is a leading cause of sickness or even death for girls, mothers, and infants, and a major cause of infertility, infection, and maternal-fetal and marital complications. They conclude that these facts are not confronted because these societies do not speak openly of such matters. Abdalla writes, "There is no longer any reason, given the present state of progress in science, to tolerate confusion and ignorance about reproduction and women's sexuality" (1982:2). Female circumcision/genital mutilation is intended to honor women as male circumcision honors men, and members of cultures where the surgery is practiced are shocked by the analogy of clitoridectomy to removal of the penis (El Dareer 1982).

Third, the belief that the practice advances health and hygiene is incompatible with stable data from surveys done in these cultures, where female circumcision/genital mutilation has been linked to mortality or morbidity such as shock, infertility, infections, incontinence, maternal-fetal complications, and protracted labor. The tiny hole generally left for blood and urine to pass is a constant source of infection (El Dareer 1982; Koso-Thomas 1987; Abdalla 1982; Calder et al. 1993; Ntiri 1993). Koso-Thomas writes, "As for cleanliness, the presence of these scars prevents urine and menstrual flow escaping by the normal channels. This may lead to acute retention of urine and menstrual flow, and to a condition known as *hematocolpos*, which is highly detrimental to the health of the girl or woman concerned and causes odors more offensive than any that can occur through the natural secretions" (Koso-Thomas 1987:10). Investigators completing a recent study wrote: "The risk of medical complications after female circumcision is very high as revealed by the present study [of 290 Somali women, conducted in the capital of Mogadishu]. Complications which cause the death of the young girls must be a common occurrence especially in the rural areas.... Dribbling urine incontinence, painful menstruations, haematocolpos and painful intercourse are facts that Somali women have to live with—facts that strongly motivate attempts to change the practice of female circumcision" (Dirie and Lindmark 1992:482).

Fourth, investigators found that circumcision is thought necessary in these cultures to preserve virginity and family honor and to prevent immorality. Type 3 circumcision [in which the clitoris and most or all of the labia minora are removed] is used to keep women from having sexual intercourse before marriage and conceiving illegitimate children. In addition, many believe that Types 2 [in which the clitoris, the labia minora, and parts of the labia majora are removed] and 3 circumcision must be done because uncircumcised women have excessive and uncontrollable sexual drives. El Dareer, however, believes that this view is not consistently held—that women in the Sudan are respected and that Sudanese men would be shocked to apply this sometimes-held cultural view to members of their own families. This reason also seems incompatible with the general view, which investigators found was held by both men and women in these cultures, that sex cannot be pleasant for women (El Dareer 1982; Koso-Thomas 1987; Abdalla 1982). In addition, female circumcision/genital mutilation offers no foolproof way to promote chastity and can even lead to promiscuity because it does not diminish desire or libido even where it makes orgasms impossible (El Dareer 1982). Some women continually seek experiences with new sexual partners because they are left unsatisfied in their sexual encounters (Koso-Thomas 1987). Moreover, some pretend to be virgins by getting stitched up tightly again (El Dareer 1982).

Fifth, interviewers found that people practicing female circumcision/genital mutilation believe that it furthers marriage goals, including greater sexual pleasure for men. To survive economically, women in these cultures must marry, and they will not be acceptable marriage partners unless they have undergone this ritual surgery (Abdalla 1982; Ntiri 1993). It is a curse, for example, to say that someone is the child of an uncircumcised woman (Koso-Thomas 1987). The widely held belief that infibulation enhances women's beauty and men's sexual pleasure makes it difficult for women who wish to marry to resist this practice (Koso-Thomas 1987; El Dareer 1992). Some men from these cultures, however, report that they enjoy sex more with uncircumcised women (Koso-Thomas 1987). Furthermore, female circumcision/genital mutilation is inconsistent with the established goals of some of these cultures because it is a leading cause of disability and contributes to the high mortality rate among mothers, fetuses, and children. Far from promoting the goals of marriage, it causes difficulty in consummating marriage, infertility, prolonged and obstructed labor, and morbidity and mortality.

CRITICISMS OF ETHICAL RELATIVISM

Examination of the debate concerning female circumcision suggests several conclusions about the extent to which people from outside a culture can understand or contribute to moral debates within it in a way that has moral force. First, the fact that a culture's moral and religious views are often intertwined with beliefs that are open to rational and empirical evaluation can be a basis of cross-cultural examination and intercultural moral criticism (Bambrough 1979). Defenders of female circumcision/genital mutilation do not claim that this practice is a moral or religious requirement and end the discussion; they are willing to give and defend reasons for their views. For example, advocates of female circumcision/genital mutilation claim that it benefits women's health and well-being. Such claims are open to cross-cultural examination because information is available to determine whether the practice promotes health or cause morbidity or mortality. Beliefs that the practice enhances fertility and promotes health, that women cannot have orgasms, and that allowing the baby's head to touch the clitoris during delivery causes death to the baby are incompatible with stable medical data (Koso-Thomas 1987). Thus an opening is allowed for genuine cross-cultural discussion or criticism of the practice.

Some claims about female circumcision/genital mutilation, however, are not as easily open to cross-cultural understanding. For example, cultures practicing the Type 3 surgery, infibulation, believe that it makes women more beautiful. For those who are not from these cultures, this belief is difficult to understand, especially when surveys show that many women in these cultures, when interviewed, attributed to infibulation their keloid scars, urine retention, pelvic infections, puerperal sepsis, and obstetrical problems (Ntiri 1993; Abdalla 1982). Koso-Thomas writes: "None of the reasons put forward in favor of circumcision have any real scientific or logical basis. It is surprising that aesthetics and the maintenance of cleanliness are advanced as grounds for female circumcision. The scars could hardly be thought of as contributing to beauty. The hardened scar and stump usually seen where the clitoris should be, or in the case of the infibulated vulva, taut skin with an ugly long scar down the middle, present a horrifying picture" (Koso-Thomas 1987:10). Thus not everyone in these cultures believes that these rituals enhance beauty; some find such claims difficult to understand.

Second, the debate over female circumcision/genital mutilation illustrates another difficulty for defenders of this version of ethical relativism concerning the problem of differentiating cultures. People who brought the practice of female circumcision/genital mutilation with them when they moved to another nation still claim to be a distinct cultural group. Some who moved to Britain, for example, resent the interference in their culture represented by laws that condemn the practice as child abuse (Thompson 1989). If ethical relativists are to appeal to cultural approval in making the final determination of what is good or bad, right or wrong, they must tell us how to distinguish one culture from another.

How exactly do we count or separate cultures? A society is not a nation-state, because some social groups have distinctive identities within nations. If we do not define societies as nations, however, how do we distinguish among cultural groups, for example, well enough to say that an action is child abuse in one culture but not in another? Subcultures in nations typically overlap and have many variations. Even if we could count cultural groups well enough to say exactly how to distinguish one culture from another, how and when would this be relevant? How big or old or vital must a culture, subculture, group, or cult be in order to be recognized as a society whose moral distinctions are self-contained and self-justifying?

A related problem is that there can be passionate disagreement, ambivalence, or rapid changes within a culture or group over what is approved or disapproved. According to ethical relativism, where there is significant disagreement within a culture there is no way to determine what is right or wrong. But what disagreement is significant? As we saw, some people in these cultures, often those with higher education, strongly disapprove of female circumcision/genital mutilation and work to stop it (El Dareer 1982; Koso-Thomas 1987; Ntiri 1993; Dirie and Lindmark 1992; Abdalla 1982). Are they in the same culture as their friends and relatives who approve of these rituals? It seems more accurate to say that people may belong to various groups that overlap and have many variations. This description, however, makes it difficult for ethical relativism to be regarded as a helpful theory for determining what is right or wrong. To say that something is right when it has cultural approval is useless if we cannot identify the relevant culture. Moreover, even where people agree about the rightness of certain practices, such as these rituals, they can sometimes be inconsistent. For example, in reviewing reasons given within cultures where female circumcision/genital mutilation is practiced, we saw that there was some inconsistency concerning whether women needed this surgery to control their sexual appetites, to make them more beautiful, or to prevent morbidity or mortality. Ethical relativists thus have extraordinary problems offering a useful account of what counts as a culture and establishes cultural approval or disapproval.

Third, despite some clear disagreement such as that over the rightness of female circumcision/genital mutilation, people from different parts of the world share common goals like the desirability of promoting people's health, happiness, opportunities, and cooperation, and the wisdom of stopping war, pollution, oppression, torture, and exploitation. These common goals make us a world community, and using shared methods of reasoning and evaluation, we can discuss how well they are understood or how well they are implemented in different parts of our world community. We can use shared goals to assess whether female circumcision/genital mutilation is more like respect or oppression, more like enhancement or diminishment of opportunities, or more like pleasure or torture. While there are, of course, genuine differences between citizens of the world, it is difficult to comprehend how they could be identified unless we could pick them out against a background of our similarities. Highlighting our differences, however useful for some purposes, should not eclipse the truth that we share many goals and values and are similar enough that we can assess each other's views as rational beings in a way that has moral force. Another way to express this is to say that we should recognize universal human rights or be respectful of each other as persons capable of reasoned discourse.

Fourth, this version of ethical relativism, if consistently held, leads to the abhorrent conclusion that we cannot make intercultural judgments with moral force about societies that start wars, practice torture, or exploit and oppress other groups; as long as these activities are approved in the society that does them, they are allegedly right. Yet the world community believed that it was making a cross-cultural judgment with moral force when it criticized the Communist Chinese government for crushing a pro-democracy student protest rally, the South Africans for upholding apartheid, the Soviets for using psychiatry to suppress dissent, and the Bosnian Serbs for carrying out the siege of Sarajevo. And the judgment was expressed without anyone's ascertaining whether the respective actions had widespread approval in those countries. In each case, representatives from the criticized society usually said something like, "You don't understand why this is morally justified in our culture even if it would not be in your society." If ethical relativism were convincing, these responses ought to be as well.

Relativists who want to defend sound social cross-cultural and moral judgments about the value of freedom and human rights in other cultures seem to have two choices. On the one hand, if they agree that some cross-cultural norms have moral authority, they should also agree that some intercultural judgments about female circumcision/genital mutilation may have moral authority. Some relativists take this route (see, for example, Sherwin 1992), thereby abandoning the version of ethical relativism being criticized herein. On the other hand, if they defend this version of ethical relativism yet make cross-cultural moral judgments about the importance of values like tolerance, group benefit, and the survival of cultures, they will have to admit to an inconsistency in their arguments. For example, anthropologist Scheper-Hughes (1991) advocates toler-

ance of other cultural value systems; she fails to see that she is saying that tolerance between cultures is *right* and that this is a cross-cultural moral judgment using a moral norm (tolerance). Similarly, relativists who say it is wrong to eliminate rituals that give meaning to other cultures are also inconsistent in making a judgment that presumes to have genuine cross-cultural moral authority. Even the sayings sometimes used by defenders of ethical relativism—such as "When in Rome do as the Romans" (Scheper-Hughes 1991)—mean it is *morally permissible* to adopt all the cultural norms in operation wherever one finds oneself. Thus it is not consistent for defenders of this version of ethical relativism to make intercultural moral judgments about tolerance, group benefit, intersocietal respect, or cultural diversity.

The burden of proof, then, is upon defenders of this version of ethical relativism to show why we cannot do something we think we sometimes do very well, namely, engage in intercultural moral discussion, cooperation, or criticism and give support to people whose welfare or rights are in jeopardy in other cultures. In addition, defenders of ethical relativism need to explain how we can justify the actions of international professional societies that take moral stands in adopting policy. For example, international groups may take moral stands that advocate fighting pandemics, stopping wars, halting oppression, promoting health education, or eliminating poverty, and they seem to have moral authority in some cases. Some might respond that our professional groups are themselves cultures of a sort. But this response raises the... problem of how to individuate a culture or society....

COMMENT

We have sufficient reason. Therefore, to conclude that these rituals of female circumcision/genital mutilation are wrong. For me to say they are wrong does not mean that they are disapproved by most people in my culture but wrong for reasons similar to those given by activists within these cultures who are working to stop these practices. They are wrong because the usual forms of the surgery deny women orgasms and because they cause medical complications and even death. It is one thing to say that these practices are wrong and that activists should be supported in their efforts to stop them; it is another matter to determine how to do this effectively. All agree that education may be the most important means to stop these practices. Some activists in these cultures want an immediate ban (Abdalla 1982). Other activists in these cultures encourage Type 1 circumcision (pricking or removing the clitoral hood) in order to "wean" people away from Types 2 and 3 by substitution. Type 1 has the least association with morbidity or mortality and, if there are no complications, does not preclude sexual orgasms in later life. The chance of success through this tactic is more promising and realistic, they hold, than what an outright ban would achieve; and people could continue many of their traditions and rituals of welcome without causing so much harm (El Dareer 1982). Other activists in these countries, such as Raquiya Abdalla, object to equating Type 1 circumcision in the female with male circumcision: "To me and to many others, the aim and results of any form of circumcision of women are quite different from those applying to the circumcision of men" (1982:8). Because of the hazards of even Type 1 circumcision, es-

pecially for infants, I agree with the World Health Organization and the American Medical Association that it would be best to stop all forms of ritual genital surgery on women. Bans have proven ineffective: this still-popular practice has been illegal in most countries for many years (Rushwan 1990; Ntiri 1993; El Dareer 1982). Other proposals by activists focus on education, fines, and carefully crafted legislation (El Dareer 1982; Abdalla 1982; Ozumba 1992; Dirie and Lindmark 1992; WHO 1992).

The critique of the reasons given to support female circumcision/genital mutilation in cultures where it is practiced shows us how to enter discussions, disputes, or assessments in ways that can have moral authority. We share common needs, goals, and methods of reasoning and evaluation. Together they enable us to evaluate many claims across cultures and sometimes to regard ourselves as part of a world community with interests in promoting people's health, happiness, empathy, and opportunities as well as desires to stop war, torture, pandemics, pollution, oppression, and injustice. Thus, ethical relativism—the view that to say something is right means it has cultural approval and to say it is wrong means it has cultural disapproval —is implausible as a useful theory, definition, or account of the meaning of moral judgments. The burden of proof therefore falls upon upholders of this version of ethical relativism to show why criticisms of other cultures always lack moral authority. Although many values are culturally determined and we should not impose moral judgments across cultures hastily, we sometimes know enough to condemn practices approved in other cultures. For example, we can understand enough of the debate about female circumcision/genital mutilation to draw some conclusions: it is wrong, oppressive, and not a voluntary practice in the sense that the people doing it comprehend information relevant to their decision. Moreover, it is a ritual, however well-meant, that violates justifiable and universal human rights or values supported in the human community, and we should promote international moral support for advocates working to stop the practice wherever it is carried out.

NO
P. Masila Mutisya

A SYMBOLIC FORM OF FEMALE CIRCUMCISION SHOULD BE ALLOWED FOR THOSE WHO WANT IT

In recent years, the issue of female circumcision has provoked heated discussion here in the United States and far from its cultural origins in Africa. As controversial as it is, the issue of female circumcision raises a very important point that needs attention across the board when we are dealing with cultural behaviors, traditions, and practices that are brought by immigrants into a foreign culture. Whether we are dealing with a sexual practice like female circumcision, parentally arranged marriages, child marriages, or a non-sexual custom, we must deal clearly with the implications of cross-cultural, inter-cultural and multicultural education. This need for cross-cultural sensitivity and understanding is fairly obvious from the blanket condemnations of all forms of female circumcision as a brutalization of women, and the parallel silence about its cultural meaning as an important rite of passage for women. There is certainly a lot of ignorance about African cultures among Americans, both in the general population with its vocal feminist advocacy groups as well as among our legislators and health care professionals. There is a real need for better understanding of these rich cultural traditions.

The issue here is not one of cultural relativism, or the lack of it. What I am concerned about is that it is all too easy to misinterpret the symbolism and meaning of a traditional cultural rite. Unless we understand the various forms of female circumcision and its cultural importance as part of a girl's rite of passage to womanhood we run the serious risk of doing more harm than good. Lack of understanding of the values of one culture leads to the imposition of the views and interpretations of the cultural majority on new minorities within a nation. This has often been the case in the United States with the miseducation and misinterpretation of many aspects of African cultures, as well as other cultures in this nation. This in turn leads to conflicts in social and psychological awareness that affect the identities of different people in our multicultural society. People of African descent seem to be more affected by this than others.

Loretta Kopelman's call for the abolition of all forms of female circumcision is a clear example of this cultural imperialism. This misunderstanding is also evident in ongoing discussions of female circumcision on the internet and in various journals.

In her discussion of female circumcision, Kopelman, a professor of medical humanities, attacks the cultural relativism theory. She argues that certain moral absolutes apply across the board to all cultures and that these principles clearly dictate that all forms of female circumcision should be banned regardless of its particular form and its symbolic role as a rite of passage in some African cultures. She maintains that the reasons given to explain why these rituals exist have no validity or value. For her, female circumcision falls in the same category as murder of the innocent and therefore should be totally banned.

I speak as an educator who understands the symbolism of the African rites of passage very well because I am part of one African culture in which this educational rite of passage is practiced. I find no evidence in Kopelman's arguments to indicate that she has any understanding of or appreciation for objective cross-cultural, intercultural, and multicultural interpretations. Her arguments are a classic example of how most westerners, rooted in the cultures of Europe and North America, so easily assume the role of dictating and imposing their morality on non-westerners without offering any viable alternative or accommodation. I think this is a way of saying that the people who have practiced these and other rituals for thousands of years before and after coming in contact with westerners, must abolish their culture and be assimilated into the dominant western Euro-American value and moral system, even though—and this is one of my major arguments—the western Euro-American culture which she seeks to impose on all others has very few if any educational culturally-based rites of passage for their youth. Barring marriage and death rituals, it is practically devoid of all rites of passage.

Most of the traditional education of African boys and girls for adulthood is informal. However, initiation rites, such as female circumcision, can be considered formal because they occur in a public community setting with specific symbolic activities and ceremonies, which differ according to the individual society. In those cultures where female circumcision is practiced, this community-based ritual is a formal recognition that the girl has successfully completed her preparation for womanhood and is ready for marriage. (The examples I cite below are mostly from the Kamba and Gikuyu people and Bantu ethnic groups.)

An African child's education for adulthood is matched with its cognitive development and readiness, and may begin anywhere between ages 4 and 12. Young girls are taught the skills of a woman, learning to cook, manage a home and handle other chores related to their domestic responsibilities. They are also taught the social importance of these responsibilities in terms of women's role as the pillars of society. They learn respect for their elders and their lineage, how to communicate without being offensive, an appreciation of their tribal or clan laws and their ethnic identity. An African child's education for adult responsibilities includes learning about their sexuality and the taboos of their culture related to sexual relationships. Such taboos include sexual abstinence until marriage and ways of dealing with temptations. Girls learn who they should and should not marry, how to make love to a man while enjoying themselves, how to avoid pregnancy because there are terrible consequences if one becomes pregnant before marriage, and also how to avoid divorce for irresponsible reasons. In our cultures, grandparents and aunts are usually responsible for educating girls for womanhood. Boys are given similar gender appropriate education in their youthful years.

Depending on the particular tribal culture, completion of this educational process is certified by a formal ritual such as female circumcision. Both the educational process and the formal ritual are essential because together they prepare the boy or girl for marriage. Without this education and a declaration of adulthood provided by a formal ritual capping the education, one is not eligible for marriage and is still considered a child.

I strongly disagree with Kopelman's position that *all* forms of female circumcision should be banned. I do agree, however, with her call for a ban on any mutilation and/or infibulation that involves cutting or severing of any part of a female genitalia for whatever reasons given, when this is known to result in any health or fertility complication or disorder whether minor or major.

My proposed solution stems from an understanding of the symbolic function female circumcision plays in the passage of an African girl into womanhood, and the reinforcement this ritual cutting plays in affirming the responsibilities of the African male. Kopelman's argument is based on a total distortion of the vital function female circumcision plays in the education girls from some African traditions need in their transition to womanhood. The reasons Kopelman cites are widely accepted by non-Africans (and some Africans) who do not truly understand or appreciate the depths of African rites of passage. I have provided details on this distortion elsewhere, in an article published in the *Journal of Black Studies* on "Demythologization and Demystification of African Initiation Rites: A Positive and Meaningful Education Aspect Heading for Extinction." In that article I pointed out the stereotypes critics of the African rites of passage use in misinterpreting this practice. Most of the stereotyped arguments do not acknowledge the considerable education that precedes the circumcision ceremony. This education provides an essential base of knowledge for the young woman to make the transition from childhood to adulthood. This education incorporates sex education, discipline, moral foundation, and gender awareness, a rare aspect in the socialization of today's youth in the United States of America.

My argument is that the education that precedes female circumcision enhances the psychological and social aspects that help shape the identity of African womanhood. This will be lost if the ritual is discontinued. These rites of passage provide a foundation of one's entire life which involves the awareness of the rules of the society and philosophy that guides such rules. This foundation provides young women—and men— with the essence of who they are and the framework of what they aspire to be. It provides the young person with confidence, efficacy and self-respect, which enhances the capacity to respect and value others as human beings. After this lesson, it is hard for the young person to take someone else's life or his/her own, a common occurrence in western societies. It is also establishes ownership of property, beginning with the gifts the initiates receive. This leads to developing responsible management skills needed to survive throughout a woman's life. The initiation and the knowledge achieved before and after circumcision give a young woman (or man) a sense of belonging or permanence. Consequently, one is very unlikely to find a young initiate feeling alienated from her or his society as we see in today's societies where children and teens find their identity in joining gangs or cults. Even in Africa today teenage pregnancies and youth violence, which were unheard of in precolonial times, are on the rise. Unfortunately these pregnancies are mostly caused by older men with teenage girls. Before the colonial powers began their campaign against African rites of passage, teen pregnancies were rare because both the teenagers and the older men knew that it was taboo to have sex before marriage and to have children one is not going to be responsible for.

STEREOTYPICAL REASONS GIVEN BY KOPELMAN AND OTHERS

Kopelman begins her argument for banning all female circumcision by citing several studies conducted by people who come from places where female infibulation and genital mutilation are widely practiced. Using these studies, she lists five reasons she attributes to those seeking to justify this practice: (1) This ritual satisfies a religious requirement, (2) It preserves group identity, (3) It helps maintain cleanliness, (4) It preserves virginity and family honor and prevents immorality, and (5) It furthers marriage goals, including greater sexual pleasure. Invalid as these reasons may be in supporting the morality and acceptability of female circumcision, the problem is that they are common "straw men" arguments set up by opponents of all female circumcision because they are easily refuted. In focusing on these stereotyped and culturally biased reasons, Kopelman and other critics totally ignore and fail to deal with the main purpose of why the circumcision ritual is performed by most Africans.

Of course, anyone who is presented with these five superficial arguments and is not informed about the true core meaning of female circumcision would be easily convinced that the ritual is barbarous and should be stopped immediately. Kopelman fails to point out why this ritual has prevailed for such a long time. Instead, she focuses on the most brutal and inhumane aspects (infibulation and mutilation), which are practiced by just a few African groups. She refers to these groups as Islamic-influenced peoples, even though she admits that among the few people who practice the extreme version, their practice predates the Islamic era. Nor does she explain which particular group of people or pharonic era first practiced these extremes. This careless reference leads people to forget that there are many other forms of the ritual which have the same symbolic meaning but do not involve the extremes of infibulation or clitoridectomy. These practices are performed safely. Some do not even involve circumcision but scarification for the purpose of shedding a little blood, a symbol of courage that is a universal component of male adolescent rites of passage. It is easy for someone like Kopelman not too see the importance of this symbolism, especially when she does not have any similar positive educational experience with which to compare it. Her argument therefore paints with a broad brush on the diversity within the African continent, and her position takes away the very essence of being of most Africans. Also, like other insensitive commentators on African cultures, she fails to point out how the influence of chastity and preservation of virginity for "man's pleasure" has been introduced in both cultural and religious perspectives from outside black Africa. European missionaries and colonialists, preceded by Arabs, followed the same pattern she adopts. Such attitudes have resulted in many Africans abandoning their traditional ways of life. This has created the many identity crises that Africans experience today.

As Africans have adopted attitudes alien to their culture when they interact with the non-Africans who reject and penalize their practice of traditional rites of passage, identity crises have gripped African societies. Examples of such crises are the increase of violence, teen pregnancies, and genocide, which were rare when the rites of passage were in effect. These crises have culminated in the destruction of the base foundation that guides Africans in conceptualizing who they are as human beings. This destruction of traditional cultures and their rites of passage has also resulted in Africans being viewed as objects of exploitation marginal to European culture, and becoming subjects to be acted upon rather than actors of their own way of life, for example, defining who they are as opposed to being defined by others. Kopelman adds wounds to the deep destruction of African cultures that has been imposed on them through miseducation. Like the colonialists before her, she is driven by hegemony in her value system and judgments of other cultures.

A CULTURALLY SENSITIVE ALTERNATIVE

In calling for the total abolition of all forms of female circumcision, Kopelman fails to offer any alternative that might be culturally accepted by both African immigrants and those adhering to the dominant Euro-American values of the United States. Instead of suggesting a substitute ritual that would fulfill the main purpose of female circumcision, Kopelman describes all forms of this varied cultural practice, even the most simple and symbolic, as a brutal ritual. She obviously does not think the people who practice this ritual are capable of making adjustments to end the atrocities and sometimes deadly consequences that frequently accompany this rite when practiced in lands where the majority of people have little or no knowledge of sterile techniques or access to modern medical care. She ignores the possibility that an alternative ritual might be accepted by peoples who have practiced female circumcision for centuries.

Let me cite an example of what I mean by a mutually acceptable form of female circumcision that would respect the ancient traditions of some African immigrants and at the same time avoid all the negative consequences of genital mutilation and infibulation. This simple but elegant alternative emerged from discussions between the staff at one American hospital and a group of Somali and other African refugees who have recently settled in Seattle, Washington, clinging to their traditions and insisting that their daughters undergo the ritual of genital cutting.

The staff at Seattle's Harborview Medical Center faced this problem when refugee mothers were asked before delivery if they wanted their baby circumcised if it was a boy. Some mothers responded, "Yes, and also if it is a girl." The hospital, which has a long history of sensitivity to diverse cultures and customs, convened a committee of doctors to discuss what to do about the requests. The hospital staff proposed a compromise, a simple, symbolic cut in the clitoral hood to draw a couple of drops of blood, which could be used in the ritual to bond the girl with the earth, her family and clan. Despite the sensationalized publicity given to the more brutal forms of genital mutilation and infibulation, this symbolic nicking of the clitoral hood to shed a few drops of blood is in fact what most Africans outside Somalia, the Sudan, and Ethiopia do in their female circumcisions.

However, when this suggested alternative became public knowledge, it threw the liberal city of Seattle into turmoil.

Mazurka Ramsey, an Ethiopian immigrant whose San Jose–based group, Forward USA, seeks to eliminate the ritual completely, asked: "How dare it even cross their mind? What the Somali, what the immigrants like me need is an education, not sensitivity to culture." Unlike Ramsey, who is eager to cast off her cultural heritage and adopt American values, other refugee parents continue to press to have their daughters circumcised, even though the Seattle So-

mali community has essentially agreed that the practice should be ended.

"You cannot take away the rights of families and women," Hersi Mohamed, a Somali elder, said. "As leaders and elders of the community we cannot force a mother to accept the general idea of the community. She can say, 'I want my girl to have letting of blood.' "

Though this is an issue physicians and hospitals across the country are facing with increasing regularity, Harborview is the only hospital so far to discuss the problem openly as a public health issue, rather than treating it simply as an outdated barbaric rite that should be wiped out and totally banned.

A new federal law, in effect since April 1997, sets a prison sentence of up to 5 years for anyone who "circumcises, excises, or infibulates" the genitals of girls under age 18. With some 150,000 females of African origin in the United States having already been cut or facing the possibility of being cut, the compromise suggested by Harborview Hospital makes good sense as an attempt to save girls from the most drastic forms of this ritual.

As the *Chicago Tribune* reported:

"It would be a small cut to the prepuce, the hood above the clitoris, with no tissue excised, and this would be conducted under local anesthetic for children old enough to understand the procedure and give consent in combination with informed consent of the parents," said Harborview spokeswoman Tina Mankowski.

"We are trying to provide a relatively safe procedure to a population of young women who traditionally have had some horrendous things done to them," she said, but added, "We are not now doing female circumcisions at Harborview, nor are we considering doing female circumcisions."

Whether the proposal would be prohibited by the new law is one of the legal questions being reviewed by the Washington state attorney general. The hospital's medical director will make no final decision on the proposal until the legal review is completed and a community-wide discussion is held, Mankowski said.

The Seattle area is home to about 3,500 members of a fast-growing Somali community. Some Somali and other African immigrants here have made it clear how deeply ingrained the practice is in their cultural and religious views.

Somali men and women told *The Seattle Times* their daughters would be shamed, dishonored and unmarriageable if they were not cut, an act they believe shows their purity.

They also said that if they could not get it done in the U.S. they would pay the $1,500 fare to fly their daughters to their homeland, where they face the extreme version of the cutting ritual. Some, but not all, of them said a symbolic cut on their daughters would be enough.

Unfortunately, the compromise collapsed when a group of feminists threatened to file a lawsuit charging the hospital staff with violation of the new federal law.

Instead of being creative and flexible like the staff at Harborview Hospital, Kopelman takes a dogmatic culturally-biased stance and calls on us to get rid of a cultural practice that predates European cultures, a custom that provides a foundation for many Africans' cultural identity. In essence, she suggests that Africans should abandon their way of life and become culture-less or ritual-less societies just as American society is. When a culture has no meaningful rites of passage for its youth, the young grow up without a sense of belonging, continuity and permanence, an experience of many youth and adults in both contemporary Africa and present American societies. As a result, psychologists and other mental health professionals are needed to provide a substitute ritual and rite of passage for many youth and adults looking for their identity. This search was unnecessary and rare in traditional African societies because they had meaningful rites of passage. Without a good foundation of identity development based on meaningful traditional rites of passage, many recent young immigrants from Africa try to cope or compensate with facial reconstructions, liposuctions, changing of skin color or bleaching (melanin) destruction, self-hate, bulemia, obesity, suicides and other types of self-abuse. Without rituals to confirm their respect for women, immigrant African males may come to treat women as objects as opposed to equal human beings.

The alternative I propose is a careful interpretation of the meaning of other peoples' cultures and examining them from their own perspective before jumping to judgments. Failure to take this approach only makes the situation worse. I therefore propose an alternative of just nicking the clitoris enough to perform the symbolic rituals. This would be preceded by the most important part, the education of a girl for the responsibilities of womanhood and a full explanation of the importance of the practice. This nicking would of course be done in a sanitized condition by a licensed physician. A careful analysis, as free of cultural bias as possible, should allow the continuation of many rites of passage that are an ancient part of immigrant cultures.

I also suggest that before we make sweeping generalizations about cultural practices, we should try to look into the perspective of the people we are trying to critique. Some practices may be a little difficult to understand, but with a careful, sensitive approach, it may be simpler than one might think. A great way to attempt to understand others is to learn their language as an avenue to a better understanding of the values and philosophical perspective. This is close to "walking in someone else's shoes," the best practice in cross-cultural and inter-cultural awareness.

POSTSCRIPT

Should All Female Circumcision Be Banned?

Sociologists and cultural anthropologists talk about "enculturation" as the process whereby people from one society and culture migrate from their homeland to another place where they have to adjust to a new culture with different values, attitudes, and behaviors.

Enculturation is a two-sided process. The obvious side involves the adjustments that the immigrants must make as they become acquainted with and part of the new society. The immigrants slowly, sometimes painfully, adjust their attitudes, behaviors, and values to accommodate the dominant majority society in which they are one of perhaps many minorities. They also gradually adopt some of the majority values and behaviors, even as they modify their own traditions. Sometimes, to avoid conflict, they may conceal from outsiders some of their more "unusual" attitudes and behaviors—"unusual" meaning unfamiliar to the majority—to avoid being singled out and discriminated against.

The less obvious side of enculturation is the inevitable adjustments that occur among people in the majority culture as they encounter and interact with minority immigrants who are in the process of moving into the mainstream and becoming part of the general culture. The issue of female genital cutting is typical of this process.

In late 1997 a report from Kenya illustrated the advantages of cultural sensitivity and the need to avoid imposing our values on other cultures. This report was published by Maendeleo ya Wanawake, the Kenyan national women's organization, and the Seattle, Washington–based Program for Appropriate Technology in Health, a nonprofit international organization for women's and children's health. They reported that a growing number of rural Kenyan families are turning to a new ritual called *Ntanira na Mugambo*, or "Circumcision Through Words." Developed by several Kenyan and international nongovernmental agencies working together for six years, "Circumcision Through Words" brings young girls together for a week of seclusion during which they learn traditional teachings about their coming roles as women, parents, and adults in the community, as well as more modern messages about personal health, reproductive issues, hygiene, communications skills, self-esteem, and dealing with peer pressure. A community celebration of song, dance, and feasting affirms the girls and their new place in the community.

As more and more immigrants enter the United States and become part of its ethnic and cultural diversity, the challenges of enculturation are likely to become more complex and demanding. Hence the importance of understanding the current debate over female circumcision. Most articles on the subject denounce the practice and call for a complete ban on any form of female circumcision. This side has now been canonized by enactment of the federal ban. As of late 1997 only P. Masila Mutisya has dared to raise the possibility of some kind of accommodation. What do you think of this seemingly one-sided debate?

SUGGESTED READINGS

R. Abcaria, "Rite or Wrong: Female Circumcisions Are Still Performed on African Continent," *Fayetteville Observer Times* (June 14, 1993), pp. C1, C2.

A. M. A'Haleem, "Claiming Our Bodies and Our Rights: Exploring Female Circumcision as an Act of Violence," In M. Schuler, ed., *Freedom from Violence: Women's Strategies from Around the World* (OEF International, 1992).

T. Brune, "Compromise Plan on Circumcision of Girls Gets Little Support," *Chicago Tribune* (October 28, 1996), News Section, p. 1.

E. Dorkenoo, *Cutting the Rose: Female Genital Mutilation—The Practice and Its Prevention* (Minority Rights Group, 1994).

O. Koso-Thomas, *The Circumcision of Women: A Strategy for Eradication* (Zed Books, 1992).

M. C. Lewis, *Herstory: Black Female Rites of Passage* (African American Images, 1988).

P. M. Mutisya, "Demythologization and Demystification of African Initiation Rites: A Positive and Meaningful Educational Aspect Heading for Extinction," *Journal of Black Studies* (September 1996), pp. 94–103.

C. M. Nangoli, *No More Lies About Africa* (African Heritage, 1990).

A. Walker, *Possessing the Secret of Joy* (Harcourt Brace Jovanovich, 1992).

ISSUE 11

Is Abstinence-Only Education Effective?

YES: Thomas Lickona, from "Where Sex Education Went Wrong," *Educational Leadership* (November 1993)

NO: Peggy Brick and Deborah M. Roffman, from " 'Abstinence, No Buts' Is Simplistic," *Educational Leadership* (November 1993)

ISSUE SUMMARY

YES: Thomas Lickona, a developmental psychologist and professor of education, argues that several studies show that teens who were given a value-free, nondirective, comprehensive sex education were significantly more likely to initiate sexual intercourse than teenagers whose sex education did not include discussion of contraceptives. Lickona concludes that only a program that stresses abstinence and does not discuss contraceptives will reduce premature sex, pregnancy, and sexual diseases among teenagers.

NO: Peggy Brick and Deborah M. Roffman, consultants and sexuality educator trainers, maintain that abstinence-only education "does not adequately address the developmental needs of children and adolescents, the reality of their lives, or the societal forces that condition their view of the world." They contend that only a comprehensive sex education that includes both abstinence education and contraceptive use can begin to meet the needs of young people.

In spring 1997 a little-noticed provision in a congressional bill to overhaul the nation's welfare program suddenly touched off a heated, nationwide debate that will likely continue for some years. This hidden provision set aside $500 million in the next five years to teach children about sexual abstinence. State legislators and local health education officials quickly became embroiled in trying to decide how they might use this money. More important, states had to decide whether to even bother applying for the money.

The money for abstinence education comes with strong guidelines. A state that received this money, for example, would have to match every four federal dollars with three state dollars. With state budgets shrinking, this would most likely mean taking funds from more comprehensive teen programs already in place and working. Second, any program funded by this provision would have to teach the virtues of sexual abstinence only and not mention or provide information about any other contraceptive methods. The course material developed with funds from this law must include eight basic "facts."

These include the statements, "Sexual activity outside the context of marriage is likely to have harmful psychological and physical effects," and, "Monogamous relationships in the context of marriage is the expected standard of all human sexual activity."

In Maine, one of the more conservative U.S. states, officials decided that the limits on what you can say were so restrictive that they could not use the money for classroom programs or any other programs where counselors or teachers would be in face-to-face situations with teens and be open to their questions. They could, however, use the money for public service announcements encouraging sexual abstinence. Michigan, for example, used the money to launch a "Sex Can Wait" media campaign, while Maryland sponsored billboards proclaiming, "VIRGIN: Teach Your Kid It's Not a Dirty Word."

Legislators in Congress clearly and consistently favor sexual abstinence and frown on or loudly condemn contraceptive education in the schools. According to Congress, sex education must teach "abstinence from sexual activity outside marriage as the expected standard for all school-age children." Some health officials are quick to point out that such language would make it difficult, if not impossible, to respond honestly to many of the questions that inevitably arise in a classroom of teenagers where some are sexually active, some are homosexual, and some have been or are unwed parents.

Although sexual activity among teenagers is declining, while the use of contraceptives, particularly condoms, is increasing, 1 million teenagers still become pregnant each year. Four out of 10 American girls will become pregnant at least once before they turn 20.

The abstinence-only sex education provision in the welfare reform law raises a fundamental question that American society must address. Whether we opt for abstinence-only or comprehensive sexuality education, we have to acknowledge the fact that half of African American girls and one in six white girls begin to develop sexually by age eight, with the development of breasts and pubic hair. Menstruation begins later, at 12 years, 2 months for black girls and a little over 8 months later for white girls.

Despite this early onset of puberty, marriage in the early or middle teen years is frowned on by our society. In the late teens it is still fraught with serious risks and problems. The average age for first marriage today is in the late 20s and rising. The fundamental question, then, is whether or not society's expectation of total premarital virginity for 15 or 20 years is realistic, especially considering such factors as adolescent hormones and the mass media's glamorizing and celebrating the pleasures of being sexually active.

As you weigh the following arguments by Thomas Lickona and by Peggy Brick and Deborah M. Roffman for and against abstinence-only sex education, try to sort out the facts from the claims. Analyze the evidence and note any claims that need to be checked and substantiated.

YES

Thomas Lickona

WHERE SEX EDUCATION WENT WRONG

Most of us are familiar with the alarming statistics about teen sexual activity in the United States. Among high school students, 54 percent (including 61 percent of boys and 48 percent of girls) say they have had sexual intercourse, according to a 1992 Centers for Disease Control study. The number of 9th graders who say they have already had sex is 40 percent.

In the past two decades, there has been an explosion in the number of sexually transmitted diseases. Twelve million people are infected each year; 63 percent of them are under 25.

Each year, 1 of every 10 teenage girls becomes pregnant, and more than 400,000 teenagers have abortions. One in 4 children is born out of wedlock, compared to 1 in 20 in 1960.

But statistics like these do not tell the whole story. The other side—one that should concern us deeply as moral educators—is the debasement of sexuality and the corruption of young people's character.

A LEGACY OF THE SEXUAL REVOLUTION

A 1993 study by the American Association of University Women found that four out of five high school students say they have experienced sexual harassment ("unwanted sexual behavior that interferes with your life") in school. Commented one 14-year-old girl: "All guys want is sex. They just come up to you and grab you."

In suburban Minneapolis, a mother filed state and federal complaints because 3rd and 4th grade boys on the school bus had tormented her 1st grade daughter daily with obscene comments and repeated demands for sexual acts. A 6th grade teacher taking my graduate course in moral education said, "The boys bring in *Playboy*, the girls wear make-up and jewelry, and the kids write heavy sexual notes to each other."

From Thomas Lickona, "Where Sex Education Went Wrong," *Educational Leadership*, vol. 51, no. 3 (November 1993), pp. 84–89. Copyright © 1993 by The Association for Supervision and Curriculum Development. All rights reserved. Reprinted by permission. Notes omitted.

At an Indiana high school, a teacher said, "Kids in the halls will call out— boy to girl, girl to boy—'I want to f— you.'" At Lakewood High School in an affluent Los Angeles suburb, a group of boys formed the "Spur Posse," a club in which participants competed to see how many girls they could sleep with.

Growing up in a highly eroticized sexual environment—a legacy of the sexual revolution—American children are preoccupied with sex in developmentally distorted ways and increasingly likely to act out their sexual impulses. The widespread sexual harassment in schools and the rising rates of teen sexual activity are not isolated phenomena but an outgrowth of the abnormal preoccupation with sex that children are manifesting from the earliest grades.

The sexual corruption of children reflects an adult sexual culture in which the evidence continues to mount that sex is out of control. In 1990, 29 states set records for the sex-and-violence crime of rape. By age 18, more than a quarter of girls and one-sixth of boys suffer sexual abuse. One in four female students who say they have been sexually harassed at school were victimized by a teacher, coach, bus driver, teacher's aide, security guard, principal, or counselor. By various estimates, sexual infidelity now occurs in a third to one-half of U.S. marriages.

Sex is powerful. It was Freud who said that sexual self-control is essential for civilization. And, we should add, for character.

Any character education worthy of the name must help students develop sexual self-control and the ability to apply core ethical values such as respect and responsibility to the sexual domain. Against that standard, how do various contemporary models of sex education measure up?

The history of modern sex education offers three models. The first two are variations of the nondirective approach: the third, by contrast, is a directive approach.

COMPREHENSIVE SEX EDUCATION

"Comprehensive sex education," which originated in Sweden in the 1950s and quickly became the prototype for the Western world, was based on four premises:

1. Teenage sexual activity is inevitable.
2. Educators should be value-neutral regarding sex.
3. Schools should openly discuss sexual matters.
4. Sex education should teach students about contraception.

The value-neutral approach to sex soon showed up in American sex education philosophy, as in this statement by the author of the *Curriculum Guide for Sex Education in California*: "'Right' or 'wrong' in so intimate a matter as sexual behavior is as personal as one's own name and address. No textbook or classroom teacher can teach it."

What was the impact of nondirective, value-neutral, comprehensive sex education on teenage sexual behavior?

- From 1971 to 1981, government funding at all levels for contraceptive education increased by 4,000 percent. During that time teen pregnancies increased by 20 percent and teen abortions nearly doubled.
- A 1986 Johns Hopkins University study concluded that comprehensive sex education did not reduce teen

pregnancies, a finding replicated by other studies.

- A 1986 Lou Harris Poll, commissioned by Planned Parenthood (a leading sponsor of comprehensive sex education), found that teens who took a comprehensive sex education course (including contraceptive education) were significantly *more likely* to initiate sexual intercourse than teens whose sex education courses did not discuss contraceptives.

THE "ABSTINENCE, BUT" MODEL

Negative results like those cited did not lead comprehensive sex educators to alter their approach—but AIDS did. AIDS led to two modifications: (1) teaching students to practice "safe [or "safer"] sex" through the use of barrier contraception (condoms); and (2) grafting an abstinence message onto the old comprehensive model. These changes resulted in what can be called the "Abstinence, But" approach, which says two things to students:

- Abstinence is the only 100 percent effective way to avoid pregnancy, AIDS, and other sexually transmitted diseases.
- But if you are sexually active, you can reduce these risks through the consistent, correct use of condoms.

This hybrid model, still found in many public and private schools, seems to many like a "realistic" compromise. But closer examination revels fundamental problems in the "Abstinence, But" model.

1. It sends a mixed message. "Don't have sex, but here's a way to do it fairly safely" amounts to a green light for sexual activity. The problem is that "Abstinence, But" is still nondirective sex education. Abstinence is presented as the safest contraceptive option, but "protected sex" is offered as a "responsible" second option. The emphasis is on "making your own decision" rather than on making the right decision.

As a rule, if educators believe that a given activity is ethically wrong—harmful to self and others (as teen sexual activity clearly is)—we help students understand why that is so and guide them toward the right decision. We don't say, for example, "Drug abuse is wrong, but make your own decision, and here's how to reduce the risks if you decide to become drug active."

2. An abstinence message is further weakened when schools provide how-to condom instructions and/or distribute condoms. Teachers providing condom instruction will commonly demonstrate how to fit a condom to a model (or students may be asked to put a condom on a banana). In the same nonjudgmental atmosphere, discussion often includes the pros and cons of different lubricants, special precautions for oral and anal sex, and so on. Some schools also take what seems like the next logical step of actually distributing condoms to students. Both actions signal approval of "protected sex" and further undermine an abstinence message.

3. Condoms do not make sex physically safe. For all age groups, condoms have a 10 percent annual failure rate in preventing pregnancy; for teens (notoriously poor users), the figure can go as high as 36 percent. By one estimate, a 14-year-old girl who relies on condoms has more than a 50 percent chance of becoming pregnant before she graduates from high school.

Contraceptive sex educators often cite AIDS as the main justification for "safe sex" education, but research shows that condoms do *not* provide adequate protection against AIDS (and, especially among teens, may generate a false sense of security). In a 1993 University of Texas study, the average condom failure rate for preventing AIDS was 31 percent.

While AIDS is still relatively infrequent among teens, other sexually transmitted diseases are epidemic. Many of these diseases—and 80 percent of the time there are no visible symptoms—can be transmitted by areas of the body that are not covered by contraceptive barriers. Human Papilloma Virus, once very rare, is perhaps the most common STD among teens, infecting 38 percent of sexually active females ages 13 to 21. Victims may suffer from venereal warts, painful intercourse, or genital cancer. The virus can also cause cancer of the penis. Condoms provide no protection against this virus.

Chlamydia infects 20 to 40 percent of sexually active singles; teenage girls are most susceptible. In men, chlamydia can cause infertile sperm; in women, pelvic inflammatory disease and infection of the fallopian tubes. A single infection in a woman produces a 25 percent chance of infertility; a second infection, a 50 percent chance. Medical research has found that condoms do not significantly reduce the frequency of tubal infection and infertility stemming from this disease.

Given teenagers' vulnerability to pregnancy despite the use of condoms and the fact that condoms provide inadequate protection against AIDS and no protection against many STDs, it is irresponsible to promote the myth that condoms make sex physically safe.

4. Condoms do not make sex emotionally safe. The emotional and spiritual dimensions of sex are what make it distinctively human. If we care about young people, we will help them understand the destructive emotional and spiritual effects that can come from temporary, uncommitted sexual relationships.

These psychological consequences vary among individuals but include: lowered self-esteem (sometimes linked to sexually transmitted diseases), a sense of having been "used," self-contempt for being a "user," the pain of loss of reputation, compulsive sexual behavior to try to shore up one's damaged self-image, regret and self-recrimination, rage over rejection or betrayal, difficulty trusting in future relationships, and spiritual guilt if one has a faith tradition that prohibits sex outside marriage (as world religions typically do). Condoms provide zero protection against these emotional consequences.

5. Nondirective sex education undermines character. From the standpoint of character education, the nondirective "Abstinence, But" model fails on several counts:

- It doesn't give unmarried young people compelling ethical reasons to abstain from sexual intercourse until they are ready to commit themselves to another person. Instead, students learn that they are being "responsible" if they use contraception.

- It doesn't help students develop the crucial character quality of self-control —the capacity to curb one's desires and delay gratification. To the extent that sex education is in any way permissive toward teenage sexual activity, it fosters poor character and feeds into the societal problem of sex-out-of-control.

- It doesn't develop an ethical understanding of the relationship between sex and love.

- It doesn't cultivate what young people desperately need if they are to postpone sex: a vision of the solemn, binding commitment between two people in which sex is potentially most meaningful, responsible, and safe (physically and emotionally)—namely, marriage.

DIRECTIVE SEX EDUCATION

By any ethical, educational, or public health measure, nondirective sex education has been a failure. As a result, schools are turning increasingly toward directive sex education—just as the national character education movement is embracing a more directive approach to promoting core ethical values as the basis of good character.

A directive approach means helping young persons—for the sake of their safety, happiness, and character—to see the logic of an "Abstinence, No Buts" standard, often called "chastity education." This standard says three things:

1. Sexual abstinence is the *only* medically safe and morally responsible choice for unmarried teenagers.

2. Condoms do not make premarital sex responsible because they don't make it physically safe, emotionally safe, or ethically loving.

3. The only truly safe sex is having sex *only* with a marriage partner who is having sex *only* with you. If you avoid intercourse until marriage, you will have a much greater chance of remaining healthy and being able to have children.

There are now many carefully crafted curriculums, books, and videos that foster the attitudes that lead teens to choose chastity—a moral choice and a lifestyle that is truly respectful of self and others. Here are some examples:

1. Decision-making: Keys to total success. Facing a serious teen pregnancy problem (147 high school girls known to be pregnant in 1984–85), the San Marcos, California, school system implemented a multifaceted program, which included six-week courses for junior high students on developing study skills, self-esteem, and positive moral values; daily 10-minute lessons on "how to be successful"; a six-week course for 8th graders using Teen Aid's curriculum on the advantages of premarital abstinence and how to regain them (for example, self-respect and protection against pregnancy and disease) after having been sexually active; *Window to the Womb,* a video providing ultrasound footage of early fetal development to show students the power of their sexuality to create human life; and summaries of all lessons for parents plus a parent workshop on teaching sexual morality to teens.

After San Marcos implemented this program, known pregnancies at the high school dropped from 20 percent in 1984 to 2.5 percent in 1986 to 1.5 percent in 1988. Meanwhile, scores on tests of basic skills went up, and in 1988 San Marcos won an award for the lowest drop-out rate in California.

2. Teen S.T.A.R. (Sexuality Teaching in the context of Adult Responsibility) is currently used with more than 5,000 teens in various regions of the United States and in other countries. The program teaches that fertility is a gift and a power to be respected. Its premise is that "decisions about sexual responsibility will arise from inner conviction and knowledge of the self." More than half of the teens who enter the program sexually active stop sexual activity; very few initiate it.

3. *The loving well curriculum,* a literature-based program, uses selections from the classics, folktales, and contemporary adolescent literature to examine relationships from family love to infatuation and early romance to marriage. An evaluation finds that of those students who were not sexually active when they started the curriculum, 92 percent are still abstinent two years later, compared to 72 percent abstinent in a control group not exposed to the curriculum.

4. *Postponing sexual involvement* was developed by Emory University's Marion Howard specifically for low-income, inner-city 8th graders at risk for early sexual activity. Of students in the program, 70 percent said it taught them that they "can postpone sexual activity without losing their friends' respect." Participants were *five times less likely* to initiate sexual activity than students who did not take the program.

Other useful resources for directive sex education include:

• *Safe Sex: A Slide Program.* This extremely persuasive slide picture/audiotape presentation argues from medical facts alone that the only truly safe sex is within marriage. Available from the Medical Institute for Sexual Health, P.O. Box 4919, Austin, TX 78765-4919.

• *Let's Talk—Teens and Chastity.* In this humorous, dynamic video, Molly Kelly—an award-winning educator and mother of eight—addresses a high school

assembly on safe sex and chastity. Available from The Center for Learning, Box 910, Villa Maria, PA 16155.

• *Sex, Lies, and the Truth* is a riveting, for-teens video tht stresses the hard truths about sex in the '90s. Available from Focus on the Family, Colorado Springs, CO 90955. Also excellent and available from Focus on the Family is *Has Sex Education Failed Our Teenagers? A Research Report* by Dinah Richard.

• *Foundations for Family Life Education: A Guidebook for Professionals and Parents,* by Margaret Whitehead and Onalee McGraw, includes abstinence-based sex education objectives for grades K–10 and a superb annotated bibliography of age-appropriate curriculums and videos. Available from Educational Guidance Institute, 927 S. Walter Reed Dr., Suite 4, Arlington, VA 22204. Forthcoming from the same Institute: *Love and Marriage at the Movies: Educating for Character Through the Film Classics.*

• George Eager's *Love, Dating, and Sex* is one of the best-written books for teens. Available from Mailbox Club Books, 404 Eager Rd., Valdosta, GA 31602.

ANSWERS TO COMMON QUESTIONS

Educators committing to directive sex education must be prepared to answer some common questions. Among them:

What about all the teens who will remain sexually active despite abstinence education? Shouldn't they be counseled to use condoms? Obviously, if a person is going to have sex, using a condom will reduce the chance of pregnancy and AIDS, but not to an acceptable level. Condoms offer no protection against many other STDs and their long-term consequences, such as infertility. Schools have the mission of teaching the truth and developing right values—which means helping students understand why the various forms of contraception do not make premarital sex physically or emotionally safe and how premature sexual activity will hurt them now and in the future.

Isn't premarital sexual abstinence a religious or cultural value, as opposed to universal ethical values like love, respect, and honesty? Although religion supports premarital abstinence, it can be demonstrated, through ethical reasoning alone, that reserving sex for marriage is a logical application of ethical values. If we love and respect another, we want what is in that person's best interest. Does sex without commitment meet that criterion? Can we say that we really love someone if we gamble with that person's physical health, emotional happiness, and future life? Given the current epidemic of sexually transmitted diseases, it's possible to argue on medical grounds alone that premarital sexual abstinence is the only ethical choice that truly respects self and other.

Isn't the recommendation to save sex for marriage prejudicial against homosexual persons, since the law does not permit them to marry? All students can be encouraged to follow the recommendation of the U.S. Department of Education's guidebook, *AIDS and the Education of Our Children:*

> Regardless of sexual orientation, the best way for young people to avoid AIDS and other STDs is to refrain from sexual activity until as adults they are ready to establish a mutually faithful monogamous relationship.

Is abstinence education feasible in places, such as the inner city, where poverty and family breakdown are harsh realities? Programs like Atlanta's Postponing Sexual Involvement have a track record of making abstinence education work amid urban poverty. Virginia Governor Douglas Wilder has argued that "the black family is teetering near the abyss of self-destruction" and that "our young, male and female alike, must embrace the self-discipline of abstinence." Sylvia Peters, who won national acclaim for her work as principal of the Alexander Dumas School (K-8) in inner-city Chicago, made the decision to tell her students (6th graders were getting pregnant before she arrived), "Do not have sex until you are married—you will wreck your life." These two black leaders know that the problem of black illegitimate births— up from 35 to 65 percent in little more than two decades— won't be solved until there is a new ethic of sexual responsibility.

Sexual behavior is determined by value, not mere knowledge. Studies show that students who have value orientations (for example, get good grades in school, have high self-regard, consider their religious faith important, have strong moral codes), are significantly less likely to be sexually active than peers who lack these values. These internally held values are more powerful than peer pressure.

Our challenge as educators is this: Will we help to develop these values and educate for character in sex, as in all other areas? If we do not move decisively—in our schools, families, churches, government, and media—to promote a higher standard of sexual morality in our society, we will surely see a continued worsening of the plague of sex-related problems —promiscuity, sexual exploitation and rape, unwed pregnancy, abortions, sexually transmitted diseases, the emotional consequences of uncommitted sex, sexual harassment in schools, children of all ages focused on sex in unwholesome ways, sexual infidelity in marriages, pornography, the sexual abuse of children, and the damage to families caused by many of these problems.

Non directive sex education obviously didn't cause all of these problems, and directive sex education won't solve all of them. But at the very least, sex education in our schools must be part of the solution, not part of the problem.

NO

Peggy Brick and
Deborah M. Roffman

"ABSTINENCE, NO BUTS" IS SIMPLISTIC

There are no easy answers to the sexual health crisis afflicting our society, including those advocated by Thomas Lickona. The "Abstinence, No Buts" approach does not adequately address the developmental needs of children and adolescents, the reality of their lives, or the societal forces that condition their view of the world.

First, Lickona undermines rational dialogue by dividing educators into artificial, polar camps: "values-free-intercourse promoters," who push for contraception-based "comprehensive" sex education (the bad guys), and "values-based-intercourse preventers," who espouse chastity-based "character" education (the good guys). It is neither accurate nor helpful for him to imply that one particular interest group has a corner on instilling character, core values, and ethical thought; on wanting young people to grow up emotionally, socially, physically, and spiritually healthy; on working toward a day when developmental and social problems—such as premature sexual activity, teenage pregnancy, abortion, STD, HIV, sexism, and sexual harassment/abuse/exploitation—no longer threaten our children.

Second, Lickona's definition of "comprehensive" sex education bears little resemblance to the actual approach. Comprehensive sexuality education encompasses not only the complexities of sex and reproduction, but the enormously complicated subjects of human growth and development, gender roles, intimacy, and social and cultural forces that influence our development as males and females (Roffman 1992). Such an approach seeks to help young people understand sexuality as integral to their identity and enables them to make responsible lifelong decisions (SIECUS 1991).

More than 60 mainstream organizations support this approach through membership in the National Coalition to Support Sexuality Education. These include the American Medical Association, American School Health Association, American Association of School Administrators, National School Boards Association, and the Society for Adolescent Medicine. The majority of American adults support such a strategy as well. For example, recent surveys in New Jersey and North Carolina found that at least 85 percent of

From Peggy Brick and Deborah M. Roffman, " 'Abstinence, No Buts' Is Simplistic," *Educational Leadership*, vol. 51 (November 1993), pp. 90–92. Copyright © 1993 by The Association for Supervision and Curriculum Development. All rights reserved. Reprinted by permission. References omitted.

those surveyed approved of comprehensive sexuality education (Firestone 1993, North Carolina Coalition on Adolescent Pregnancy 1993).

A truly comprehensive approach is ongoing and begins during the preschool and elementary years (Montfort 1993). Curriculums of this type educate, rather than propagandize, children about sexuality. Youngsters learn to ask questions, predict consequences, examine values, and plan for the future. They confront real-life dilemmas: What would happen if? What would you do if? By the middle grades, students learn to take action on issues such as: What can we do to reduce teen pregnancies in this school? To educate students about HIV/AIDS? (See Reis 1989, Kirby et al. 1991, Center for Population Options 1992, O'Neill and Roffman 1992, SIECUS 1993.) Ideally, this approach to sexuality education will be integrated throughout the entire curriculum (Brick 1991).

WHY DIRECTIVE APPROACHES FAIL

Those of us committed to comprehensive sex education and to public education in a pluralistic society are not persuaded by the arguments for "directive," ideological sex education for several reasons.

1. It is hypocritical and futile to expect efforts directed at adolescents to solve the nation's myriad sexual problems. Powerful social forces contribute to the early development of unhealthy sexual scripts—about who we are as males or females, how we should act, and issues of right and wrong.

For example, the early learning of male gender roles, often linked with violence and the need to dominate, is fundamentally related to problems of rape and harassment (Miedzian 1991). The manipulation of the sexuality of both males and females from an early age, and the stimulation of sexual desires by advertising and other media, are fundamental to the operation of our economic system (D'Emilio and Freedman 1988). Adolescent child-bearing, sexually transmitted diseases, and the spread of HIV are highly correlated with poverty and lack of hope for the future (National Research Council 1987). Further, many problems attributed to teens are not just teen problems: the majority of *all* pregnancies in this country are unplanned (Heller 1993). Seventy percent of adolescent pregnancies are fathered by adult men (Males 1993).

2. Directive approaches require a delay of intercourse 10 or more years beyond biological maturity, which is contrary to practice in virtually all societies—unless there is a strict tradition segregating unmarried males and females and chaperoning women (Francoeur 1991).

3. The success of these proposals requires an immediate, fundamental change in the sexual attitudes and behaviors of a society through mere educational intervention. Such a radical change has never been accomplished. Traditionally, the majority of American males have accepted premarital intercourse, and as early as 1973, a study showed 95 percent of males and 85 percent of females approved of it (DeLamater and MacCorquodale 1979).

4. Advocates of the directive approach do not prepare youth to make decisions in a highly complex world. They permit no choice but *their* choice and deliberately deny potentially life-saving information to those who do not conform to their viewpoint.

5. The curriculums espoused are fear-based, characterized by devastating de-

scriptions of the dangers of all nonmarital intercourse and medical misinformation about abortion, sexually transmitted diseases, HIV/AIDS, and the effectiveness of condoms. For example, the major cause of condom failure is incorrect usage. Knowledge of proper condom use, of the variations in quality among brands, and of the substantial increase in effectiveness when condoms are used in combination with spermicides greatly reduces the risk for those who choose to have sexual intercourse (Kestelman and Trussell 1991). These sex-negative, emotionally overwhelming, and potentially guilt-producing strategies may well induce problems rather than ameliorate them by leading to unhealthy sexual attitudes, irrational decision making, denial, or rebellion (Fisher 1989).

Moreover, these curriculums are promoted by groups such as Concerned Women for America, the Eagle Forum, Focus on the Family, and the American Life League, which are lobbying heavily to impose Fundamentalist Christian doctrine on public schools (Kantor 1993, Hart 1993).

DISTORTED AND MISREPRESENTED DATA

Given these concerns, claims about the success of abstinence-only programs must be examined with extreme caution. Take, for example, the claim that a program in San Marcos, California, greatly reduced teen pregnancies in the mid-80s. In fact, this claim was not based on a scientific study but on the observation of the high school principal reporting the number of students who *told* the school counselor they were pregnant. After a much-publicized program condemning premarital intercourse, far fewer students reported their pregnancies to school staff; actual census figures for San Marcos indicated that from 1980-1990, the birth rate for mothers aged 14-17 more than doubled (Reynolds 1991). Many other evaluators have challenged the integrity of research documenting these extraordinary claims in support of abstinence-only curriculums (Trudell and Whatley 1991, Kirby et al. 1991, Alan Guttmacher Institute 1993). Such programs may change attitudes temporarily (at least as reported to a teacher), but they do not change behavior in any significant way.

Similar statistical distortions have been used to discredit programs that are not abstinence-only in approach. Seriously flawed is the conclusion, based on data collected in a 1986 Lou Harris Poll, that "teens who took a comprehensive sex education course (defined as one including contraceptive education) were subsequently 53 percent more likely to initiate intercourse than teens whose sex education courses did not discuss contraceptives."

First, the survey not did ask when intercourse was initiated in relation to the timing of the program; therefore, the word "subsequently" (implying causation) is patently misleading. Second, the analysis ignored the crucial variable of chronological age. Sexual intercourse among teenagers increases with age, as does the experience of having had a "comprehensive" program. Therefore, causation was implied, when in reality, correlation was the appropriate interpretation.

Besides the use of distorted data, groups demanding an abstinence-only approach dismiss people whose values regarding sexual behaviors differ from their own, asserting that these people are "without values." In fact, comprehensive sex education is based upon core human values that form the foundation of all ethical behavior, such as personal responsibility, integrity, caring for others, and mutual respect in relationships.

Moreover, comprehensive sex education is based on values appropriate to our democratic and pluralistic society —including respect for people's diverse viewpoints about controversial issues.

A WAKE-UP CALL FOR SOCIETY

Our entire society, not just sex education, has failed to provide children and youth with the educational, social, and economic conditions necessary to grow toward sexual health. In fact, truly comprehensive K-12 sexuality education, which at most exists in only 10 percent of schools nationwide, has hardly been tried

(Donovan 1989). Sexuality education—of whatever kind—is neither the cause, nor the cure, for our nation's sexual malaise.

In a society where children's consciousness is permeated by virulent images of sex—where their sexuality is manipulated by advertising and the media, where few adults provide helpful role models—we cannot expect sex education to perform a miracle. Curriculums that provide as their primary or sole strategy admonitions against nonmarital intercourse are destined to be ineffective and, in fact, insult the real-life needs of children and youth. In a society that conveys complex, confusing messages about sexuality, only comprehensive sexuality education can begin to address the diverse needs of youth and promote healthy sexual development.

POSTSCRIPT

Is Abstinence-Only Education Effective?

In mid-1997 the National Campaign to Prevent Teen Pregnancy, a private, nonpartisan initiative created by the Clinton administration, found no evidence that abstinence-only education delays sexual activity. The analysis revealed that "some abstinence programs are probably inadequate, and others probably do a fair amount of good." According to the campaign's research review, there is some evidence that broad sex education programs are more helpful to teenagers than abstinence-only programs are. Contrary to the fears expressed by many groups, the research reported by the Applied Research Center in Oakland, California, and the Public Media Center of San Francisco shows that broad sex education programs do not increase teenage sexual activity and that they can decrease intercourse and increase contraceptive use.

Several of the United States' most popular abstinence-only curricula came under attack in the campaign's report as inaccurate, fear-mongering, and biased. The report cited examples in which programs exaggerated the failure rate of condoms, implied that the AIDS virus passes through latex condoms, and suggested that after sex for which a condom was used, the genitals should be washed with Lysol disinfectant. The report also gave examples of what it called "scare tactics." In one educational video, when a student asks, "What if I want to have sex before I get married?" the instructor replies, "Well, I guess you'll just have to be prepared to die. And you'll probably take with you your spouse and one or more of your children."

Advocates of abstinence-only education dismissed the California findings. Commenting on the campaign's report, Amy Stephens, of Friends of the Family, claimed that this "report is a just a biased media campaign to discredit the Federal money for abstinence education.... These programs are not fear-based efforts that tell teenagers to just say no. They include character education and relationship education, and we believe they work. And Congress believes it will cut down welfare by reducing illegitimacy."

Where does the solution to this controversial issue lie? Which side offers the best argument? While each side argues over what is the best approach to decreasing teen pregnancy and sexual diseases, kids continue to get pregnant. Is it possible for the opposing advocates to stop criticizing one another and start working out a compromise? What might that compromise be? Or are the two sides so diametrically opposed that a compromise is impossible?

SUGGESTED READINGS

R. Brown et al., "Opinions in Pediatric and Adolescent Gynecology: Opinions on Abstinence Programs for Adolescents," *Journal of Pediatric and Adolescent Gynecology* (vol. 9, 1996), pp. 165–168.

R. Eisenman, "Conservative Sexual Values: Effects of an Abstinence Program on Student Attitudes," *Journal of Sex Education and Therapy* (Summer 1994), pp. 75–78.

J. J. Frost and J. Darroch Forrest, "Understanding the Impact of Effective Teenage Pregnancy Prevention Programs," *Family Planning Perspectives* (September 1995), pp. 188–195.

L. M. Kantor, "Attacks on Public School Sexuality Education Programs: 1993–94 School Year," *SIECUS Report* (August/September 1994), pp. 11–16.

T. Lewin, "States Slow to Take U.S. Aid to Teach Sexual Abstinence," *The New York Times* (May 8, 1997), pp. A1, A22.

K. L. Nelson, "The Conflict Over Sexuality Education: Interviews With Participants on Both Sides of the Debate," *SIECUS Report* (August/September 1996), pp. 12–16.

J. Olsen, S. Weed, D. Daly, and L. Jensen, "The Effects of Abstinence Sex Education on Virgin Versus Nonvirgin Students," *Journal of Research and Development in Education* (Winter 1992), pp. 69–75.

J. Olsen, S. Weed, A. Nielson, and L. Jensen, "Student Evaluation of Sex Education Programs Advocating Abstinence," *Adolescence* (Summer 1992), pp. 369–380.

J. Stryker, "Abstinence or Else!" *The Nation* (June 16, 1997), pp. 19–21.

B. Dafoe Whitehead, "The Failure of Sex Education," *The Atlantic Monthly* (October 1994).

On the Internet . . .

http://www.dushkin.com

Constitutional Law News
This Web site offers detailed overviews of constitutional law issues.
http://www.ljx.com/practice/constitutional/index.html

Feminists Against Censorship
Feminists Against Censorship was formed in 1989 by a group of longtime feminist academics and campaigners who wished to fight censorship from a feminist perspective. *http://www.fiawol.demon.co.uk/FAC*

Pornography and Sexual Violence
At this site, the National Coalition for the Protection of Children and Families provides information regarding the connections between pornography and sexual violence. *http://www.rain.org/~sbc-cap/html/porn_and_sexual_violence.html*

Santa Barbara County Citizens Against Pornography
Santa Barbara County Citizens Against Pornography (SBC-CAP) is a broad-based coalition of citizens concerned about the harmful effects of pornography. Their mission is to raise public awareness about the harms of pornography and thereby reduce sexual violence and victimization of adults and children.
http://www.rain.org/~sbc-cap/

The Ethical Spectacle
According to Jonathan Wallace, the publisher of this site, the goal of *The Ethical Spectacle* is to "shine a lantern on the intersection at which ethics, law and politics meet (or collide) in... the United States of America." Issues such as pornography and Internet censorship are discussed at this site. *http://www.spectacle.org/*

The Home Page of Dr. Laurie Shrage
Dr. Shrage writes frequently on issues of prostitution.
http://www.is.csupomona.edu/~ljshrage/

PART 3

Legal and Social Issues

According to the democratic ideal, the government should make only those laws that are absolutely necessary to preserve the common good. Unless government can demonstrate a "compelling need," it should not infringe on the privacy and personal rights of individual citizens. This principle raises some perplexing questions when applied to the rights of individuals to access sexual information and entertainment on the Internet, in print, or on videotape, as well as the effectiveness of chemical castration in preventing sex offenders from repeating their crimes. Two issues in this section deal with the rights of gay males and lesbians: the right to serve in the military and the right to receive the same benefits that the state accords married heterosexuals. This section also examines the implications of recent social controversies regarding date rape, sexual harassment, and dealing with HIV infections.

■ Should Sex Be Banned on the Internet?

■ Should Society Recognize Gay Marriages?

■ Is Chemical Castration an Acceptable Punishment for Male Sex Offenders?

■ Should Pornography Be Banned as a Threat to Women?

■ Is Homosexuality Incompatible With Military Service?

■ Have the Dangers of Date Rape Been Exaggerated?

■ Should Privacy Rights Yield to Public Health Concerns in Dealing With HIV Infections?

■ Is Sexual Harassment a Pervasive Problem?

ISSUE 12

Should Sex Be Banned on the Internet?

YES: Simon Winchester, from "An Electronic Sink of Depravity," *The Spectator* (February 4, 1995)

NO: Lisa Mason, from "The Elephant and the Net Cruiser: Regulating Communications on the Net," *Information Technology and Libraries* (December 1995)

ISSUE SUMMARY

YES: Social commentator Simon Winchester argues that society must take measures to regulate and control the dissemination of sexual barbarism and criminal perversion on the over 5,000 online newsgroups and equally numerous chat groups on the Internet.

NO: Lisa Mason, a science fiction writer, concludes that Internet censorship will not work, based on the Internet's global nature, its complex and different functions, the limits we already have on free speech, the fact that free speech is not always pretty, and the Internet's ability to enhance the freedom of citizens in a democracy.

On March 25, 1997, a parent whose child witnessed someone downloading a pornographic Web site at the local public library told the Warren Michigan City Council, "We should be sending a message to representatives in Washington and Lansing that there should be a chip or some other method of blocking pornography on the Internet at public education centers."

In Ohio, Cuyahoga County Public Library officials informed residents that anyone caught looking at obscene pictures on the library's new Internet terminals will be denied further access. Council members hailed the zero-tolerance policy.

Since 1995 Illinois citizens have been trying and several times have come very close to passing "neighborhood protection" legislation that would amend the statewide standard for obscenity. These bills would enable each of Illinois's 102 counties to create its own definition of obscenity. Since many libraries in Illinois serve residents in more than one county, librarians would be required to restrict Internet access based on each library user's county of residence. Libraries would also have to monitor users' Internet access through their facilities and restrict access according to the different obscenity definitions in force in the user's county and the library's location.

If this all sounds terribly complex and confusing, it is. But it is also typical of the heated debates now raging over efforts to restrict access to sexual material on the Internet.

Throughout history, people who are interested in sexual topics have always been quick to exploit new modes of communication. During the Renaissance, for example, the invention of movable type was quickly exploited by citizens interested in getting around the control of the nobility and the church over what was available in the previously hand-copied books. The inventions of photography, the radio, cinema, and television were quickly adapted by people who were interested in sexual materials. Twenty years ago inexpensive, high-quality hard-core videocassettes fueled the sale of video cameras, VCRs, and videocassettes. In 1994 hard-core interactive CD-ROMs racked up $260 million in sales, pushing the popularity of this electronic medium.

The latest topic of controversy in this area is sex on the Internet (or simply, the Net) and the World Wide Web. One difference between the Internet and other modes of communication that have been exploited sexually is that the Internet is global, not local. With the Internet hundreds of people around the world can share sex talk at one time. From its birth the Net has made images of erotica and pornography available to anyone, anywhere. However, many people are convinced that it is dangerous for "anyone," "anywhere," "anytime" to be able to access any information about sexuality that he or she finds interesting, helpful, or just curious. On the positive side, sex researchers, sex educators, sex therapists, health educators, psychologists, and doctors can find a wealth of reliable information about sexual attitudes and behaviors on the Internet. Furthermore, average men and women can find the latest information on breast cancer, male impotence and prostate problems, and other personal health issues. However, children, pornographers, and pedophiles can also use the Net for information and to make connections that society in general or some minority populations believe they should not have.

In 1995 Senators James Exon (D-Nebraska) and Daniel Coats (R-Indiana) introduced federal legislation to expand Federal Communications Commission regulations on obscene and indecent audio text. This law covered all content carried over all forms of electronic communication networks. When enacted, the Communications Decency Act of 1995 (S. 314) imposed fines as much as $100,000 and two-year prison terms on anyone who knowingly transmits any "obscene, lewd, lascivious, filthy, or indecent" communications on the nation's telecommunications networks, including the Internet. The law was immediately appealed and ended up being reviewed by the U.S. Supreme Court in June 1997.

Although written early in the debate over the Exon-Coats provisions in the Communications Decency Act, the following selections by Simon Winchester and Lisa Mason bring to the fore the many complicated aspects of this ongoing controversy.

YES

Simon Winchester

AN ELECTRONIC SINK OF DEPRAVITY

If last year it was merely modish to be seen speeding down the information superhighway, this year it is fast becoming essential, at least in America. Hitch your wagon to cyberspace, says the new Speaker of the House, Mr Newt Gingrich, and your democracy will become absolute, with all America joined together for the first time into one vast and egalitarian town meeting.

Mr Gingrich made this all clear two weeks ago when he unveiled a new system for bringing Congress to the electronically connected populace, which in honour of President Jefferson is called 'Thomas'. Anyone with a computer and a modem at home or in the office (or even up in the skies, courtesy of USAir's new back-of-seat telescreens) may now, with only the click of a few buttons, find the text of any bill, any resolution, any government statement.

Mr Gingrich is hugely excited by this idea—going so far as to suggest, and not at all facetiously, that perhaps every citizen be given a thousand-dollar tax deduction to allow him to buy himself a laptop computer. Thus will all America be conjoined, he argues, and thus will its democracy be ever strengthened as in no other country on earth.

Fine, say I, and not just because I will become richer by $1,000. For the last three years or so I have been a dedicated and enthusiastic user of the Internet. (The Internet—'the net' to those in the know—began innocently enough 20 years ago as a vast worldwide network of computers, linked together by government-funded telephone lines, with high-powered government-funded 'exchanges' to speed calls on their way, which enabled universities and governments to swap information. Five years or so ago, its controllers opted to make it more democratic, and now anyone is able to connect to it; tens of thousands of new subscribers join every day, and the net is becoming truly global, with at least 20 million regular users.)

I am a typical enough user. I send electronic mail—e-mail—to everyone who is similarly hooked up (it is lightning fast and essentially free); and I browse through the world's libraries and data-bases to do research for whatever book I happen to be writing. I bask happily in the Panglossian principle that the Internet seems to enshrine. By virtue of the net, I have complete freedom to explore and trawl for anything I want in what has become by custom an untrammelled, uncontrolled, wholly liberated ocean of information. The Internet seems and sounds to be something almost noble. One can understand why the US Congress named its own portion of the net after Jefferson: all knowledge there is is on hand for all the people—just the kind of thing the great man would have liked.

But this week, while I was peering into an area of the Internet where I have hitherto not lingered, I discovered something so appalling as to put all such high-minded sentiments into a quite different perspective.

I had stumbled, not entirely accidentally, into a sinkhole of electronic but very real perversion. The first thing I read, almost as soon as I entered it, was a lengthy, very graphic and in stylistic terms quite competently composed narrative that presented in all its essentials the story of a kidnapping, and the subsequent rape, torture, mutilation and eventual murder of the two victims. The author called himself by a code-name, Blackwind; and while it is quite likely that he is American, almost as certain that he is well-educated and quite possible that he is at least a peripheral member of the academic community, we know, and are allowed to know, nothing else about him.

His anonymity is faultlessly safeguarded by a system of electronics which has been built into the Internet, and which even the police and the other agents of the state are unable, technically or in law, to penetrate. This is, from their point of view, highly regrettable. Blackwind's offerings—and the very similar stories currently being published on the Internet by scores of men who are in all likelihood as deranged as he seems to be —should be subject to some kind of legal sanction, and for one very understandable reason: the victims of the story he has written are small children.

One is a six-year-old boy named Christopher, who, among other indignities, suffers a castration—reported in loving detail—before being shot. The other is a girl named Karen, who is seven years old and is raped repeatedly by no fewer than nine men, before having her nipples cut off and her throat slashed.

At the moment of my writing this, I find that there are perhaps 200 similar stories presently circulating and available on one of the so-called 'newsgroups' on the Internet. The choice of tales is endlessly expanded and refreshed by new and ever more exotic stories that emerge into this particular niche in the ether every day, almost every hour. You want tales of fathers sodomising their three-year-old daughters, or of mothers performing fellatio on their prepubescent sons, or of girls coupling with horses, or of the giving of enemas to child virgins? Then you need do no more than visit the newsgroup that is named 'alt.sex.stories' and all will reliably be there, 24 hours a day, for everyone with a computer and a telephone, anywhere on (or above) the face of the earth.

There are about 5,000 separate newsgroups on the net, each one of them presenting chatter about some scintilla of human knowledge or endeavour. I have long liked the system, and found it an agreeable way to discover people around the world who have similar interests. I used to tell others who were not yet signed up to the net that using newsgroups was like going into a hugely crowded pub, finding in milliseconds those who wanted to talk about what you wanted to know, having a quick drink with them before leaving, without once having encountered a bore.

And so, with an alphabetical list running from 'ab.fen'—which shows you how much fun you can have in Alberta—down to something in German called 'zer.z-metz.wissenschaft.physik', the enthusiasms of the world's Internet-connected population are distilled into their electronic segments. Alberta-philes can chat with each other, as can German physicists, and those who would bore these are left to chat among themselves. In theory, an admirable arrangement.

By Jeffersonian rights it should be uplifting to the spirit. In reality it is rather less so. In far too many groups the level of discussion is execrable and juvenile. Arguments break out, insults are exchanged, the chatter drifts aimlessly in and out of relevance. This is a reality of the electronic world that few like to admit. It is prompting many browsers to suspect, as I do, that a dismayingly large number of users of this system are not at all the kind of sturdy champions of freedom and democracy and intellect that Mr Gingrich and Mr Gore would like them to be.

More probably, to judge from the tone and the language in many of the groups, they are pasty-faced and dysfunctional men with halitosis who inhabit damp basements. And it is for them, in large measure, that the newsgroups whose titles begin with the code-letters 'alt.sex' seem to exist.

There are 55 of these, offering manna for all diets. Some are fairly light-hearted: alt.sex.anal, for example, contains much spirited chat about amusing uses to which you can put the colonic gateway; 'alt.sex.-voyeurism' seems to contain reasonably harmless chatter between a whole worldful of civic-minded Peeping Toms, who like to advise one another which public loos in which national parks have eye-sized knotholes in their doors. There is also 'alt.sex.nasal.hair', into which I have not thus far been tempted.

There are a number of the groups, though, which are not so amusing. There is 'alt.sex.intergen', where the last letters stand for 'intergenerational', which is the current paedophile bulletin-board; and there is my current target, 'alt.sex.stories'. I came across it by accident, and I double-clicked my mouse to open it, briefly enthralled. It did not take many seconds before I realised I had been ill-prepared for what was on offer.

There is a kind of classification system. Each story entry lists a title, an author (invariably either a pseudonym, or posted via an anonymous computer that had laundered the words and made the detection of the author impossible), and a series of code-words and symbols that indicate the approximate content.

Blackwind's many offerings—there were about 200 stories in all, with Blackwind contributing perhaps 15 of them —usually fell into the categories that are denoted by the codes 'm-f, f-f, scat.pedo.snuff', meaning that they contain scenes of male-female sex, female-female sex, scatological imagery, paedophiliac description and the eventual killing of the central victim. You quickly get, I think, the drift. Others are more horrifying still—those that end with the invariable 'snuff' scene, but whose enticements on the way include 'best', 'torture', 'gore' or 'amputees', and which refer to sex with animals, bloodlettings, sadistic injury, and the limitless erotic joy of stumps.

It is important to note that no one polices or, to use the Internet word, 'moderates', this group. (Some of the more obscure and non-sexual newsgroups do have a volunteer, usually a specialist in the field, who tries to keep order in what might, if unchecked, become an unruly discussion.) On 'alt.sex.stories' there is only one man, a Mr Joshua Laff of the University of Illinois at Urbana, who oversees the group, in a somewhat lethargic way. He helpfully suggests the codewords for the various kinds of perverse interests. He indicates to people who want to talk about sex stories, rather than actually contributing them, that they would be better advised to post their gripes on 'alt.sex.stories.discussion', next door, and so on.

But Mr Laff has no admitted scruples about what is permitted to go out over the air. So far as he is concerned, the First Amendment to the Constitution protects all that is said on 'alt.sex.stories' as free speech. What is demonstrated on these thousands of electronic pages is a living exhibition of the birthright of all who are fortunate enough to be born in the land that has given us the National Rifle Association, the Reverend Jimmy Swaggart, and Blackwind.

In truth, Mr Laff and those who support the published existence of such writings are technically right. No obscene pictures are published—these could be banned in law. No obscene truths are proffered, so far as we know—no confessions of real rapes, nor of actual acts of pederasty. And since all the stories are prefaced with warnings that those under 18, or those of a sensitive disposition, should read no further—devices that presumably attract precisely those they purport to deter—so, the authors seem to agree, their ramblings do no harm at all.

Most individual states legislate firmly or less so against printed pornography:

but so far no one has successfully prosecuted the Internet—not least for the reason that with so amorphous, so global and so informal a linking of computers, who out there can be held responsible? People like Blackwind simply open accounts at what are known as 'anonymous posting systems', and their words become filtered through two or three computers in such a way that the original source can never be known, and the perpetrator of any possible crime becomes impossible to find. And, anyway, those who endlessly cry First Amendment! here are wont to say that the publishing of mere words, even those from so clearly depraved an individual as Blackwind, can do no harm at all.

Commonsense would argue otherwise. A long and graphic account of exactly how and at what hour you wait outside a girls' school, how best to bundle a seven-year-old into your van, whether to tell her at the start of her ordeal that she is going to be killed at the end of it (Blackwind's favoured *modus operandi*), how best to tie her down, which aperture to approach first, and with what—such things can only tempt those who verge on such acts to take a greater interest in them.

Surely such essays tell the thinker of forbidden thoughts that there exists somewhere out there a like-minded group of men for whom such things are really not so bad, the enjoyment of which, if no one is so ill-starred as to get caught, can be limitless. Surely it is naive folly—or, at the other end of the spectrum, gross irresponsibility—to suppose otherwise.

Such material is not, I am happy to say, universally available. Some of the big corporations which offer public access to the Internet—American On-Line, CompuServe, Prodigy, Mr Murdoch's Delphi —have systems in place that filter out the more objectionable newsgroups. On America On-Line you may read the ramblings on 'alt.sex.voyeurism' and probably even 'alt.sex.nasal.hair', but you may read no 'alt.sex.stories', nor may you learn techniques for having real relationships, as paedophiles like to say they have, with young children.

But for those with the wherewithal to find more robust and uncontrolled access to cyberspace—and the means, quite frankly, most of the world's computer users, be they 90 years old or nine—all newsgroups are equally available, the evil along with the excellent. The question we have to ask is whether that should continue to be the case.

One might not mind so much if the material were being confined to the United States, where most of it originates. But in fact it manages to seep its electronic way everywhere, from Wiltshire to Waziristan. And crucially, no mechanism is yet in place allowing foreigners—whose laws might well be far less tolerantly disposed to it—to filter it out.

A computer-owner in Islington or Islamabad can have easy and inexpensive access to material over the net which would be illegal for him or her to read or buy on any British or Pakistani street. In China, pornographers would be imprisoned for publishing material that any Peking University students can read at the click of a mouse; and the same is true in scores of other countries and societies. The Internet, we smugly say, has become a means of circumventing the restrictive codes of tyrannies. But the reverse of this coin is less attractive: it also allows an almost exclusively American contagion to ooze outwards, unstoppable, like an oil spill, contaminating everyone and everything in its path.

We cannot, of course, prevent such things being thought. We may not prevent them being written for self-gratification alone. But, surely, science and the public can somehow conspire and cooperate to see that such writings as are represented by 'scat.pedo.torture.snuff' and the like are neither published nor read, and that they do not in consequence have the opportunity to spread outwards as an electronic contagion from the minds of those who, like Blackwind, first create them.

The Jeffersonian model for universal freedom which Mr Gingrich so rightly applauds could not take into account the barbarisms of the modern mind. Nor could it imagine the genius by which such barbarisms can be disseminated as they are today, in seconds, to the remotest and still most innocent corners of the world. Someone, perhaps even the Speaker of the House of Representatives, is going to have to consider soon the implications, for ill as well as good, of our venture out onto the information superhighway, or else there are going to be some very messy electronic traffic accidents.

NO

Lisa Mason

THE ELEPHANT AND THE NET CRUISER

The Way You Think...

"The way you think about things shapes the way your reality is." Ruby Maverick, a character in my novel, *Summer of Love*, says that when she challenges a far-future time traveler to examine the assumptions underlying his ontology of spacetime. The concept could very well be applied to recent attempts by the United States government to censor speech on the Net.

I'm honored to submit this address to the Library and Information Technology Association. In 1992, I attended the American Library Association conference in San Francisco where I heard presentations by Hans Moravec, Bruce Sterling, and David Brin at the LITA President's Program. Among other things, the discussion then raised the issue of censorship of speech on the Net, but focused more on the censorship implicit in the commercialization of cyberspace, the increasing dependence of university libraries on funding from big business, and the domination of the public's attention span by a dwindling number of hugely powerful arbiters of taste.

When talking about big business, I've developed Neil Postman's wonderful term "technopoly" into my own buzzword, "the technopolistic plutocracy," and I think librarians and academics should never waver in their vigilance against encroachment by the technopolistic plutocracy upon the intellectual integrity and experimentation that have been the benchmark of scholarship in the United States. Now, three years later, censorship of speech on the Net is still an issue of vital concern. ... I want to shift the focus from the censorship implicit in technopolization to a nasty and quite explicit piece of proposed legislation in the U.S. Senate known as the Exon Bill.

The Exon Bill: What Is the Senator Thinking?

The Exon bill mandates that anyone using a modem who makes, transmits, or otherwise makes available any comment, request, suggestion, proposal, image, or any other communication that is obscene, lewd, lascivious, filthy, or indecent will be subject to up to two years in jail or $100,000 in fines. The Senate... passed the telecommunications deregulation bill [in February 1996], of which the Exon bill is a part, and observers believe that the House is likely to pass some form of the bill, as well. Similar bills have been proposed in New Zealand and Singapore, so Senator [James] Exon [D.-Nebraska] is not alone in the effort to mandate morality on the Net.

The way you think about things... Listen to enthusiasts of the Net and you would conclude the online experience is the most exciting intellectual development since, say, the Renaissance. Mike Godwin, online counsel for the Electronic Frontier Foundation writes, "For the first time in history we have a many-to-many medium in which you don't have to be rich to have access and in which you don't have to win the approval of an editor or publisher to speak your mind. UseNet and the Internet...hold the promise of guaranteeing for the first time in history that the First Amendment's protection of freedom of the press means as much to each individual as it does to... the *New York Times*."

The way you think about things... But what if extremist anti-government militias use e-mail to distribute hate speech, together with instructions on how to make a bomb? What if sexually explicit materials of questionable literacy value are distributed over a network maintained by a distinguished university library? What if a university student broadcasts on a bulletin board a fictional account of a violent assault using a fellow student's name? What if publishers located in Finland distribute in Iowa computer-generated graphic images simulating child pornography? What if your ten-year-old daughter is cruising the Net looking for information about koala bears and she stumbles onto the *Penthouse* Web site? What if your eleven-year-old son is cruising the Net and he's looking for the *Penthouse* Web site?

Well, several of these scenarios have actually happened, and the others may be disturbing. I'm pretty confident no opponent of the Exon bill would argue that you shouldn't be concerned about exposing your child to materials you deem inappropriate for him or her. I'm fairly certain there are opponents of the Exon bill who have little interest in smut and who themselves never ever go to the *Penthouse* Web site. I'm quite sure most opponents of the Exon bill neither endorse hate speech nor approve of that university student's pathetic attempt at fiction. And I'm positive your child can go find your issues of *The New Yorker* in the magazine rack right next to *Scientific American* for some pretty sizzling short stories by Mary Gaitskill or Jamaica Kincaid far more easily than he or she can turn on your computer and access adult bulletin boards wallowing in obscenity.

Of course, you have to determine whether a communication in question is obscene, and we generally assume that stories in *The New Yorker* are literature. On the other hand, one reader's obscenity may be another reader's *Ulysses, Lolita,* "Howl," or "Love Book." Lest anyone think that the seizure of books is a relic of autocratic zeal half a century ago, remember it was the late sixties when Allen Cohen, the editor of the *San Francisco Oracle,* was arrested and jailed for distributing Lenore Kandel's poetry on San Francisco streets for ten cents a book.

It really does get down to the way you think about things, and I can think of at least five fundamentals that cybercops, cyberlibrarians, systems administrators, and especially senators should contemplate before they decide how they're going to shape the reality of the Net. The first two fundamentals speak to the ontology of the Net, the third and fourth address existing regulation of communication, and the fifth goes to us, we the people.

THE FIRST FUNDAMENTAL

Globalism Defies Traditional Notions of Jurisdiction

The first fundamental turns on the sheer global nature of the Net, which defies traditional legal notions of jurisdiction. This nonlocality may be a delight to net cruisers but is clearly a bane to the like of Senator Exon. Perhaps tiny Singapore, whose government cares little for civil liberties and also controls the island's only Internet gateway, may be able to clamp down on "obscene" or other "subversive" materials there, but the United States government and other governments in the global village will be hard-pressed to enforce such control.

The sheer ontological problem of the Net is that traditional legal notions of jurisdiction don't easily fit. Traditional jurisdiction is defined as the authority by which the court may take cognizance of a case, the power a court possesses to compel parties to appear before it, or a court's power to render judgment over specific subject matter or a specific person. But the "store-and-forward" nature of data distribution on computer systems means that data may exist on a system at some point in time (or place) even though the data did not originate there and will not ultimately end up there.

Attorneys have already careened full speed into the problem of jurisdiction in the Thomas case, in which systems operators based in California were tried and convicted in Tennessee when a postal inspector in the latter state downloaded images from the sysops' bulletin board. The court found that the images were obscene under the community standards of Tennessee. The Thomases are appealing because the images would not have been considered obscene under the community standards of California.

"Where" were the images, exactly, before the postal inspector pulled them down, and which community standards should prevail? If you decide that the community standards of the physical location where electronic data is ultimately downloaded prevail, then everyone everywhere who uploads anything on the Net will have to conform to the standards of the most conservative and restrictive jurisdiction to which any data could possibly end up—or face potential criminal prosecution of the most serious kind.

If anyone is worried about our proper sister state of Tennessee, what about Singapore? What about Saudi Arabia? How about Beijing? Or Iraq?

Such a scheme is not only unconstitutional, it's an administrative nightmare. It just won't work.

THE SECOND FUNDAMENTAL

The Elephant and Your E-mail

Remember the parable of the elephant and the four vision-challenged people —also known as the four blind men? Each blind man touched the elephant on only one part of its anatomy. Since the elephant is a huge beast and each man is comparatively small, each blind man conceived of the elephant according to his sensory perception of that one part. The elephant was either a rope, a brick wall, a tree stump, or a big, leathery fan depending on whether the man touched the elephant's tail, its ribcage, its leg, or its ear.

The Net is a lot like that elephant. At times, the Net functions as a one-to-one medium, sometimes as a one-to-many medium, and often as a many-to-many medium. E-mail is sort of like the postal system and sort of like the telephone system. Bulletin boards and newsgroups are sort of like talk radio. Some commentators compare the World Wide Web, where companies and others display commercial information, to a magazine publisher or perhaps a newsagent. Software archives and electronic libraries are a lot like traditional publishers or traditional libraries.

Would you tolerate it if our government could and did open every piece of mail or wiretapped every telephone call to make sure you weren't sending or receiving something obscene under who knows what sort of community standard? Essentially that's the modus operandi of the Exon bill.

The American Civil Liberties Union has stated that it "would most like to see the method of constitutional analysis... closely track that applied to the phone system, where censorship is essentially nonexistent, anyone can talk to anyone else, and there is a requirement of universal service. This would be preferable to that applied to cable TV where censorship is more common, all information flows in one direction from the cable company to the consumer,... and service is less universal."

Hopefully, the Exon bill notwithstanding, the future of the Net will lie closer to the elephant and the blind men. The moral of the parable is that none of the blind men understood what an elephant really is because none of the parts described the whole beast. So, too, with regulation of the Net. Regulation of the whole cannot be governed by regulation suitable for just a part. And we must find the appropriate analogy for each of those parts.

THE THIRD FUNDAMENTAL

Free Speech Isn't Free, Anyway

Free speech isn't free in the United States. Myriad laws already regulate seditious speech, libel, and obscenity. A sale may be fraudulent regardless of whether some huckster makes it through the mail, in cyberspace, or at your front door. Threatening to kill the President is illegal whether you do so through the postal service or in cyberspace. Conspiring to make bombs or distribute information about making bombs will surely win the attention of the FBI whether you use the Net or not. A harassing phone caller can be legally enjoined. Every medium through which ideas are distributed or communicated is subject to some regulation of content.

Some commentators believe that the various existing laws regulating communications may be adapted to interactive media. Some believe that the nature of the Net undermines the very basis of some regulations, rendering their application over broad.

For example, traditional libel law is grounded in the nature of traditional publishing, a one-to-many medium of communication, and addresses the typical inequality between the libeler and the victim. But in a many-to-many medium like the Net, victims of libel may far more easily provide an effective rebuttal that will reach as wide an audience as the libeler. Considering the policy of libel law, then, there are less compelling reasons to hold a systems operator to the same standard of liability as a newspaper publisher. And considering again the nature of that fabled elephant, it seems absurd to hold an online service to a standard applicable to a publisher, who edits everything, when a service may more appropriately be characterized as a common carrier like a telephone company, that doesn't regulate content at all.

And obscenity law? As we saw in the Thomas case, the traditional constitutional test for determining whether a communication is obscene turns in part on an application of "local community standards." The policy behind the community standards test is that what is acceptable in New York City, San Francisco, or Chicago should not govern what is acceptable in Memphis. But the converse is true as well: what is acceptable in a small conservative community cannot constitutionally narrow the standard of what is acceptable in Chicago.

Clearly, we need to examine whether the traditional laws governing communication are constitutionally sound when applied to this new medium.

THE FOURTH FUNDAMENTAL

Free Speech Isn't Always Pretty
Free speech isn't free in another way, too, and the cost may be tallied in emotional distress. The principle of free speech permits not only minority political opinion, but also speech that may be provocative, outrageous, juvenile, mean, or downright ugly.

I don't just mean the phenomenon of flaming, but incidents such as the university student I mentioned above who uploaded a fictional account of a violent assault using the name of another student and the discovery of personal insults on a men-only online conference at a West coast junior college. The student has been arrested; the online conference has been subjected to a "code of conduct" imposed campuswide and has recently been shut down.

These incidents are part of a disturbing trend in the scholastic community to impose "speech codes." It's quite true that the online speech involved was odious. I can understand that the policy driving speech codes and the desire to censor bigoted and sexist speech on campus are decent and good-hearted. Speech codes are intended to prevent harassment and spare victims' feelings. I'm not unsympathetic to good intentions. Harassment, like libel and obscenity, is legally actionable. Personally, I wish all the jerks of the world would grow up. Maybe they could stand to have their mouths washed out with soap.

But constitutionally you cannot throw the jerks of the world in jail or turn off their bulletin board for having foul mouths. And emotional distress, however painful, cannot override the constitutional protection of speech, however nasty. In the end, speech codes amount to impermissible censorship and must be challenged.

Offensive free speech may not encourage tolerance, but it does educate us about pluralism. It does put you on notice of just what you may be up against. And who knows; a brilliant comeback to a small-minded bigot may actually teach the bigot something. We can hope, anyway. The principle that "the way you think about things shapes the way your reality is" is intended to encourage everyone to face the facts, however ugly, and discover your own truth.

THE FIFTH FUNDAMENTAL

Human Nature and Democracy

The way you think about human nature will shape how you think human beings should be governed. The autocrat assumes that human nature is essentially weak, stupid, and easily manipulated. Thus, the autocrat seeks to control from above, to protect us from ourselves. By contrast, the basic assumption of democracy and the Constitution is that we human beings are essentially strong, intelligent, and capable of thinking for ourselves. We're especially capable of thinking for ourselves when we're fully educated and informed, when we're exposed to all sides of an issue. That's exactly what the First Amendment is designed to ensure.

Because the nature of the Net is a decentralized, many-to-many medium—a remarkably democratic medium—it would appear to be far more effective to empower net users to protect themselves rather than impose intrusive governmental regulation from the top down. The nature of the Net is consonant with the democratic view of human nature. The Net doesn't push content at consumers in quite the same way that television, movies, and radio do. Instead, consumers exercise their ability to think for themselves because they pull content out of the Net at will.

Let's enhance that control, not debilitate it.

Fortunately, some legislators and private developers have recognized this. Senator Patrick Leahy of Vermont has proposed the "Child Protection, User Empowerment, and Free Expression in Interactive Media Study Bill" that specifically aims at empowering the user to control commercial and noncommercial information received over interactive telecommunications systems. And just to show you how fast things are moving in this area, as of June 27, [1995,] charges were dropped against the university student I mentioned. As of June 28, Newt Gingrich himself has stated he does not support the Exon bill because he believes it is unconstitutional.

It seems to me that parents concerned about who their kids are chatting with have *got* to be the ones who monitor those chats. So far, I've heard of two home censorship programs, Kid Account in Sacramento, California, and SurfWatch in Los Altos, California. Other programs enabling private imposition of censorship based on purely personal choice are sure to be swiftly developed. If censorship has got to be imposed somewhere, I'd much rather it be imposed in *your* home—not in your home *and* my home *and* everyone else's.

Just as educated voters are enlightened voters, so empowered net users are protected net users. Reality may not always live up to theory, but that's the democratic ideal. I think it's an ideal worth defending as we speed into the digital future.

POSTSCRIPT

Should Sex Be Banned on the Internet?

In June 1997 the U.S. Supreme Court unanimously declared the Communications Decency Act of 1995 unconstitutional. Far from ending the debate, this decision sent advocates of restricting sex on the Internet back to their supporters in an effort to achieve their goals in some way that would be constitutionally acceptable. The debate now seems to be focusing on the use of filtering software programs, both for use by parents to protect children in their homes and as a requirement for computers in public libraries and schools. One problem is that filters can block sites of a sexual nature that are not legally obscene as well as informational sites on topics like sex education or drug use. The question here is, Do we really want to judge how old someone must be to access factual information on sexual orientation via the public library's computer?

The debate on this issue continues because it affects the privacy of every American citizen who surfs the Net or uses electronic mail and because it also reaches around the world. In June 1997 Germany launched an effort to prosecute America Online, Inc. for aiding in the distribution of pornography and violent computer games that violated Germany's obscenity laws. The international business community responded by pointing out that their executives would not be interested in opening or maintaining branches or doing business at all in countries where "multimedia laws" put their employees at risk of being arrested for violating some law regulating the content of Internet communications.

SUGGESTED READINGS

B. Branch and G. Conable, "To Filter or Not to Filter," *American Libraries* (June/July 1997), pp. 100–102.

D. Burt, "In Defense of Filtering," *American Libraries* (August 1997), pp. 46–48.

J. Gear, "Arguments for Library Self-Censorship Rebutted from a Conservative Standpoint," *Librarians at Liberty* (June 1997).

S. Levy, "No Place for Kids? A Parent's Guide to Sex on the Net," *Newsweek* (July 3, 1995).

M. G. Mason, "Sex, Kids, and the Public Library," *American Libraries* (June/July 1997), pp. 104–105.

R. S. Peck and A. K. Symons, "Kids Have First Amendment Rights, Too," *American Libraries* (September 1997), pp. 64–65.

ISSUE 13

Should Society Recognize Gay Marriages?

YES: Christine Pierce, from "Gay Marriage," *Journal of Social Philosophy* (Fall 1995)

NO: Robert H. Knight, from "How Domestic Partnerships and 'Gay Marriage' Threaten the Family," *Insight* (June 1994)

ISSUE SUMMARY

YES: Philosophy professor Christine Pierce argues that lesbian and gay couples should not be denied the monetary and social benefits that married heterosexuals enjoy. She contends that allowing gay and lesbian couples to register as domestic partners but not to marry leaves homosexuals as second-class citizens with unequal rights.

NO: Robert H. Knight, director of cultural studies at the Family Research Council, argues that recognizing gay marriages would destroy society's traditional protection of marriage and family as the best environment for children, legitimize same-sex activity, allow homosexuals to adopt children, and undermine the crucial kinship structure that gives continuity, community, and stability to our society.

In December 1990 a gay male couple and two lesbian couples filed suit against the state of Hawaii, charging that the state had violated the equal protection clause of the state constitution by denying them marriage licenses. On May 27, 1993, the state supreme court, in *Baehr v. Lewin*, overturned a lower court decision and held that Hawaii had in fact violated the equal protection clause of its own constitution by denying marriage licenses to these same-sex couples. In December 1995 a Hawaii legislative committee recommended legalizing same-sex marriage by a vote of 5–2. In case the legislature was not willing to legalize same-sex marriages, the committee offered a backup recommendation that the state implement a comprehensive domestic partnership law. A year later, in December 1996, a circuit court judge ruled that the state had failed to demonstrate any compelling state interest for not granting marriage licenses to homosexual couples. On April 29, 1997, the Hawaii legislature voted to grant gay couples the rights and benefits of married couples but stopped short of legalizing same-sex marriage.

Under this domestic partnership law, homosexual couples would be eligible for spousal benefits for insurance and state pensions, inheritance rights, the right to sue for wrongful death, and other benefits. Meanwhile, the legislature agreed to ask Hawaii's voters to approve a constitutional amendment in November 1998 that would give lawmakers the power to reserve marriage for heterosexual couples only.

Over a dozen states have hurried to adopt laws that would define marriage as the "union of a man and a woman" and deny recognition of gay and lesbian marriages, in the event Hawaii recognizes same-sex marriages. In January 1996 the U.S. Congress enacted the Defense of Marriage Act, allowing any individual U.S. state, territory, possession, or Indian tribe to ignore same-sex marriages legally recognized by Hawaii or any other state. Without the Defense of Marriage Act, all states would be required to give "full faith and credit" to a gay or lesbian marriage recognized by a single state, such as Hawaii.

In recent years American corporations have also been adapting to changing social values. About half of the *Fortune* 500 companies have policies barring discrimination against homosexuals, while half of the *Fortune* 1000 companies have domestic partnership health benefits. These companies include Microsoft, the International Business Machines (IBM) Corporation, the Walt Disney Company, Apple Computer, and Time Warner. A growing number of corporations go beyond offering employees with domestic partners basic health benefits. Domestic partner benefits, previously given only to heterosexual married couples, may include life, disability, and dental insurance; tax relief; bereavement and dependent care leave; tuition; use of recreational facilities; and purchase discounts on memberships at local health clubs, airline tickets, and other services.

Few issues in American society today generate as much heat and emotion as the debate over gay and lesbian marriages. In the following selections, Christine Pierce argues that gay men and lesbians should have the same right to marry and form a family as heterosexuals do, while Robert H. Knight contends that such recognition would destroy the stability of the family and society.

YES

Christine Pierce

GAY MARRIAGE

INTRODUCTION

"The effort to legalize gay marriage will almost certainly emerge as a major issue in the next decade," says law professor Nan D. Hunter in the October 1991 *Nation*. Why is this so? In part, what drives this issue is the practice of most United States employers and many institutions (such as the IRS) to give *significant* benefits including health, life, disability and dental insurance, tax relief, bereavement and dependent care leave, tuition, use of recreational facilities, and purchase discounts on everything from memberships at the local Y to airline tickets only to those in conventional heterosexual families. Although employee benefits are sometimes referred to as "fringe" benefits, they, in fact, make up a hefty portion of compensation. As such, married people are paid more than their nonmarried counterparts. Whether or not favoring the institution of marriage is justified, there remains the problem that those in heterosexual relationships at least have the option (indeed, the right) to marry, whereas lesbians and gay men in relationships do not (at least in the United States.)

Although I find monetary and benefit arguments convincing, what follows is a discussion of other types of considerations—legal, historical, ethical, and psychological—that are relevant to the issue of gay marriage. Of these, I find the so-called psychological ones most persuasive. Moreover, since some benefits can be gained by domestic partnership plans, the question of the comparative merits of marriage and domestic partnership needs to be addressed.

LEGAL ARGUMENTS

Although I will not dwell on the subject of law, a May 1993 Hawaii Supreme Court decision described by the Lambda Legal Defense and Education Fund as "astonishing" and possibly opening the door to gay marriage is worthy of mention. In *Baehr* v. *Lewin*, the first same-sex marriage case to reach a State Supreme Court in twenty years, the Hawaii Supreme Court held that

From Christine Pierce, "Gay Marriage," *Journal of Social Philosophy*, vol. 26, no. 2 (Fall 1995). Copyright © 1995 by *Journal of Social Philosophy*. Reprinted by permission. Notes omitted.

"denying marriage licenses to same-sex couples appears to violate the State constitutional guarantee of equal protection on the basis of sex." Overturning a lower court decision, the Hawaii Supreme Court sent the issue back for a trial at which the state must show compelling reasons for its discriminatory policy. According to Lambda, the Hawaii court refused to be satisfied with the "tortured and conclusory sophistry" of past court hearings on gay marriage and rejected the "tautological and circular nature" of the state's arguments that same-sex couples cannot marry because marriage is inherently for opposite-sex couples. Indeed, the argument from definition cited so recently in the Hawaii case has been around for a long time. In 1971, the Minnesota Supreme Court defined marriage as "a union of man and woman..." and in 1974, two men were denied a marriage license "because of the nature of marriage itself." As Richard Mohr puts it so nicely, "the courts [have held] that gay access to marriage must be a form of grand theft." The charge, says Mohr, is "theft of essence." "... [S]traights wouldn't really be married," he says, "if gays were ... the meaning of marriage would be revised beyond recognition if gays could marry...." Similar claims about the concept of "family" are commonplace in right-wing rhetoric today; it is said that so-called true families will be undermined if the concept of family is extended to include lesbian and gay couples.

Other possibilities for legal argument include privacy rights and Kenneth Karst's interesting suggestion that the Constitutional freedom of intimate association "... extends to homosexual associations...." These ideas I simply mention, concluding my remarks on le-

gal reasoning by noting the importance of a 1967 Supreme court case, *Loving* v. *Virginia*, which established the right to marry as a fundamental legal right. *Loving* overturned laws against interracial marriage in the United States. Presumably one can make an equal protection argument to the effect that even as the government cannot restrict choice of a marital partner by insisting on a particular race, so the government cannot restrict such a choice on the basis of sex. Of course, such an argument would only work in a state like Hawaii where the category of sex is constitutionally protected from discrimination. In sum, what is new on the legal scene is that gay advocates of gay marriage are making serious arguments that are at long last being taken seriously.

QUEER VS. STRAIGHT: HISTORICAL ARGUMENTS

As the title of a recent article conveys, however, "Some Gays Aren't Wedded to the Idea of Same-Sex Marriage." Journalist Anna Quindlen expands on this issue when she says, "Gay marriage is a radical notion for straight people and a conservative notion for gay ones. After years of being sledgehammered by society, some gay men and [lesbians] are deeply suspicious of participating in an institution that seems to have 'straight world' written all over it." Queer things—queer theory, Queer Nation, the protest chant, "we're here, we're queer, we're fabulous, get used to us"—assume that respect for distinctiveness, an opportunity to pursue a life that is "not straight" is what is wanted. While some traditionalists have called same-sex marriage a slap in the face of tradition and some queer theorists have repudiated the institution of marriage as not queer, both may have reason to pause. If Yale historian John Boswell is right, Christian marriage rites between same-sex partners date back to the fourth century, earlier than the widespread performance of heterosexual ceremonies in the eleventh century. Boswell claims to have found gay marriage rites in liturgical manuals and early legal documents that constitute clear evidence that " ... gay unions were comparable to heterosexual marriage." Both men and women were married using these rites, though evidence for lesbian unions is not as geographically widespread nor as ancient," Boswell says. He theorizes that "gay marriage rites ... appear to have started as a religious ceremony and were based principally on love ... includ[ing] an erotic dimension." He contrasts this history with heterosexual marriage which he says started as a civil ceremony with property exchange and later, when appropriated by the church, emphasized progeny and worldly success. So, it appears that queer theorists could claim or reclaim an institution that is part of their history. Indeed, the good history—the part about love and eroticism—is queer.

EQUALITY, JUSTICE, LIBERATION

Whether being able to marry is a desirable political goal is a question pretty much outside of law and history. At the least, it is a question that requires ethical analysis of matters such as equality, justice, oppression, and dignity. Attorney Paula Ettelbrick, who doubts that marriage is the path to liberation for anyone, argues against lesbian and gay marriages on the grounds that they will not alter the elitist character of marriage, that they will at best "minimally transform" the oppressive character of marriage by "diluting its patriarchal dynamic," and that they will not transform society or bring about a just world.

On the subject of a just world, Ettelbrick says,

> Gay marriage will not help us address the systematic abuses inherent in a society that does not provide decent health care to all of its citizens... nor will it address the pain of the unmarried lesbian who is prohibited from entering the intensive care unit... solely because she is not a spouse or a family member. Likewise, marriage will not help the gay victim of domestic violence who, because he chose not to marry, finds no protection under the law to keep his violent lover away.

Of course, allowing lesbians and gay men to marry will not address the issue of decent health care. Why, one might (indeed, *should*) ask, must one be employed by a company or an institution of a certain size or be married to someone who is in order to get health insurance? Presumably, in a just world, folks could get health care because they are valuable. Ettelbrick is absolutely correct in her view about the notions of "equality" or "rights" or "equal rights" when she says, "A pure 'rights' analysis often fails to incorporate a broader understanding of the underlying inequities that operate to deny justice to a fuller range of people and groups." Despite her claim that rights and justice should be combined, she goes on to argue that gay marriage will gain rights for a few, will make some lesbians and gays "insiders," but will not correct the imbalance of power between the married and the nonmarried. Thus, "justice would not be gained."

One answer to Ettelbrick is that she herself has put her finger on the way equality arguments usually work. They work on a limited scale. They do not do big jobs such as bring about a just society. As Mary Midgley puts it so clearly,

> ... equality... is a rather abstract ideal.... Who is to be made equal to whom, and in what respect? Historically the answers given have mostly concerned rather narrow groups.... The formula needed is something like, 'let those who are already equal in respect x be, as is fitting, equal also in respect y." ... Outsiders... who are currently not equal in respect x, cannot benefit from this kind of argument.... The notion of equality is a tool for rectifying injustices within a given group, not widening that group or deciding how it ought to treat those outside it.

Ettelbrick least understands the limited and painfully slow way that equality arguments normally work when she suggests that "... more marginal members of the lesbian and gay community (women, people of color, working class and poor) are less likely [than those more acceptable to the mainstream] to see marriage as having relevance to our struggles for survival." The fact that achieving the right to marry will not benefit everyone or everyone equally or solve all the world's problems is not an argument against it. What good, asks Ettelbrick, "... is the affirmation of our relationships (that is, marital relationships) if we are rejected as women, blacks, or working class?" The answer to the question, "What good is a job in philosophy if I am discredited as a woman?" is "A lot." Moreover, the exclusion of lesbian relationships from legal recognition directly affects survival issues that cut across class and race. As attorney Ruthann Robson notes, "... a member of a lesbian couple who becomes inca-

pacitated can be controlled by a person determined in accordance with relationships recognized under the rule of law, such as the father who does not believe she is a lesbian, the brother who abused her, or the husband she has not seen for twenty years but never divorced." The recent long and well-publicized estrangement between partners Karen Thompson and Sharon Kowalski (after a car accident which left Kowalski partially paralyzed, her father assumed her guardianship and denied Thompson even any visitation rights) is a textbook example of Robson's point.

Ettelbrick dismisses the importance of equality not only because it is of more use to those "... closer to the norm or to power...," but also because "... the concept of equality... only supports sameness." She continues: "The moment we argue... that we should be treated as equals because we are really just like married couples and hold the same values to be true, we... begin the dangerous process of silencing our different voices." I have argued elsewhere against the assumption that equality is similarity. In brief, whether or not differences are relevant depends on what kind of equality one is talking about. If one is talking about equal opportunity, then differences should be ignored, however, if one is talking about equal representation, differences are important. Even if equality did entail similarity, sameness is not always bad. Of course, sometimes sameness *is* bad, and that is part of Ettelbrick's worry. She says, "[Lesbians and gay men] end up mimicking all that is bad about the institution of marriage in our effort to appear to be the same as straight couples."

Others who disagree with Ettelbrick think that the participation of lesbians and gay men in the institution of marriage will alter the institution for the better. For example, Thomas Stoddard says, "... marriage may be unattractive and even oppressive as it is currently structured and practiced, but enlarging [it] to embrace same-sex couples would necessarily transform it into something new." Susan Moller Okin in her recent book *Justice, Gender and the Family* certainly makes a strong case against what she calls *gender-structured* marriage, thereby tempting others to suggest that an alternative, especially an alternative that is not gender-structured, has to to be better. Marriage and the family as currently practiced in our society, Okin says, "... constitute the pivot of a... system of gender that renders women vulnerable to dependency, exploitation, and abuse." The conventional family, she says, "is the linchpin of gender"; and gendered relationships, private and public, are thoroughly unjust. Martha Nussbaum in her review of Okin's book says, "[Okin] plainly has a strong preference for the nuclear family in something like its modern Western form.... But she never tells us what benefits she believes the modern Western family provides, or why, in view of the many alternatives that have been conceived, she still prefers the pattern that has proven, as she herself demonstrates, so resistant to reform in the name of justice."

If same-sex couples could marry, says Nan Hunter,

> ... the profoundly gendered structure at the heart of marriage would be radically disrupted. Who *would* be the "husband" in a marriage of two men, or the "wife" in a marriage of two women? And either way—if there can be no such thing as

a female husband or a male wife, as the right-wing argues with contempt; or indeed in some sense there *can* be, as lesbian and gay couples reconfigure these roles on their own terms—the absolute conflation of gender with role is shattered. What would be the impact on heterosexual marriage?

Unfortunately, Hunter does not answer this question. As we have seen, Thomas Stoddard is hopeful, Paula Ettelbrick is doubtful, and Martha Nussbaum wants to try something new because heterosexual marriage and the nuclear family are unjust institutions. I would not rest a case for the legalization of lesbian and gay marriage on the possibility that lesbians and gay men might improve the institution of marriage, for transformative values may not come about. Nonetheless, I am with Nussbaum here. We ought to pull the pin and see what happens. However, at the least arguments against lesbian and gay marriages based on the oppressive character of marriage should be rejected if the oppressive character referred to is due to the currently accepted gender requirements of marriage. This type of argument, exemplified in the following remarks by Ruthann Robson and S. E. Valentine, is widespread in lesbian writings: "Underlying the lesbian critique of marriage is the gendered perspective of marriage developed by feminists.... Marriage has remained interwoven with both the development and the perpetuation of patriarchy and women's status within the patriarchy." Even if the oppressive nature of marriage historically did count as a reason for devaluing marriage per se, and therefore gay marriage, it still could be argued that lesbians and gay men should have the right to marry. It is perfectly coherent to assert that lesbians and gay men should have the option to marry without claiming a necessary value for marriage, even as one can coherently claim that lesbians and gay men should have the option to serve in the military without valuing the military.

Paula Ettelbrick has one last formulation of her anti-equality argument. She says the idea of marriage is inconsistent with the goal of gay liberation which is to recognize the legitimacy of many different kinds of relationships. Interestingly, she favors domestic partnership plans which, she argues, better accomplish this goal. Such plans—on the part of municipalities and employers—almost universally define domestic partners to include lesbian and gay couples as well as unmarried heterosexual partners and extend to them some of the rights accorded to married couples. The qualifications for benefits approximate the qualifications for marriage, although in many instances they are more stringent. For example, domestic partnership requires couples to give evidence of commitment, whereas marriage does not. [I]n Ettelbrick's view, marriage is a "two-tier system of the 'haves' and the 'have-nots,'" and same-sex marriage simply perpetuates "the elevation of married relationships and of 'couples' in general ... further eclipsing other relationships of choice." Domestic partnership plans, on the other hand, "validate nonmarital relationships," thereby contributing to the goal mentioned above of recognizing many different kinds of relationships. It does seem that the idea of domestic partnership is more inclusive of diverse relationships than is marriage, although domestic partnership does not abolish the privileging of some relationships. Sisters who are really sisters and not closeted lesbians posing as sisters could get minimal benefits if they set up a household and are financially interdependent.

KINSHIP ARGUMENTS

Despite the attractive potential of registered partnerships, I think a separate and compelling argument can be made for lesbian and gay marriages. Although lesbians and gay men have made some progress in the area of individual rights in the United States, until very recently there has been an almost total nonrecognition of gay families. A chapter title of a recent book illustrates the exile of gays from kinship: "Is Straight to Gay as Family Is to No Family?" And Justice White, speaking for the Supreme Court's majority view that homosexual sex between consenting adults in their own bedroom is not protected by the right to privacy, said, in the *Bowers* v. *Hardwick* decision in 1986, "No connection between family, marriage, or procreation on the one hand and homosexual activity on the other has been demonstrated." The right to privacy in *Bowers* protects only marital privacy. Gay people were not seen by Justice White as being in relationships. Lesbians and gay men were not visible to him as couples, partners, families, kin. Had the Court interpreted the right to privacy as a right to sexual autonomy, gay people might have been seen, for all the Court had to be able to see was individuals who desired autonomy and who had some kind of a sexual life. But when the Court said the right to privacy is the right to marital privacy, then they saw no connection between marriage and gay people. A legal system or an ethical system based on principle will not be of any use to lesbians and gay men if they are not seen as the sorts of folks to whom these principles can apply.

Worse yet, think about an ethic based on sentiment. Take, for example, Mary Midgley's view: those nearest to us have special claims—claims which diminish in proportion to distance, either physical or social. Fortunately, Midgley says that those most distant need not always come at the end of the queue. Unfortunately, priority rankings among various kinds of claims are determined by the cultural maps worked out by individual societies, and nearness and kinship are real and important factors in our psychological makeup. The psychology presented here seems right to me. I care more about Morgan, my Maine Coon cat, than I do about the child I don't know who lives six blocks down the street. These feelings I have really matter, however much those folks who believe in universalizing ethical principles say that physical and social distance should not matter. However, appealing to sentiment as a way of justifying behavior as *ethical* can be as dangerous as it is comforting. It is, of course, comforting to hear that those folks one already cares about are just the ones that one ought to care about (or ought to care most about). Such a psychology explains, at least in part, why ethical views based on sentiment have not been applied positively to lesbians and gay men who are perceived as strangers and not as kin in our society.

One would expect lesbians and gay men to get a better deal from ethics based on principle, but arguments based on principle often do not work for gay people—evidenced by the 1986 *Bowers* case. A more recent example is the debate over Colorado Amendment 2 which illustrates how all civil rights of lesbians and gay men can be jeopardized because lesbians and gay men are not perceived as kin or as having important relationships. In July 1993, the state supreme court ruled that the voter initiative to outlaw gay rights laws must prove a compelling state interest in order to meet constitutional standards. The state's attorney general argued that "the State's desire to promote 'family values' provide[s] such a compelling interest." Amendment 2 was declared unconstitutional by a district court judge on December 13, 1993, on the grounds that it violated equal protection by usurping "the fundamental right of an identifiable group to participate in the political process," and it may be that the Colorado Supreme Court and the United States Supreme Court will continue in this lead. Nevertheless, the fact that anyone would offer "family values" as a good reason for the denial of equal rights is a measure of just how far lesbians and gay men are from being viewed as kin in our society. As one California court put it, in rejecting a similar initiative in Riverside, California, "All that is lacking is a sack of stones for throwing."

In short, moral arguments based on existing sentiment will not work for gay people; arguments based on principle should work but often do not, in part because sentiment plays a role in even principled ethics and law. Until current sentiments in our society are changed, lesbians and gay men will not be able to expect that ethical (and legal) principles will be applied fairly to them. Thus, it is important for the sake of creating new sentiments to press for gay marriage so that lesbians and gay men can become visible as couples, partners, families, and kin. Pressing for registered partnerships —or what some have called gay near-marriage—may not do the job. Those folks who in 1986 could not even imagine lesbians and gay men in relationships need to know that many lesbians and gay men—to quote the Supreme Court—view their relationships as "noble" and "intimate to the degree of being sacred."

CONCLUSION

In sum, I have raised the following issues: Married people are paid more than their nonmarried counterparts, while the possibility of choice regarding whether or not to marry has not been extended to lesbians and gay men. Marriage has been rejected as an undesirable political goal on the grounds that it is not queer, presumably meaning to a degree that marriage is not part of lesbian and gay history. But John Boswell's new discoveries of historical evidence indicate that marriage is in a very important sense queer. I have argued that the pursuit of equality should not be abandoned simply because it is often compatible with injustice. Nor should equality be discarded because it supposedly means "sameness" and sameness is bad. I have suggested that our assessment of the comparative merits of marriage and domestic partnership is to some extent a reflection of the respective values we place on equality and diversity. Although I have expressed my doubts about the transformative power of same-sex marriage, it seems to me that objections to gay marriage based on the gender structure of heterosexual marriage are misplaced. Lastly, I have argued that Americans have been allowed for too long to view lesbians and gay men only as individuals, i.e., not in relationships and as strangers, i.e., not as kin. I think that gay marriage needs to be on the political agenda for the sake of gaining a certain level of social awareness and acceptance of serious lesbian and gay relationships. I do not worry, as do some queer theorists, that pursuing a goal such as marriage will result in assimilation into invisibility or as Ettelbrick puts it, "[let us] fade into the woodwork." I think it is a far greater worry that the current invisibility as family is threatening to destroy any kind of a decent life at all for lesbians and gay men in the United States.

NO

Robert H. Knight

HOW DOMESTIC PARTNERSHIPS AND "GAY MARRIAGE" THREATEN THE FAMILY

For several years, homosexual activists have promoted the extension of marital benefits to same-sex couples (and, in some cases, unmarried heterosexual couples) in corporations and in the law. This practice, called "domestic partnerships" is billed as an extension of tolerance and civil rights, but would actually undermine the institutions of marriage and family.

So, too, is the drive to confer actual marital status on same-sex relationships through the legalization of so-called gay marriage.

Policies and laws that confer partner benefits or marital status on same-sex couples should be opposed because they:

• send a clear signal that companies or cities no longer consider marriage a priority worth encouraging above other kinds of relationships;

• deny the procreative imperative that underlies society's traditional protection of marriage and family as the best environment in which to raise children;

• seek to legitimize same-sex activity and homosexuals' claim that they should be able to adopt children, despite the clear danger this poses to children's development of healthy sexual identities;

• injure the crucial kinship structure, which is derived from marriage and family and imparts continuity, community, and stability to societies;

• violate freedom of religion, as more and more devout Christian, Jewish and Muslim employees and citizens are told that they must accept as "moral" what their faiths teach is immoral;

• mock the idea of commitment, since most domestic partner laws allow for easy dissolution of the relationship and the registry of several partners (consecutively) a year;

• breed cynicism, because they defy common understanding about the relative worth of particular relationships. Societies must have intact families to survive; societies do not need any homosexual relationships in order to flourish. To equate them is to lie about them.

From Robert H. Knight, "How Domestic Partnerships and 'Gay Marriage' Threaten the Family," *Insight* (June 1994). Copyright © 1994 by The Family Research Council, 801 G Street, NW, Washington, DC 20001. Reprinted by permission. Notes omitted.

Furthermore, the drive for homosexual status is undergirded by faulty assertions of scientifically based findings, such as the now-discredited, Kinsey-derived 10 percent estimate of homosexuality in the population; the media-touted but unproven "genetic link" to homosexual behavior; and the deliberate misinterpretation of key psychological studies about homosexuality.

A GROWING CAMPAIGN

Across America, cities, corporations and universities are being lobbied or intimidated into conferring marital benefits on same-sex couples.

• Several cities, including Seattle, Madison (Wisconsin) and the California cities of Los Angeles, San Francisco, Berkeley, Laguna Beach, Santa Cruz and West Hollywood, have extended employee family benefits to same-sex partners. In the District of Columbia, the City Council voted in 1992 to add domestic partners to the city's health insurance policy, but the policy was deleted by Congress in an appropriations bill. Proponents plan to try again to enact the extension.

• In 1990, Stanford University adopted rules granting unmarried couples, including homosexuals, access to dormitories and other campus facilities. Later, "family housing," which had been set aside primarily for married couples with children, was officially opened to homosexuals. Several other campuses have extended benefits such as campus housing to same-sex couples, including the University of Chicago, Harvard, Columbia, Dartmouth, Iowa, Iowa State, the University of Wisconsin, Minnesota, Northwestern, Indiana, and the Massachusetts Institute of Technology.

• Several corporations have extended family benefits to same-sex partners, although most corporations have resisted doing so. Only six of the Fortune 1000 companies have instituted domestic partner plans, and about seventy companies nationwide permit unmarried partners to join company health plans. The co-chair of the National Gay and Lesbian Task Force, Elizabeth Birch, is also senior litigation counsel at Apple Computer. She says, "No area has more potency than the advancement of gay rights in the workplace." Companies/institutions with same-sex benefits include Time Warner, Levi-Strauss, Apple, Lotus, Microsoft, MCA, Inc., Viacom Inc., Oracle Systems Corp., Digital, Ben & Jerry's, Minnesota Public Radio, Montefiore Hospital in New York, the *Village Voice* newspaper, Borland International Inc., and the Federal National Mortgage Association. Institutions that promote homosexuality through diversity training and officially sanctioned homosexual employees' groups include many major universities, AT&T (with a 1,000-member homosexual employees group), U.S. West, Xerox, and federal agencies, such as the departments of Transportation, Agriculture, Health and Human Services, and Housing and Urban Development.

• In Hawaii, the state Supreme Court has ruled that the state must show a "compelling interest" in denying marital status to homosexual couples. A constitutional conflict looms should the Hawaii court legalize "gay marriage," because under the U.S. Constitution's full faith and credit clause, states must accord reciprocity to other states in such matters as marriage and drivers' licenses. So, theoretically, a homosexual couple could marry in Honolulu, move to California, and demand that the Golden State recognize their "marriage."

THE HOMOSEXUAL AGENDA

Why is all this happening right now? It seems like only yesterday that homosexual activists wanted only "tolerance," demanding no special rights to compete with the prevailing moral order. But now, activists are on the verge of actually changing the definitions of marriage and family.

Homosexual activist Michelangelo Signorile speaks with a candor not found in most media portrayals of the issue. Discussing ways to advance homosexuality, he urges activists:

> ... to fight for same-sex marriage and its benefits and then, once granted, redefine the institution of marriage completely, to demand the right to marry not as a way of adhering to society's moral codes but rather to debunk a myth and radically alter an archaic institution that as it now stands keeps us down. The most subversive action lesbians and gay men can undertake—and one that would perhaps benefit all of society— is to transform the notion of "family" entirely.

Signorile is right about the subversive nature of the goal of "gay marriage," but homosexuals would not have to go to any lengths to "redefine" marriage once granted that status. The very act of obtaining recognition for same-sex relationships on a par with marriage would transform the notion of "family" entirely.

While Signorile might be dismissed as just one voice, his views are in keeping with those of other high-profile homosexual activists. Franklin Kameny, a Washington, D.C.-based leader of the

homosexual rights movement for three decades, has this to say about families:

> ... the "traditional" family has been placed upon such a lofty pedestal of unquestioning and almost mindless, ritualistic worship and endlessly declared but quite unproven importance that rational discussion of it is often well-nigh impossible.... There is no legitimate basis for limiting the freedom of the individual to structure his family in nontraditional ways that he finds satisfying.

Thomas Stoddard, leader of the drive to lift the military's ban on homosexuals and former president of the Lambda Legal Defense Fund, now known as the Lambda Legal Defense and Education Fund, a homosexual legal foundation, sees marriage as the prime vehicle to advance societal acceptance of homosexuality:

> I must confess at the outset that I am no fan of the "institution" of marriage as currently constructed and practiced.... Why give it such prominence? Why devote resources to such a distant goal? Because marriage is, I believe, the political issue that most fully tests the dedication of people who are not gay to full equality for gay people, and also the issue most likely to lead ultimately to a world free from discrimination against lesbians and gay men. Marriage is much more than a relationship sanctioned by law. It is the centerpiece of our entire social structure, the core of the traditional notion of "family."

Lesbian activist Paula Ettelbrick, former legal director of the Lambda Legal Defense and Education Fund and now policy director for the National Center for Lesbian Rights, supports the "right" of homosexuals to marry, but opposes marriage as oppressive in and of itself. She says homosexual marriage does not go far enough to transform society:

> Being queer is more than setting up house, sleeping with a person of the same gender, and seeking state approval for doing so.... Being queer means pushing the parameters of sex, sexuality, and family, and in the process, transforming the very fabric of society.... As a lesbian, I am fundamentally different from non-lesbian women.... In arguing for the right to legal marriage, lesbians and gay men would be forced to claim that we are just like heterosexual couples, have the same goals and purposes, and vow to structure our lives similarly.... We must keep our eyes on the goals of providing true alternatives to marriage and of radically reordering society's views of reality.

MARRIAGE, DOMESTIC PARTNERSHIPS AND THE LAW

No jurisdictional unit in the United States —town, city, or state—recognizes same-sex couples as "married." Protections favoring marriage are built into the law and the culture because of the central importance of the family unit as the building block of civilization. In 1888, the U.S. Supreme Court described marriage "as creating the most important relation in life, as having more to do with the morals and civilization of a people than any other institution."

However, some jurisdictions are moving toward redefining the family to include same-sex relationships, and there is a movement within the legal community to overhaul the definitions of marriage and family. A note in the *Harvard Law Review* in 1991 advocated replacing the formal definition of family with an elastic standard based "mainly on the strength or duration of emotional bonds," regard-less of sexual orientation. The note recommends redefining the family through "domestic partner" or family "registration" statutes that go beyond the limited benefits now conferred by existing domestic partnership laws so as to "achieve parity" between marriage and other relationships.

In 1990, San Francisco Mayor Art Agnos appointed lesbian activist Roberta Achtenberg (currently assistant secretary of the U.S. Department of Housing and Urban Development) to chair the Mayor's Task Force on Family Policy. The final report of the task force defines the family this way:

> A unit of interdependent and interacting persons, related together over time by strong social and emotional bonds and/or by ties of marriage, birth, and adoption, whose central purpose is to create, maintain, and promote the social, mental, physical and emotional development and well-being of each of its members.

In this definition, which could reasonably be described as a formulation by homosexual activists, marriage is no longer the foundation for families but secondary to "strong social and emotional bonds." This definition is so vague that multiple-partner unions are not excluded, nor any imaginable combination of persons, including a fishing boat crew. The whole point is to demote marriage to a level with all other conceivable relationships.

The Task Force's definition of "domestic partners" is almost as vague, but limits the relationship to two partners: "Two people who have chosen to share all aspects of each other's lives in an intimate and committed relationship of mutual caring and love."

The District of Columbia City Council legislation defines "domestic partner" as "a person with whom an individual maintains a committed relationship," which is defined as "a familial relationship between two individuals characterized by mutual caring and the sharing of a mutual residence." One of the partners must be a city employee "at least eighteen years old and is competent to contract"; "not be related by blood closer than would prohibit marriage in the District"; "be the sole domestic partner of the other person"; and "not be married."

Applicants would qualify by signing a "declaration of domestic partnership" to be filed with the mayor, and which could be terminated by filing a termination statement with the mayor, which takes effect six months after filing. After that, another partner could be registered. Benefits include granting of sick leave, health insurance, and funeral leave.

Domestic partnership laws have been imposed or enacted by governmental agencies without much say from the public. When citizens do get a chance to give their views, they reject the notion. In May 1994, the city of Austin, Texas, became the first U.S. jurisdiction to overturn an existing domestic partners law when the citizenry voted 62 percent to 38 percent to undo what the city council had enacted. In other jurisdictions, notably Cincinnati, Tampa, and Lewiston, Maine, voters overwhelmingly voted to roll back homosexual rights laws, which are the foundation of the claim for the "right" of domestic partnership status. Even in liberal San Francisco, voters rejected domestic partnerships in 1991, although the policy was later approved.

In the courts, the issue has returned repeatedly since 1976, when the famous "palimony" case of *Marvin* v. *Marvin*

held that a property agreement between two unmarried adults who live together and engage in sex is enforceable in a court of law. In most cases, judges, with some notable exceptions, have rejected claims made by homosexual partners to marital-type recognition concerning property allocation and custody of children. In September 1993, a Virginia judge awarded custody of a boy to his grandmother, removing him from his mother's lesbian household. An appeals court overturned that ruling, however, and the case is making its way toward the Supreme Court. In California, a lesbian lost her bid to enforce a "co-parenting" agreement with a biological mother after the couple terminated their relationship. In West Virginia, the state supreme court in July 1993 granted a lesbian mother a stay of an order to remand custody of her children to their father. A circuit court had issued the order, citing as cause that the mother had moved in with her lesbian companion.

HAWAII

In May 1993, the Hawaiian Supreme Court ruled three to one that the state's exclusion of same-sex couples from marital status may be unconstitutional because it amounts to sex discrimination. Marriage is a civil right, the court said, and when the state says who may marry (and by implication, who may not), it violates the guarantee of equal protection under the law. The court invited the state to offer compelling reasons why marriage should be limited to opposite-sex couples.

In April 1994, the state legislature overwhelmingly passed a bill defining marriage in the traditional sense and defending it as the time-honored foundation for procreating and raising children. But many observers expect the liberal Hawaiian court to mandate "gay marriage." Also pending in Hawaii is a domestic partnership bill, which State Senator Ann Kobayashi, a homosexual rights supporter, praised as "a foot in the door" toward legalization of same-sex "marriage."

Homosexual activists, including those in Hawaii, often compare their quest for marital status with an interracial couple's legal victory in *Loving* v. *Virginia*. In that 1967 case, the Supreme Court struck down laws preventing marriage between people of different races as violating the equal protection and due process clauses of the Fourteenth Amendment to the Constitution.

But the court never came close to redefining the institution of marriage itself, which is what would have to occur for same-sex relationships to be accorded marital status. The false equation of a benign, nonbehavioral characteristic such as skin color with an orientation based precisely on behavior finds no support within the law.

In the 1970s, homosexuals unsuccessfully challenged marriage laws in Minnesota, Kentucky, and Washington state. In the Minnesota case, the state supreme court noted, "The institution of marriage as a union of man and woman, uniquely involving the procreating and rearing of children within a family, is as old as the book of Genesis.... This historic institution is more deeply founded than the asserted contemporary concept of marriage and societal interests for which petitioners contend."

Only relationships have not been accorded the same status as marriage because they do not contribute in the same way to a community. To put it bluntly,

societies can get along quite well without homosexual relationships, but no society can survive without heterosexual marriages and families. In fact, because the term "heterosexual marriage" is redundant, the term "marriage" will mean in this paper what it has always meant: the social, legal, and spiritual union of a man and a woman. "Gay marriage" is an oxymoron, an ideological invention designed to appropriate the moral capital of marriage and family toward the goal of government-enforced acceptance of homosexuality.

THE IMPORTANCE OF DEFINITION

Marriage / a: the state of being united to a person of the opposite sex as husband or wife; b: the mutual relation of husband and wife: wedlock; c: the institution whereby men and women are joined in a special kind of social and legal dependence for the purpose of founding and maintaining a family.

———*Webster's Third New International Dictionary of the English Language Unabridged*, Merriam-Webster Inc., Springfield, Mass., 1981, p. 1284.

To place domestic partner relationships on a par with marriage denigrates the marital imperative. But to describe such relationships as "marriage" destroys the definition of marriage altogether. When the meaning of a word becomes more inclusive, the exclusivity that it previously defined is lost. For instance, if the state of Hawaii decided to extend the famous—and exclusive—"Maui onion" appellation to all onions grown in Hawaii, the term "Maui onion" would lose its original meaning as a specific thing. Consumers would lack confidence in buying a bag of "Maui onions" if all onions could be labeled as such. The same goes for any brand name or even wine from Bordeaux as opposed to wine from California. Likewise, if "marriage" in Hawaii ceases to be the term used solely for the social, legal and spiritual bonding of a man and a woman, the term "marriage" becomes useless. Other states rightly could challenge Hawaii's marriage licenses as meaning something entirely different from what is meant in Pennsylvania or California.

Homosexual activist Tom Stoddard acknowledges that "enlarging the concept to embrace same-sex couples would necessarily transform it into something new.... Extending the right to marry to gay people—that is, abolishing the traditional gender requirements of marriage —can be one of the means, perhaps the principal one, through which the institution divests itself of the sexist trappings of the past."

In other words, while many homosexual spokesmen say they want only to be left alone to enjoy the benefits of marriage, Stoddard rightly sees the expanded definition as a way of attacking the institution itself.

Once the "one man, one woman" definition is abandoned, there is no logical reason for limiting it to two people or even to people. Back to the Maui onion example: Hawaii's garlic growers could demand that the exclusive use of the term "Maui onions" gives onion farmers an advantage, and is therefore "discrimination." Of course, garlic growers could qualify for the "Maui onion" label by growing onions in Maui under the Maui requirements. Likewise, homosexuals are not denied the right to marry. Like anybody else, they can qualify for the appellation of marriage by fulfilling its requirements. But they cannot call same-sex relationships "marriage" since

they are lacking a basic requirement; they are missing an entire sex. The joining of the two sexes in permanence is the very essence of marriage. Once the "one man, one woman" definition is abandoned, there is no logical reason for limiting "marriage" to two people or even to people. Why not have three partners? Or why not a man and his daughter? Or a man and his dog? The logical reason to extend "marriage" to homosexual couples has nothing to do with marital integrity, but only reflects the fact that homosexuals want the same status regardless of its real meaning. Anything less, they say, is a denial of human rights. If so, then a threesome or a foursome seeking marital status can similarly claim that their sexual proclivities must be recognized by society and the law as the equal of marriage or they are facing discrimination.

Destroying definitions does enormous damage not only to marriage but to the idea of truth. Calling two lesbians a "marriage" is telling a lie, and official recognition of this lie breeds the sort of cynicism found in totalitarian societies, where lies are common currency.

THE MYTH OF HOMOSEXUAL MONOGAMY

In 1992, organizers of the homosexuals' 1993 March on Washington met in Texas to draft a platform of demands. Known as "the Texas platform," it was later toned down to make it more palatable to a mass audience. The original section on "family," however, is revealing as to the intentions of the movement. In addition to Demand No. 40, "the recognition and legal protection of all forms of family structures," the writers called for Demand No. 45, "legalization of same-sex marriages," and Demand No. 46, "legalization of multiple partner unions."

An enormous body of research indicates that monogamy is not the norm for the average homosexual. But even when it is, the result is not necessarily healthier behavior. A study published in the journal *AIDS* found that men in steady relationships practiced more anal intercourse and oral-anal intercourse than those without a steady partner. In other words, the exclusivity of the relationship did not diminish the incidence of unhealthy behavior that is the essence of homosexual activity. Curbing promiscuity would help curb the spread of AIDS and the many other sexually transmitted diseases that are found disproportionately among homosexuals, but there is little evidence that "monogamous" homosexual relationships function that way. An English study also published in the journal *AIDS* found that most "unsafe" sex acts occur in steady relationships.

In April 1994, the homosexual-oriented magazine *Genre* examined current practices among male homosexuals who live with partners. The author concluded that the most successful relationships are possible largely because the partners have "outside affairs."

An excerpt:

"I think we are seeing a new phenomenon in the gay community," announces Guy Baldwin, an L.A.-based psychologist whose practice is mostly comprised [sic] of gay men. "It is the appearance of the well-adjusted open gay marriage." Historically, Baldwin argues, gay men have always engaged in erotic experiences outside a primary relationship, "but they have done so with a great deal of trepidation, soul-searching, and lots of beating up on themselves." For Baldwin's part, what's new is that gay

men are no longer holding themselves up to the rigorous standards offered by mainstream society, which equates emotional fidelity with erotic exclusivity.... "With all the talk about legalizing marriage for gays, there's an assumption in the minds of most people I talk to that only rarely does that legalization include monogamy."

According to the *Genre* article, in 1993, David P. McWhirter and Andrew M. Mattison, authors of *The Male Couple*, "reported that in a study of 156 males in loving relationships lasting from one to thirty-seven years, only seven couples considered themselves to have been consistently monogamous. Most understood outside sex, and even outside love, as the norm. 'It should be recognized that what has survival values in a heterosexual context may be destructive in a homosexual context,' argues a couple in the McWhirter and Mattison study. They add, 'Life-enhancing mechanisms used by heterosexual men and women should not necessarily be used as a standard by which to judge the degree of a homosexual's adjustment.' In other words, to adapt heterosexual models to homosexual relations is more than just foolhardy; it's an act of oppression."

Former homosexual William Aaron explains why "monogamy" has a different meaning among homosexuals:

In the gay life, fidelity is almost impossible. Since part of the compulsion of homosexuality seems to be a need on the part of the homophile to "absorb" masculinity from his sexual partners, he must be constantly on the lookout for [new partners]. Consequently the most successful homophile "marriages" are those where there is an arrangement between the two to have affairs on the side while maintaining the semblance of permanence in their living arrangement.

SEXUAL REVOLUTION: LEVELER OF CIVILITY

As the research of the late Harvard sociologist Pitirim Sorokin reveals, no society has loosened sexual morality outside of marriage and survived. Analyzing studies of cultures spanning several thousand years on several continents, Sorokin found that virtually all political revolutions that brought about societal collapse were preceded by sexual revolutions in which marriage and family were no longer accorded premier status. To put it another way, as marriage and family ties disintegrated, the social restraints learned in families also disintegrated. Chaos results, and chaos ushers in tyrants who promise to restore order by any means, Sorokin notes.

Self-governing people require a robust culture founded on marriage and family, which nurture the qualities that permit self-rule: deferred gratification, self-sacrifice, respect for kinship and law, and property rights. These qualities are founded upon sexual restraint, which permits people to pursue longterm interests, such as procreating and raising the next generation, and security benefits for one's children.

According sex outside marriage the same protections and status as the marital bond would destroy traditional sexual morality, not merely expand it. One can no more "expand" a definition or moral principle than one can continually expand a yardstick and still use it as a reliable measure.

The drive to delegitimize marriage by hijacking its status for other relationships, including unmarried opposite-sex couples, is being funded and directed by the homosexual rights movement. Lawsuits filed against landlords unwilling to rent to unmarried couples out of religious conviction are largely the work of the Lambda Legal Defense and Education Fund, the American Civil Liberties Union's homosexual legal project, and other homosexual activist organizations intent on using government power to force acceptance of their agenda. If the rights of landlords to refuse to aid and abet what they consider sinful behavior are abridged, it is a small legal step to force landlords, even in households with children, to rent to anyone regardless of sexual orientation. In this way, freedom for homosexuals would be expanded, but at the expense of the freedom of those who find homosexuality destructive, immoral, and unhealthy.

So far, the courts have rejected the claims of homosexuals and unmarried couples in this regard. In a series of recent cases, the courts have ruled that landlords cannot be compelled by law to betray their religious objections to fornication. In May 1994, a California appeals court ruled that the California Fair Employment and Housing Commission erred in fining a sixty-one-year-old landlady, Evelyn Smith, $954 for refusing to rent a duplex to an unmarried couple. The agency had also required Mrs. Smith to post a sign saying she would not discriminate against unmarried people. The three-judge panel found that the order "penalizes [Mrs. Smith] for her religious belief that fornication and its knowing facilitation are sinful."

The Boston-based Gay and Lesbian Advocates and Defenders had filed an amicus brief in the case, and Lambda Legal Defense Fund senior staff attorney Evan Wolfson denounced the verdict, saying that religious beliefs should retreat "when it comes to public good, such as public housing and access to public housing." In saying this, Mr. Wolfson ignored the distinction between government-run "public housing" and private property, as owned by Mrs. Smith.

Courts also have upheld the rights of landlords in Massachusetts, Minnesota, Illinois, and in other California jurisdictions.

THE IMPORTANCE OF FAMILY TIES

For thousands of years, in all successful cultures, homosexuality has been discouraged through social norms and legal prohibition. Cultures have always found it necessary to encourage new marriages and protect existent marriages by extending rewards and privileges for this productive behavior and by extending sanctions and stigmas to unproductive behavior, such as promiscuous sex and homosexual sex. Research and common sense show that the health of any given society depends largely on the number of intact, mom-and-dad families. People living in other arrangements benefit from the social order derived from the marital order.

Marriage-based kinship is essential to stability and continuity. A man is more apt to sacrifice himself to help a son-in-law than some unrelated man (or woman) living with his daughter. Kinship entails mutual obligations and a commitment to the future of the community. Homosexual relationships are a negation of the ties that bind—the continuation of kinship through procreation of children. To accord same-sex relationships the same status as a marriage is to accord them a value that they cannot

possibly have. Marriages benefit more than the two people involved, or even the children that are created. Their influence reaches children living nearby, as young minds seek out role models. The stability they bring to a community benefits all. And the best chance for having a successful, strong marriage is to grow up in a family with a strong marriage as its foundation. This does not mean that people in divorced families or single-parent homes are unable to achieve their own strong family, just that it is more difficult since their role models did not reflect the mom-and-dad family on a daily, longterm basis. A homosexual household compounds the problem by not only lacking one entire sex in the household's foundational relationship but by presenting an aberrant form of sexuality as something "normal."

PROTECTING CHILDREN

A major reason for discouraging societal recognition of homosexual relationships on the partnership level or as "marriages" is the boost such arrangements give to the concept of homosexual adoption of children. Currently, only two states, Florida and New Hampshire, have laws preventing homosexuals from adopting children. This is because it has been considered unthinkable and unnecessary, not because people favor adoption of children by homosexuals. Polls over the past two decades indicate strong societal disapproval of homosexual adoptions. But approval of same-sex relationships undermines much of the moral argument against same-sex couples adopting children. If two same-sex people are seen as the equivalent of husband and wife, it becomes easier for homosexuals to argue, falsely, that a same-sex couple provides the same environment for raising children.

BREAKING MORE WINDOWS

The purpose of marriage is to stabilize sexuality and to provide the best environment in which to procreate and raise children. Sex outside marriage traditionally has been discouraged not only because of the dangers of sexually transmitted diseases and out-of-wedlock births but also because of the dangers it poses to stable families. Crime scholar James Q. Wilson describes "the broken window effect," in which failure to curb breaches in civil order leads to more breaches. He noticed that a building in a tough part of a city had all its windows intact, unlike others around it. After one window was broken, however, all the other windows soon met the same fate. Likewise, if a culture does not discourage extramarital sexuality, the stable marriages are threatened because of the erosion of cultural, social, and, finally, legal support. Plagued by a high rate of divorce, teen pregnancies and STD epidemics, America can only unravel the social fabric further by legitimizing homosexuality.

CONCLUSION

"Domestic partnerships" and "gay marriages" are being advocated as an extension of tolerance and as a matter of civil rights, but these are really wedges designed to overturn traditional sexual morality, as is acknowledged by many homosexual activists themselves. There is little or no support within the law for such formulations, and there is no U.S. jurisdiction that recognizes homosexual "marriage." Voters and corporations should resist the demands made upon them to equate family life with behavior that has been deemed unhealthy, immoral, and destructive to individuals and societies in cultures the world over.

POSTSCRIPT

Should Society Recognize Gay Marriages?

In 1994 the Union of American Hebrew Congregations, a Reform Jewish group, called on government at all levels to provide the means of legally acknowledging "committed lesbian and gay partnerships." In March 1996 another liberal Reform group, the Central Conference of American Rabbis, voted to support civil marriage for lesbian and gay men and to oppose governmental efforts to bar such unions. The Union of Orthodox Rabbis of the United States and Canada quickly responded by announcing its opposition: "We cannot give any recognition [to same-sex marriages]. This is another breakdown of the family unit, which only leads, of course, to the dissolution of the Jewish people."

A similar debate exists among Christians. Many Episcopalian, United Church of Christ (Congregational), Unitarian/Universalist, Presbyterian, Methodist, and other Protestant ministers, along with some Catholic priests, will witness and bless gay unions. Others in the same churches find gay unions totally unacceptable. In 1996 and 1997 several church-affiliated and private universities had heated debates about whether or not denying gay and lesbian couples requests to be married in campus chapels violated their university's antidiscrimination ban. In mid-1997 the Alabama legislature proposed a bill imposing a fine of $1,000 on any clergy who officiated at a same-sex wedding. In response, the Reverend Troy Perry, founder of the Universal Fellowship of Metropolitan Community Churches, threatened to hold a mass wedding for homosexuals on the steps of the state capital.

How should we define and structure marriage for the postindustrial twenty-first century? What is the nature and purpose of marriage today? And what will it be 10 or 20 years from now?

SUGGESTED READINGS

K.A. Appiah, "The Marrying Kind," *The New York Review* (June 20, 1996).

R. M. Baird and S. E. Rosenbaum, eds., *Same-Sex Marriage: The Moral and Legal Debate* (Prometheus Books, 1997).

W. N. Eskridge, *The Case for Same-Sex Marriage* (Free Press, 1996).

G. Rotello, "To Have and to Hold: The Case for Gay Marriage," *The Nation* (June 24, 1996).

J. Q. Wilson, "Against Homosexual Marriage," *Commentary* (March 1996).

ISSUE 14

Is Chemical Castration an Acceptable Punishment for Male Sex Offenders?

YES: Douglas J. Besharov, from "Sex Offenders: Yes: Consider Chemical Treatment," *ABA Journal* (July 1992)

NO: Andrew Vachhs, from "Sex Offenders: No: Pragmatically Impotent," *ABA Journal* (July 1992)

ISSUE SUMMARY

YES: Douglas J. Besharov, a resident scholar at the American Enterprise Institute in Washington, D.C., argues that carefully conducted research in Europe and the United States shows that chemical castration is effective, more humane, and much less expensive than imprisonment for some convicted compulsive sex offenders.

NO: Andrew Vachhs, a juvenile justice advocate and novelist, asserts that chemical and surgical castration both fail to address aggression as an underlying motive for repeat sex offenders.

Until 1996 the issue of whether or not convicted rapists and child molesters should be able to choose chemical castation in lieu of a prison sentence surfaced now and then, but it never quite received serious public attention. That situation is changing, as research continues with Depo-Provera, a synthetic form of the hormone progesterone that suppresses the male hormone testosterone and thus eliminates sex drive. As news of this research spreads, convicted sex offenders are starting to ask the courts to allow them to choose between being sent to prison or being sentenced to counseling and ongoing treatment with Depo-Provera.

It is important to note that the procedure in question here is *chemical* castration, not permanent *surgical* castration. In Texas, for instance, Steven Allen Butler, who had raped a 13-year-old girl, asked for surgical castration and 10 years of probation as his punishment instead of imprisonment. The district court initially agreed to his request but later withdrew its approval after protests by civil liberties groups and the refusal of physicians to perform the procedure. Butler himself had second thoughts about the operation. While some view surgical castration as "a return to the Dark Ages," chemical castration with antiandrogenic hormones has been an accepted treatment for many sex offenders.

A case study reported by John Money, founder and director of the Psychohormonal Research Unit at the Johns Hopkins Medical Institutions, illustrates the ambivalence raised by this issue: A young man came to the Hopkins clinic seeking help with a compulsive behavior he did not understand. At intervals he would find himself driving around searching for a church. He then went into an trance state where he could not recall what he did between finding the church and some time later. For 18 months, with counseling and a weekly shot of Depo-Provera, his compulsive behavior was eliminated. Then, while on his way to an appointment at the clinic, he felt a need to follow a school bus that had triggered his compulsion as it passed a church.

The patient's premonition had been only partly fulfilled on this particular occasion for, on the far side of the church, there was only a little boy playing. "I didn't stop," the patient said. "I went on past, but I had to come back again. And after I came back the third time, I just, I just like, uh, relaxed; and I was able to pull myself together, and come on into the city. I don't know what happened. There was a change. Just all of a sudden I quit driving around."

The patient's agitation over this relapse to his compulsive driving around in search of a church allowed Money to uncover what had been happening during his trance states. Before being treated with Depo-Provera, when the patient found a church he would look around to "find a youth at the age of puberty with whom he would strike up a friendly conversation, and then, utterly without warning, punch and kick him, and drive away." For 18 months, Depo-Provera freed him of his compulsive search and the trance-state and subsequent assault that followed his finding a church. Money was then able to uncover the childhood history behind the compulsive assault behavior and treat it. However, as successful as the Depo-Provera was for 18 months, there was still the chance of a mild or even dangerous relapse.

This risk of relapse is a major factor in the following debate between Douglas J. Besharov and Andrew Vachhs. Watch for other points of disagreement and concern as you read their brief statements.

YES

Douglas J. Besharov

SEX OFFENDERS: CONSIDER CHEMICAL TREATMENT

Surgical castration has never been very popular in this country, although it has been used sporadically in a number of states for more than 100 years, and was a common remedy in Germany and Denmark as late as the 1960s.

Although many castrated men may be capable of intercourse, the limited research that exists suggests that the repeat-offense rate is low. On humanitarian and civil liberties grounds, however, most experts now oppose the procedure and it is unlikely that many courts will turn to it as an alternative to incarceration—especially since there is a better option.

First tried more than 25 years ago, the use of hormone suppressors—also known as "chemical castration"—has proven highly effective for certain sex offenders. The most common drug used is medroxyprogesterone acetate, a synthetic progesterone originally developed as a contraceptive marketed as Depo-Provera.

According to a 1990 article in the *American Journal of Criminal Law*, this treatment, when given to men, "reduces the production and effects of testosterone, thus diminishing the compulsive sexual fantasy. Formerly insistent and commanding urges can be voluntarily controlled." It creates what another writer called "erotic apathy." Fifty sex offender clinics in this country now use chemical therapy, and it is even more widely used in Europe.

LOW RECIDIVISM

Carefully conducted research indicates that hormone therapy works—when coupled with appropriate counseling—for most paraphiliacs (sex offenders driven by overwhelming sexual fantasies). Recidivism rates are under 5 percent.

Just as in surgical castration, the subject can still have erections, and many successfully impregnate their wives. For this reason, hormone treatment does not work for antisocial personalities or for those whose sex offenses are motivated by feelings of anger, violence or power. The treatment does not reach the causes of their harmful behavior. Thus, proper diagnosis is essential.

Some may argue that hormone treatment as an alternative to incarceration is too lenient for serious sex crimes. First, it is possible to combine treatment with incarceration. But more importantly, we should remember how frequently serious offenders serve very short sentences. Nationally, convicted rapists serve less than 6 years in jail, and that does not include all those who plead guilty to a lesser offense. For too many offenders, the sexual abuse and violence in prisons merely heightens their propensity to commit further crime.

Recognizing the sexual side of some rapes in no way seeks to blame the victim, or denies the violent, hateful aspect of rape. Promoting an apparently effective therapy does not condone the behavior, but it does protect future victims.

Others will oppose using these drugs because, even though they work, they are an invasion of bodily integrity and re-productive freedom. (Side effects include weight gain, hot flashes and hypertension.) But it is more accurate to see them as equivalent to the psychotropic drugs, which include antidepressants, antipsychotics and tranquilizers, now routinely used to treat many mental disorders.

Some would even deny defendants the right to accept the treatment in lieu of imprisonment—because the choice is inherently coercive. Perhaps it is. But the question is this: When faced with the certainty of incarceration, wouldn't we all want to be able to make such a choice? To ask the question is to answer it.

After all the sensationalism, the use of hormone-suppressing drugs, in certain cases, holds great promise for reducing the level of sexual violence against women and children. As a voluntary alternative, it is in both the defendant's and society's interest.

NO

Andrew Vachhs

SEX OFFENDERS: PRAGMATICALLY IMPOTENT

As a criminal justice response to the chronic, dangerous sexual psychopath, castration of any kind is morally pernicious and pragmatically impotent. Even if we could ignore the implications of mutilation-as-compensation for criminal offenses, castration must be rejected on the most essential of grounds: The "cure" will exacerbate the "disease."

Proponents of castration tell us: 1) It will heal the offender (and thus protect society), and 2) it would be the offender's own choice.

Violent sex offenders are not victims of their heightened sex drives. Rapists may be "expressing their rage." Predatory pedophiles may be "replaying their old scripts." But any sexual sadist, properly interviewed, will tell you the truth: They do what they do because they want to do it. Their behavior is not the product of sickness—it is volitional.

Castration will not remove the source of a violent sex offender's rage— only one single instrument of its expression. Rapes have been committed with broomsticks, coke bottles—any blunt object. Indeed, most criminal statutes now incorporate just such a possibility.

And imagine a violent rapist whose hatred of women occupies most of his waking thoughts. Imagine him agreeing to castration to avoid a lengthy prison sentence. Imagine his rage festering geometrically as he stews in the bile of what "they" have done to him. Does anyone actually believe such a creature has been rendered harmless?

An escalating pattern is characteristic of many predatory sex offenders— castration is likely to produce an internal demand for even higher levels of stimulation.

The castration remedy implies some biomedical cause for sexual offenses. Once fixed, the offender ceases to be a danger. This is nonsense—the motivation for sexual assault will not disappear with the severed genitalia or altered hormones.

In Germany, Klaus Grabowski avoided a life sentence by agreeing to castration. Released, he began covert hormone injections. In 1980, he strangled a 7-year-old girl and buried her body. At trial, his defense was that the cas-

From Andrew Vachhs, "Sex Offenders: No: Pragmatically Impotent," *ABA Journal* (July 1992). Copyright © 1992 by The American Bar Association. Reprinted by permission of the *ABA Journal*.

tration had removed any sexual feelings, that he had lured the child to his apartment because he loved children and killed her in response to blackmail threats.

HIGH PREDATORY DRIVE

Even the most liberal of Americans have become suspicious of a medical model to explain sex offenders. Such offenders may plot and plan, scheme and stalk for months, utilize the most elaborate devices to avoid detection, even network with others and commercially profit from their foul acts.

But some psycho-apologist can always be found to claim the poor soul was deep in the grip of irresistible impulse when he was compelled to attack. Imagine the field day the expert-witness fraternity will have explaining how the castrated child molester who later killed his new victims was rendered insane as a result of the castration itself.

Sex offender treatment is the growth industry of the 1990s. Chemical castration already looms as a Get-Out-of-Jail-Free Card.

Castration validates the sex offender's self-portrait: He is the victim; he can't help himself. It panders to our ugliest instincts, not the least of which is cowardice—the refusal to call evil by its name.

Nor can castration be defended because the perpetrator chooses it. Leaving aside the obvious issue of coercion, under what theory does a convicted criminal get to select his own (non-incarcerative) sentence?

America loves simple solutions to complex problems, especially solutions with political utility, like boot camp for youthful offenders. The last thing our cities need is muggers in better physical shape.

When it comes to our own self-interest (and self-defense), the greatest sickness is stupidity. Castration qualifies . . . on all counts.

POSTSCRIPT

Is Chemical Castration an Acceptable Punishment for Male Sex Offenders?

The history of castration as a penalty for sexual assaults in America can be traced back to colonial times, when laws and courts sought to protect American society from "unnatural and inordinate copulations" between black men and white women. All of the 13 colonies prohibited sexual relations between black men (both freemen and slaves) and white women (but not between white men and black women). Although black men who were convicted of raping white women were usually hanged, most colonies also allowed vigilantes, as well as the courts, to castrate black men who raped, attempted to rape, or had consensual sex with white women.

In September 1996 California became the first state to require *chemical* castration of child molesters who have been convicted of committing a second sexual assault against a child under 13 years of age. Within a few months, Montana and Georgia became the second and third states to require chemical castration of child molesters. Other states are trying to pass similar measures.

In May 1997 Texas became the first state to make *surgical* castration available as an option for repeat child molesters serving time in prison. Governor George W. Bush signed into law a bill that allows voluntary surgical castration for inmates 21 or older who have been convicted of sexual offenses against children two or more times. In signing the law, Bush predicted that it will reduce child sex offenses in Texas, where an estimated 7,000 people are imprisoned for sex crimes.

Advocates of surgical castration are quick to point out that 50–60 percent of convicted sex offenders who go through the standard prison rehabilitation program become repeat offenders after they are paroled. Also, whereas untreated sex offenders have an 80 percent recidivism rate, only 3 percent of surgically castrated sex offenders repeat their offenses. California legislators were reminded that repeat offender rates among child molesters in Europe dropped from almost 100 percent to just 2 percent when chemical castration was instituted.

Among the arguments cited against chemical castration is the fact that sex offenders who undergo this treatment as a condition for parole can walk into almost any training gym and buy steroids to counter the effects of the Depo-Provera treatment. This argument says that taxpayers will be paying millions of dollars for treatment that has not been proven to work, can easily be circumvented, and will wear off quickly at the end of the offender's parole.

Sorting out the facts and finding comparable examples of the effectiveness of chemical and surgical castration is only part of resolving this controversial issue. It is an issue that society is just beginning to deal with. The arguments raised by Besharov and Vachhs provide us with a starting point for debate, but more facts and much more discussion is needed before this issue can be resolved.

SUGGESTED READINGS

"Castration or Incarceration?" *New Scientist* (September 21, 1996), p. 3.

V. T. Cheney et al., *The Advantages of Castration, Vol 1* (Library Binding, 1997).

V. T. Cheney et al., *A Brief History of Castration, Vol 1* (Library Binding, 1996).

A. J. Malcomb, J. Gunn, and D. A. G. Cook et al., "Should a Sexual Offender Be Allowed Castration?" *British Medical Journal* (September 25, 1993), pp. 790–793.

J. Money, *Love and Love Sickness: The Science of Sex, Gender Differences, and Pairbonding* (Johns Hopkins University Press, 1980), pp. 205–207.

J. Money, *Lovemaps: Clinical Concepts of Sexual/Erotic Health and Pathology, Paraphilia, and Gender Transposition in Childhood, Adolescence, and Maturity* (Irvington Publishers, 1986).

ISSUE 15

Should Pornography Be Banned as a Threat to Women?

YES: Andrea Dworkin, from *Letters from a War Zone: Writings, 1976–1987* (Secker & Warburg, 1988)

NO: Nadine Strossen, from "The Perils of Pornophobia," *The Humanist* (May/June 1995)

ISSUE SUMMARY

YES: Feminist author Andrea Dworkin describes the numerous ways in which pornography is used by men in American culture to degrade women and to violate their civil rights.

NO: Professor of law Nadine Strossen argues that "political correctness" movements on college campuses and misguided feminist assaults on pornography have resulted in the naive belief that pornography is a major weapon used by men to degrade and dominate women.

Although the First Amendment of the U.S. Constitution protects freedom of speech, Americans have always had restraints on what they can say and write in public. Over 70 years ago U.S. Supreme Court chief justice Oliver Wendell Holmes ruled that the First Amendment does not give someone the right to shout "Fire!" in a crowded theater because of the harm such an act could cause. This court ruling, although frequently ignored in current debates, supports antipornography feminists such as Andrea Dworkin and Catharine MacKinnon, who contend that the violence and degrading descriptions of women found in pornography can be physically harmful and should therefore be illegal. Dworkin calls for banning not only "traditional" pornography but also publications, acts, and verbalizations that can be construed as offensive or demeaning to women. In the following selection, Dworkin presents pornography as a major weapon in a cultural war between females and males that permeates every aspect of our lives and society.

At the root of the pornography debate is how we define pornography. Lesbian feminist Pat Califia argues that Dworkin, MacKinnon, and Women Against Violence in Pornography and the Media (WAVPM) have adopted a very broad definition. According to their definition, Califia has said, "Pornography can include a picture of a woman whose body is smeared with honey, a woman stabbing a man in the back, or a woman dressed in leather towering over two men as well as films showing various sex acts. This vague definition allowed them to support their contention that pornography objectifies and demeans women, since any image that is objectifying or demeaning is called pornographic." This definition also allows Dworkin and others to claim that they are fighting against sexist stereotypes of women, not trying to censor sexually explicit material. In their view, misogyny (the hatred of women) is more prevalent and pernicious in pornography than in any other type of media.

Nadine Strossen counters in the second selection that the focus and efforts of Dworkin and WAVPM to censor all pornography is actually damaging the women's rights movement more than it is helping. Instead of trying to determine what is pornographic, Strossen wants to focus on gaining greater political and economic equality for women.

As you read the two selections, try to develop a classification of different types of pornography. How do you view the new feminist-produced soft-core pornography that portrays women as people who enjoy sexual pleasure as much as men do? How about pornography produced by gays and lesbians for gay and lesbian readers? Or the widely popular erotic romance novels that are enthusiastically embraced by women of all classes? Decide which types (if any) you would want to make illegal. For instance, should soft-core pornography, involving nudity and depictions of genitalia, be treated the same as hard-core productions, which contain graphic presentations of sexual play, intercourse, and oral sex? What about pornography that depicts anal sex, light or heavy bondage, bestiality, or some other fetishistic behavior? What about topless dancers at bars, strippers on stage or at parties, and live sex acts on stage? How should suggestive advertisements, telephone sex, and "alt.sex" talk groups on the Internet be handled?

As you think through your position on this issue, you will need to define the terms *violence, exploitation, objectification,* and *degrading.* You might also want to think about what role pornography plays in our society. Why does much pornography depict violent sex or the degradation and victimization of women? Is author Susan Brownmiller on target when she contends that "pornography promotes a climate of opinion in which hostility against women is not only tolerated but ideologically encouraged"? Is pornography a symptom of a sick society, or is it a healthy safety valve in a society that is basically uncomfortable with sexuality? If people had a more positive view of sex and allowed it a natural place in daily life, would hard-core pornography continue to sell as well as it does today?

YES

Andrea Dworkin

AGAINST THE MALE FLOOD: CENSORSHIP, PORNOGRAPHY, AND EQUALITY

In the amendment to the Human Rights Ordinance of the City of Minneapolis written by Catharine A. MacKinnon and myself, pornography is defined as the graphic, sexually explicit subordination of women whether in pictures or in words that also includes one or more of the following: women are presented dehumanized as sexual objects, things, or commodities; or women are presented as sexual objects who enjoy pain or humiliation; or women are presented as sexual objects who experience sexual pleasure in being raped; or women are presented as sexual objects tied up or cut up or mutilated or bruised or physically hurt; or women are presented in postures of sexual submission; or women's body parts are exhibited, such that women are reduced to those parts; or women are presented being penetrated by objects or animals; or women are presented in scenarios of degradation, injury, abasement, torture, shown as filthy or inferior, bleeding, bruised, or hurt in a context that makes these conditions sexual.

This statutory definition is an objectively accurate definition of what pornography is, based on an analysis of the material produced by the $8-billion-a-year industry, and also on extensive study of the whole range of pornography extant from other eras and other cultures. Given the fact that women's oppression has an ahistorical character—a sameness across time and cultures expressed in rape, battery, incest, and prostitution—it is no surprise that pornography, a central phenomenon in that oppression, has precisely that quality of sameness. It does not significantly change in what it is, what it does, what is in it, or how it works, whether it is, for instance, classical or feudal or modern, Western or Asian; whether the method of manufacture is words, photographs, or video. What has changed is the public availability of pornography and the numbers of live women used in it because of new technologies: not its nature. Many people note what seems to them a qualitative change in pornography—that it has gotten more violent, even grotesquely violent, over the last two decades. The change is only in what is publicly visible: not in the range or preponderance of violent pornography (e.g., the place of rape in pornography stays constant and central, no matter where, when, or how the pornography is produced); not in the character, quality, or content of what the pornographers actually produce; not in the harm caused; not in the valuation of women in it, or the metaphysical definition of what women are; not in the sexual abuse promoted, including rape, battery, and incest; not in the centrality of its role in subordinating women. Until recently, pornography operated in private, where most abuse of women takes place.

The oppression of women occurs through sexual subordination. It is the use of sex as the medium of oppression that makes the subordination of women so distinct from racism or prejudice against a group based on religion or national origin. Social inequality is created in many different ways. In my view, the radical responsibility is to isolate the material means of creating the inequality so that material remedies can be found for it.

This is particularly difficult with respect to women's inequality because that inequality is achieved through sex. Sex as desired by the class that dominates women is held by that class to be elemental, urgent, necessary, even if or even though it appears to *require* the repudiation of any claim women might have to full human standing. In the subordination of women, inequality itself is sexualized: made into the experience of sexual pleasure, essential to sexual desire. Pornography is the material means of sexualizing inequality; and that is why pornography is a central practice in the subordination of women.

Subordination itself is a broad, deep, systematic dynamic discernible in any persecution based on race or sex. Social subordination has four main parts. First, there is *hierarchy*, a group on top and a group on bottom. For women, this hierarchy is experienced both socially and sexually, publicly and privately. Women are physically integrated into the society in which we are held to be inferior, and our low status is both put in place and maintained by the sexual usage of us by men; and so women's experience of hierarchy is incredibly intimate and wounding.

Second, subordination is *objectification*. Objectification occurs when a human being, through social means, is made less than human, turned into a thing or commodity, bought and sold. When objectification occurs, a person is depersonalized, so that no individuality or integrity is available socially or in what is an extremely circumscribed privacy (because those who dominate determine its boundaries). Objectification is an injury right at the heart of discrimination: those who can be used as if they are not fully human are no longer fully human in social terms; their humanity is hurt by being diminished.

Third, subordination is *submission*. A person is at the bottom of a hierarchy because of a condition of birth; a person on the bottom is dehumanized, an object or commodity; inevitably, the situation of that person requires obedience and compliance. That diminished person is expected to be submissive; there is no longer any right to self-determination, because there is no basis in equality for any such right to exist. In a condition of inferiority and objectification, submission is usually essential for survival. Oppressed groups are known for their abilities to anticipate the orders and desires of those who have power over them, to comply with an obsequiousness that is then used by the dominant group to justify its own dominance: the master, not able to imagine a human like himself in such degrading servility, thinks the servility is proof that the hierarchy is natural and that objectification simply amounts to seeing these lesser creatures for what they are. The submission forced on inferior, objectified groups precisely by hierarchy and objectification is taken to be the proof of inherent inferiority and subhuman capacities.

Fourth, the subordination is *violence*. The violence is systematic, endemic enough to be unremarkable and normative, usually taken as an implicit right of the one committing the violence. In my view, hierarchy, objectification, and submission are the preconditions for systematic social violence against any group targeted because of a condition of birth. If violence against a group is both socially pervasive and socially normal, then hierarchy, objectification, and submission are already solidly in place.

The role of violence in subordinating women has one special characteristic congruent with sex as the instrumentality of subordination: the violence is supposed to be sex for the woman too— what women want and like as part of our sexual nature; it is supposed to give women pleasure (as in rape); it is supposed to mean love to a woman from her point of view (as in battery). The violence against women is seen to be done not just in accord with something compliant in women, but in response to something active in and basic to women's nature.

Pornography uses each component of social subordination. Its particular medium is sex. Hierarchy, objectification,

submission, and violence all become alive with sexual energy and sexual meaning. A hierarchy, for instance, can have a static quality; but pornography, by sexualizing it, makes it dynamic, almost carnivorous, so that men keep imposing it for the sake of their own sexual pleasure—for the sexual pleasure it gives them to impose it. In pornography, each element of subordination is conveyed through the sexually explicit usage of women: pornography in fact is what women are and what women are for and how women are used in a society premised on the inferiority of women. It is a metaphysics of women's subjugation: our existence delineated in a definition of our nature; our status in society predetermined by the uses to which we are put. The woman's body is what is materially subordinated. Sex is the material means through which the subordination is accomplished. Pornography is the institution of male dominance that sexualizes hierarchy, objectification, submission, and violence. As such, pornography creates inequality, not as artifact but as a system of social reality; it creates the necessity for and the actual behaviors that constitute sex inequality.

Subordination can be so deep that those who are hurt by it are utterly silent. Subordination can create a silence quieter than death. The women flattened out on the page are deathly still, except for *hurt me*. *Hurt me* is not women's speech. It is the speech imposed on women by pimps to cover the awful, condemning silence. The Three Marias of Portugal went to jail for writing this: "Let no one tell me that silence gives consent, because whoever is silent dissents."[1] The women say the pimp's words: the language is another element of the rape; the language is part of the humiliation; the language is part of the forced sex. Real silence might signify dissent, for those reared to understand its sad discourse. The pimps cannot tolerate literal silence—it is too eloquent as testimony—so they force the words out of the woman's mouth. The women say pimp's words: which is worse than silence. The silence of the women not in the picture, outside the pages, hurt but silent, used but silent, is staggering in how deep and wide it goes. It is a silence over centuries: an exile into speechlessness. One is shut up by the inferiority and the abuse. One is shut up by the threat and the injury. In her memoir of the Stalin period, *Hope Against Hope*, Nadezhda Mandelstam wrote that screaming "is a man's way of leaving a trace, of telling people how he lived and died. By his screams he asserts his right to live, sends a message to the outside world demanding help and calling for resistance. If nothing else is left, one must scream. Silence is the real crime against humanity."[2] Screaming is a man's way of leaving a trace. The scream of a man is never misunderstood as a scream of pleasure by passers-by or politicians or historians, nor by the tormentor. A man's scream is a call for resistance. A man's scream asserts his right to live, sends a message; he leaves a trace. A woman's scream is the sound of her female will and her female pleasure in doing what the pornographers say she is for. Her scream is a sound of celebration to those who overhear. Women's way of leaving a trace is the silence, centuries' worth: the entirely inhuman silence that surely one day will be noticed, someone will say that something is wrong, some sound is missing, some voice is lost; the entirely inhuman silence that will be a clue to human hope denied, a shard of evidence that a crime has occurred, the crime that created the silence; the entirely inhuman

silence that is a cold, cold condemnation of what those who speak have done to those who do not.

But there is more than the *hurt me* forced out of us, and the silence in which it lies. The pornographers actually use our bodies as their language. We are their speech. Our bodies are the building blocks of their sentences. What they do to us, called speech, is not unlike what Kafka's Harrow machine—"The needles are set in like the teeth of a harrow and the whole thing works something like a harrow, although its action is limited to one place and contrived with much more artistic skill"[3]—did to the condemned in "In the Penal Colony":

> "Our sentence does not sound severe. Whatever commandment the prisoner has disobeyed is written upon his body by the Harrow. This prisoner, for instance"—the officer indicated the man—"will have written on his body: HONOR THY SUPERIORS!"[4]

> ... The Harrow is beginning to write; when it finishes the first draft of the inscription on the man's back, the layer of cotton wool begins to roll and slowly turns the body over, to give the Harrow fresh space for writing.... So it keeps on writing deeper and deeper...[5]

Asked if the prisoner knows his sentence, the officer replies: " 'There would be no point in telling him. He'll learn it on his body.' "[6]

This is the so-called speech of the pornographers, protected now by law.

Protecting what they "say" means protecting what they do to us, how they do it. It means protecting their sadism on our bodies, because that is how they write: not like a writer at all; like a torturer. Protecting what they "say" means protecting sexual exploitation, because they cannot "say" anything without diminishing, hurting, or destroying us. Their rights of speech express their rights over us. Their rights of speech require our inferiority: and that we be powerless in relation to them. Their rights of speech mean that *hurt me* is accepted as the real speech of women, not speech forced on us as part of the sex forced on us but originating with us because we are what the pornographers "say" we are.

If what we want to say is not *hurt me*, we have the real social power only to use silence as eloquent dissent. Silence is what women have instead of speech. Silence is our dissent during rape unless the rapist, like the pornographer, prefers *hurt me*, in which case we have no dissent. Silence is our moving, persuasive dissent during battery unless the batterer, like the pornographer, prefers *hurt me*. Silence is a fine dissent during incest and for all the long years after.

Silence is not speech. We have silence, not speech. We fight rape, battery, incest, and prostitution with it. We lose. But someday someone will notice: that people called women were buried in a long silence that meant dissent and that the pornographers—with needles set in like the teeth of a harrow—chattered on.

NOTES

1. Maria Isabel Barreno, Maria Teresa Horta, and Maria Velho da Costa, *The Three Marias: New Portuguese Letters*, trans. Helen R. Lane (New York: Bantam Books, 1976), p. 291.

2. Nadezhda Mandelstam, *Hope Against Hope*, trans. Max Hayward (New York: Atheneum, 1978), pp. 42–43.

3. Franz Kafka, "In the Penal Colony," pp. 191–227, *The Penal Colony*, trans. Willa and Edwin Muir (New York: Schocken Books, 1965), p. 194.

4. Kafka, "In the Penal Colony," p. 197.

5. Kafka, "In the Penal Colony," p. 203.

6. Kafka, "In the Penal Colony," p. 197.

NO

Nadine Strossen

THE PERILS OF PORNOPHOBIA

In 1992, in response to a complaint, officials at Pennsylvania State University unceremoniously removed Francisco de Goya's masterpiece, *The Nude Maja*, from a classroom wall. The complaint had not been lodged by Jesse Helms or some irate member of the Christian Coalition. Instead, the complainant was a feminist English professor who protested that the eighteenth-century painting of a recumbent nude woman made her and her female students "uncomfortable."

This was not an isolated incident. At the University of Arizona at Tucson, feminist students physically attacked a graduate student's exhibit of photographic self-portraits. Why? The artist had photographed *herself* in her *underwear*. And at the University of Michigan Law School, feminist students who had organized a conference on "Prostitution: From Academia to Activism" removed a feminist-curated art exhibition held in conjunction with the conference. Their reason? Conference speakers had complained that a composite videotape containing interviews of working prostitutes was "pornographic" and therefore unacceptable.

What is wrong with this picture? Where have they come from—these feminists who behave like religious conservatives, who censor works of art because they deal with sexual themes? Have not feminists long known that censorship is a dangerous weapon which, if permitted, would inevitably be turned against them? Certainly that was the irrefutable lesson of the early women's rights movement, when Margaret Sanger, Mary Ware Dennett, and other activists were arrested, charged with "obscenity," and prosecuted for distributing educational pamphlets about sex and birth control. Theirs was a struggle for freedom of sexual expression and full gender equality, which they understood to be mutually reinforcing.

Theirs was also a lesson well understood by the second wave of feminism in the 1970s, when writers such as Germaine Greer, Betty Friedan, and Betty Dodson boldly asserted that women had the right to be free from discrimination not only in the workplace and in the classroom but in the

From Nadine Strossen, "The Perils of Pornophobia," *The Humanist*, vol. 55, no. 3 (May/June 1995), pp. 7–9. Copyright © 1995 by Nadine Strossen. Reprinted by permission.

bedroom as well. Freedom from limiting, conventional stereotypes concerning female sexuality was an essential aspect of what we then called "women's liberation." Women should not be seen as victims in their sexual relations with men but as equally assertive partners, just as capable of experiencing sexual pleasure.

But it is a lesson that, alas, many feminists have now forgotten. Today, an increasingly influential feminist pro-censorship movement threatens to impair the very women's rights movement it professes to serve. Led by law professor Catharine MacKinnon and writer Andrea Dworkin, this faction of the feminist movement maintains that sexually oriented *expression*—not sex-segregated labor markets, sexist concepts of marriage and family, or pent-up rage—is the preeminent cause of discrimination and violence against women. Their solution is seemingly simple: suppress all "pornography."

Censorship, however, is never a simple matter. First, the offense must be described. And how does one define something so infinitely variable, so deeply personal, so uniquely individualized as the image, the word, and the fantasy that cause sexual arousal? For decades, the U.S. Supreme Court has engaged in a Sisyphean struggle to craft a definition of *obscenity* that the lower courts can apply with some fairness and consistency. Their dilemma was best summed up in former Justice Potter Stewart's now famous statement: "I shall not today attempt further to define [obscenity]: and perhaps I could never succeed in intelligibly doing so. But I know it when I see it."

The censorious feminists are not so modest as Justice Stewart. They have fashioned an elaborate definition of *pornography* that encompasses vastly more material than does the currently recognized law of *obscenity*. As set out in their model law (which has been considered in more than a dozen jurisdictions in the United States and overseas, and which has been substantially adopted in Canada), pornography is "the sexually explicit subordination of women through pictures and/or words." The model law lists eight different criteria that attempt to illustrate their concept of "subordination," such as depictions in which "women are presented in postures or positions of sexual submission, servility, or display" or "women are presented in scenarios of degradation, humiliation, injury, torture... in a context that makes these conditions sexual." This linguistic driftnet can ensnare anything from religious imagery and documentary footage about the mass rapes in the Balkans to self-help books about women's health. Indeed, the Boston Women's Health Book Collective, publisher of the now-classic book on women's health and sexuality, *Our Bodies, Ourselves*, actively campaigned against the MacKinnon-Dworkin model law when it was proposed in Cambridge, Massachusetts, in 1985, recognizing that the book's explicit text and pictures could be targeted as pornographic under the law.

Although the "MacDworkinite" approach to pornography has an intuitive appeal to many feminists, it is *itself* based on subordinating and demeaning stereotypes about women. Central to the pornophobic feminists—and to many traditional conservatives and right-wing fundamentalists, as well—is the notion that *sex* is inherently degrading to women (although not to men). Not just sexual expression but sex itself—even consensual, nonviolent sex—is an evil from which women, like children, must be protected.

MacKinnon puts it this way: "Compare victims' reports of rape with women's reports of sex. They look a lot alike.... The major distinction between intercourse (normal) and rape (abnormal) is that the normal happens so often that one cannot get anyone to see anything wrong with it." And from Dworkin: "Intercourse remains a means or the means of physiologically making a woman inferior." Given society's pervasive sexism, she believes, women cannot freely consent to sexual relations with men; those who do consent are, in Dworkin's words, "collaborators... experiencing pleasure in their own inferiority."

These ideas are hardly radical. Rather, they are a reincarnation of disempowering puritanical, Victorian notions that feminists have long tried to consign to the dustbin of history: woman as sexual victim; man as voracious satyr. The MacDworkinite approach to sexual expression is a throwback to the archaic stereotypes that formed the basis for nineteenth-century laws which prohibited "vulgar" or sexually suggestive language from being used in the presence of women and girls.

In those days, women were barred from practicing law and serving as jurors lest they be exposed to such language. Such "protective" laws have historically functioned to bar women from full legal equality. Paternalism always leads to exclusion, discrimination, and the loss of freedom and autonomy. And in its most extreme form, it leads to purdah, in which women are completely shrouded from public view.

* * *

The pro-censorship feminists are not fighting alone. Although they try to distance themselves from such traditional "family-values" conservatives as Jesse Helms, Phyllis Schlafly, and Donald Wildmon, who are less interested in protecting women than in preserving male dominance, a common hatred of sexual expression and fondness for censorship unite the two camps. For example, the Indianapolis City Council adopted the MacKinnon-Dworkin model law in 1984 thanks to the hard work of former council member Beulah Coughenour, a leader of the Indiana Stop ERA movement. (Federal courts later declared the law unconstitutional.) And when Phyllis Schlafly's Eagle Forum and Beverly LaHaye's Concerned Women for America launched their "Enough Is Enough" anti-pornography campaign, they trumpeted the words of Andrea Dworkin in promotional materials.

This mutually reinforcing relationship does a serious disservice to the fight for women's equality. It lends credibility to and strengthens the right wing and its anti-feminist, anti-choice, homophobic agenda. This is particularly damaging in light of the growing influence of the religious right in the Republican Party and the recent Republican sweep of both Congress and many state governments. If anyone doubts that the newly empowered GOP intends to forge ahead with anti-woman agendas, they need only read the party's "Contract with America" which, among other things, reintroduces the recently repealed "gag rule" forbidding government-funded family-planning clinics from even discussing abortion with their patients.

The pro-censorship feminists base their efforts on the largely unexamined assumption that ridding society of pornography would reduce sexism and violence against women. If there were any evidence that this were true, anti-censorship feminists—myself included—would be compelled at least to reexamine our opposition to censorship. But there is no such evidence to be found.

A causal connection between exposure to pornography and the commission of sexual violence has never been established. The National Research Council's Panel on Understanding and Preventing Violence concluded in a 1993 survey of laboratory studies that "demonstrated empirical links between pornography and sex crimes in general are weak or absent." Even according to another research literature survey that former U.S. Surgeon General C. Everett Koop conducted at the behest of the staunchly anti-pornography Meese Commission, only two reliable generalizations could be made about the impact of "degrading" sexual material on its viewers: it caused them to think that a variety of sexual practices was more common than they had previously believed, and to more accurately estimate the prevalence of varied sexual practices.

Correlational studies are similarly unsupportive of the pro-censorship cause. There are no consistent correlations between the availability of pornography in various communities, states and countries and their rates of sexual offenses. If anything, studies suggest an inverse relationship: a greater availability of sexually explicit material seems to correlate not with higher rates of sexual violence but, rather, with higher indices of gender equality. For example, Singapore, with its tight restrictions on pornography, has experienced a much greater increase in rape rates than has Sweden, with its liberalized obscenity laws.

There *is* mounting evidence, however, that MacDworkinite-type laws will be used against the very people they are supposed to protect—namely, women. In 1992, for example, the Canadian Supreme Court incorporated the MacKinnon-Dworkin concept of pornography into Canadian obscenity law. Since that ruling, in *Butler v. The Queen*—which Mac-Kinnon enthusiastically hailed as "a stunning victory for women"—well over half of all feminist bookstores in Canada have had materials confiscated or detained by customs. According to the *Feminist Bookstore News*, a Canadian publication, "The *Butler* decision has been used... only to seize lesbian, gay, and feminist material."

Ironically but predictably, one of the victims of Canada's new law is Andrea Dworkin herself. Two of her books, *Pornography: Men Possessing Women* and *Women Hating*, were seized, custom officials said, because they "illegally eroticized pain and bondage." Like the MacKinnon-Dworkin model law, the *Butler* decision makes no exceptions for material that is part of a feminist critique of pornography or other feminist presentation. And this inevitably overbroad sweep is precisely why censorship is antithetical to the fight for women's rights.

The pornophobia that grips MacKinnon, Dworkin, and their followers has had further counterproductive impacts on the fight for women's rights. Censorship factionalism within the feminist movement has led to an enormously wasteful diversion of energy from the real cause of and solutions to the ongoing problems of discrimination and violence against women. Moreover, the "porn-made-me-do-it" defense, whereby convicted rapists cite MacKinnon and Dworkin in seeking to reduce their sentences, actually impedes the aggressive enforcement of criminal laws against sexual violence.

A return to the basic principles of women's liberation would put the feminist movement back on course. We women are entitled to freedom of expression—to read, think, speak, sing, write, paint, dance, photograph, film, and fantasize as we wish. We are also entitled to our dignity, autonomy, and equality. Fortunately, we can—and will—have both.

POSTSCRIPT

Should Pornography Be Banned as a Threat to Women?

The issue of pornography and its potential harms—especially in reinforcing the subjugation and humiliation of females, as Dworkin argues—is a perplexing one. Both Dworkin and Strossen make salient points, but neither discusses elements of their debate within a broader historical framework. That historical perspective is important to understanding the current debate.

Efforts to censor speech, writing, and pictorial material (including classical art) have been a recurring part of the American landscape. The success of censorship efforts depend very much on the dominating political views in the particular era in which the efforts are made; specifically, whether conservative or liberal views dominate that period. In the conservative Victorian era, with its repression of female sexuality, for instance, Anthony Comstock persuaded Congress to adopt a broadly worded law banning "any book, painting, photograph, or other material designed, adapted, or intended to explain human sexual functions, prevent conception, or produce abortion." That 1873 law stayed in effect for 100 years, until the U.S. Supreme Court finally declared its last remnants unconstitutional by allowing the sale of contraceptives to married women in 1963 and to single women in 1972.

Editor and critic H. L. Mencken (1880–1956) once defined "puritan" as someone who wakes up in the night with a haunting fear that someone, somewhere just might be having a good time! American society has never been comfortable celebrating people's sexuality or sexual pleasure. Yet there have been some significant changes. Notable are the more limited definitions of pornography outlined by the U.S. Supreme Court in the 1957 *Roth v. United States* and the 1973 *Miller v. United States* decisions.

In 1986 the U.S. Attorney General's Commission on Pornography, headed by then–attorney general Edwin Meese, maintained that the "totality of evidence" clearly documents the social dangers of pornography and justifies severe penalties and efforts to restrict and eliminate it. At the same time, C. Everett Koop, the conservative U.S. Surgeon General, arrived at conclusions quite the opposite of those of the Meese commission. Koop claimed that "we still know little about the patterns of use or the power of attitudes in precipitating sexual aggression. Much research is still needed in order to demonstrate that the present knowledge [of laboratory studies] has significant real world implications for predicting [sexual] behavior."

As you ponder the points raised by Dworkin and Strossen, keep in mind that well-intentioned laws frequently bring unintended consequences. For instance, as Strossen notes, after Canada adopted an antipornography law based on the Dworkin–Catharine MacKinnon model, the new law has been used to censure feminist artists and to censor lesbian, gay, and feminist books. Two of Dworkin's own books have been banned by Canadian customs using her own law. In another disturbing application, Canadian customs officials confiscated a book entitled *Hot, Hotter, Hottest*, thinking it was a book about sex rather than the cookbook about spicy food that it was. In Ohio law enforcement officials confiscated *Doing It Debbie's Way*, an exercise videotape featuring Debbie Reynolds, thinking it was a sequel to the pornographic video *Debbie Does Dallas*.

SUGGESTED READINGS

R. M. Baird and S. E. Rosenbaum, eds., *Pornography: Private Right or Public Menace?* (Prometheus Press, 1991).

M. French, *The War Against Women* (Ballantine Books, 1992).

C. Greek and W. Thompson, *Porn Wars* (Aldyne, 1995).

C. Hoff Sommers, *Who Stole Feminism? How Women Have Betrayed Women* (Simon & Shuster, 1994).

A. Leuchtag, "The Culture of Pornography," *The Humanist* (May/June 1995).

C. MacKinnon, "Pornography Left and Right," *Harvard Civil Rights–Civil Liberties Law Review* (Winter 1995).

E. Schlosser, "The Business of Pornography," *U.S. News and World Report* (February 10, 1997), pp. 42–52.

N. Strossen, *Defending Pornography: Free Speech, Sex, and the Fight for Women's Rights* (Scribner, 1995).

K. Swisher et al., *Violence Against Women* (Greenhaven Press, 1994).

B. Thompson, *Soft Core: Moral Crusades Against Pornography in Britain and America* (Cassell, 1995).

S. Tisdale, *Talk Dirty to Me: An Intimate Philosophy of Sex* (Doubleday, 1994).

E. Willis, *Beginning to See the Light: Sex, Hope, and Rock-and-Roll* (University Press of New England, 1992).

ISSUE 16

Is Homosexuality Incompatible With Military Service?

YES: Eugene T. Gomulka, from "Why No Gays?" *Proceedings* (December 1992)

NO: Charles L. Davis, from "Lifting the Gay Ban," *Society* (November/ December 1993)

ISSUE SUMMARY

YES: Eugene T. Gomulka, a commander in the U.S. Navy Chaplain Corps, argues that gays should be banned from the military because of "widespread sexual compulsion," a higher rate of suicide, and high rates of alcoholism, sexually transmitted diseases, and HIV infection among gay men, as well as "behavioral problems" and tensions that come with housing gay and heterosexual personnel together in close quarters.

NO: Charles L. Davis, a political scientist, argues that any policy that does not grant full rights to gays to serve in the military is discriminatory, stigmatizes the gay community, and fosters distrust and suspicion that weakens the military and its effectiveness both in times of war and peace.

The military has always been a major cultural institution in American society. For many men, being in the military is a mark of masculinity. Small wonder, then, that the issue of recognizing and accepting the presence of homosexuals (to whom some attribute unmasculine traits) in the military has stirred such emotional reactions on every side.

In 1943 the U.S. Department of Defense (DoD) instituted regulations barring gays from military service and requiring their "undesirable discharge" if discovered. Within two years, as America prepared for the final European offensive against the Third Reich, the secretary of war ordered a review of all gay discharges to "salvage" as many homosexuals as possible for the war effort. As soon as the war ended, gays were again discharged. During the Korean War, the number of homosexuals issued undesirable discharges plunged dramatically. When an armistice was signed in 1953, the military again cracked down on homosexuals with vigor.

Pentagon statistics show that during the Vietnam War, field and staff commanders consistently refused to reject gay inductees and refused to discharge known homosexuals. When the Vietnam War ended, the DoD reinstated its regulations that anyone who even hinted that he or she was gay must be discharged. No exceptions were allowed.

In 1991 America rushed to prepare for Operation Desert Storm, the international effort to drive Iraqi forces out of Kuwait. In another reversal of policy, the military informed gay and lesbian reservists that they could not use their sexual orientation to escape mobilization. "Once stationed in the gulf," reported Randy Shilts, a journalist for the *San Francisco Chronicle*, "many gay military personnel found a remarkably accepting environment."

In 1993 Senator Sam Nunn (D-Georgia), head of the Armed Services Committee, advocated a "Don't ask, Don't tell" compromise that could allow homosexuals to serve in the military "if they're dedicated to that purpose, as long as they keep their private life private." Congressman Barney Frank (D-Massachusetts), who is gay, stated that he would prefer completely lifting the ban, but he admitted, "We don't have the votes for that in Congress." His compromise was to allow gay men and lesbians to serve in the military and to be open about their sexual orientation off duty, so long as they keep quiet about this side of their life while on duty. Under Frank's proposal, if someone reported a sailor or soldier going to a gay bar or a gay support meeting in civilian clothes while off duty, the military's response should be, "None of your business or ours."

That this debate is far from settled is evident in the varied responses to Frank's proposal. Congressman Gerry E. Studds, also a Massachusetts Democrat and a homosexual, suggested that Frank was "prematurely raising the white flag on this issue." Thomas Stoddard, coordinator of the Campaign for Military Service, a gay rights group, found Frank's proposal "a creative gambit which, while preferable to the deeply offensive policy now in effect, perpetuates the underlying policy of discrimination."

In the following selections, Eugene T. Gomulka asserts that homosexuals compromise the effectiveness of the military. Charles L. Davis, in opposition, maintains that integrating gays into the military does not harm the workings of the service.

YES

Eugene T. Gomulka

WHY NO GAYS?

Secretary of Defense Dick Cheney and other governmental and military leaders have been under pressure to change the long-standing policy that excludes homosexuals from military service.[1] Critics liken the policy to the past exclusion of blacks and women and call for an end to the "discrimination." The *News Tribune* of Tacoma, Washington, for example, published a story on 5 June 1992 concerning Seattle Mayor Norm Rice's criticism "equating the military's ban on homosexuals with racial segregation." In a written response to Mayor Rice, General Colin Powell distinguished between race—as an uncontrollable factor relating to personhood—and homosexual behavior—as a controllable factor relating to conduct. General Powell wrote, "Skin color is a benign, nonbehavioral characteristic.... Comparison of the two is a convenient but invalid statement."

Even if it is shown that some homosexuals have not "chosen" their orientation, it is fair to state that homosexual behavior is a choice; one that most people do not view as normal conduct, in or out of the military.[2]

A fundamental flaw in the argument for allowing homosexuals to serve in the military is the failure to recognize the link between "nonthreatening" sexual orientation and sexual behavior. More frequently today, practicing homosexuals do not consider their orientation a private matter, but are inclined to seek public affirmation for their lifestyle. It can be argued that the deliberate manifestation by word or deed of one's homosexual orientation marks the beginning of behavioral change because the announcement itself is the demand for a social infrastructure to support the behavior.[3]

The military believes for a number of sound reasons that many persons with a homosexual orientation would experience difficulty controlling their behavior in the unique circumstances of military life.[4] Unlike living conditions in most civilian circumstances, private moments on board ship or while deployed are few or nonexistent. As Secretary Cheney has noted on previous occasions, the line between public and private for those who wear the uniform is very small indeed.[5]

SERIOUS QUESTIONS TO CONSIDER

Critics of the Department of Defense (DoD) policy question the validity of the arguments used by the military to justify the exclusion of homosexuals from its ranks. These same critics (many of whom are civilian), who downplay the behavioral aspects of homosexuality, should be prepared to discuss some concerns that might be raised by the military personnel whose lives would be affected by a change in the current policy.

- Given the uniquely close living conditions of military life, would forcing heterosexuals to compromise their privacy and be looked upon as sexual objects by some homosexuals impact recruitment and retention?
- Without the current exclusion, couldn't the military service, with its predominantly young male population, be an attractive occupation for homosexuals who see no reason to restrict their behavior?
- In light of what some would argue is an innate orientation, would it be wise for a liquor store manager to hire an alcoholic who does not see that condition as a problem and who may abuse his situation?
- How might we expect a heterosexual to behave while sharing a small room with an attractive person of the opposite sex in a ship deployed at sea for six months?
- If homosexuals were allowed to serve in the military and occupy the same quarters, wouldn't it be discriminatory for an unmarried heterosexual couple to be denied permission to share quarters in barracks, base housing, or even at sea?[6]

- It is ironic that some lawmakers who have been outspoken in regard to sexual harassment in the military also endorse homosexuals serving in those same armed forces. Would any of these lawmakers be comfortable having a 17-year-old son billeted in a three-man barracks room with two homosexuals, for a four-year tour of duty?

Unfortunately, these are but a few questions that opponents of the current DoD policy do not wish to consider.

STATISTICS

A recent General Accounting Office (GAO) report, *Defense Force Management: DoD's Policy on Homosexuality,* notes statistics regarding the number of homosexuals who have been discharged from the military.[7] Opponents of the current DoD policy like to quote this report in regard to the amount of money expended in discharging homosexuals. They give the impression that homosexuals are separated simply because of a discovered non-threatening orientation. However, many separation cases involve instances of homosexual behavior, which will only increase if known homosexuals are allowed to enlist. Consequently, the amount of money expended on separating people because of homosexual behavior actually could increase if homosexuals were admitted. The GAO report should persuade those concerned with finances to think twice before endorsing a policy that could result in separation costs far greater than today's.

There are a number of other statistics that the GAO report did not include.

Here are a few others that should be considered:

- There is evidence of widespread sexual compulsion among homosexual men. A recent University of Chicago survey revealed that, for the U.S. population as a whole, the estimated number of sex partners since age 18 is 7.15 (8.67 for those never married).[8] These numbers stand in striking contrast to the results of a major study by the Kinsey Institute that revealed that 43% of the homosexual men surveyed estimated they had sex with 500 or more partners; 28% with 1,000 or more partners.[9] In the same study, 79% of the white male homosexuals surveyed said that more than half of their partners were strangers; 70% said more than half of the sexual partners were men with whom they had sex only once.[10] Since the onset of the AIDS epidemic, there does not appear to be a significant decrease in homosexual partnering behavior. In one study, the number of different partners reported fell from 70 to 50 per year; in another study, the number went from 76 to 47 per year.[11]
- Homosexual men are six times more likely to have attempted suicide than are heterosexual men.[12]
- Studies indicate that between 25% and 33% of homosexual men and women are alcoholics.[13]
- In a survey by the American Public Health Association, 78% of the gay respondents reported they had been infected with a sexually transmitted disease at least one time.[14]
- The latest figures available from the Centers for Disease Control show that two thirds of all AIDS cases are directly attributable to homosexual conduct.[15] Admitting homosexuals into the military surely would bring about an increase in the number of AIDS cases and would put additional financial and personnel demands on an already strained military medicine program.[16]

CONCLUSION

American society is experiencing increasing sensitivity with respect to human rights, accompanied by a growing rejection of sexual morality. The movement to approve homosexual conduct as an acceptable lifestyle is not surprising in today's permissive society. Military leaders are in a position to influence the attitudes of their subordinates—by their words and their example (lifestyle)—and can profoundly affect the direction and lives of those they lead. This fact was articulated by General John Lejeune, the 13th Commandant of the Marine Corps, who noted that "a large portion of those enlisting are under 21 years of age" and "are in a very formative period of their lives. We owe it to them, to their parents, and to the nation, that when discharged from the services they should be far better physically, mentally, and morally than they were when they enlisted." Military personnel themselves and the parents of young service men and women cannot help but be concerned about this matter. Legislators and military leaders have a legitimate role to play in providing positive, acceptable role models, especially for young people whose minds and characters are in formative stages.

In summary, the DoD homosexual-exclusion policy is designed to preserve, promote and protect legitimate military interests, including the personal privacy rights of service members. Discussions with active-duty personnel whose lives would be affected by a policy change give evidence that recruitment of avowed homosexuals could erode morale and have a negative impact on recruitment and retention. Heterosexual military personnel should not be forced to interface with homosexuals without recourse to other living arrangements, as would be available to most civilians. Just as the military excludes persons because of physical handicap or age for the good of the service, so too is it justified in excluding homosexuals from its ranks.

While opponents of the current DoD policy prefer to discount behavioral aspects, in favor of presenting homosexuality as a nonthreatening orientation, the fact is that lifelong, or even career-long celibacy among those with a homosexual orientation is a rare exception rather than the rule. Today—when militant homosexuals not only reveal their liaisons and lifestyles, but also actively and articulately promote the homosexual relationship as a morally acceptable alternative to marriage—legislation that would require the military to accept homosexuals would do much more to violate the rights of heterosexual military personnel than it would to promote the rights of homosexuals. Consequently, legislation that would threaten the rights of military personnel by allowing acknowledged homosexuals into the military should not be enacted.

NOTES

1. Colbert I. King, "Debunking the Case Against Gays in the Military," *The Washington Post*, 7 July 1992, p. 19. The argument in this and so many other articles attempts to define the DoD ban as primarily concerned with sexual orientation. The article cites presidential candidates who are swayed by this attempt to portray the military as preoccupied with orientation vice the negative effects that homosexual behavior would have upon military good order, morale, and discipline. "Bill

Clinton has already said ... if denied the right [to serve in the military], it should be on the basis of behavior, not status." Given the high degree of sexual compulsion on the part of male homosexuals, the defective presumption is that people with a homosexual orientation (status) will remain celibate on ships, in barracks, etc., and not actualize their orientation through homosexual behavior.

2. Henry Robinson, "They Came to Reclaim Asheville," *Asheville Citizen Times*, 27 June 1992, p. 5B. When 1,500 people participated in a Gay Pride March, a counter demonstration was organized the following week that drew more than 20,000 marchers. Current DoD policy mirrors the fact that most Americans strongly disapprove of homosexual behavior, which they do not view as an acceptable alternative to marriage and family life.

3. Steve Scott, "Gay Church Wants Its Clergy to be Chaplains," *Dallas Morning News*, 3 July 1992, p. 36. This article demonstrates a provision for a "social infrastructure" in a religious body that does not perceive the behavior as morally or socially reprehensible.

4. The numerous reasons for excluding homosexuals from military service are contained in DoD Directive 1332.14 H(1), which reads: "Homosexuality is incompatible with military service. The presence in the military environment of persons who engage in homosexual conduct, or who, by their statements, demonstrate a propensity to engage in homosexual conduct, seriously impairs the accomplishments of the military mission. The presence of such members adversely affects the ability of the military services to maintain discipline, good order and morale, foster mutual trust and confidence among service members, to ensure the integrity of the system of rank and command, to facilitate assignment and worldwide deployment of service members who frequently must live and work under close conditions affording minimal privacy, to recruit and retain members of the military services, to maintain public acceptability of military service, and to prevent breaches of security."

5. In *Steffan v. Cheney*, the United States District Court for the District of Columbia ruled on 19 December 1991 in favor of the Secretary of Defense. The judge noted that, "in the military establishment ... the policy of separating men and women while sleeping, bathing, and using the bathroom seeks to maintain the privacy of officers and the enlisted while in certain cases of undress. The embarrassment of being naked as between the sexes is prevalent because sometimes the other is considered a sexual object. The quite rational assumption in the Navy is that with no one present who has a homosexual orientation, men and women alike can undress,

sleep, bathe, and use the bathroom without fear or embarrassment that they are being viewed as sexual objects."

6. Charles Moskos, "Why Banning Homosexuals Still Makes Sense," *Navy Times*, 30 March 1992, p. 27. Rather than drawing an analogy between homosexuality and racism, the writer argues that the more correct analogy is between homosexuality and heterosexuality. He writes, "Anybody who wants to allow homosexuals into the military must make the same argument for breaking down the barrier between the sexes."

7. U.S. General Accounting Office, "Defense Force Management: DoD's Policy on Homosexuality" (Washington, D.C.), 12 June 1992, pp. 16–26.

8. Tom W. Smith, *Adult Sexual Behavior in 1989: Number of Partners, Frequency, and Risk*, presented to the American Association for the Advancement of Science, February 1990, published by NORC, University of Chicago.

9. Alan P. Bell and Martin S. Weinberg, *Homosexualities: A Study of Diversity Among Men and Women* (New York: Simon and Schuster, 1978), p. 308.

10. Ibid., p. 308.

11. S. A. Stewart, *USA Today*, 21 November 1984; L. McKusick, et al., "AIDS and Sexual Behavior Reported by Gay Men in San Francisco," *American Journal of Public Health*, 1985, pp. 493–496.

12. Ibid., Table 21.12.

13. Robert J. Kus, "Alcoholics Anonymous and Gay American Men," *Journal of Homosexuality*, Volume 14, No. 2 (1987), p. 254.

14. Enrique T. Rueda, *The Homosexual Network* (Old Greenwich, CT: The Devin Adair Company, 1982), p. 53.

15. "The HIV/AIDS Surveillance Report," Department of Health and Human Services, Public Health Service, Centers for Disease Control, National Center for Infectious Diseases, Division of HIV/AIDS, January 1992, p. 9.

16. *Steffan v. Cheney*, op. cit., p. 28. The threat of AIDS was a factor in ruling in favor of the current DoD policy. The judge wrote, "There is another justification for the policy of excluding homosexuals from service in the U.S. armed forces... Far and away the highest risk category for those who are HIV-positive, a population who will with a high degree of medical certainty one day contract AIDS, is homosexual men."

AUTHOR'S NOTE

The purpose of this paper is to help focus the current discussion on the issue of homosexuality and military service. It is not a criticism or an attack on homosexual persons as individuals or as a group. Personally, I know and care very much for persons who have confided in me that they have a homosexual orientation. I am pastorally aware of problems and challenges they experience, and I pray that God may help them to experience a happy, healthy, and full life.

Although critics of the current DoD policy on homosexuality attempt to frame the discussion of this issue along the lines of sexual orientation, many homosexuals are separated from the military because of their behavior—and a change in the current policy may well result in more behavior problems.

This paper's arguments in defense of the current DoD policy are not primarily religious. They are based upon the commonly accepted belief in American society that homosexual activity is not an acceptable alternative to marriage and family life. The issues of family values and heterosexual and homosexual rights lie at the heart of this matter. I hope this paper will help stimulate a rational and profitable discussion of the issue.

NO

Charles L. Davis

LIFTING THE GAY BAN

Marine Colonel Fred Peck, who served as the military spokesman for the operation in Somalia, captured public attention recently in testimony before the Senate Arms Services Committee investigating the ban on homosexuals in the armed forces. Colonel Peck, a staunch foe of lifting the ban, revealed that one of his sons was a homosexual and that he would counsel all his sons to stay out of the military if the ban were lifted. He expressed particular concern for his homosexual son, whose life, the Colonel believed, would be in jeopardy were he to enter military service (*The New York Times*, May 12, 1993).

Underlying Colonel Peck's attitude toward the gay ban is a particular view of U.S. military community and its culture that seems to be widely shared by proponents of the gay ban. The military community is presumed to be less tolerant of social and cultural diversity than is civilian society. Intolerance is presumed to be rooted in both the institutional needs of the military and its social composition. Group cohesion and unity are paramount institutional needs for maintaining "discipline, good order, and morale." Cohesion and unity cannot be achieved if the boundaries of social diversity are extended to include "out-groups" —those whose values and behavior patterns conflict with those of the larger military community. Furthermore, the boundaries of acceptable behavior and values are more narrowly drawn in the military than in civilian society because of the social composition of the military.

The military is presumed to attract a relatively homogeneous group in terms of cultural values and perspectives. The social and political outlooks of the military community are characterized as narrow, parochial, conservative, and conventional. The boundaries of what is socially acceptable in military communities, therefore, is more narrowly drawn than in civilian society. The proponents of the gay ban, therefore, argue that the military cannot be "a laboratory for social experimentation" unless one were willing to sacrifice its group cohesion and unity and, thus, its effectiveness. Perhaps, Colonel Peck goes to the extreme in arguing that violence would result, but he shares the view that the military community will not accept declared homosexuals. That assumption is central to the thinking of proponents of the ban.

From Charles L. Davis, "Lifting the Gay Ban," *Society* (November/December 1993). Copyright © 1993 by Transaction Publishers. Reprinted by permission.

Even those who, like Senator Sam Nunn and other senators, favor the "Don't ask, Don't tell" policy hold this view. This policy means that the military no longer asks recruits about their sexual orientation nor will it conduct investigations to identify homosexuals. However, gay men and women could not be open about their sexuality at the risk of being discharged from the military. Also a strict code of conduct would be imposed on overt behavior—same-sex dancing and the like would be prohibited. The underlying assumption is the same, open homosexuality is outside the norms of acceptable behavior in military communities. To protect legally the right to such behavior or even the right to declare one's sexual orientation would disrupt group cohesion and prevent the emotional bonding upon which the military so vitally depends for its effectiveness.

Such views are reflected in the Department of Defense policy that bans homosexuals from military service. According to the current department directive, as revised on February 12, 1986:

> Homosexuality is incompatible with military service... The presence of such members adversely affects the ability of the Military Services to maintain discipline, good order, and morale; to foster mutual trust and confidence among service-members; to ensure the integrity of the system of rank and command; to facilitate assignment of worldwide deployment of service members who frequently must live and work under close conditions affording minimal privacy; to recruit and retain members of the Military Services; to maintain public acceptability of military services; and to prevent breaches of security.

While issues such as national security and privacy are invoked, the exclusionary policy is justified primarily in terms of the unacceptability of homosexuality to the military community and the general populace. Persuasive opinion data can be marshalled in support of this view. For example, one poll, completed in December 1992, found that 45 percent of the soldiers at two Texas Army bases indicated that they would resign if forced to serve with openly gay soldiers (*Lexington Herald-Leader*, April 30, 1993).

Other polls have also found widespread opposition within the military to lifting the ban. Within the general population, polls show the public has become more tolerant of gays, but even though, there is still substantial support for restricting the rights and opportunities of homosexuals. These data can be used to support the argument that recruitment, group cohesion, public support for the military, and so on would suffer as a consequence of lifting the ban.

An implicit assumption in this argument favoring the ban is that negative attitudes toward gays are not likely to change in the military community. Indeed, this assumption is central to much of the argument for retaining the ban. If it is granted that negative attitudes and stereotypes of gays could change, then one would have to grant that many of the dire consequences that are predicted need not occur. If the military community were to become tolerant of open gays in the ranks, there would be no threat to the "discipline, good order, and morale" of the military. The central issue is whether the larger military community is capable of the attitude change needed to facilitate the integration of declared gays into military service. My argument is that the military services may be far better able to adapt to such a policy change than proponents of the current ban claim.

No one can argue that attitude change on the gay issue is easily achieved. Homophobic attitudes are deeply rooted in the military culture as well as in the general American culture. Furthermore, negative attitudes toward gays tend to be more deeply rooted in emotions than for other "out-groups" in American society, as a recent empirical study has shown. Yet, attitude change in the military on the gay issue may not be so difficult as proponents of the ban suggest.

It would be unrealistic to expect homophobic elements in the military (or in civilian life) to condone homosexuality. But homophobic attitudes toward behavior need not change for attitudes to change about the rights of gay men and women. One need not like or approve of homosexuality in order to accept the premise that rights of consenting adults to privacy in their sexual conduct and to be free from discrimination based on sexual orientation ought to be respected. If such rights are accorded and respected, it is difficult to see why gay men and women would not be accepted in the work world of the military without disruption to "discipline, good order, and morale." The issue is not acceptance of homosexual behavior, as General Colin Powell and other proponents of the gay ban argue, but acceptance of gay rights in accordance with American liberal culture.

But would acceptance of gay rights lead military personnel to accept gays in their ranks as colleagues? The nature of contact experiences would be partly determinative. Positive experiences would contribute to reduction of prejudice and negative stereotyping while negative experiences would reinforce existing prejudices and stereotypes. The nature of the work environment would seem to dictate what types of experiences would most likely occur. Positive experiences would seem more likely if harassment and intimidation of gays were not tolerated and existing norms about fraternization and intimacy in the military workplace respected. There is no reason to believe that such norms would be less respected by the entry of gays into the military. Allport's classic study of prejudice reduction suggests that close contact involving cooperative interdependence in the workplace helps to reduce prejudice and negative stereotyping of "out-groups"—not to increase hostility and conflict as suggested by proponents of the gay ban.

Racial integration of the military provides an instructive example. As Charles Moskos has made clear, conflict between black and white troops was common in the segregated armed forces. However, racial hostility disappeared among white and black troops who fought together in the Battle of the Bulge in 1944 in what was to be the first experiment with a racially integrated fighting force in American history. In "From Citizens' Army to Social Laboratory," *(The Wilson Quarterly,* Winter 1993) Moskos writes, "The soldiers who stepped forward performed exceptionally well in battle, gaining the respect of the white soldiers they fought next to and the high regard of the white officers under whom they served." The military has since become a model institution of racial harmony, Moskos notes. This case fully supports Allport's theory; it is not clear why integration of declared gays into the military would not also lead to prejudice reduction rather than to conflict.

The case of racial integration—and more than simply integration, the high degree of racial harmony that Moskos notes—illustrates that attitudes toward "out-groups" can and do change in the military community. What is not clear is why a similar attitude change toward gays in the military could not also occur. Those who view the military community as incapable of integrating gays may be overlooking the highly diverse character of the military and its demonstrated capacity to integrate individuals from highly diverse social and cultural backgrounds.

The military imposes a high degree of unity and uniformity on its personnel through its hierarchical structure of authority. But at the same time it recruits from a very broad base of American society, though perhaps less so since compulsory military service has ended. Individuals from diverse social, religious, cultural, and regional backgrounds are placed in a close working situation of cooperative interdependence in which they must learn to interact with each other and, in many cases, live together.

Furthermore, military personnel frequently move to different places all over the world. With manpower cutbacks, the military has increasingly been able to recruit a more educated force (though not as educated as during compulsory military service) and it utilizes various incentives to encourage further education of its members once they are inducted into the services. In short, the contemporary U.S. military is comprised of individuals who have experienced considerable social and cultural diversity, who have traveled widely, and who tend to be relatively well educated. In many ways, the United States military is already a laboratory in social and cultural diversity by virtue of the fact that it draws recruits from all strata of an extremely diverse society. The American soldier may thus be better prepared to deal with the lifting of the gay ban than many expect.

Moskos recognizes that the era of compulsory universal military service promoted cultural and social diversity: "It brought together millions of Americans who otherwise would have lived their lives in relative social and geographic isolation. No other institution has accomplished such an intermingling of diverse classes, races, and ethnic groups."

My own experience with the military leads me to believe that an usual degree of cultural and social diversity still exists in the post-draft military. What I encountered was a social and cultural diversity that was far greater than in other institutions, including institutions of higher learning. I was a college professor at the University of Kentucky Center at Fort Knox from 1977 to 1989 rather than a recruit or draftee. When I began teaching full-time at Fort Knox in the fall of 1977, I brought with me the full baggage of stereotypes about the United States military. I was not sure whether I would find an excessively deferential type of student or the narrow-minded, authoritarian type. I was also concerned about soldiers pulling rank in class discussions and the overall atmosphere of academic freedom. In short, I was afraid of pressures, both direct and subtle, to tow the line.

I do not wish to suggest that the University of Kentucky Center at Fort Knox was an academician's mecca. Our program was a very low priority with both the military and the University of Kentucky administration in Lexington. We were housed in an old WPA school building from the 1930s along with several other institutions of higher learning that offered programs at Fort Knox. Little of the elaborate and sophisticated equipment or modern facilities, used for military training, were available to us. Before the University of Kentucky program was pulled from Fort Knox, our offices were even shifted to an unused, run-down army barracks.

Whatever my reservations about the facilities and the priority of our program may have been, I soon began questioning my own negative stereotypes about the military community. Indeed, my experience is further confirmation of Allport's theory of prejudice reduction via social contact. Admittedly the student body at the Fort Knox Center was not a representative cross-section of the Fort Knox community, but I suspect that the social diversity of students reflected the diverse military community from which most students came. (It should be pointed out that students included civilian employees and spouses of military personnel as well as soldiers. Most students were connected to the military base at Fort Knox, even if not on active duty in the U.S. Army.) In any case, the diversity was far greater than what I have even experienced in conventional institutions of higher learning.

Not surprisingly, a significant number of students came from ethnic and racial minority groups, among them African-Americans, Koreans, and Hispanics. Minority groups were probably not proportionately represented in the student body, but their number was significantly greater than in more conventional institutions of higher learning. There was also a large number of students who did not come from the middle and upper-middle classes as do so many traditional college students. Many students represented the first generation in their families that attended college. In short, there was a higher degree of social and cul-

tural diversity than one typically finds on most college or university campuses. Surprising too was the high degree of ideological diversity among the students—from one enlisted soldier who had joined a Democratic Socialist branch in nearby Louisville to a major who considered Milton Friedman too liberal.

What was particularly striking was the ability of these students to get along and to respect each other despite differences in social, cultural, or racial background, military rank, and even ideological orientation. Indeed, I suspect that informal norms that stress tolerance and mutual respect in the face of diversity were operative in this military community. Such norms may be vital for achieving the degree of cohesion and unity that the U.S. military needs to carry out its mission and may be the glue that holds military communities together.

My impressions of one military community are consistent with various sociological studies of the military with which I am familiar. While the available systematic research on the social and political attitudes of military personnel is still limited and not conclusive, there is nothing in that research to suggest that military personnel are more intolerant of "out-groups" or anti-democratic than their civilian counterparts.

Using a panel design for a larger study of political socialization of American youths, M. Kent Jennings and Gregory B. Markus compared attitude changes among respondents who had served in the military with those who had not. The panel consisted of a national probability sample of high school seniors, male and female, interviewed in 1965 and then reinterviewed in 1973 (N = 674 male respondents in the panel). These researchers found no evidence that prior military service results in a failure to acquire participatory skills and motivations, in spite of a time lag before many veterans become active voters. Nor did they uncover any evidence that military service is associated with heightened political intolerance. These findings are consistent with other research that shows that military service actually reduces authoritarian tendencies, as measured on Adorno's F-scale.

It might be objected that these findings are based on samples of inductees who served only briefly in the military and never acquired a syndrome of attitudes and beliefs more typical of the non-conscripted military. Furthermore, most respondents in the Jennings Markus study had been reintegrated into civilian life. To account for these possibilities, Ronald D. Taylor and I conducted a study of students enrolled at the University of Kentucky Center at Fort Knox during the 1984/85 academic year (N = 116). The military sub-sample included non-conscripted soldiers currently serving in the U.S. Army, most of whom intended to remain in the service for an extended period of time. This sub-sample of active-duty soldiers was found to be more interested in politics, better informed about politics, and more politically tolerant than either the veteran or civilian sub-samples. These findings suggest that active military service might result in more democratic and tolerant behavior than proponents of the gay ban would lead one to believe.

It would be rash to conclude that, because of its social diversity, the U.S. military provides an ideal laboratory of social experimentation for integrating gays into the mainstream of American life. Homophobic attitudes are entrenched in military communities as elsewhere in American society. Certainly there are elements in the military that are not likely to change long-held beliefs about homosexuals, and there are no assurances that events like the murder of the gay sailor, Allen R. Schindler, in 1992 will not happen again. Nevertheless, there are reasons to believe that the United States military is much better able to manage the task without significant disruption of "discipline, good order, and morale" than proponents of the ban would grant.

It seems that successful integration of declared gay men and women into the military depends on leadership more than anything else. If the military leadership continues to project their own homophobic fears and to manipulate popular stereotypes about the U.S. military, homophobic attitudes are not likely to change in military communities. Indeed, the cues that are now emanating from some of the leaders suggest that to be pro-gay rights is to be anti-military. An implicit linkage to President Clinton and the views on the military he expressed during the Vietnam era is also being made. Some military leaders seem intent on creating a self-fulfilling prophecy that negative attitudes and stereotypes regarding gays are not going to change in military communities.

The official Department of Defense policy of excluding homosexuals might also reinforce and justify negative attitudes and stereotypes regarding gays. Similarly, any policy that does not recognize and protect the rights of gays to privacy and to non-discrimination because of sexual orientation is likely to reinforce and justify existing attitudes and stereotypes as well as to create an environment of distrust and suspicion toward gays in the military.

To accord less than full rights to gays who serve in the military, as the "Don't ask, Don't tell" policy does, is to continue to stigmatize the gay community and to justify continued distrust and suspicion. If attitude change is to occur within the heterosexual community in the military, it is essential that the official policy unambiguously protect the rights of gay military personnel and that the leadership be fully committed to implementation of those rights.

I grew up in a southern community in the 1950s where it was frequently asserted that "the southern way of life" would never change. Racial mores and attitudes were presumed to be too deeply ingrained to permit peaceful integration. As with Colonel Peck, the fear of violence was used to justify the status quo. It was amazing how peacefully and quickly racial integration came once federal and state civil rights laws were passed and the political leadership endorsed racial equality.

Integrating declared gays into the military may not follow as smooth a course, but the posture of the military leadership and the nature of the official policy will certainly make a difference. The basic problem facing the military is not that rank-and-file soldiers or sailors are inherently incapable of handling social and cultural diversity and change.

POSTSCRIPT

Is Homosexuality Incompatible With Military Service?

Discrimination and prejudice are not eliminated simply by changing a law or by issuing a presidential executive order. President Harry S. Truman's executive order to eliminate racial segregation in the U.S. military during the Korean War required many years of education and positive leadership to achieve its goal. Similarly, as one commentator wrote in *New York Magazine* (November 30, 1992), lifting the ban on homosexuals in the military may be as big a boon in the long run to the U.S. military's effectiveness as racial integration has been. However, the author goes on to say, "It seems safe to say that the most prominent feature of the military when the ban against gays is lifted [assuming it is lifted] will not be homosexual orgies in the barracks. It will instead be increased violence against gays by soldiers whose identity as straight warriors is threatened. In response, gay grievance groups will demand protection and privileges and freely resort to litigation when they feel frustrated. Lifting the ban on gays in the military solves one problem but also creates a host of new, more complex ones."

While Americans continue to debate the issue of homosexuals in the military, 14 of the 16 nations in the North Atlantic Treaty Organization (NATO) either have laws protecting homosexuals from discrimination, including those in the military, or follow policies that make no distinction between homosexuals and nonhomosexuals, even for highly sensitive, special security military duty. In October 1992 Canada eliminated all barriers to gays and lesbians in its military. Soon after, Australia followed suit. In NATO, only the United States and Great Britain maintain a ban on homosexuals in the military.

Opponents of banning homosexuals from the military cite the success of Holland, Denmark, Switzerland, Norway, Sweden, Spain, Italy, and (to a lesser extent) France, where gays and lesbians have already been integrated into the armed forces. Supporters of the ban argue that whether or not any of these nations allow homosexual men and women in their militaries is irrelevant because most of these nations have never had a top-notch army, and those that did ceased to be major powers long ago.

Opponents of the ban cite the experience of the German and Israeli militaries. Germany maintains a ban on sexual relations between military personnel while on duty but is not concerned with what goes on off duty and off base. In Israel, mandatory service requirements mean that every 18-year-old man and woman enlists, with the only exception being religious students. As one Americanized Israeli soldier recalled, "I had thought Israel was less tolerant than the United States, but when I enlisted, I never witnessed any morale problems caused by homosexuals and didn't hear any homophobic talk.... There were openly gay soldiers I encountered, but no one seemed to resent it. It's not even an issue. I don't know why it is in America." Traditionalists, in response, emphasize the perils of mixing gay and lesbian soldiers and sailors with heterosexual personnel.

Adding to the complexity of the current debate is a financial issue: The General Accounting Office (GAO) has pointed out that enforcing the ban on homosexuals in the military wastes about $27 million in training costs every year. Calling the ban too costly, the GAO argued that "experts believe the policy is unsupported, unfair and counterproductive; has no validity according to current scientific research and opinions; and appears to be based on the same type of prejudicial suppositions [once] used to discriminate against blacks and women."

SUGGESTED READINGS

"Homosexuality and the Military Culture" [Special issue], *Society* (November/December 1993).

D. Jackson, "I Just Don't Want to Go," *Time* (July 6, 1992).

R. Shilts, *Conduct Unbecoming: Gays and Lesbians in the U.S. Military* (St. Martin's Press, 1993).

J. Steffan, *Honor Bound: An American Fights Against Prejudice and for the Right to Serve His Country* (Random House, 1992).

J. M. Wall, "Gays and the Armed Forces," *Christian Century* (December 2, 1992).

ISSUE 17

Have the Dangers of Date Rape Been Exaggerated?

YES: Camille Paglia, from *Sex, Art and American Culture* (Vintage, 1992)

NO: Robin Warshaw, from *I Never Called It Rape: The Ms. Report on Recognizing, Fighting, and Surviving Date and Acquaintance Rape* (Harper & Row, 1988)

ISSUE SUMMARY

YES: Professor of humanities Camille Paglia argues that feminists have grossly distorted the facts about date rape and that date rape propaganda actually puts women in greater danger of being raped. "The only solution to date rape," she states, "is female self-awareness and self-control."

NO: Robin Warshaw, a journalist who specializes in social issues, examines survey data indicating that about one in three college women is the victim of rape or attempted rape and over half experience some form of sexual victimization by age 21. She concludes that date rape is extremely pervasive but that relatively few victims are aware that they have been raped.

Thirty years ago, rape meant one thing: a male jumping out of the dark to confront a woman he had stalked or laid in wait for where she would be unable to resist his forcing sexual intercourse on her. Women might also be raped if they inadvertently interrupted a male robbing their house or apartment. Rape did not occur in marriage or a dating situation. A husband or a boyfriend might press a little hard or use a little force, but only because he knew "she really wanted it."

One consequence of the sexual revolution of the 1960s and 1970s was that women began to reject the assumption of many men that dating, courtship, or marriage gave them a right to have sexual intercourse even if the woman decided, after going along with some intimate love play, "No more, I want to stop." Growing tension led to women's pressing for legal recognition of the limits of a male's "conjugal rights" and the crime of marital rape. Traditional male prerogatives were more slowly challenged in the dating situation, even as premarital sex became more acceptable for both men and women. Traditionally, many men and women accepted the right of men to their sexual satisfaction when they spent money on a date, when they had been dating a woman for some time, when a woman was under the influence, or when a woman's flirting indicated that she wanted sex, even when she said, "Stop."

In 1969, just as the sexual revolution was peaking in the United States, sociologist Eugene Kanin published a paper in the *Journal of Sex Research* reporting on aspects of male aggression that affected couples. In 1975, in her book *Against Our Will: Men, Women, and Rape* (Simon & Schuster), feminist pioneer Susan Brownmiller gave a name to one particular type of male aggression briefly examined by Kanin. "Date rape," forced sexual assault by an acquaintance when on a date, was thus introduced.

The term *date rape*, however, seemed to limit this form of male aggression to couples actually going together in some kind of ongoing courtship. A broader designation was needed to cover situations in which the aggressor and victim were not courting or dating but knew each other or went out casually and occasionally as a couple. So we now have date rape and the broader term *acquaintance rape*.

Date and acquaintance rape came into public view with a 1985 *Ms.* magazine survey, directed by Professor Mary P. Koss and funded by the National Institute of Mental Health. In 1988 Robin Warshaw's slim volume *I Never Called It Rape: The* Ms. *Report on Recognizing, Fighting, and Surviving Date and Acquaintance Rape*, which examines data from the survey, became a national best-seller. It also generated prevention workshops and therapy groups for date rape victims on college campuses across the nation.

Prior to this new conception, rape had been understood to involve a man using or threatening to use a weapon or physical strength to force some sexually intimate act on an unwilling woman. Date and acquaintance rape have introduced the more nebulous and vaguely defined factor of "psychological force," or "coercion," to the concept of rape.

Individual perceptions of what differentiates psychological coercion (emotional force) from seduction and persuasion in a dating relationship or a casual friendship often differ, depending both on one's gender and one's social class. With men and women today often engaging in casual sex for fun, relaxation, or curiosity, it is difficult to spell out clearly when and why some forms of persuasion are acceptable at one time in one relationship and unacceptable (and worthy of being labeled "rape") at another time in another relationship. The issue becomes even more complicated the morning, 1 year, or 10 years after a casual sexual experience, when recollection and reflection can give the experience new interpretations.

It is little wonder that both women and men are confused today about the signals they send and receive in dating and acquaintance situations. The following selections by Camille Paglia and Robin Warshaw highlight the confusion about date rape, how to interpret its meaning and causes within a social context, and how to reduce its frequency in our society.

YES

Camille Paglia

RAPE AND THE MODERN SEX WAR

Rape is an outrage that cannot be tolerated in civilized society. Yet feminism, which has waged a crusade for rape to be taken more seriously, has put young women in danger by hiding the truth about sex from them.

In dramatizing the pervasiveness of rape, feminists have told young women that before they have sex with a man, they must give consent as explicit as a legal contract's. In this way young women have been convinced that they have been the victims of rape. On elite campuses in the Northeast and on the West Coast, they have held consciousness-raising sessions, petitioned administrations, demanded inquests. At Brown University, outraged, panicky "victims" have scrawled the names of alleged attackers on the walls of women's rest rooms. What marital rape was to the seventies, "date rape" is to the nineties.

The incidence and seriousness of rape do not require this kind of exaggeration. Real acquaintance rape is nothing new. It has been a horrible problem for women for all of recorded history. Once, fathers and brothers protected women from rape. Once, the penalty for rape was death. I come from a fierce Italian tradition where, not so long ago in the motherland, a rapist would end up knifed, castrated, and hung out to dry.

But the old clans and small rural communities have broken down. In our cities, on our campuses far from home, young women are vulnerable and defenseless. Feminism has not prepared them for this. Feminism keeps saying the sexes are the same. It keeps telling women they can do anything, go anywhere, say anything, wear anything. No, they can't. Women will always be in sexual danger.

One of my male students recently slept overnight with a friend in a passageway of the Great Pyramid in Egypt. He described the moon and sand, the ancient silence and eerie echoes. I will never experience that. I am a woman. I am not stupid enough to believe I could ever be safe there. There is a world of solitary adventure I will never have. Women have always known these somber truths. But feminism, with its pie-in-the-sky fantasies about the perfect world, keeps young women from seeing life as it is.

We must remedy social injustice whenever we can. But there are some things we cannot change. There are sexual differences that are based in biology. Academic feminism is lost in a fog of social constructionism. It believes we are totally the product of our environment. This idea was invented by Rousseau. He was wrong. Emboldened by dumb French language theory, academic feminists repeat the same hollow slogans over and over to each other. Their view of sex is naive and prudish. Leaving sex to the feminists is like letting your dog vacation at the taxidermist's.

The sexes are at war. Men must struggle for identity against the overwhelming power of their mothers. Women have menstruation to tell them they are women. Men must do or risk something to be men. Men become masculine only when other men say they are. Having sex with a woman is one way a boy becomes a man.

College men are at their hormonal peak. They have just left their mothers and are questing for their male identity. In groups they are dangerous. A woman going to a fraternity party is walking into Testosterone Flats, full of prickly cacti and blazing guns. If she goes, she should be armed with resolute alertness. She should arrive with girlfriends and leave with them. A girl who lets herself get dead drunk at a fraternity party is a fool. A girl who goes upstairs alone with a brother at a fraternity party is an idiot. Feminists call this blaming the victim. I call it common sense.

For a decade feminists have drilled their disciples to say, "Rape is a crime of violence but not of sex." This sugar-coated Shirley Temple nonsense has exposed young women to disaster. Misled by feminism, they do not expect rape from the nice boys from good homes who sit next to them in class.

Aggression and eroticism are deeply intertwined. Hunt, pursuit, and capture are biologically programmed into male sexuality. Generation after generation, men must be educated, refined, and ethically persuaded away from their tendency toward anarchy and brutishness. Society is not the enemy, as feminism ignorantly claims. Society is woman's protection against rape. Feminism, with its solemn Carry Nation repressiveness, does not see what is for men the eroticism or fun element in rape, especially the wild, infectious delirium of gang rape. Women who do not understand rape cannot defend themselves against it.

The date-rape controversy shows feminism hitting the wall of its own broken promises. The women of my sixties generation were the first respectable girls in history to swear like sailors, get drunk, stay out all night—in short, to act like men. We sought total sexual freedom and equality. But as time passed, we woke up to cold reality. The old double standard protected women. When anything goes, it's women who lose.

Today's young women don't know what they want. They see that feminism has not brought sexual happiness. The theatrics of public rage over date rape are their way of restoring the old sexual rules that were shattered by my generation. Because nothing about the sexes has really changed. The comic film *Where the Boys Are* (1960), the ultimate expression of fifties man-chasing, still speaks directly to our time. It shows smart, lively women skillfully anticipating and fending off the dozens of strategies with which horny men try to get them into bed. The agonizing subplot and climax are brilliantly done. The victim, Yvette Mimieux, makes mistake after mistake, obvious to the other girls. She allows herself to be lured away from her girlfriends and into isolation with boys whose character and intentions she misreads. *Where the Boys Are* tells the truth. It shows courtship as a dangerous game in which the signals are not verbal but subliminal.

Neither militant feminism, which is obsessed with politically correct language, nor academic feminism, which believes that knowledge and experience are "constituted by" language, can understand preverbal or nonverbal communication. Feminism, focusing on sexual politics, cannot see that sex exists in and through the body. Sexual desire and arousal cannot be fully translated into verbal terms. This is why men and women misunderstand each other.

Trying to remake the future, feminism cut itself off from sexual history. It discarded and suppressed the sexual myths of literature, art, and religion. Those myths show us the turbulence, the mysteries, and the passions of sex. In mythology we see men's sexual anxiety, their fear of woman's dominance. Much sexual violence is rooted in men's sense of psychological weakness toward women. It takes many men to deal with one woman. Woman's voracity is a persistent motif. Clara Bow, it was rumored, took on the USC football team on weekends. Marilyn Monroe, singing "Diamonds Are a Girl's Best Friend," rules a conga line of men in tuxes. Half-clad Cher, in the video for "If I Could Turn Back Time," deranges a battleship of screaming sailors and straddles a pink-lit cannon. Feminism, coveting social power, is blind to woman's cosmic sexual power.

To understand rape, you must study the past. There never was and never will be sexual harmony. Every woman must take personal responsibility for her sexuality, which is nature's red flame. She must be prudent and cautious about where she goes and with whom. When she makes a mistake, she must accept the consequences and, through self-criticism, resolve never to make that mistake again. Running to Mommy or Daddy on the campus grievance committee is unworthy of strong women. Posting lists of guilty men in the toilet is cowardly, infantile stuff.

The Italian philosophy of life espouses high-energy confrontation. A male student makes a vulgar remark about your breasts? Don't slink off to whimper and simper with the campus shrinking violets. Deal with it. On the spot. Say, "Shut up, you jerk! And crawl back to the barnyard where you belong!" In general, women who project this take-charge attitude toward life get harassed less often. I see too many dopey, immature, self-pitying women walking around like melting sticks of butter. It's the Yvette Mimieux syndrome: Make me happy. And listen to me weep when I'm not.

The date-rape debate is already smothering in propaganda churned out by the expensive northeastern colleges and universities, with their overconcentration of boring, uptight academic feminists and spoiled, affluent students. Beware of the deep manipulativeness of rich students who were neglected by their parents. They love to turn the campus into hysterical psychodramas of sexual transgression, followed by assertions of parental authority and concern. And don't look for sexual enlightenment from academe, which spews out mountains of books but never looks at life directly.

As a fan of football and rock music, I see in the simple, swaggering masculinity of the jock and in the noisy posturing of the heavy-metal guitarist certain fundamental, unchanging truths about sex. Masculinity is aggressive, unstable, combustible. It is also the most creative cultural force in history. Women must reorient themselves toward the elemental powers of sex, which can strengthen or destroy.

The only solution to date rape is female self-awareness and self-control. A woman's number-one line of defense is herself. When a real rape occurs, she should report it to the police. Complaining to college committees because the courts "take too long" is ridiculous. College administrations are not a branch of the judiciary. They are not equipped or trained for legal inquiry. Colleges must alert incoming students to the problems and dangers of adulthood. Then colleges must stand back and get out of the sex game.

NO   Robin Warshaw

THE REALITY OF ACQUAINTANCE RAPE

Women raped by men they know—acquaintance rape—is not an aberrant quirk of male-female relations. If you are a woman, your risk of being raped by someone you know is *four times greater* than your risk of being raped by a stranger.

A recent scientific study of acquaintance rape on 32 college campuses conducted by *Ms.* magazine and psychologist Mary P. Koss showed that significant numbers of women are raped on dates or by acquaintances, although most victims never report their attacks.

Ms. Survey Stats

- 1 in 4 women surveyed were victims of rape or attempted rape.
- 84 percent of those raped knew their attacker.
- 57 percent of the rapes happened on dates.

Those figures make acquaintance rape and date rape more common than left-handedness or heart attacks or alcoholism. These rapes are no recent campus fad or the fantasy of a few jilted females. They are real. And they are happening all around us.

THE EXTENT OF "HIDDEN" RAPE

Most states define rape as sexual assault in which a man uses his penis to commit vaginal penetration of a victim against her will, by force or threats of force or when she is physically or mentally unable to give her consent. Many states now also include unwanted anal and oral intercourse in that definition and some have removed gender-specific language to broaden the applicability of rape laws.

In acquaintance rape, the rapist and victim may know each other casually—having met through a common activity, mutual friend, at a party, as neighbors, as students in the same class, at work, on a blind date, or while traveling. Or they may have a closer relationship—as steady dates or former sexual partners. Although largely a hidden phenomenon because it's the least reported type of rape (and rape, in general, is the most underreported crime

From Robin Warshaw, *I Never Called It Rape: The* Ms. *Report on Recognizing, Fighting, and Surviving Date and Acquaintance Rape* (Harper & Row, 1988). Copyright © 1988 by The Ms. Foundation for Education and Communication, Inc., and Sarah Lazin Books. Reprinted by permission of HarperCollins Publishers, Inc.

against a person), many organizations, counselors, and social researchers agree that acquaintance rape is the most prevalent rape crime today.

Only 90,434 rapes were reported to U.S. law enforcement agencies in 1986, a number that is conservatively believed to represent a minority of the actual rapes of all types taking place. Government estimates find that anywhere from three to ten rapes are committed for every rape reported. And while rapes by strangers are still underreported, rapes by acquaintances are virtually nonreported. Yet, based on intake observations made by staff at various rape-counseling centers (where victims come for treatment, but do not have to file police reports), 70 to 80 percent of all rape crimes are acquaintance rapes.

Those rapes are happening in a social environment in which sexual aggression occurs regularly. Indeed, less than half the college women questioned in the *Ms.* survey reported that they had experienced *no* sexual victimization in their lives thus far (the average age of respondents was 21). Many had experienced more than one episode of unwanted sexual touching, coercion, attempted rape, or rape. Using the data collected in the study... the following profile can be drawn of what happens in just one year of "social life" on America's college campuses:

Ms. **Survey Stats**

In one year 3,187 women reported suffering:

- 328 rapes (as defined by law)
- 534 attempted rapes (as defined by law)
- 837 episodes of sexual coercion (sexual intercourse obtained through the ag-

gressor's continual arguments or pressure)

- 2,024 experiences of unwanted sexual contact (fondling, kissing, or petting committed against the woman's will)

Over the years, other researchers have documented the phenomenon of acquaintance rape. In 1957, a study conducted by Eugene J. Kanin of Purdue University in West Lafayette, Indiana, showed that 30 percent of women surveyed had suffered attempted or completed forced sexual intercourse while on a high school date. Ten years later, in 1967, while young people donned flowers and beads and talked of love and peace, Kanin found that more than 25 percent of the male college students surveyed had attempted to force sexual intercourse on a woman to the point that she cried or fought back. In 1977, after the blossoming of the women's movement and countless pop-culture attempts to extol the virtues of becoming a "sensitive man," Kanin found that 26 percent of the men he surveyed had tried to force intercourse on a woman and that 25 percent of the women questioned had suffered attempted or completed rape. In other words, two decades had passed since Kanin's first study, yet women were being raped by men they knew as frequently as before.

In 1982, a doctoral student at Auburn University in Auburn, Alabama, found that 25 percent of the undergraduate women surveyed had at least one experience of forced intercourse and that 93 percent of those episodes involved acquaintances. That same year, Auburn psychology professor and acquaintance-rape expert Barry R. Burkhart conducted a study in which 61 percent of the men said they had sexually touched a woman against her will.

Further north, at St. Cloud State University in St. Cloud, Minnesota, research in 1982 showed 29 percent of women surveyed reported being physically or psychologically forced to have sexual intercourse.

In 1984, 20 percent of the female students questioned in a study at the University of South Dakota in Vermillion, South Dakota, said they had been physically forced to have intercourse while on a date. At Brown University in Providence, Rhode Island, 16 percent of the women surveyed reported they were raped by an acquaintance and 11 percent of the men said they had forced sexual intercourse on a woman. And another study coauthored by Auburn's Burkhart showed 15 percent of the male respondents reporting having raped a date.

That same year, the study of acquaintance rape moved beyond the serenity of leafy college quadrangles into the hard reality of the "dangerous" outside world. A random sample survey of 930 women living in San Francisco, conducted by researcher Diana Russell, showed that 44 percent of the women questioned had been victims of rape or attempted rape —and that 88 percent of the rape victims knew their attackers. A Massachusetts Department of Public Health study, released in 1986, showed that two-thirds of the rapes reported at crisis centers were committed by acquaintances.

These numbers stand in stark contrast to what most people think of as rape: that is, a stranger (usually a black, Hispanic, or other minority) jumping out of the bushes at an unsuspecting female, brandishing a weapon, and assaulting her. The truth about rape—that it usually happens between people who know each other and is often committed by "regular" guys—is difficult to accept.

Most people never learn the truth until rape affects them or someone they care about. And many women are so confused by the dichotomy between their acquaintance-rape experience and what they thought rape really was that they are left with an awful new reality: Where once they feared strange men as they were taught to, they now fear strange men *and* all the men they know....

RAPE IS RAPE

Rape that occurs on dates or between people who know each other should not be seen as some sort of misguided sexual adventure: Rape is violence, not seduction. In stranger rape *and* acquaintance rape, the aggressor makes a decision to force his victim to submit to what he wants. The rapist believes he is entitled to force sexual intercourse from a woman and he sees interpersonal violence (be it simply holding the woman down with his body or brandishing a gun) as an acceptable way to achieve his goal.

"All rape is an exercise in power," writes Susan Brownmiller in her landmark book *Against Our Will: Men, Women and Rape*. Specifically, Brownmiller and others argue, rape is an exercise in the imbalance of power that exists between most men and women, a relationship that has forged the social order from ancient times on.

Today, that relationship continues. Many men are socialized to be sexually aggressive—to score, as it were, regardless of how. Many women are socialized to submit to men's wills, especially those men deemed desirable by society at large. Maintaining such roles helps set the stage for acquaintance rape.

But despite their socialization, most men are not rapists. That is the good news.

The bad news, of course, is that so many are.

Ms. **Survey Stat**

1 in 12 of the male students surveyed had committed acts that met the legal definitions of rape or attempted rape.

BLAMING THE ACQUAINTANCE-RAPE VICTIM

Without question, many date rapes and acquaintance rapes could have been prevented by the woman—if she hadn't trusted a seemingly nice guy, if she hadn't gotten drunk, if she had acted earlier on the "bad feeling" that many victims later report they felt but ignored because they didn't want to seem rude, unfriendly, or immature. But acknowledging that in some cases the woman might have prevented the rape by making a different decision does not make her responsible for the crime. Says a counselor for an Oregon rape-crisis agency: "We have a saying here: 'Bad judgment is not a rapeable offense.'"

As a society, we don't blame the victims of most crimes as we do acquaintance-rape survivors. A mugging victim is not believed to "deserve it" for wearing a watch or carrying a pocketbook on the street. Likewise, a company is not "asking for it" when its profits are embezzled; a store owner is not to blame for handing over the cash drawer when threatened. These crimes occur because the perpetrator decides to commit them.

Acquaintance rape is no different. There are ways to reduce the odds, but, like all crimes, there is no way to be certain that it will not happen to you.

Yet acquaintance-rape victims are seen as responsible for the attacks, often more responsible than their assailants. "Date rape threatens the assumption that if you're good, good things happen to you. Most of us believe that bad things don't happen out of the blue," says psychologist Koss, chief investigator of the *Ms.* study, now affiliated with the department of psychiatry at the University of Arizona Medical School in Tucson, Arizona. Society, in general, is so disturbed by the idea that a "regular guy" could do such a thing— and, to be sure, many "regular guys" are made uncomfortable by a concept that views their actions as a crime—that they would rather believe that something is wrong with the woman making such an outlandish claim: She is lying, she has emotional problems, she hates men, she is covering up her own promiscuous behavior. In fact, the research in the *Ms.* survey shows that women who have been raped by men they know are not appreciably different in any personal traits or behaviors than women who are not raped.

Should we ask women not to trust men who seem perfectly nice? Should we tell them not to go to parties or on dates? Should we tell them not to drink? Should we tell them not to feel sexual? Certainly not. *It is not the victim who causes the rape.*

But many persist in believing just that. An April 1987 letter to syndicated columnist Ann Landers from a woman who had been raped by two different men she dated reportedly drew heavy negative reader mail after Landers responded supportively to the woman. "Too bad you didn't file charges against those creeps," Landers wrote. "I urge you to go for counseling immediately to rid yourself of the feeling of guilt and rage. You must get it through your head that you were not to blame."

So far, so good, but not for long. Three months later, Landers published a letter from an irate female reader who noted that the victim said she and the first man had "necked up a storm" before he raped her. Perhaps the raped woman hadn't intended to have intercourse, the reader said, "but she certainly must accept responsibility for encouraging the guy and making him think she was a willing partner. The trouble starts when she changes her mind after his passions are out of control. Then it's too late."

Landers bought this specious argument—a variant on the old "men can't help themselves" nonsense. In her reply to the follow-up letter she wrote, "Now I'm convinced that I must rethink my position and go back to telling women, 'If you don't want a complete sexual experience, keep a lively conversation going and his hands off you.'"

In other words, if you get raped, it's your own fault.

DATE RAPE AND ACQUAINTANCE RAPE ON COLLEGE CAMPUSES

Despite philosophical and political changes brought about by the women's movement, dating relationships between men and women are still often marked by passivity on the woman's part and aggression on the man's. Nowhere are these two seen in stronger contrast than among teenagers and young adults who often, out of their own fears, insecurity, and ignorance, adopt the worst sex-role stereotypes. Such an environment fosters a continuum of sexual victimization— from unwanted sexual touching to psychologically coerced sex to rape—that is tolerated as normal. "Because sexu-

ally coercive behavior is so common in our male-female interactions, rape by an acquaintance may not be perceived as rape," says Py Bateman, director of Alternatives to Fear, a Seattle rape-education organization....

Not surprising, then, that the risk of rape is four times higher for women aged 16 to 24, the prime dating age, than for any other population group. Approximately half of all men arrested for rape are also 24 years old or younger. Since 26 percent of all 18- to 24-year-olds in the United States attend college, those institutions have become focal points for studying date rape and acquaintance rape, such as the *Ms.* research.

Ms. Survey Stat

For both men and women, the average age when a rape incident occurred (either as perpetrator or victim) was 18½ years old.

Going to college often means going away from home, out from under parental control and protection and into a world of seemingly unlimited freedoms. The imperative to party and date, although strong in high school, burgeons in this environment. Alcohol is readily available and often used in stultifying amounts, encouraged by a college world that practically demands heavy drinking as proof of having fun. Marijuana, cocaine, LSD, methamphetamines, and other drugs are also often easy to obtain.

Up until the 1970s, colleges adopted a "substitute parent" attitude toward their students, complete with curfews (often more strict for females than males), liquor bans, and stringent disciplinary punishments. In that era, students were punished for violating the three-feet-on-the-floor rules during coed visiting hours in dormitories or for being caught with alcohol on college property. Although those regulations did not prevent acquaintance rape, they undoubtedly kept down the number of incidents by making women's dorms havens of no-men-allowed safety.

Such regulations were swept out of most schools during the Vietnam War era. Today, many campuses have coed dorms, with men and women often housed in alternating rooms on the same floor, with socializing unchecked by curfews or meaningful controls on alcohol and drugs. Yet, say campus crisis counselors, many parents still believe that they have properly prepared their children for college by helping them open local bank accounts and making sure they have enough underwear to last until the first trip home. By ignoring the realities of social pressures at college on male and female students—and the often catastrophic effects of those pressures—parents help perpetuate the awareness vacuum in which date rape and acquaintance rape continue to happen with regularity.

"What's changed for females is the illusion that they have control and they don't," says Claire P. Walsh, program director of the Sexual Assault Recovery Service at the University of Florida in Gainesville. "They know that they can go into chemical engineering or medical school and they've got their whole life planned, they're on a roll. They transfer that feeling of control into social situations and that's the illusion."

When looking at the statistical results of the *Ms.* survey, it's important to remember that many of these young people still have years of socializing and dating ahead of them, years in which they may encounter still more acquaintance rape. Students, parents of college students, and college administrators should be concerned. But many are not, lulled by the same myths that pervade our society at large: Rape is not committed by people you know, against "good" girls, in "safe" places like university campuses.

THE OTHER VICTIMS OF ACQUAINTANCE RAPE

Date rape and acquaintance rape aren't confined to the college population, however. Interviews conducted across the country showed that women both younger and older than university students are frequently acquaintance-rape victims as well.

A significant number of teenage girls suffer date rape as their first or nearly first experience of sexual intercourse... and most tell no one about their attacks. Consider Nora, a high school junior, who was raped by a date as they watched TV in his parents' house or Jenny, 16, who was raped after she drank too much at a party. Even before a girl officially begins dating, she may be raped by a schoolmate or friend.

Then there are the older women, the "hidden" population of "hidden" rape victims—women who are over 30 years old when their rapes occur. Most are socially experienced, yet unprepared for their attacks nonetheless. Many are recently divorced and just beginning to try the dating waters again; some are married; others have never married. They include women like Helene, a Colorado woman who was 37 and the mother of a 10-year-old when she was raped by a man on their third date, and Rae, who was 45 when she was raped by a man she knew after inviting him to her Oklahoma home for coffee.

"I NEVER CALLED IT RAPE"

Ms. **Survey Stat**

Only 27 percent of the women whose sexual assault met the legal definition of rape thought of themselves as rape victims.

Because of her personal relationship with the attacker, however casual, it often takes a woman longer to perceive an action as rape when it involves a man she knows than it does when a stranger assaults her. For her to acknowledge her experience as rape would be to recognize the extent to which her trust was violated and her ability to control her own life destroyed.

Indeed, regardless of their age or background, many women interviewed... told no one about their rapes, never confronted their attackers, and never named their assaults as rape until months or years later.

POSTSCRIPT

Have the Dangers of Date Rape Been Exaggerated?

One of the more intriguing outcomes of the new awareness of date rape and sexual harassment can be found in the eight-page Sexual Offense Policy developed by the students and administration of Antioch College in Yellow Springs, Ohio. According to this policy, "All sexual contact and conduct on the Antioch College campus and/or occurring with an Antioch community member [student, faculty or staff] must be consensual. . . . Verbal consent should be obtained with each new level of physical and/or sexual contact/conduct. . . . Asking 'Do you want to have sex with me?' is not enough. The request for consent must be specific to each act."

The Antioch policy went into effect in February 1991, with a revised form adopted in June 1992. The policy spells out six categories of offenses: rape, sexual assault, sexual imposition ("Non-consensual. . . touching of thighs, genitals, buttocks, pubic region or breast/chest area"), insistent and/or persistent sexual harassment, nondisclosure of sexually transmitted diseases, and nondisclosure of positive HIV status. Although the penalties for violating the policy can be stiff, including suspension and dismissal, many regard the detailed policy not as law but as a set of guidelines that encourage communication and dialogue that help lay the groundwork for a healthy sexual relationship.

While few Antioch students actually follow the rules step-by-step, many admit that it has prompted them to at least think about how they relate sexually to others. The policy does not inhibit sex, and it does not make it more difficult to move from a casual acquaintance to a sexual, intimate relationship. It just makes the process more thoughtful.

SUGGESTED READINGS

A. Parrot and L. Bechhofer, eds., *Acquaintance Rape: The Hidden Crime* (John Wiley, 1991).

N. Podhoretz, "Rape in Feminist Eyes," *Commentary* (October 1991).

K. Roiphe, "Date Rape's Other Victim," *The New York Times Magazine* (June 13, 1993).

K. Roiphe, *The Morning After: Sex, Fear and Feminism on Campus* (Little, Brown, 1993).

G. Will, "Sex Amid Semicolons," *Newsweek* (October 4, 1993).

ISSUE 18

Should Privacy Rights Yield to Public Health Concerns in Dealing With HIV Infections?

YES: Tom A. Coburn, from *The HIV Prevention Act of 1997* (U.S. House of Representatives, 1997)

NO: Christopher DeMarco, from "Privacy Rights Should *Not* Yield to Public Health Concerns in Dealing With HIV Infection," An Original Essay Written for This Volume (1998)

ISSUE SUMMARY

YES: Tom A. Coburn, a Republican U.S. representative from Oklahoma, argues that we are not making as much progress as we should and could be making in controlling the spread of HIV, because we have given privacy rights priority over traditional, tried and proven tools of public health policy.

NO: Christopher DeMarco, an AIDS specialist, agrees that traditional public health measures will help reduce the spread of HIV infection. However, he maintains that some of these measures carry serious risks to the civil rights of infected individuals and that we must ensure equal access to medications and avoid reducing prevention education.

Controlling any epidemic spread by bacteria or a virus requires the development of an effective, inexpensive test to identify infected people in order to determine where the disease is showing up and how many people are infected. Traditional public health policy for handling an epidemic also relies heavily on educating infected and at-risk people so they will change their behavior to reduce the chance of spreading the disease. All this requires a delicate balancing of the harsh realities of public health concerns and protecting the civil liberties of people whose rights may be affected or limited by public health policies.

Fifty or more years ago, when knowledge about bacterial and viral diseases was much more limited, there were far fewer ways of coping with outbreaks of typhoid, diphtheria, tuberculosis, polio, influenza, scarlet fever, whooping cough, measles, and other infectious diseases that threatened the welfare and lives of tens of thousands of Americans. Because there were no antibiotics, traditional public health policy sometimes required the extreme step of putting infected people into quarantine or isolating them in sanitariums.

Other effective ways of reducing the spread of bacterial and viral diseases were developed. For example, *routine testing* was carried out on all at-risk individuals, often without explicit patient consent. Doctors, laboratories, and public health personnel were also required to *report* to local health centers the names of those who tested positive for an infection. A third practice was *contact tracing*, or identifying anyone who may have been exposed to the infection and *notifying* those people that they may have been exposed and should get tested.

When AIDS (acquired immunodeficiency syndrome) was first identified in the early 1980s, it appeared as a disease rampant among urban male homosexuals and intravenous drug users. Faced with a fatal, communicable disease, and not knowing how it was spread, public health authorities desperately sought the cooperation of the people who were infected with this deadly virus. In *The Gravest Show on Earth* (St. Martin's Press, 1996), Elinor Burkett notes why people with the disease were so concerned about not letting others know they had AIDS: The nation was in panic.

Early discovery of the human immunodeficiency virus (HIV, the virus that causes AIDS) and development of a test for that virus came at a time of growing persecution of homosexuals. Terrified by the violence aimed at them, the gay community extracted a price when public health officials sought their help in learning more about the disease. That price was ironclad anonymity. In 1985, just before the first test to detect HIV was to be announced, the National Gay Task Force and the gay civil rights organization Lambda Legal Defense and Education Fund went to court to delay the announcement until the government guaranteed that the test would not be used in widespread screening of gay men. Health authorities and the gay community were already aware that some school districts were hoping to use the test to identify and fire gay teachers. To gain cooperation from the gay community, the Food and Drug Administration and Centers for Disease Control agreed that the HIV test would not be used to screen and identify people infected with HIV. The test would only be used to screen the blood in blood banks.

This compromise meant that traditional public health procedures were not used for AIDS. There would be no routine testing for HIV, and the names of infected individuals would be reported to authorities only in a few places. Therefore, the epidemic's hot spots would not be identified until the infection was well-established. And there would be little contact tracing and notification.

Today growing numbers of public health authorities and politicians are convinced that the threats to civil rights that existed 15 years ago have been resolved and that it is now time to apply the whole arsenal of policies that are known to be important in managing any epidemic. This is Tom A. Coburn's position in the following selection. In the second selection, Christopher DeMarco argues that the current policy is still the best policy.

YES
Tom A. Coburn

THE HIV PREVENTION ACT OF 1997

It has been just 16 years since the first cases of AIDS were recognized. The initial thousand cases were reported to the Centers for Disease Control and Prevention (CDC) by February 1983. By the end of June 1996, the cumulative incidence of reported AIDS cases reached a total of 548,102. Of these, 343,000 are known to have died. Clearly, this is an epidemic of historic proportion that is continuing to grow.

While no cure exists for AIDS, we know enough about the disease to prevent its spread. For instance, we know that AIDS is caused by the Human Immunodeficiency Virus (HIV) and is actually the end stage of HIV infection. We also know that the disease is transmitted through exchange of body fluids and it attacks the body's immune system eventually leaving the body unable to fend off infection.

What we do not know is the extent of the epidemic. We have failed to employ the public health procedures which have been successful in curtailing other epidemics in our efforts against HIV. These include confidential HIV reporting and partner notification.

We have made an effort to report cases of AIDS on a state and national level but not cases of HIV. We do not make it a priority to notify those who may have been exposed that their lives may be endangered.

Put simply, the federal government and the public health community have been AWOL in the battle against HIV. Sound medical practices have been abandoned and replaced with political correctness. HIV has been treated as a civil rights issue instead of the public health crisis that it is.

The HIV Prevention Act of 1997 (H. R. 1062/ S. 503) will return sound medical practices to our Nation's public health policy and curtail the spread of the deadly HIV epidemic.

Recent scientific breakthroughs make prompt passage of this bill extremely important. Many of the world's top HIV scientists have suggested that it may be possible to "eradicate" the virus from the body and completely suppress it by using a combination of new HIV drugs. Most believe that these drugs may transform HIV for many from a terminal disease into a chronic disease

From Tom A. Coburn, *The HIV Prevention Act of 1997*, U.S. House of Representatives (1997). References omitted.

like diabetes or heart disease. However, researchers agree that *the success of these drugs depends upon starting treatment early.*

This bill aims at protecting the uninfected and at helping those who are infected to discover their status as early as possible to maximize the opportunities now available.

In addition to numerous public health officials across the country, the American Medical Association—the nation's largest doctors group—has announced its "strong support" for the HIV Prevention Act of 1997.

The following is a section-by-section summary of the proposal.

IMPROVED HIV EPIDEMIC MEASUREMENT

The HIV Prevention Act refocuses our epidemic measurement on HIV infection rather than AIDS.

Currently *every* state reports cases of AIDS, which is merely the end state of HIV infection. By confidentially reporting new cases of HIV, which is already required by 28 states, those responsible for control of the disease can more accurately determine the current extent of the epidemic as well as future trends, rates of progression, direction of spread, possible changes in transmissibility and other critical factors of disease control. Such information allows for the development of long-term prevention strategies based on reliable data. It is no coincidence that the states which require HIV reporting have a lower median incidence of AIDS than states that only report AIDS.

Reporting is used to study and access many diseases. In addition to AIDS, other infectious diseases such as gonorrhea, hepatitis and syphilis are currently reported to CDC. To protect confidentiality, some states use codes rather than personal identifiers such as name and address. This bill does *not* specifically require name reporting.

PARTNER NOTIFICATION

The HIV Prevention Act would require states to inform individuals if they may have been exposed to HIV by a current or past partner.

CDC estimates that up to 950,000 Americans are currently HIV-positive. Sadly, most of those infected do not know it and will not get tested until they are already sick with AIDS-related disease. By this point, they have been denied the medical care that can prolong their lives and stave off illness and may have infected others unknowingly.

Partner notification is the only timely way to alert those in danger of infection. It is the standard public health procedure for curtailing the spread of virtually all other sexually transmitted diseases.

Partner notification essentially requires two steps. The first is to counsel all infected individuals about the importance of notifying their partner or partners that they may have been exposed. The second is for their doctor to forward the names of any partners named by the infected person to the Department of Health where specially trained public health professionals complete the notification.

In all cases, the privacy of the infected is—and must be—protected by withholding the name of the infected person from the partner being notified. Because names are never revealed, the infected retain their anonymity.

Partner notification has proved to be highly effective and there is *no* evidence that partner notification programs discourage individuals from being tested. Between *50% and 90%* of those who tested positive cooperate voluntarily with notification. Further, even higher proportions of those partners contacted—usually 90% or more—voluntarily obtain an HIV test. But only *10% or less* of people who have recently tested HIV-positive manage, by themselves, to notify their partners.

Legislation requiring *spousal notification* has already been signed into law (Public Law 104–146). It applies only to those partners who are or had been married. It makes perfect sense to expand notification to all of those who may have been exposed to HIV.

The CDC currently requires every state to establish procedures for partner notification for AIDS. At least 32 states have already enacted HIV/AIDS-specific partner notification laws, but most do not mandate or impose a duty to notify.

Partner notification is especially important for women because many HIV-infected women (50% to 70% in some studies) do not engage in high risk behaviors but were infected by a partner who does.

Jack Wroten, who heads Florida's program, said that "I would hope that the controversy surrounding partner notification would cease" because "it works" and "it's very, very productive. And the fact is that the majority [of people], if you ask them, 'Do you want to be notified?'—absolutely."

Notification allows for early medical treatment which can prolong and improve lives. It curtails the spread of HIV, and therefore, saves lives. It is also widely supported by most Americans according to a poll published in the *New York Post* and will bring greater safety to our nation's blood supply.

In addition to saving lives, partner notification also saves money. The CDC has concluded that even if only one in 80 notifications results in preventing a new case of HIV-infection, given the huge medical and social costs of every case (lifetime cost for HIV treatment is $119,000), notification pays for itself.

HIV TESTING FOR SEXUAL OFFENDERS

The HIV Prevention Act requires that those accused of sexual offenses be tested for HIV.

Many times the victims of rape and other sexual assaults also become victims of HIV. HIV testing of those accused of rape and other sexual offenses empowers victims to protect themselves and others from HIV.

Primarily, it is important to the victim's physical and psychological well-being. Studies indicate that treatment with anti-HIV drugs immediately following HIV exposure can significantly reduce the chance of infection. However, because of the toxicity and long-term side effects of anti-HIV therapies, these drugs should not be administered without knowing if HIV exposure has occurred. Otherwise, the victim's health may be unnecessarily endangered. Knowing the status of the assailant also relieves much of the victim's agonizing anxiety.

Victims cannot rely solely on testing themselves because it can take weeks, sometimes months, before HIV antibodies can be detected and infection determined. Therefore, testing the assailant is the only timely manner in which to determine if someone has been exposed to HIV.

Mandatory HIV testing prevents sexual offenders from further abusing victims and the legal system by bargaining for lighter sentences if they volunteer to be tested.

Finally, if the assailant does test positive, this knowledge allows both the victim and alleged attacker to get counseling, receive treatment and take precautions to protect others from infection.

The AMA supports this policy because "early knowledge that a defendant is HIV infected would allow the victim to gain access to the ever-growing arsenal of new HIV treatment options. In addition, knowing that the defendant was HIV infected would help the victim avoid conduct which might put others at risk of infection."

Almost every state provides HIV testing of *convicted* sex offenders at the victim's request. This does little to aid the victim because waiting until conviction can often take many months or even years and the window of opportunity to prevent infection has been lost.

A recent Colorado study found that while 3,250 arrests were made forcible rape, *less than a dozen tests were ordered.* And in Alabama, because of the lengthy delay in bringing rape cases to trial, no one has used a law that allows victims to find out whether or not their attackers are infected with HIV.

Opponents of mandatory testing for those accused of rape and sexual assault have claimed that it is a violation of the Fourth Amendment which protects against unreasonable search and seizure.

However, the Supreme Court has drawn a different conclusion in regards to law enforcement taking blood samples. Stating that the "Fourth Amendment's proper function is to constrain, not against all intrusions as such, but against intrusions which are not justified in the circumstances, or which are made in an improper manner," the Court found nothing inherently unreasonable about taking blood samples from those *accused* of a crime.

Clearly, knowing whether or not someone was exposed to the deadly HIV virus is justifiable.

Most recently, the New Jersey appeals court upheld the state's law requiring pre-conviction testing when three teenage boys who gang raped a mentally retarded girl were required to undergo HIV testing.

The other argument is that testing may provide a false sense of security if the accused does not test positive or alarm a victim if he does. This is just plain ridiculous. Both the assailant and victim should undergo both an initial and a follow-up test along with counseling.

The AIDS Action Council, which claims to be the nation's leading AIDS advocacy organization, has even stated that "this provision is unnecessary" and that "rape and sexual assault survivors need to take care of themselves and not concentrate on the HIV status of their assailant." Survivors of rape and assault deserve better than this cold and uncaring attitude; they deserve the right to know if they have been exposed to HIV.

HIV AND MEDICAL PROCEDURES

The HIV Prevention Act protects both health care patients and professionals from inadvertent exposure to HIV. It would do this by encouraging states and medical associations to establish policies to be followed by providers with HIV in the performance of any risk prone invasive medical procedure on a patient. It also allows providers to test a patient for HIV before performing such a procedure.

Q & A ABOUT THE HIV PREVENTION ACT

1.) Will the HIV Prevention Act require states to report the names of HIV-positive individuals to the Centers for Disease Control and Prevention (CDC)?

No. The names of patients are *not* reported to the CDC, only relevant demographic and personal information such as age, sex, race or ethnic group plus transmission or risk category. Names are never reported to CDC as part of an established program of surveillance of widespread disease such as HIV. Names or surrogate identifiers are reported to the respective state health departments to ensure partner notification and contact follow-up.

2.) Will this bill frighten or discourage individuals from getting tested for HIV?

No. AIDS activists made these same claims in 1989 when name reporting and partner notification went into effect in Virginia, but testing for HIV actually INCREASED. More recently, when anonymous testing was eliminated in North Carolina, HIV testing INCREASED by 45%.

There is no evidence in any of the 28 states with partner notification that reporting or notification discourage people from getting tested for HIV.

3.) Does the bill allow physicians to refuse to treat HIV infected patients?

No. The bill specifically states that health professionals, at their discretion, may request that a patient be tested for HIV before performing an invasive medical procedure.

Testing patients for HIV is primarily aimed at protecting the health of the patient. Doctors do not want to prescribe immunosuppressant drugs if the patient is HIV positive. Protecting health care workers from infection is important, but the real key is that doctors need the ability to fully diagnose a patient. A health care provider needs to know if a patient is HIV positive in order to give the patient the best possible care.

Federal law prohibits providers from refusing care to anyone who has tested positive for HIV. The HIV Prevention Act would not change this.

4.) Does the bill require doctors to be tested for HIV before performing invasive procedures on patients?

No, but it does take the first step in this direction by expressing the Sense of the Congress that HIV infected health professionals should notify their patients of their status.

Many states have already addressed this issue. Some even require health care personnel who perform invasive procedures to be tested for HIV. The French Order of Doctors announced earlier this year that it was the "moral duty" of surgeons infected with HIV to "stop operating" and switch to general medicine or administrative work.

(Box continued on next page)

5.) Does this bill contain an unfunded mandate? Will the testing, reporting and partner notification be expensive? Where will the money come from?

This is *not* an unfunded mandate. Because many states are already conducting partner notification for HIV and all states conduct partner notification for other STDs, the cost of the partner notification proposal in the bill would not be terribly costly (possibly $10 to $20 million). CDC receives $140 million for HIV counseling and testing. The additional $10–20 million could come from this existing amount which has already been budgeted.

6.) What provisions will be in place to protect confidentiality?

Every state already has strict confidentiality laws in place for all medical diseases. In addition, many states have enacted special laws to protect HIV-status information. Every state has reported AIDS cases to their state public health department and to the CDC for 16 years without incident. Why would this change with reporting HIV? In fact, all existing reporting systems (for example, blood banks, military, CDC, and state health departments) have been conducted with only a single documented breach of confidentiality. Additionally, this bill expresses the Sense of the Congress that "strict confidentiality" should be maintained in carrying out the provisions of the bill.

7.) AIDS activists say that this bill does not treat HIV-infected persons like those infected with other communicable diseases. What other diseases have these same reporting and partner notification requirements?

CDC currently designates 52 infectious diseases as notifiable at the national level. Although AIDS and pediatric HIV infections are included on this list, adolescent and adult HIV infection are conspicuously absent.

Partner notification programs are already in place for other STDs and federal law requires spousal notification for HIV. This bill would notify anyone who may have been exposed to HIV by a past or present partner.

As of June 30, 1996, 18,014 of the AIDS cases reported to the CDC were people employed in health care, including 1,178 physicians and 3,019 nurses. The CDC knows of 51 health care workers in the United States who have been documented as having seroconverted to HIV following occupational exposure. CDC is also aware of 108 other cases of HIV infection in occupationally exposed health care workers whose seroconversion after exposure was not documented. Clearly, a danger of HIV transmission does exist in the performance of some medical procedures.

Both patients and health care providers would benefit from full medical diagnoses, which should include routine testing for HIV. This is especially true in the performance of risk prone invasive procedures.

Knowledge of HIV infection of a patient is critical for a health provider to avoid compromising the condition of the patient. Prescribing immunosuppressant drugs to a patient who is HIV-positive, for example, could be lethal.

Routine testing also allows a provider to avoid transmission by taking added precautions. Universal precautions (requiring that all patients be treated as if they are infected) do not provide enough protection. Health care workers have been infected with HIV after being stuck with needles or after infected blood entered the workers' bloodstream through an open cut or splashes onto a mucous membrane (like the eyes or inside the nose). Additionally, a new study found that 17% to 25% of health care workers experience adverse reactions such as contact dermatitis from latex gloves used as routine precautions. Some can even suffer life-threatening reactions, including respiratory problems and shock.

A recent study of hospital nurses concluded that workplace stress due to the fear of HIV contagion is high and the most effective way to reduce fear is to inform staff of the HIV status of patients.

The public would like doctors and dentists with AIDS or HIV to be legally required to inform their patients of their health status according to 93% of those polled in a New York Post survey. Seventeen states have already passed legislation to protect patients from HIV-infected health care workers.

Because an HIV-infected body is still infectious even after death, and can remain so for several days, embalmers and other funeral-service practicioners may also be at risk. In fact, it is not unprecedented for HIV infection to occur during an autopsy. The HIV Prevention Act would offer protection for those who work on corpses by allowing testing to determine whether or not a body is infected.

Similar proposals regarding patients and health care providers passed the Senate overwhelmingly in 1991, but were later dropped in conference.

HIV NOTIFICATION

The HIV Prevention Act requires that if an insurance issuer requires an HIV test as a condition of application, the applicant is entitled to the results. It also permits adoptive parents to learn the HIV status of a child that they are considering for adoption.

Twenty-two states do *not* require insurers to disclose HIV test results to applicants. Therefore, applicants who test positive but are unaware of their status are denied the opportunity to learn their status, seek medical care and prevent exposure to others.

Many states do not permit potential adoptive parents to know the HIV status of a child they are prepared to adopt. Because of the enormous financial and emotional commitment that is necessary when caring for any one who is HIV-positive, this provision provides fairness to both the infected child and the adoptive parents.

INTENTIONAL TRANSMISSION OF HIV

The HIV Prevention Act expresses the sense of the Congress that states should criminalize the intentional transmission of HIV.

Those who are infected with any communicable disease have a responsibility to prevent transmitting the disease to others. Because no cure exists for HIV, transmitting the disease is the equivalent of delivering a death sentence.

79% of Americans believe that those who knowingly infect another person with HIV should face criminal charges. Half of those surveyed said that people who knowingly transmit the virus should be charged with murder.

While 27 states have already enacted laws which address HIV transmission, other states have not enacted laws to punish those who intentionally seek to do harm by infecting others with HIV.

CONFIDENTIALITY AND HIV

The HIV Prevention Act expresses the sense of Congress that strict confidentiality must be observed at all times in carrying out the provisions of this Act.

Because of the stigma associated with HIV, those with the disease have legitimate concerns about discrimination. That is why every state has strict confidentiality laws in place for all medical records and at least 39 states have specific laws providing for confidentiality of HIV/AIDS related information. The Americans With Disabilities Act also ensures additional protections against discrimination.

This provision would not pre-empt any of these protections, but rather underscore their importance.

NO

Christopher DeMarco

PRIVACY RIGHTS SHOULD *NOT* YIELD TO PUBLIC HEALTH CONCERNS IN DEALING WITH HIV INFECTION

With the HIV Prevention Act of 1997, Representative Thomas Coburn of Oklahoma (R) proposes to improve America's public health record with regard to HIV transmission. While we both agree that there is a need to enact measures that can stem the transmission of HIV, Coburn's prevention suggestions need to be scrutinized to determine whether or not these are the best measures possible. I propose to review Coburn's bill, pointing out possible flaws, potential consequences of some of the measures if implemented, and opposing views from the public health literature and workers in the HIV/AIDS field.

BACKGROUND

Coburn argues that we have not been faithful to the sound principles of public health and his bill calls for more fully using traditional public health measures and ensuring medications for infected persons to decrease HIV transmission. By traditional public health measures he means routine testing without consent, reporting results to authorities, contact tracing, and partner notification. He states that it is important to get medication to those who are infected as soon as possible to ensure that they will receive the most help. But reducing HIV prevention will take more than public health measures and medication; it will take addressing some of the more general societal concerns such as civil and privacy rights of infected individuals, equal access to health care and medications, prevention education for those unlikely to complete high school or attend college, a decent standard of living, and good work conditions.

Adequate public education has to be the first item in a national health program. Inadequate education, resulting in formal and functional illiteracy, is a serious obstacle to learning the use of preventative measures such as personal hygiene, immunization, and lifestyle changes. U.S. data on the number of persons in a population who die of particular diseases (morbidity) indicate serious class differences in incidence of illness and disability. In 1989, the poorest fifth of Americans, when compared to the richest fifth, had more than twice as many persons limited in activity due to chronic conditions, more than twice as many days of restricted activity, more than twice as many days in bed due to illness/injury/impairment, and four times as many persons reported to be in fair or poor health.

In Canada, the Ottawa Charter for Health Promotion of 1986 maintains that "health promotion policy combines diverse but complementary approaches including legislation, fiscal measures, taxation, and organizational change... the prerequisites and prospects for health cannot be ensured by the health sector alone... it demands coordinated action by all concerned: by governments, by health and other social and economic sectors, by non-governmental and voluntary organizations, by local authorities, by industry and by the media." This approach to health promotion is consistent with the epidemiologic concept of the "web of causation." By taking both general and specific causative factors into account we can be more effective in treating any disease.

Traditional public health measures should have been proposed for HIV/AIDS from the start but they were not because our society could not assure gay men, who feared that their civil rights were a low priority, that their names would not be reported and that they would not be arrested. I think that our avoiding civil rights before we were struck with HIV put us into a position in which civil and privacy rights had to be shored up before more traditional public health measures could be taken. I think that we could not fully focus on the epidemiology of HIV until we could assure those for whom the epidemiologic effort was intended that the effort would not expose them as part of a hated group and they would be harmed for that. I think that without progress in civil and privacy rights, we will never get to a place in which HIV status did not matter. I do not think that we should say that the higher the level of civil rights, the lower the level of epidemiologic control. The higher the level of civil rights, the more cooperation epidemiologic effort will receive.

Coburn states that we do not know enough about the epidemic because we have failed to employ public health measures. The fact is that over the last 15 years, billions of dollars have been spent by thousands of dedicated workers in programs similar to the ones he calls for. He calls for testing without consent and we provide testing with consent; he calls for reporting to state and federal authorities and we report to state authorities, and he calls for contact tracing and we conduct partner notification. It is a gross exaggeration for him to state that "the Federal government and public health community have been AWOL in the battle against HIV."

HIV has not stopped spreading because we don't know about it; we know plenty. There are other reasons it has not stopped spreading—there is not enough money in the right places such as tailored prevention programs. Also we have ignored some general concerns that prevent people from coming forward. These concerns include lack of access to adequate health care, lack of knowledge of how to get adequate health care, lack of language ability to maximize a ten-minute physician exam, etc.

HIV REPORTING

Coburn calls for improved epidemic measurement in the specific form of HIV reporting rather than AIDS-only reporting. He states that it is no coincidence that states which require HIV reporting have a lower median incidence of AIDS than states that only report AIDS. I doubt if these lower incidence rates can be attributed solely to required reporting or any other single factor. Reporting is used on many diseases, including syphilis. However, we have been reporting syphilis for decades but still have periodic increases in the disease.

Coburn says that the effectiveness of new therapies is reason to report. These treatments offer the potential to control the disease but not for over half of those infected for whom the treatments are unavailable. Treatments are unavailable to many poor and uneducated persons we have already identified with HIV because they may not believe in the importance of medication counseling services or because these and other types of counseling services are seen as luxuries by the medical establishment.

Mandatory reporting could lead to reduction and/or elimination of anonymous testing and then we may lose these individuals to testing for years to come. Various studies have shown that persons tested in anonymous sites are more likely to test positive than clients at confidential sites. Many people would avoid general health care if mandatory HIV reporting existed because they still fear breaches in confidentiality and/or have already had negative experiences or have witnessed negative experiences in forms of denial of medical coverage, housing, and employment.

PARTNER NOTIFICATION AND CONTACT TRACING

According to Coburn, partner notification consists of two steps. The physician counsels infected individuals and then forwards to the Department of Health (DOH) the names of sexual partners given by the infected individual. Although the names are registered at the DOH, the infected person's name is not revealed to the partners when they are informed that they have been exposed and should be tested.

Contact tracing is a more aggressive form of partner notification in which a trained health professional contacts an individual named by an infected person without using the infected person's name. The potentially infected individual may give additional names of individuals and these individuals are followed-up by the health professional.

Contact tracing has limitations which include the time-intensive nature of the work and the special training for staff which must be done to prepare the staff to work with life and death issues. Successful tracing depends on the skills of the health professional to elicit sensitive, personal information, as well as the willingness of the individual(s) contacted to change his/her behaviors. Without the ability to offer a cure for HIV (as there is with syphilis), contacted individuals have an abundance of questions and concerns about complicated medical treatments, why there's no cure, how to pay for expensive medical treatments, supporting and counseling services, and confidentiality issues. Staff commitment to confidentiality is essential to its success.

Partner notification is considered important to Coburn's bill because it will help identify HIV cases for epidemiologic purposes, but mandatory name reporting is not needed to determine incidence. Surveillance studies and sentinel studies are conducted already. Some states have implemented name reporting; others do not report names and have kept anonymous testing sites open.

Coburn adds that partner notification is important because it is the only timely way to alert those in danger of infection to get them medical treatment as soon as possible. In our society we have difficulty educating those who are identified with HIV to take medications. Even if we do educate individuals to take medications, we must also educate these persons to take them with the proper diet to ensure bioavailability and to reduce the possibility of resistance. If increased numbers of individuals will be identified, increased funds will be needed to provide proper education about the medications and the restrictions associated with the medications.

Partner notification is already in place in all states. Will mandating another layer of partner notification on the national level yield enough new HIV-infected individuals to justify using up scarce prevention education resources? Although we have long had aggressive partner notification and contact tracing for syphilis and gonorrhea control, these STDs [sexuality transmitted diseases] have not been eliminated.

Minnesota has a partner notification program which has worked, but I don't know if the Minnesota program can work in other states in which there are pockets of persons willing to perpetrate anti-AIDS, anti-gay, and/or anti-drug user assaults or violence. Minnesota's program has worked and has since evolved into a community-based response that includes many HIV prevention and treatment organizations in the state. Coburn suggests a one-size-fits-all national mandate, instead of locally-tailored solutions. This may be a step backward.

Instead of mandating a national partner notification program, greater HIV prevention resources should be provided to the states and localities to implement strategies that work for their communities. Such strategies can focus on controlling the spread of HIV infection through tailored behavioral change interventions, encouraging voluntary partner notification, and providing assistance for individuals who want to notify their partners themselves.

Implementing a national partner notification program may well be premature in some areas where fear of prejudice and discrimination exist for valid reasons. Even if a national program were implemented, it would be at the mercy of confidentiality concerns. We should do more than require a sense of Congress to request confidentiality. We should ensure that the existing laws are strong enough to ensure that confidentiality is kept. Also, as with syphilis and gonorrhea, we must understand that partner notification is not going to eliminate HIV, even if we had a cure for it. Expanded prevention education will still be needed to support any notification program's efforts.

HIV TESTING FOR SEX OFFENDERS

Coburn claims his bill will protect the victims of sexual assault by requiring HIV testing for the alleged offender. The Omnibus Crime Control Act of 1994 already provides for a victim to request a court order to have the alleged perpetrator in federal sexual assault cases tested for HIV. Many states have passed similar laws.

Testing sexual offenders using HIV antibody tests does not provide definitive proof of the perpetrator's status if the test result is negative. If the result is negative, it could mean that the person is HIV-infected but that the antibodies have not had sufficient time to build to a level that is detected by the test. This level can take weeks and even months. If the perpetrator's test result is positive, meaning the individual has HIV, there is no guarantee the HIV was passed from the attacker to the attacked. In either case, the attacked will need to be tested anyway. Coburn's proposals on testing indicted rapists focuses on victims' rights rather than on scientific risks faced by the victims. Obviously rape victims should be given immunotherapy and psychological treatment for HIV as soon as they report the attack. In addition, when dealing with HIV in sex offense situations, we must be sure to maintain a focus on the survivor and enable her or his sense of redeveloping control over a situation. It may damage a victim's recovery process to be focused on the results of HIV tests of the perpetrator or to mandate their own testing.

HIV AND MEDICAL PROCEDURES

Coburn calls for increased epidemiology that includes testing health care providers. However, epidemiologists themselves find practitioner testing problematic. The Society for Health care Epidemiology of America (SHEA) states that having HIV-infected practitioners report their infection statuses to prospective patients is unwarranted. Risk of provider-to-patient transmission is extremely low according to the Society for Health care

Epidemiology of America (1997). HIV testing of patients is problematic for several reasons. First, universal precautions are a very important part of medicine. Universal precautions exist to protect medical providers from being infected both by the infections they know about and by those they do not yet know about. Virologists understand that new viruses develop and manifest themselves on a regular basis. Even if HIV did not exist, there would be a need to have universal precautions to protect against unknown viruses. The perceived need for universal precautions may decrease because the underlying message is that when someone is HIV-positive measures should definitely be taken but are not otherwise needed. We must be vigilant in maintaining universal precautions.

Second, what about emergency situations? What test can be used in the energy room to determine whether the potential patient has HIV antibodies? Testing takes precious time and emergency cases cannot be stalled. Even if an antibody test were done, the patient may be in the window period and infection would be undetectable. It seems inhumane to wait for an HIV test result before providing lifesaving services. Third, the Coburn legislation interferes with current law prohibiting health care professionals from conditioning the performance of a needed medical service on the patient's agreement to be tested for HIV.

INTENTIONAL TRANSMISSION OF HIV

Every state and Washington, DC has a law to address intentional transmission. About half of the states make it a felony and/or misdemeanor to knowingly transmit HIV. Coburn suggests a sense of Congress to criminalize knowingly transmitting the virus. We must make sure that any law enacted does not single out persons with HIV because those individuals have HIV. Laws should be kept general enough to include cases in which HIV and other STDs are used as a weapon just as cases in which other agents are used as weapons to hurt others.

CONFIDENTIALITY AND HIV

Coburn states that HIV confidentiality should be maintained by a sense of Congress; however, a sense of Congress does not criminalize breaches of confidentiality. It may be more effective to specifically identify areas in which discrimination can occur and to make sure that laws address discrimination in health care insurance, housing, and employment rather than to call for something with no teeth. By seeming to address a general concern about confidentiality without addressing specific areas, this bill could potentially weaken states' confidentiality laws.

PROBLEMS WITH THE COBURN BILL

Prevention could be de-emphasized by a focus on testing and notification. Money spent on testing would take away funds from treatment and prevention —testing hospital patients alone could cost $1.65 billion per year. These funds could educate just those persons afraid to be HIV tested about the need for testing and how to maintain rights and dignity throughout the process. The bill would subvert the ability of the local communities to pursue disease control strategies that are appropriate for local

conditions. State health directors report that 265 statutory/regulatory changes would be needed and these changes would cost $420 million to implement. No funding is given to states to do this. With no funding allocated for these changes, the prevention coffers could be raided.

One assumption of the bill is that the availability of medications has led to the decrease in the number of AIDS deaths. Although the overall death rate decreased, the death rate for women increased by 3% reminding us that treatment access is unequal. Government-sponsored HIV research has included only 12% females. At a recent conference I attended in which spokespersons from a variety of major pharmaceutical companies spoke, females in the audience were frustrated that not one spokesperson could answer how many women were included in tests, much less whether or not the drugs were safe for females.

Even if females had equal testing and equal access to drugs, access to care means more than providing drugs. Drugs alone are not the answer; there is no magic bullet. Over 50% of persons will not be helped by the new class of drugs called protease inhibitors. We cannot underestimate the side effects which prevent continuing treatment nor the fact that resistance can occur.

Although early intervention is important, the individual has already been infected with HIV and no victory can be claimed. Prevention is still important.

The bill uses Medicaid funding as leverage to bring states on board; however, many with HIV use Medicaid. Those HIV-infected individuals currently on Medicaid may lose it if a state decides not to follow the bill. The Federal and state Medicaid partnership which finances health care services for over 37 million low income and disabled individuals, including the 53% of the adults and 90% of the children living with AIDS may be jeopardized. If Medicaid is lost, how will these individuals acquire costly medications? How long will it be until individuals in states opposed to the bill regain the ability to receive treatments they cannot afford?

WHAT TO DO?

Prevention goals are better served by concentrating on education and access to care. A comprehensive strategy that uses multiple approaches, tailored to the needs of different populations is needed to prevent HIV infection in the first place. We need an approach which includes widespread and consistent provision of information which helps people learn what behaviors place them at risk and how they can modify their behaviors to reduce risk. Greater community-based efforts and easier access to HIV counseling and anonymous testing are needed. The importance of this link is the nuts and bolts and should not be eliminated. True prevention of infections among those who are being infected the most is needed—many new infections are among women, people of color, adolescents, and needle sharers. Substance abuse treatment and needle exchange programs are important HIV prevention strategies. Prevention that is comprehensive and targeted is needed. The National Institutes of Health Consensus Conference on HIV Prevention made clear that there are prevention strategies scientifically shown to work but our politics have gotten in the way. The Center for AIDS Prevention Studies at University of California, San Francisco, showed that

adding $500 million to the prevention budget would save $1.25 billion in medical care. We must make sure communities have the information and resources needed to implement community-based prevention strategies geared to the specific demographics of the epidemic locally.

The public health response to HIV has roots in the public health response to syphilis engineered by Dr. Parran in 1938. One legacy of Parran's plan was to maintain the integrity of public health precepts such as post-intercourse treatment in the face of criticism from moralistic quarters. Another legacy is that STD prevention has become linked with early identification of cases and contacts followed by referral and treatment, rather than the promotion of behavioral change per se. Since we have no cure for HIV, we have to rely on behavioral health strategies. Typically, it is more efficient, when we have the option to treat by medication, to use that method. Add to this the fact that we know less about methods of behavioral change than we do about microbe control.

However, we do not have a cure for HIV and so we must rely on behavioral change. What is a good behavioral change end point—abstinence or prevention (prophylaxis)? In 1938 it was perhaps more acceptable to state that abstinence was the social norm to which behavioral change programs should strive. Today, our society struggles more openly with the question about which is a more appropriate endpoint. Perhaps both points are appropriate goals for different segments of society. In one location, abstinence may be the better the goal; in another, prophylaxis may be more appropriate. Seropositive individuals may benefit from early medical intervention as therapies become available. Seronegative individuals may benefit from reduction in anxiety levels. Intervention techniques aimed at self-preservation of individuals not yet infected may be more effective than relying solely on altruism. In the end it is clear that for any counseling and testing program to be accepted, there must be adequate legislation protecting confidentiality and prohibiting discrimination against those who are willing to participate.

CONCLUSION

The Coburn bill calls for increased use of some traditional public health interventions which can be viewed as measures that address specific causes of HIV (e.g., make sure contacts know they may have been HIV infected). However, we must remember that decreasing the importance of public health interventions that address general causes of HIV (e.g., fear about losing rights if I access health care so I do not) will likely lead to a lack of support for measures that address more specific causes of HIV. Public health literature suggests then that we must focus on both specific and general public health measures. To date, it appears that two camps have developed. Opponents of Coburn's bill view the mandatory provisions as a threat to civil liberties, while supporters consider them sound public health science. Confidentiality and maintenance of individual rights are needed to promote public health. If we sacrifice individual rights we will not achieve our public health objectives.

The Coburn bill asks us to focus on specific (e.g., contact tracing) rather than general public health measures (e.g., prevention workshops). Implementing these specific measures may cost so much that general measures including prevention would undoubtedly suffer. It is essential to understand that these prevention and education programs which provide information, counseling, and support to those who most need it are strained. Without these programs, the very individuals who need public health the most may be forced back into their closets, making them unavailable if there were ever a Coburn contact tracing program.

POSTSCRIPT

Should Privacy Rights Yield to Public Health Concerns in Dealing With HIV Infections?

In this debate about which public health policies would be most effective in limiting the spread of HIV and AIDS, Coburn argues that our current social awareness of HIV and AIDS no longer justifies the anonymous voluntary testing policy that was necessary 15 years ago. He identifies seven areas where he believes significant benefits would be gained if we applied traditional health care policies of routine testing without patient consent, reporting names of infected individuals to local health authorities, tracing contacts, and notifying people who are at risk of their possible exposure.

Coburn's first point is that a traditional policy would provide valuable information about how widespread the HIV virus is—not just where the AIDS hot spots are, but where AIDS hot spots are developing. Coburn claims that routine testing, confidentially reporting the names of infected individuals, tracing contacts, and notifying at-risk people would provide greater protection for people exposed to HIV by a current or previous partner, allow for routine HIV testing of rapists and sex offenders, improve protection for both patients and health care providers, protect the rights of insurance applicants to know their test results when an insurer requires an HIV test, and reinforce infected people's moral and legal responsibility not to infect others. Finally, Coburn maintains that the current Americans With Disabilities Act and state laws provide HIV-positive people with adequate protection against discrimination and confidentiality of their HIV- and AIDS-related information.

How convincing are the positions taken by Coburn and DeMarco? How strong are their arguments? How does the concept of the "web of causation" mentioned by DeMarco affect your view of this issue? Where do you think Coburn and DeMarco miss the mark? To what extent do you think the possible long-term negative consequences of particular policies should affect policymakers' decisions? What might be done to reduce the possible risks associated with changing the way in which HIV and AIDS are dealt with?

SUGGESTED READINGS

AIDS Action Analysis: The Coburn HIV Prevention Act of 1997 (AIDS Action Council, 1997).

"AIDS: Late Diagnoses Deprive People of Medical Care," *Healthline* (February 1, 1996).

L. K. Altman, "Sex, Privacy and Tracking H.I.V. Infections," *The New York Times* (November 4, 1997), pp. F1, F2.

C. Burr, "The AIDS Exception: Privacy vs. Public Health," *The Atlantic Monthly* (June 1997), pp. 57–67.

HIV Prevention Act of 1997: A Costly Misguided Approach to Disease Control (Gay Men's Health Crisis, 1997).

M. Johnson, *Working on a Miracle* (Bantam Books, 1997).

C. Norwood, "Mandated Life Versus Mandatory Death: New York's Disgraceful Partner Notification Record," *Journal of Community Health* (April 1995).

S. Stapleton, "Treating HIV Like Any Epidemic: Improved Therapies Bolster Argument for Public Health Strategies," *American Medical News* (March 24/31, 1997).

S. G. Stolberg, "Critics Challenging Special Status for AIDS Patients," *The New York Times* (November 12, 1997), pp. A1, A26.

ISSUE 19

Is Sexual Harassment a Pervasive Problem?

YES: Catharine R. Stimpson, from "Over-Reaching: Sexual Harassment and Education," *Initiatives* (vol. 52, no. 3, 1989)

NO: Gretchen Morgenson, from "May I Have the Pleasure," *National Review* (November 18, 1991)

ISSUE SUMMARY

YES: Catharine R. Stimpson, a former graduate dean of Rutgers University, claims that sexual harassment is epidemic in American society and will remain epidemic as long as males are in power and control. Although some significant progress has been made in creating resistance to sexual harassment, she maintains that the only way to create a harassment-free society is to redefine the historical connections between sexuality, gender, and power.

NO: Gretchen Morgenson, senior editor of *Forbes* magazine, argues that statistics on the prevalence of sexual harassment are grossly exaggerated by "consultants" who make a good livelihood instituting corporate antiharassment programs. She argues that, in reality, the problem of sexual harassment has and will continue to become less of a problem.

In fall 1991 stories of sexual harassment began splashing daily across the front pages of newspapers and opening nearly every television news broadcast. For example, Anita F. Hill, a law professor, charged that Judge Clarence Thomas had sexually harassed her when she worked for him at the Equal Employment Opportunity Commission. This charge came close to derailing Thomas's nomination to the U.S. Supreme Court. In the sports world, three members of the New England Patriots football team (and the team itself) were fined nearly $50,000 for making lewd gestures and remarks to *Boston Herald* reporter Lisa Olson in their locker room.

Sexual harassment charges have also been leveled at America's political leaders. The majority leader of Florida's House of Representatives lost his position for allowing an "offensive, degrading and inappropriate" atmosphere of sexual innuendo among his staff. Senator Bob Packwood (R-Oregon) faced a more personal attack, as a congressional ethics committee investigated charges that he had regularly sexually harassed female colleagues. As a result, Packwood was forced to resign from the Senate in September 1995.

In late 1991 and through most of 1992, the infamous Tailhook Association convention of U.S. Navy and Marine Corps pilots made national news. After interviewing more than 1,500 officers and civilians, investigators implicated more than 70 officers in sexual harassment and assault incidents against at least 26 women and several men (including 14 officers), either directly or in covering up the affair. The 70 officers were referred for disciplinary reviews and possible dismissal from the service. Top admirals were charged with tacitly approving such behavior for years, and major promotions for two admirals were lost because of sexual harassment questions.

In 1993 the American Association of University Women Education Foundation polled 1,632 teenagers in grades 8 to 11 on sexual harassment. They found that 76 percent of the girls and 56 percent of the boys reported receiving unwanted sexual comments or looks; 65 percent of the girls and 42 percent of the boys said they were touched, grabbed, or pinched in a sexual way. Some questioned whether all the behaviors included in the survey can legitimately be considered sexual harassment. Christina Hoff Sommers, at Clark University, said, "They're committed to finding gender bias everywhere, behind every door, in every hallway, and they find it. What this is going to invite is we're going to begin litigating high-school flirtation. In order to find gender bias against girls, they had to ask questions so broad that they invited complaints from boys." Countering this criticism, Maryka Biaggio, at Pacific University in Oregon, defended the broad, inclusive nature of the questions: "We know that people in general tend to underreport or minimize occurrences of sexual harassment, so in order to get a good sense of an individual's experience, you have to put forth a fairly inclusive definition."

Billie Dziech, coauthor of *The Lecherous Professor,* says, "We need clear definitions. We need to recognize that they are not hard and fast. They will differ for different individuals. This is slippery terminology." Dziech suggests that we should distinguish among what we consider normal flirting and "horseplay between men and women," a "sexual hassle," and "sexual harassment." But even that distinction will likely differ with different people and with the same person in different situations. This problem is compounded in a multiethnic society; behavior that is acceptable between two persons from the same culture may be unacceptable when the two parties are from different cultures. Still, the distinction might help separate the lewd comment from the funny sexual joke, and it may better define raunchy, suggestive, seductive, complimentary, and leering comments, looks, and gestures. When, for example, should the comment "You look great today" be interpreted as a sexist remark?

In the following selections, Catharine R. Stimpson and Gretchen Morgenson explore some of the complex questions raised by sexual harassment.

YES

Catharine R. Stimpson

OVER-REACHING: SEXUAL HARASSMENT AND EDUCATION

Sexual harassment is an ancient shame that has become a modern embarrassment. Largely because of the pressure of feminism and feminists, such a shift in status took place during the 1970s. Today, the psychological and social pollution that harassment spews out is like air pollution. No one defends either of them. We have classified them as malaises that damage people and their environments. For this reason, both forms of pollution are largely illegal. In 1986, in *Meritor Savings Bank v. Vinson*, the Supreme Court held an employer liable for acts of sexual harassment that its supervisory personnel might commit.

Yet, like air pollution, the psychological and social pollution of sexual harassment persists. In the stratosphere, chlorofluorocarbons from aerosol sprays and other products break apart and help to destroy the ozone layer. Well below the stratosphere, in classrooms and laboratories sexual louts refuse to disappear, imposing themselves on a significant proportion of our students.[1] As the graduate dean at a big public university, I experience, in my everyday life, the contradiction between disapproval of sexual harassment and the raw reality of its existence. I work, with men and women of good will, to end harassment. We must work, however, because the harassers are among us.

Inevitably, then, we must ask why sexual harassment persists, why we have been unable to extirpate this careless and cruel habit of the heartless. As we know, but must continue to repeat, a major reason is the historical strength of the connections among sexuality, gender, and power. But one demonstration of the force of these connections, sexual harassment, floats at the mid-point of an ugly, long-lasting continuum. At the most glamorous end of the continuum is a particular vision of romance, love, and erotic desire. Here men pursue women for their mutual pleasure. That promise of pleasure masks the inequities of power. "Had we but world enough, and time," a poet [Andrew Marvell] sings, "This coyness, Lady, were no crime." But for the poet, there is not enough world, not enough time. The lady, then, must submit to him before "... Worms shall try/That long preserv'd Virginity."

From Catharine R. Stimpson, "Over-Reaching: Sexual Harassment and Education," *Initiatives*, vol. 52, no. 3 (1989), pp. 1–5. Copyright © 1989 by The National Association for Women in Education. Reprinted by permission.

At the other end of the continuum is men's coercion of women's bodies, the brutalities of incest and of rape, in which any pleasure is perverse.

In the mid-nineteenth century, Robert Browning wrote a famous dramatic monologue, "Andrea Del Sarto." In the poem, a painter is using his wife as a model. As he paints, he speaks, muses, and broods. He is worried about his marriage, for his model/wife is apparently faithless, a less than model wife. He is worried about his art, for his talents may be inadequate. He is, finally, worried about his reputation, for other painters may be gaining on and surpassing him. In the midst of expressing his fears, he declares, "Ah, but a man's reach should exceed his grasp/Or what's a heaven for. . . ." Traditional interpretations of his poem have praised Browning for praising the necessity of man's ambitions, of man's reaching out for grandeur. Indeed, Del Sarto, in an act of minor blasphemy, casts heaven not as God's space but as man's reminder that he has not yet achieved his personal best. Unhappily, these interpretations go on, women can hurt men in their noble quests. Fickle, feckless, the feminine often embarks on her own quest, a search-and-destroy mission against male grandeur.

A revisionary interpretation of "Andrea Del Sarto," however, can find the poem a different kind of parable about sexuality, gender, and power. In this reading, a man has at least two capacities. First, he can reach out and move about in public space and historical time. Del Sarto goes after both canvas and fame. Next, he can define a woman's identity, here through talking about her and painting her portrait. Del Sarto literally shapes the image of his wife. Ironically, he wants to believe that he is a victim. He exercises

his powers in order to demonstrate that he is powerless. A man, he projects himself as a poor baby who cannot shape up his mate.

A sexual harasser in higher education reveals similar, but more sinister, capacities. The hierarchical structure of institutions sends him a supportive message: the arduous climb up the ladder is worth it. The higher a man goes, the more he deserves and ought to enjoy the sweetness and freedoms of his place.[2] First, a man reaches out for what he wants. He makes sexual "advances." His offensive weapons can be linguistic (a joke, for example) or physical (a touch). He warns the powerless that he has the ability to reach out in order to grasp and get what he wants. He also demonstrates to himself that he is able to dominate a situation. As the psychoanalyst Ethel Spector Person has pointed out, for many men, sexuality and domination are inseparable. To be sexual is to dominate and to be reassured of the possession of the power to dominate (Person, 1980).[3]

Usually, women compose the powerless group, but it may contain younger men as well, the disadvantages of age erasing the advantages of gender. One example: a 1986 survey at the University of Illinois/Champaign-Urbana found that 19 percent of the female graduate students, 10 percent of the undergraduates, and 8 percent of the professional school students had experienced harassment. So, too, had 5 percent of the male respondents. In all but one incident, the harasser was another man (Allen & Okawa, 1987).

Second, the harasser assumes the right to define the identity of the person whom he assaults. To him, she is not mind, but body; not student, not professional, but sexual being. She is who and what the harasser says she is. Ironically, like Andrea Del Sarto, many academics project their own power onto a woman and then assert that she, not he, has power.[4] He, not she, is powerless. Her sexuality seduces and betrays him. This psychological maneuver must help to explain one fear that people express about sexual harassment policies—that such policies will permit, even encourage, false complaints against blameless faculty and staff. A recent study found 78 percent of respondents worried about loss of due process and about the fate of innocent people who might be accused of misconduct. Yet, the study concluded, less than 1 percent of all sexual harassment complaints each year *are* false. The deep problem is not wrongful accusations against the innocent, but the refusal of the wronged to file any complaint at all. In part, they believe they should handle sexual matters themselves. In part, they hope the problem will go away if they ignore it. In part, they fear retaliation, punishment for stepping out of line (Robertson, Dyer, & Campbell, 1988).

The unreasonable fear about false complaints is also a symptom of the blindness of the powerful to the realities of their own situation. They enjoy its benefits but are unable to see its nature and costs to other people. They are like a driver of an inherited sports car who loves to drive but refuses to learn where gas and oil come from, who services the car when it is in the garage, or why pedestrians might shout when he speeds through a red light. In a probing essay, Molly Hite (1988) tells a story about a harasser on a United States campus, a powerful professor who abused his authority over female graduate students. He damaged several women, psychologically and professionally. Yet even after that damage became public knowledge, he survived, reputa-

tion intact, although he did discreetly move to another campus. Hite inventories the responses of her colleagues to this event. Men, no matter what their academic rank, tended to underplay the seriousness of his behavior. They thought that he had acted "normally," if sometimes insensitively, that the women had acted abnormally and weakly. Women, no matter what their academic rank, tended to sympathize with the female victims. They could identify with powerlessness. Hite writes, "The more the victim is someone who could be you, the easier it is to be scared. By the same reasoning, it's possible to be cosmically un-scared, even to find the whole situation trivial to the point of absurdity, if you can't imagine ever being the victim" (p. 9).

So far, higher education has participated in building at least four related modes of resistance to sexual harassment. First, we have named the problem *as a problem*. We have pushed it into public consciousness as an issue. The Equal Employment Opportunity Commission guidelines, in particular, have provided a citable, national language with which to describe harassment, a justifiable entry in the dictionary of our concerns. Next, we have learned how much administrative leadership has mattered in urging an institution to address this concern. Not surprisingly, faculties have not moved to reform themselves. Next, workshops that educate people about the nature of harassment do seem to reduce its virulence. Finally, we have created grievance procedures with which we can hear complaints, investigate them, and punish harassers.[5] The most carefully designed in themselves help to empower women. The process does not itself perpetuate her sense of self as victim (Hoffman, 1986).

These modes of resistance, good in themselves, have also done good. They have shown an institution's commitment to a fair, non-polluting social environment. They have warned potential harassers to stop. They have offered some redress to the harassed. Resistance will, however, be of only limited good unless a rewriting of the historical connections among sexuality, gender, and power accompanies it. Similarly, putting up traffic lights on crowded streets is a good. Lights are, however, of only limited good unless drivers believe in the rights of other drivers, in safety, and in the limits of their machines.

In such a rewriting, an act of "overreaching" will be interpreted not as aspiration and desire, but as an invasion of another person's body, dignity, and livelihood. No one will feel the approaching grasp of the harasser as a welcome clasp. Over-reaching will be a sign not of grace but of disgrace, not of strength but of callousness and, possibly, anxiety, not of virility but of moral and psychological weakness. It will not be a warm joke between erotic equals, but a smutty titter from an erotic jerk. The rhetoric of neither romance nor comedy will be able to paint over the grammar of exploitation.[6]

One consequence of this rewriting will be to expand our modes of resistance to include a general education curriculum, not simply about harassment as a phenomenon, but about power itself, which harassment symptomizes. This will mean teaching many men to cut the ties among selfhood, masculinity, and domination. It will mean teaching many women to cut the ties among self, femininity, and intimacy at any price, including the price of submission. Occasionally, reading a sexual harassment complaint from a young woman, I have asked myself, in some rue

and pain, why she has acted *like a woman*. By that, I have meant that her training for womanhood has taught her to value closeness, feeling, relationships. Fine and dandy, but too often, she takes this lesson to heart above all others.

The first part of the curriculum, for women, will remind them of their capacity for resistance, for saying no. Telling a harasser to stop can be effective.[7] Speaking out, acting verbally, can also empower an individual woman. Less fortunately, these speech acts reconstitute the traditional sexual roles of man as hunter, woman as prey. Unlike a rabbit or doe, she is responsible for setting the limits of the hunt, for fencing in the game park. If the hunter violates these limits, it is because she did not uphold them firmly enough. Moreover, saying no to the aggressor also occurs in private space. Because of this location, both harasser and harassed can forget that these apparently private actions embody, in little, grosser structures of authority.

The second part of the curriculum will be for men and women. Fortunately, women's studies programs are now developed enough to serve as a resource for an entire institution that chooses to offer lessons about gender and power. These lessons will do more than anatomize abuses. They will also present an ethical perspective, which the practices of colleges and universities might well represent. This ethic will cherish a divorce between sexuality and the control of another person, an unbridgeable distance between a lover's pleasure and a bully's threat. This ethic will also ask us to cherish our capacities to care for each other, to attend to each other's needs without manipulating them.[8] We will reach out to each other without grasping, hauling, pushing, mauling.

The struggle against sexual harassment, then, is part of a larger struggle to replant the moral grounds of education. Our visionary hope is that we will, in clear air, harvest new gestures, laws, customs, and practices. We will still take poets as our prophets. When we do so, however, we might replace the dramatic monologue of a fraught, Renaissance painter with that of a strong-willed, late twentieth-century feminist. In 1977, in "Natural Resources," Adrienne Rich spoke for those who stubbornly continue to believe in visionary hope:

"My heart is moved by all I cannot save:
so much has been destroyed.
I have to cast my lot with those
who age after age, perversely,
with no extraordinary power,
reconstitute the world."

NOTES

1. The authors of a survey of 311 institutions of higher education, conducted in 1984, estimate that one woman out of four experiences some form of harassment as a student (Robertson et al., 1988). A survey of a single institution, a large public research university, found that 31 percent of the more than 700 respondents had been subjected to "sex-stereotyped jokes, remarks, references, or examples" ("Survey documents," 1988, pp. 41–42).

2. As Robertson et al. comment, "individuals in positions of authority... (are) used to viewing professional status as expanding privilege rather than increasing responsibility and obligation" (p. 808). An anecdote illustrates this generalization. Recently, I was chairing a meeting of the graduate faculty of my university. Our agenda item was a proposal to conduct a periodic review of faculty members, program by program, to help insure they were still qualified to be graduate teachers. A professor, well-known for his decency, stood up in opposition. He said, "When I got tenure, I became a member of a club, and no one is going to tell me what to do. If I don't want to publish, that's my business."

3. Not coincidentally, most of the sexual harassers whom I have had to investigate as graduate dean have had streaks of arrogance, flare-ups of vanity. In contrast, the men who have been most sympathetic to the necessity of my investigations have had a certain ethical poise, a balance of standards and stability.

4. An obvious parallel is a traditional response to rape, in which women are held culpable for being raped. Moreover, like versions of Jezebel, they are thought only too likely to cry rape in order to cover up their own sins.

5. I am grateful to Robertson et al. (1988) for their description of various modes of resistance to harassment. Their study also explores the reasons why public institutions have been more sensitive than private institutions. More specifically, Beauvais (1986) describes workshops that deal with harassment for residence hall staff at the University of Michigan.

6. Disguising the language of harassment as humor has several advantages. First, it draws on our old, shrewd assessment of much sexual behavior as funny and comic. Next, it simultaneously inflates the harasser to the status of good fellow, able to tell a joke, and deflates the harassed to the status of prude, unable to take one.

7. Allen and Okawa (1987) say that this worked for two-thirds of the respondents in their study of harassment at the University of Illinois.

8. Tronto (1987) suggestively outlines a theory of care that educational institutions might adopt.

REFERENCES

Allen, D., & Okawa, J. B. (1987). A counseling center looks at sexual harassment. *Journal of the National Association for Women Deans, Administrators, and Counselors,* 51(1), 9–16.

Beauvais, K. (1986). Workshops to combat sexual harassment: A case study of changing attitudes. *Signs,* 12(1), 130–145.

Hite, M. (1988). Sexual harassment and the university community. Unpublished manuscript.

Hoffman, F. L. (1986). Sexual harassment in academia. *Harvard Educational Review,* 56(2), 105–121.

Person, E. (1980). Sexuality as the mainstay of identity. In C. R. Stimpson & E. S. Person (eds.), *Women: Sex and sexuality.* Chicago: University of Chicago Press.

Robertson, C., Dyer, C. C., & Campbell, D. A. (1988). Campus harassment: Sexual harassment policies and procedures at institutions of higher learning. *Signs,* 13(4), 792–812.

Survey documents sexual harassment at U Mass. (1988). *Liberal Education,* 74(2), 41–2.

Tronto, J. C. (1987). Beyond gender differences to a theory of care. *Signs,* 12(4), 644–663.

NO

Gretchen Morgenson

MAY I HAVE THE PLEASURE

On October 11 [1991],in the middle of the Anita Hill/Clarence Thomas con-tretemps, the *New York Times* somberly reported that sexual harassment per-vades the American workplace. The source for this page-one story was a *Times*/CBS poll conducted two days earlier in which a handful (294) of women were interviewed by telephone. Thirty-eight per cent of respondents confirmed that they had been at one time or another "the object of sexual advances, propositions, or unwanted sexual discussions from men who su-pervise you or can affect your position at work." How many reported the incident at the time it happened? Four per cent.

Did the *Times* offer any explanation for why so few actually reported the incident? Could it be that these women did not report their "harassment" because they themselves did not regard a sexual advance as harassment? Some intelligent speculation on this matter might shed light on a key point: the vague definitions of harassment that make it easy to allege, hard to iden-tify, and almost impossible to prosecute. Alas, the *Times* was in no mood to enlighten its readers.

It has been more than ten years since the Equal Employment Opportu-nity Commission (EEOC) wrote its guidelines defining sexual harassment as a form of sexual discrimination and, therefore, illegal under Title VII of the Civil Rights Act of 1964. According to the EEOC there are two different types of harassment: so-called *quid pro quo* harassment, in which career or job advancement is guaranteed in return for sexual favors, and environmental harassment, in which unwelcome sexual conduct "unreasonably interferes" with an individual's working environment or creates an "intimidating, hos-tile, or offensive working environment."

Following the EEOC's lead, an estimated three out of four companies na-tionwide have instituted strict policies against harassment; millions of dollars are spent each year educating employees in the subtleties of Title VII etiquette. Men are warned to watch their behavior, to jettison the patronizing pat and excise the sexist comment from their vocabularies.

Yet, if you believe what you read in the newspapers, we are in the Stone Age where the sexes are concerned. A theme common to the media, plaintiff's lawyers, and employee-relations consultants is that male harassment of women is costing corporations millions each year in lost productivity and low employee morale. "Sexual harassment costs a typical Fortune 500 Service or Manufacturing company $6.7 million a year" says a sexual-harassment survey conducted late in 1988 for *Working Woman* by Klein Associates. This Boston consulting firm is part of a veritable growth industry which has sprung up to dispense sexual-harassment advice to worried companies in the form of seminars, videos, and encounter groups.

But is sexual harassment such a huge problem in business? Or is it largely a product of hype and hysteria? The statistics show that sexual harassment is less prevalent today than it was five years ago. According to the EEOC, federal cases alleging harassment on the job totaled 5,694 in 1990, compared to 6,342 in 1984. Yet today there are 17 per cent more women working than there were then.

At that, the EEOC's figures are almost certainly too high. In a good many of those complaints, sexual harassment may be tangential to the case; the complaint may primarily involve another form of discrimination in Title VII territory: race, national origin, or religious discrimination, for example. The EEOC doesn't separate cases involving sexual harassment alone; any case where sexual harassment is mentioned, even in passing, gets lumped into its figures.

Many of the stories depicting sexual harassment as a severe problem spring from "consultants" whose livelihoods depend upon exaggerating its extent. In one year, DuPont spent $450,000 on sexual-harassment training programs and materials. Susan Webb, president of Pacific Resources Development Group, a Seattle consultant, says she spends 95 per cent of her time advising on sexual harassment. Like most consultants, Miss Webb acts as an expert witness in harassment cases, conducts investigations for companies and municipalities, and teaches seminars. She charges clients $1,500 for her 35-minute sexual-harassment video program and handbooks.

UNFELT NEEDS

Corporations began to express concern on the issue back in the early Eighties, just after the EEOC published its first guidelines. But it was *Meritor Savings Bank v. Vinson,* a harassment case that made it to the Supreme Court in 1985, that really acted as an employment act for sex-harassment consultants. In *Vinson,* the Court stated that employers could limit their liability to harassment claims by implementing anti-harassment policies and procedures in the workplace. And so, the anti-harassment industry was born.

Naturally, the consultants believe they are filling a need, not creating one. "Harassment is still as big a problem as it has been because the workplace is not integrated," says Susan Webb. Ergo, dwindling numbers of cases filed with the EEOC are simply not indicative of a diminution in the problem.

Then what do the figures indicate? Two things, according to the harassment industry. First, that more plaintiffs are bringing private lawsuits against their employers than are suing through the EEOC or state civil-rights commissions. Second, that the number of cases filed is a drop in the bucket compared to the number of actual, everyday harassment incidents.

It certainly stands to reason that a plaintiff in a sexual-harassment case would prefer bringing a private action against her employer to filing an EEOC claim. EEOC and state civil-rights cases allow plaintiffs only compensatory damages, such as back pay or legal fees. In order to collect big money—punitive damages—from an employer, a plaintiff must file a private action.

Yet there's simply no proof that huge or increasing numbers of private actions are being filed today. No data are collected on numbers of private harassment suits filed, largely because they're brought as tort actions—assault and battery, emotional distress, or breach of contract. During the second half of the Eighties, the San Francisco law firm of Orrick, Herrington, and Sutcliffe monitored private sexual-harassment cases filed in California. Its findings: From 1984 to 1989, the number of sexual-harassment cases in California that were litigated through a verdict totaled a whopping 15. That's in a state with almost six million working women.

Of course, cases are often settled prior to a verdict. But how many? Orrick, Herrington partner Ralph H. Baxter Jr., management co-chairman of the American Bar Association's Labor Law Committee on Employee Rights and Responsibilities, believes the number of private sexual-harassment cases launched today is greatly overstated. "Litigation is not as big a problem as it's made out to be; you're not going to see case after case," says Mr. Baxter. "A high percentage of matters go to the EEOC and a substantial number of cases get resolved."

Those sexual-harassment actions that do get to a jury are the ones that really grab headlines. A couple of massive awards have been granted in recent years—five plaintiffs were awarded $3.8 million by a North Carolina jury —but most mammoth awards are re-

duced on appeal. In fact, million-dollar sexual-harassment verdicts are still exceedingly rare. In California, land of the happy litigator, the median jury verdict for all sexual-harassment cases litigated between 1984 and 1989 was $183,000. The top verdict in the sate was just under $500,000, the lowest was $45,000. And California, known for its sympathetic jurors, probably produces higher awards than most states.

Now to argument number two: that the number of litigated harassment cases is tiny compared to the number of actual incidents that occur. Bringing a sexual-harassment case is similar to filing a rape case, consultants and lawyers say; both are nasty proceedings which involve defamation, possible job loss, and threats to both parties' family harmony.

It may well be that cases of perceived harassment go unfiled, but is it reasonable to assume that the numbers of these unfiled cases run into the millions? Consider the numbers of cases filed that are dismissed for "no probable cause." According to the New York State human-rights commission, almost two-thirds of the complaints filed in the past five years were dismissed for lack of probable cause. Of the two hundred sexual-harassment cases the commission receives a year, 38 per cent bring benefits to the complainant.

What about private actions? No one keeps figures on the percentage of cases nationwide won by the plaintiff versus the percentage that are dismissed. However, the outcomes of private sexual-harassment suits brought in California from 1984 to 1989 mirror the public figures from New York. According to Orrick, Herrington, of the 15 cases litigated to a verdict in California from 1984 to 1989, slightly less than half were dismissed and slightly more than half (53 per cent) were won by the plaintiff.

Are California and New York anomalies? Stephen Perlman, a partner in labor law at the Boston firm of Ropes & Gray, who has 15 years' experience litigating sexual-harassment cases, thinks not: "I don't suppose I've had as many as a dozen cases go to litigation. Most of the cases I've seen—the vast majority —get dismissed. They don't even have probable cause to warrant further processing."

WHAT IS HARASSMENT?

A major problem is the vague definition of harassment. If "environmental harassment" were clearly defined and specifiable, lawyers would undoubtedly see more winnable cases walk through their doors. Asking a subordinate to perform sexual favors in exchange for a raise is clearly illegal. But a dirty joke? A pin-up? A request for a date?

In fact, behavior which one woman may consider harassment could be seen by another as a non-threatening joke. The closest thing to harassment that I have experienced during my 15-year career occurred in the early Eighties when I was a stockbroker-in-training at Dean Witter Reynolds in New York City. I had brought in the largest personal account within Dean Witter's entire retail brokerage system, an account which held roughly $20 million in blue-chip stocks. Having this account under my management meant I had a larger capital responsibility than any of my colleagues, yet I was relatively new to the business. My fellow brokers were curious, but only one was brutish enough to walk right up to me and pop the question: "How did you get that account? Did you sleep with the guy?"

Instead of running away in tears, I dealt with him as I would any rude person. "Yeah," I answered. "Eat your heart out." He turned on his heel and never bothered me again. Was my colleague a harasser, or just practicing Wall Street's aggressive humor, which is dished out to men in other ways? Apparently, I am in the minority in thinking the latter. But the question remains. Whose standards should be used to define harassment?

Under tort law, the behavior which has resulted in a case—such as an assault or the intent to cause emotional distress— must be considered objectionable by a "reasonable person." The EEOC follows this lead and in its guidelines defines environmental harassment as that which "unreasonably interferes with an individual's job performance."

Yet, sexual-harassment consultants argue that any such behavior—even that which is perceived as harassment only by the most hypersensitive employee —ought to be considered illegal and stamped out. In fact, they say, the subtler hostile-environment cases are the most common and cause the most anguish. Says Frieda Klein, the Boston consultant: "My goal is to create a corporate climate where every employee feels free to object to behavior, where people are clear about their boundaries and can ask that objectionable behavior stop."

Sounds great. But rudeness and annoying behavior cannot be legislated out of existence; nor should corporations be forced to live under the tyranny of a hypersensitive employee. No woman should have to run a daily gauntlet of sexual innuendo, but neither is it reasonable for women to expect a pristine work environment free of coarse behavior.

Susan Hartzoge Gray, a labor lawyer at Haworth, Riggs, Kuhn, and Haworth in Raleigh, North Carolina, believes that hostile-environment harassment shouldn't be actionable under Title VII. "How can the law say one person's lewd and another's nice?" she asks. "There are so many different taste levels.... We condone sexual jokes and innuendos in the media—a movie might get a PG rating—yet an employer can be called on the carpet because the same thing bothers someone in an office."

But changing demographics may do more to eliminate genuine sexual harassment than all the apparatus of law and consultancy. As women reach a critical mass in the workforce, the problem of sexual harassment tends to go away. Frieda Klein says the problem practically vanishes once 30 per cent of the workers in a department, an assembly line, or a company are women.

Reaching that critical mass won't take long. According to the Bureau of Labor Statistics, there will be 66 million women to 73 million men in the workplace by 2000. They won't all be running departments or heading companies, of course, but many will.

So sexual harassment will probably become even less of a problem in the years ahead than it is today. But you are not likely to read that story in a major newspaper anytime soon.

POSTSCRIPT

Is Sexual Harassment a Pervasive Problem?

For many women, the high cost of fighting sexual harassment often makes suffering in silence more appealing. As feminist Naomi Wolf points out, "Many strong, successful professional women have made conscious decisions to ignore sexual harassment in their offices because they know that as soon as they complained, there would be 50 other [women] waiting to take their jobs." Camille Paglia, author of *Sexual Personae* (Yale University Press, 1990), counters, "Women allow themselves to become victims when they don't take responsibility. If getting the guy to stop means putting a heel into his crotch, then just do it. Don't complain about it 10 years later." Yet Deborah Tannen, author of *You Just Don't Understand: Women and Men in Conversation* (William Morrow, 1990), says, "Women have learned that confrontation is to be avoided and they don't have the verbal tools to attack this kind of problem head-on as a man would."

This issue may have some chilling effects on everyday male-female relations, on dating and courtship, in the workplace, on college campuses, and even in high schools. Anthropologist Lionel Tiger predicts a "return to a kind of Victorian period" in which some men will be reluctant to try developing a relationship with any woman who initially seems aloof.

The Tailhook Association incident, which has made headlines around the world, seems to have had some global influence: the Belgian and Dutch governments have launched public information campaigns; the Spanish and French governments have recently passed laws making sexual harassment a crime; and the European Commission, the administrative arm of the 12-nation European Community, has issued a code defining sexual harassment.

Sexual harassment is fast becoming a global issue that will likely continue to have reverberations in the ways women and men relate for years to come.

SUGGESTED READINGS

F. Barringer, "School Hallways as Gantlets of Sexual Taunts," *The New York Times* (June 2, 1993).

B. W. Dziech and L. Weiner, *The Lecherous Professor: Sexual Harassment on Campus*, 2d ed. (University of Illinois Press, 1990).

M. Lawton, "Survey Paints 'Picture' of School Sexual Harassment," *Education Week* (March 31, 1993).

A. N. LeBlanc, "Harassment at School: The Truth Is Out," *Seventeen* (May 1993).

L. McMillen, "Misleading Studies Seen on Sexual Harassment," *Chronicle of Higher Education* (September 27, 1996).

P. Sharpe and F. Mascia-Lees, " 'Always Believe the Victim,' 'Innocent Until Proven Guilty,' 'There Is No Truth': The Competing Claims of Feminism, Humanism, and Postmodernism in Interpreting Charges of Harassment in the Academy," *Anthropological Quarterly* (April 1993).

N. Wolf, *The Beauty Myth: How Images of Beauty Are Used Against Women* (William Morrow, 1991).

CONTRIBUTORS
TO THIS VOLUME

EDITORS

ROBERT T. FRANCOEUR has taught human sexuality at colleges and high schools for over 20 years. He is currently a professor of biological and allied health sciences at Fairleigh Dickinson University in Madison, New Jersey, and he is the author of 7 books on human sexuality, including *Becoming a Sexual Person* (Macmillan, 1989), *A Descriptive Dictionary and Atlas of Sexology* (Greenwood, 1992), and *An International Handbook of Sexuality* (Greenwood, 1994). He has contributed to 53 handbooks and readers on human sexuality, and he has 47 technical papers and over 110 popular articles on sexual issues to his credit. He holds a doctorate in embryology and master's degrees in Catholic theology and biology, and he is a charter member of the American College of Sexology.

WILLIAM J. TAVERNER received his B.A. in psychology from SUNY Albany and his M.A. in human sexuality from New York University. He has taught human sexuality for challenging populations, including individuals with developmental disabilities, substance abusers, and other at-risk youth. He currently administers a human sexuality program that allows recovering substance abusers to address and reconcile their underlying sexual issues. He is the author of *Sexuality and Substance Abuse* (Phoenix Foundation, 1997) and *Focus Group Survival Book* (Phoenix Foundation, 1997). He is also a member of the Sexuality Information and Education Council of the United States and the North Atlantic Training Institute for Sexual Health Educators.

STAFF

David Dean   List Manager
David Brackley   Developmental Editor
Juliana Poggio   Associate Developmental Editor
Rose Gleich   Administrative Assistant
Brenda S. Filley   Production Manager
Juliana Arbo   Typesetting Supervisor
Diane Barker   Proofreader
Lara Johnson   Graphics
Richard Tietjen   Publishing Systems Manager

AUTHORS

DEBORAH ANAPOL, a psychologist, is cofounder of IntiNet Resource Center, a clearinghouse and network for people and organizations interested in sexual intimacy and family design. She drew on her experiences with polyamorous relations in writing *Love Without Limits: Responsible Nonmonogamy and the Quest for Sustainable Intimate Relationships* (IntiNet Resource Center, 1992) and *A Resource Guide for the Responsible Nonmonogamist* (IntiNet Resource Center, 1990).

DOUGLAS J. BESHAROV is a resident scholar at the American Enterprise Institute in Washington, D.C.

JAMES BOVARD is the 1996 Warren T. Brookes Fellow in Environmental Journalism with the Competitive Enterprise Institute, a free market public policy group in Washington, D.C. He is a frequent contributor to the editorial pages of the *Wall Street Journal, Playboy, The American Spectator,* and other publications. He is the author of several books, including *Shakedown: How Government Screws You from A to Z* (Viking Penguin, 1995) and *Lost Rights: The Destruction of American Liberty* (St. Martin's Press, 1994).

PEGGY BRICK is director of education at Planned Parenthood of Greater Northern New Jersey in Hackensack, New Jersey. She has taught human behavior, including sexuality education, in public high school for 17 years, and she is currently president of the Sexuality Information and Education Council of the United States (SIECUS).

WILLIAM BYNE is a research associate in the Albert Einstein College of Medicine at Yeshiva University in New York City, where he investigates the brain structure of humans and other primates, as well as an attending psychiatrist at the New York State Psychiatric Institute. His research focuses on the ways in which biological and social factors interact to influence behavior. He received his Ph.D. in 1985 from the University of Wisconsin–Madison and his M.D. in 1989 from Yeshiva University.

PAT CALIFIA has described herself as a dyke, a feminist, a pornographer, a sadomasochist, a poet, a storyteller, an omnivore, a pagan, a social critic, a sex educator, and an activist. A prolific writer in a number of mediums, she has published hundreds of articles, reviews, poems, short fictional pieces, and books, including *Public Sex: The Culture of Radical Sex* (Cleis Press, 1994) and *The Second Coming,* coedited with Robin Sweeney (Alyson Publications, 1996).

JAMES CARVILLE, a social commentator and journalist, currently serves as senior political adviser to President Bill Clinton. In the past he has successfully managed some important election campaigns for various governors and senators. He is the author of the best-seller *We're Right, They're Wrong: A Handbook for Spirited Progressives* (Simon & Schuster, 1996) and coauthor, with Mary Matalin, of *All's Fair: Love, War, and Running for President* (Simon & Schuster, 1994).

CENTER FOR POPULATION OPTIONS works to increase the opportunities for and the abilities of youth to make healthy decisions about sexuality. Since 1980 it has provided information, education, and advocacy to youth-serving agencies and professionals, policymakers, and the media.

WILLIAM J. CLINTON became the 42d president of the United States in 1993. He taught at the University of Arkansas in the early 1970s, became Arkansas state attorney general in 1976, and was elected governor of Arkansas in 1978. He is the author of *My Plans for a Second Term* (Carol Publishing Group, 1995) and coauthor, with Al Gore, of *Putting People First: How We Can All Change* (Times Books, 1992).

TOM A. COBURN is the Republican representative from the Second District in Oklahoma. He is a member of the Committee on Commerce, the Subcommittee on Telecommunications and Finance, and the Subcommittee on Health and Environment.

MARTHA CORNOG, manager of membership services at the American College of Physicians in Philadelphia, Pennsylvania, was on the panel "For Sex: See Librarian" at the American Library Association Annual Conference in New Orleans. She is the editor of *Libraries, Erotica, and Pornography* (Oryx, 1991).

CHARLES L. DAVIS is an associate professor of political science at the University of Kentucky in Lexington, Kentucky. He is the author of *Working-Class Mobilization and Political Control: Venezuela and Mexico* (University Press of Kentucky, 1989). He has also published various articles on mass political behavior in Latin America and on the political participation of soldiers in the U.S. Army.

EDWIN J. DELATTRE is dean of the School of Education and a professor of education and philosophy in the College of Liberal Arts at Boston University in Boston, Massachusetts. He is also president emeritus of St. John's College, and he is well known nationally for his work on ethics in daily public and private life.

His publications include *Education and the Public Trust: The Imperative for Common Purposes* (Ethics and Public Policy, 1988) and *Character and Cops: Ethics in Policing* (American Enterprise Institute, 1989).

CHRISTOPHER DeMARCO directs HIV/AIDS programs for a social services agency in New York City. He has been involved in the field of HIV/AIDS since 1986 and has worked in the field since 1990.

ANDREA DWORKIN, coauthor of the Indianapolis legislation that defines *pornography* as a violation of women's civil rights, is an American nonfiction writer, essayist, novelist, and short story writer. She is best known for her controversial nonfiction works that examine the status of women in modern society, including *Life and Death: Unapologetic Writings on the Continuing War Against Women* (Free Press, 1997) and *Pornography: Men Possessing Women* (E. P. Dutton, 1989).

EUGENE T. GOMULKA, a commander in the U.S. Navy Chaplain Corps, currently serves as deputy chaplain for the U.S. Marine Corps. He received a B.A. in philosophy from Saint Francis College and a licentiate in sacred theology from the Pontifical University of Saint Thomas Aquinas in Rome, Italy. He has received two Meritorious Service Medals, the Navy Commendation Medal, and the Navy Achievement Medal.

JOHN GRAY is recognized internationally as a leader in the field of relationships and personal growth. For over 20 years he has conducted public and private seminars to enrich the quality of relationships and improve communication. He earned his Ph.D. in psychology from Columbia Pacific University, and he has taught his seminars in major cities throughout the world. He is the author of many books on relationships between men and women, including *Mars and Venus in the Bedroom: A Guide to Lasting Romance and Passion* (HarperCollins, 1995) and *Mars and Venus Together Forever* (HarperPerennial, 1996).

DEAN H. HAMER received his Ph.D. in biological chemistry from Harvard University in 1977. For over 20 years, he has been at the National Institutes of Health, and he is currently chief of the section on gene structure and regulation at the National Cancer Institute. His studies focus on the role of genes in sexual orientation and in complex medical conditions, including the progression of HIV and Kaposi's sarcoma.

SUSAN HAMSON, Web master of the Internet site *Rebuttal from Uranus,* received her M.A. in American history from Rutgers University. She is currently a doctoral student in American women's history and the history of sexuality at Temple University.

DOUGLAS JOHNSON is legislative director of the National Right to Life Committee (NRLC).

ROBERT H. KNIGHT is director of cultural studies for the Family Research Council. A former news editor for the *Los Angeles Times,* he was the 1989–1990 Media Fellow at the Hoover Institution at Stanford University. He wrote and directed *The Children of Table 34,* a video documentary about sexologist Alfred Kinsey, and *Hope and Healing,* a video about people overcoming homosexuality.

LORETTA M. KOPELMAN is a professor in and chair of the Department of Medical Humanities in the School of Medicine at East Carolina University in Greenville, North Carolina. She is co-editor, with John C. Moskop, of *Children and Health Care: Moral and Social Issues* (Kluwer Academic Publishers, 1989).

PETER D. KRAMER is a clinical professor of psychiatry at Brown University in Providence, Rhode Island. He is the author of *Listening to Prozac: A Psychiatrist Explores Antidepressant Drugs and the Remaking of the Self* (Viking Penguin, 1993) and the forthcoming *Should You Leave? A Psychiatrist Explores Intimacy and Autonomy in Relationships and the Nature of Advice.*

SIMON LeVAY earned a doctorate in neuroanatomy at the University of Göttingen in Germany. His work in the early 1970s at Harvard University focused on the brain's visual system. He has worked as head of the vision center of the Salk Institute for Biological Studies in San Diego, California, and he is the founder of the Institute of Gay and Lesbian Education.

THOMAS LICKONA, a developmental psychologist, is a professor of education at the State University of New York College at Cortland and director of the Center for the Fourth and Fifth Rs (Respect and Responsibility). He is a member of the board of directors of the Character Education Partnership, a national coalition working to promote character development in schools and communities. He is a frequent consultant to schools across the United States, and he has also lectured in Canada, Japan, Switzerland, Ireland, and Latin America on teaching moral values in the school and at home.

LISA MASON, a Phi Beta Kappa scholar and a graduate of the University of Michigan Law School, is a science fiction writer. Her short fiction has appeared in such publications as *Omni, The Year's Best Fantasy and Horror,* and *Universe,* and her novels include *The Golden Nineties* (Bantam Spectra, 1995) and *Summer of Love* (Bantam Spectra, 1994).

JOHN MONEY is a profesor of medical psychology and pediatrics at Johns Hopkins University and Hospital in Baltimore, Maryland, where he cofounded and directed the Psychohormonal Research Unit. His research interests include hermaphrodites, transsexuals, and paraphilias, and he is the author of nearly 400 scientific papers and two dozen books on sexology and psychoendocrinology, including *Venuses Penuses* (Prometheus Books, 1986) and *Reinterpreting the Unspeakable: Human Sexuality 2000* (Continuum, 1994).

GRETCHEN MORGENSON is senior editor of *Forbes* magazine.

P. MASILA MUTISYA is an assistant professor in the Department of Curriculum and Instruction in the School of Education at Fayetteville State University in Fayetteville, North Carolina. He teaches courses on foundations of education, human development, and multicultural education.

CAMILLE PAGLIA is a professor of humanities at the University of the Arts in Philadelphia, Pennsylvania. She is the author of the best-seller *Sexual Personae* (Yale University Press, 1990) and *Vamps and Tramps: New Essays* (1995).

CHRISTINE PIERCE is a philosopher with an interest in seeing gay male and lesbian couples legally recognized as family units. She is coeditor, with Donald VanDeVeer, of *AIDS: Ethics and Public Policy* (Wadsworth Publishing, 1988).

DEBORAH M. ROFFMAN is a sexuality education trainer and consultant. She has taught human sexuality education at the Park School in Brooklandville, Maryland, since 1975.

JAMES L. SAUER is a librarian at Eastern College in Phoenixville, Pennsylvania.

CATHARINE R. STIMPSON is director of the Fellows Division of the John D. Catherine T. MacArthur Foundation in Chicago, Illinois. She served as dean of the graduate college at Rutgers University from 1986 to 1992, and she is a former president of the Modern Language Association as well as the founding editor of *Signs: Journal of Women in Culture and Society.* Her publications include *Where the Meanings Are* (Methuen, 1988).

NADINE STROSSEN is a professor in the School of Law at New York University in New York City and a general counsel for the American Civil Liberties Union.

ANDREW VACHHS is a juvenile advocate and widely praised crime novelist.

ANASTASIA VOLKONSKY is a writer and researcher based in San Francisco, California, and a founding director of PROMISE, an organization dedicated to combating sexual exploitation.

ROBIN WARSHAW is a freelance journalist based in Pennsauken, New Jersey, and the author of *I Never Called It Rape* (Harper & Row, 1988).

SIMON WINCHESTER is a contributor to *The Spectator.*

INDEX